Contracts not covered,
or not fully covered,
by the Public Sector Directive

Carina Risvig Hansen

Contracts not covered, or not fully covered, by the Public Sector Directive

Djøf Publishing
2012

Carina Risvig Hansen
Contracts not covered, or not fully covered, by the Public Sector Directive

1. edition

Cover: Bo Helsted
Print & Binding: Ecograf, Højbjerg

Printed in Denmark 2012
ISBN 978-87-57-2762-2

Published with support from
Jurist- og Økonomforbundets Forlags legat til støtte af videnskabelige afhandlinger

Sold and distributed in Scandinavia by:
DJØF Publishing
Copenhagen, Denmark
Email: forlag@djoef.dk
www.djoef-forlag.dk

Sold and distributed in North America by:
International Specialized Book Services (ISBS)
Portland, USA
Email: orders@isbs.com
www.isbs.com

Sold in all other countries by:
The Oxford Publicity Partnership Ltd
Towcester, UK
Email: djof@oppuk.co.uk
www.oppuk.co.uk

Distributed in all other countries by:
Marston Book Services
Abingdon, Oxon, UK
Email: trade.orders@marston.co.uk
www.marston.co.uk

Foreword

When I was about to choose my first elective course at the beginning of my Masters of Law, my stepdad advised me to choose public procurement law. He is a construction engineer and argued that knowledge of public procurement law was particular important in this field and that a lawyer would therefore always be needed. I am sure he had hoped that I would have chosen to take a more practical approach to the field of law, and had not expected that I would find public procurement law interesting in such a way that I would write a PhD Thesis about it! The latter, – more theoretical point of view – often tends to provide more questions than actual answers. Yet, I owe him for opening my eyes to this interesting and challenging area of law and for the many discussions we have had, and I promise I will also try to provide answers to most of the questions asked.

This book is a slightly amended version of my PhD Thesis submitted in February 2012, at Copenhagen Business School. The Thesis was composed on a part time basis, while also being employed part time at the Danish Competition and Consumer Authority. It has been a challenge yet awarding experience trying to balance two (almost fulltime) jobs at the same time. I appreciate having had this opportunity to be involved in academia while keeping track on the more practical world. I owe my boss at the Competition and Consumer Authority, Pia Ziegler, for being very flexible and understanding, and for making sure there has always been interesting tasks I have had trouble saying no to.

I also want to thank my supervisors, Professor Steen Treumer and Professor Jens Fejø for their fruitful advices, interesting discussions and great support a long the way (and off-course for the various footnote corrections). I have always looked forward to our meetings and will greatly miss them in the future.

In the spring 2010 I was a visiting scholar at Nottingham University, and I want to thank the Public Procurement Research Group, especially Professor Sue Arrowsmith for having me there, and the many people I met there who made my stay both interesting, educational and entertaining.

In the spring 2011 I was a visiting scholar at Turin University, and for that I owe Professor Roberto Caranta a great thanks for letting me share his office, for introducing me to many people and for generally being so nice with me. I also want to thank him for acting as the opponent at my Pre-defence in November 2011, which gave me some constructive and valuable feedback.

Many people have read small or larger parts of the work along the way and I owe them all: my colleagues at the Danish Competition and Consumer Authority, Betina Tångberg Pedersen, Peter Moesgaard Kring, Mette Olling Vang, Jesper Halvorsen and Vibeke Ulf Dumrath, as well as my Colleagues at CBS, professor Christina Tvarnø and Mette Ohm Rørdam.

I also want to thank Grith Ølykke for reading a substantial part of the Thesis and for the great invaluable feedback, as well as Albert Sanchez Graells for his constructive comments to earlier drafts, and for the many interesting discussions we have had and for support along the way.

Finally, a great thanks to family and friends for being patient with me in a busy period and for making me believe there is a life after Thesis.

Copenhagen, May 2012.

Carina Risvig Hansen

Materials published after December 2011 have only to a limited extent been taken into account.

Abbreviations

CMLR	Common Market Law Review
Commission	European Commission of the European Union
CPV	Common Procurement Vocabulary
Court of Justice	Court of Justice of the European Union
ECR	European Court Reports
ELR	European Law Review
EU	European Union
DG MARKT	Internal Market and Services Directorate General
GPA	Government Procurement Agreement
OJ	Official Journal of the European Union
PPLR	Public Procurement Law review
PPP	Public Private Partnership
SIGMA	Support of Improvement of Governance and Management.
SME	Small and Medium-sized Enterprise
TFEU	Treaty of the Functioning of the European Union
TEU	Treaty of the European Union
U	Ugeskrift for Retsvæsen (Danish legal Journal)

Contents

PART I

‘Introduction, Definitions and Foundations’

CHAPTER 1

Introduction and Methodology

1. Introduction

The EU Treaties as well as the EU Procurement Directives apply to certain public contracts when a contracting authority wishes to entrust a public task to a third party.

According to the Court of Justice such contracts are regulated by secondary EU legislation to: '... *ensure the free movement of services and the opening-up to undistorted competition in all the Member States*'.[1] Therefore, adopting common procedures applicable for contracting authorities when awarding certain public contracts was found appropriate. However, for various reasons, not all types of public contracts fall within the Public Sector Directive. Three types of contracts that are either not covered, or not fully covered, by the Public Sector Directive are service concession contracts, contracts with a value falling below the thresholds in the EU Procurement Directives (henceforth, 'contracts below the thresholds'), and contracts regarding services listed in Annex II B to the Public Sector Directive (henceforth 'B-service contracts').

The above-mentioned contract types are referred to as 'the three types of contracts'.

The Public Sector Directive does not cover these three types of contracts because the EU legislator did not intend for it to be necessary to follow the detailed procedural rules in the Directive when awarding one of these types of contracts (see chapters 3-5 for the grounds upon which the three types of contracts have been excluded). Nevertheless, not covering these contracts fully by the Public Sector Directive does not mean that these types of contracts

1. Case C-454/06, Pressetext Nachrichtenagentur GmbH v. Austria, APA-OTS Originaltext-Service GmbH and APA Austria Presse Agentur registrierte Genossenschaft mit beschränkter Haftung, [2008] ECR I-4401, paragraph 31. The aim of the EU Procurement rules is further elaborated on in chapter 2.

are entered into less frequently or are not of interest to economic operators.[2] Indeed, service concession contracts are essential, particularly when contracting authorities need to mobilise private capital and know-how in order to supplement scarce public resources. In this context these contracts are an attractive means executing projects of public interest.[3] Furthermore, the Commission has estimated the value of contracts below the threshold to 12 percent of the total government and utility expenditure on works, goods and services.[4] Finally, as concerns B-service contracts regarding sectors such as education, health and social services these have been estimated to 36 percent of the total government and utility expenditure on works, goods and services.[5]

Consequently, the three types of contracts are frequently of interest to economic operators (domestic as well as non-domestic, depending on the contract in question). The Commission even calls the lack of secondary law for service concession contracts a loophole that gives rise to: '*serious distortion of the internal market, in particular limiting access by European business (...) to the economic opportunities offered by concession contracts.*'[6]

Contracting authorities are obliged to follow the EU Treaties and the principles derived there from when awarding one of the three types of contracts (see section 3.1.1.1). The case law from the Court of Justice has shown that the principles of the EU Treaties imply certain positive obligations for contracting authorities that must be observed before a contract can be awarded

2. The term 'economic operator' is used in this Thesis to cover equally the concepts of contractor, supplier, and service provider. Once an economic operator has submitted a tender, the term 'tenderer' is used. Once an economic operator has sought an invitation to participate in a restricted or negotiated procedure the term 'candidate' is used (In line with the definition in Article 1(8) of the Public Sector Directive). The economic operator who has been granted a concession contract will be deemed 'concessionaire'. However, because the Public Sector Directive, as well as the Court of Justice, uses the terms 'undertaking', 'company' as well as 'economic operator' without any distinctions, these terms are used in the Thesis in connection with the Court's cases or literature where such terms have been used.
3. Commission's Impact Assessment on an Initiative on Concessions, SEC(2011) 1588 final, p. 4.
4. Commission's Evaluation Report *'Impact and Effectiveness of EU Public Procurement Legislation'*, part 1 SEC(2011) 853 final, p. 35.
5. Commission's Evaluation Report *'Impact and Effectiveness of EU Public Procurement Legislation'*, part 1 SEC(2011) 853 final, p. 35, bearing in mind that also goods and works in these sectors are covered by the estimate.
6. Explanatory Memorandum to the Commission's Proposal for a Directive of the European Parliament and the Council on the award of concession contracts COM (2011) 897 final, p. 2, henceforth the Proposed Concessions Directive.

and signed.[7] However, the precise content of these obligations is unclear. Overall, the principles of the EU Treaties create a sort of separate regime for the three types of contracts, which aim to ensure that contracting authorities protect the interest of economic operators by creating competition for the contract and guaranteeing that economic operators are treated equally in tandem with the overall aim of the EU procurement rules.

2. Aim of the Thesis

The aim of the Thesis is to analyse, clarify, and discuss which positive obligations derived from EU law, in a public procurement law context, a contracting authority must apply when entering into one of the three types of contracts – service concession contracts, contracts below the thresholds and contracts regarding B-services, and how these obligations can be enforced.

Thus, the Thesis will analyse, which obligations can be derived from mainly the Treaties' principle of transparency and the principle of equal treatment when a contracting authority enters into one of the three types of contracts (part II of the Thesis).

Furthermore, the Thesis will analyse how these obligations can be enforced. Effective remedies are essential to ensure that contracting authorities behave in accordance with the obligations derived from the principles of the Treaties, when entering into one of the three types of contracts. If the principles can be infringed without repercussions, the effectiveness of the principles will be endangered. Thus, effective remedies must be available when the principles have been breached.

7. Starting mainly with Case C-324/98, Telaustria Verlags GmbH and Telefonadress GmbH v. Telekom Austria AG, [2000] ECR I-10745. See chapter 7.

3. Methodology

The doctrinal legal method will be used in this Thesis.[8] This method will be applied to analyse what is valid law, *de lege lata,* for contracting authorities when awarding one of the three types of contracts. What is valid law must be determined by interpreting the legal sources available (see section 3.1 for observations on the legal sources relevant for the analysis in this Thesis). The doctrinal legal method seeks to establish how the courts would rule if the questions were presented before them. Thus, how the Court of Justice could ultimately be expected to rule on the matter, hence some observations regarding the Court of Justice's case law, the Court's interpretation method and the importance of the Court's case law for the analysis in this Thesis will be presented in section 3.2.

The Thesis will neither propose improvements of the legal rule nor, as a main rule, how the legal rule should (or could) be, *de lege ferenda.* Historic observations will be made only when necessary to understand the current legal situation. The research in this Thesis does not include any empirical work or economic approaches regarding the effectiveness of the obligations derived from the principles of the Treaties.

3.1. The sources of law as applied in this Thesis

The relevant sources of law when addressing public procurement rules at EU level include the Treaty of the European Union (TEU), the Treaty on the Functioning of the EU (TFEU), the Public Procurement Directives and the principles derived from the above sources of law. Together these sources constitute the 'EU public procurement rules'.

The principles of the Treaties – primarily the principle of transparency and the principle of equal treatment – make up the most important legal source for contracting authorities when awarding one of the three types of contracts. However, as the obligations derived from the principles of the Treaties,

8. On a more theoretical plan it has been argued that there exists no common legal method in relation to EU law, which is being used in the same manner throughout EU. Some scholars have argued that a common legal method would be desirable see, for example, Hesselink, Martjin *"A European Legal Method? On European Private Law and Scientific Method"* [2009] ELJ, Vol. 15, n° 1, pp. 20–45 who argues in a private law context that: '*Therefore, a common legal method, with a common idea concerning legal sources and interpretation, seems desirable.*' For various aspects on European legal method see Neergaard, Ulla, Nielsen, Ruth and Roseberry, Lynn (Eds) *"European Legal Method – Paradoxes and Revitalisation"* [2010] DJØF.

(which are analysed in this Thesis) are developed through the case law from the Court of Justice, the most important source for analysing what is valid law, *de lega lata,* is found in the case law from the Court of Justice and its interpretation of the principles (see section 3.2).

To conclude on the *de lega lata* analysis, various other legal sources such as the TFEU's provisions of free movement, Directives, opinions from Advocates General, the Commission's Communications and guidelines, literature, and national case law will be used as well.

EU legislation can be divided into two categories: primary and secondary legislation. Primary legislation consists of the Treaties, the principles of the Treaties, and the Charter of Fundamental Right.[9] Secondary legislation consists of Regulations, Directives, and decisions.[10]

3.1.1. Primary legislation

3.1.1.1. The EU Treaties

The European Treaties consist of the Treaty of the European Union and the Treaty of the Functioning of the European Union.[11] The Treaties do not contain any EU procurement rules.[12]

9. The Charter of Fundamental Rights of the European Union (2000/C 364/01). The Charter became a part of primary EU law when the Lisbon Treaty entered into force. See Article 6(1) TEU.
10. See Article 288 TFEU. For further on EU legal sources see, for example, Nielsen, Ruth and Tvarnø, Christina *"Retskilder & Retsteorier"* [2011] 3rd Edition, DJØF, chapter 3. Hartley, TC *"The Foundations of European Union Law"* [2010] 7th Edition, Oxford University Press, p. 214-244. Craig, Paul and Búrca, Gráinne de *"EU Law – Text, Cases and Materials"* [2011] 5th Edition, Oxford University Press, chapter 4.
11. The Treaty of Lisbon amending the EU Treaty and the EC Treaty. Reference is made to the consolidated versions of the Treaty on European Union and the Treaty on the Functioning of the European Union, [2008] C 115. The latter will be referred to as the Treaty or TFEU. The former will be referred to as the EU Treaty. References will be made to the numbering in the Treaties at the time of the ruling in the cases. However, the current numbering will be stated in brackets for example Article 12 EC [Art. 18 TFEU].
12. Besides Article 199(4) TFEU, which deals with contracts financed by the EU, and wherein it is stated that participation in tenders shall be open on equal terms to legal persons who are nationals of a Member States. Also Article 179 (2) TFEU stresses procurement and contains a statement that the EU shall encourage undertakings in their research and enable undertakings to exploit the Internal Market '*in particular through the opening-up of national public contracts (...).*'

The most relevant provisions in the TFEU regarding procurement matters are the free movement rules found in Article 34 TFEU (free movement of goods), Article 49 TFEU (freedom of establishment), Article 57 TFEU (free movement of services), and the principle of non-discrimination on grounds of nationality found in Article 18 TFEU. Thus, several provisions are relevant when addressing public procurement. In fact, the overall aim of the first Works Directive has been to remove restrictions of the free movement rules, hereby indicating that the Treaty already applied to public contracts before the adoption of the Directive (see the aim of the procurement rules in chapter 2).

Also the Commission had early on indicated that the Treaty applied for contracts outside the Procurement Directives[13] as well had the literature stated before *Telaustria* that the Treaty applied.[14] However, the general assumption in the legal literature was that the provisions on free movement did not themselves imply transparency or similar positive obligations, but rather only engendered certain 'negative' obligations. Such a negative obligation could for example be the banning of discrimination against non-domestic products, which restricted the access to the specific contract.[15] Therefore, no – further – obligations could be transferred upon contracts not covered by the Directive, because the EU legislator had already excluded certain contracts from the

13. See, for example, the Green Paper '*Public Procurement in the European Union: Exploring the way forward*' [1996] COM 1996 583, p. 12, which states: '*the principles must apply in all situations where public procurement and similar contracts are involved.*' A long the same line see the Commission's Interpretative Communication on Concessions under Community Law (2000/C121/02), which states: '*Though concessions are not directly addressed by the public contracts directives, they are nonetheless subject to the rules and principles of the Treaty.*'
14. See, for example, Arrowsmith, Sue *"The Law of Public and Utilities Procurement"* [1996] 1st Edition, London, Sweet and Maxwell, p. 158, who stated that: '*The Community Treaty provisions can affect all public procurements, however small. The regulations, on the other hand, apply only to contracts above a certain value.*'
15. Before *Telaustria* see Braun, Peter *"A Matter of Principle(s) – The Treatment of Contracts Falling Outside the Scope of the European Procurement Directives"* [2000] PPLR n° 1, pp. 39-49, who stated: '*... it is not possible to assume, as the Commission does, that contracting authorities are under a positive obligation to publish contracts arising from the Treaty.*' Arrowsmith, Sue *"Public Private Partnerships and the European Procurement rules: EU Policies in Conflict?"* [2000] CMLR n° 37, pp. 709-737.

Public Procurement Directives.[16] The Commission did not share this common opinion.[17]

Thus, the Court's finding in *Telaustria* – that the Treaties' principles also imply positive obligations (the transparency obligation analysed in chapter 7), prior to entering into a contract outside the Directive, surprised the most.[18] Nevertheless, despite the judgment in *Telaustria* academics did not immediately accepted the ruling that positive obligations applied.[19]

16. However, it was to some extent expected by some authors. See, for example, Nielsen, Ruth *"Udbud af offentlige kontrakter"* [1998] 1st Edition, DJØF, p. 83 who states '*Thus, there presumably exists a duty to publish procurements ones covered by the EC Treaty despite being covered or outside the specific Procurement Directives.*' [My translation]. See also Treumer, Steen *"Ligebehandlingsprincippet i EU's udbudsregler"* [2000] DJØF, pp. 78-79 who argues that it was most likely that the Court of Justice, based on the principle of equal treatment, would come to the conclusion to apply some of the basics provisions in the procurement directives outside the Directive.
17. Green Paper '*Public Procurement in the European Union: Exploring the way forward*' [1996] COM 1996 583, p. 12. See the Commission's Interpretative Communication on Concessions under Community Law (2000/C121/02), which states: '*the principle of non-discrimination on grounds of nationality, implies that there is an obligation to be transparent so that the contracting authority will be able to ensure it is adhered to.*' (See also chapter 7, section 2.1.)
18. For comments after *Telaustria* see, for example, Steinicke, Michael *"Varernes frie bevægeligthed og offentlige indkøb"* [2001] DJØF p. 164; Treumer, Steen and Werlauff, Erik *"The Leverage Principle: Secondary Law as a Lever for the Development of Primary Community Law"* [2003] ELR n° 1, 28(1), pp. 124-133, who state that: '*This result is at variance with the view, generally shared until now, that a contracting entity whose contract falls outside the scope of the procurement Directives is in principle free to decide whether to undertake a tender procedure or not.*'; Hordijk, Erik Pijnacker & Meulenbelt, Maarten *"A Bridge Too Far: Why the Commission's Attempts to Construct an Obligation to Tender Outside the Scope of the Public Procurement Directives Should be Dismissed"* [2005] PPLR n° 3, pp. 120-130; Krüger, Kai *"Critical comments on the new procurement directives, preceding the Nordic adaption"* in Treumer, Steen and Fejø, Jens (Eds) *"EU's Udbudsregler – implementering og håndhævelse i norden"* [2006] DJØF, p. 13, Krüger refer to '*The remarkable trend to require transparency.*'; Brown, Adrian *"Seeing Through Transparency: the Requirement to Advertise Public Contracts and Concessions Under the EC Treaty"* [2007] PPLR n° 1, pp. 1-21, p. 12 calls the Court's development: '*important and controversial*'; Arrowsmith, Sue and Kunzlik, Peter (Eds) *"Social and Environmental Policies in EC Procurement Law"* [2009] Cambridge University Press, p. 82.
19. See, for example, Krugner, Matthias *"The principles of equal treatment and transparency and the Commissions Interpretative Communication on Concessions"* [2003] PPLR n° 5, pp. 181-207, who states: '*The conclusion to be drawn from this*

3.1.1.2. The principles derived from the EU Treaties

The principles derived from the EU Treaties are part of primary legislation. They possess equivalent status to the Treaties because they originate in the Treaties.[20]

In relation to the analysis of the obligations derived from the principles of the Treaties in this Thesis, emphasis will be placed on the principle of equal treatment and the principle of transparency (see further discussion of these principles in procurement matters in chapter 2). The Court of Justice has used these two principles to create positive obligations for contracting authorities even when the legislator did not provide for such obligations in secondary legislation.

The principle of proportionality and the principle of mutual recognition are other principles important for the analysis in this Thesis (see chapter 8).

Generally, the principles' functions outside EU public procurement situations will not be pursued in this Thesis.[21]

Regarding enforcement of the obligations derived from the principles of the Treaties, other principles derived from the Treaties play a significant role in establishing enforcement mechanism and remedies. These principles being: the principle of national procedural autonomy, the principle of equivalence and the principle of effectiveness. Another principle relevant to enforcement is the principle of right to judicial review, which is also found in

case law seems to be, at least at first sight, that the criticism outlined is not convincing. On the other hand, nowhere in the Treaty is a general principle of equal treatment mentioned. It is therefore necessary to clarify the meaning of the principle of equal treatment and the principle of transparency as set up by the Court of Justice, and to assess the arguments of both the Commission and its critics on this subject. It can then be considered what effects, if any, the principles of equal treatment and transparency have in the case of award of concessions.' See also Hordijk, Erik Pijnacker & Meulenbelt, Maarten *"A Bridge Too Far: Why the Commission's Attempts to Construct an Obligation to Tender Outside the Scope of the Public Procurement Directives Should be Dismissed"* [2005] PPLR n° 3, pp. 120-130.

20. Tridimas, Takis *"The General Principles of EU Law"* [2006] 2nd Edition, Oxford University Press, p. 51.
21. For example, the principle of equal treatment has played a great role in many fields of law, and the principle can be seen throughout the Treaties in various contexts such as for example Article 157 TFEU regarding equality between men and women with regard to labour market opportunities and treatment at work. Also the Charter of Fundamental Rights contains various provisions of equal treatment. For a historic perspective and general overview of the principle of equal treatment in different context see for example Tridimas, Takis *"The General Principles of EU Law"*, [2006] 2nd Edition, Oxford University Press, chapter 5.

the Article 47 of the Charter. These principles will be further addressed in chapters 9, 10, and 11.

3.1.2. Secondary legislation

3.1.2.1. Regulations

Only in relation to minor issues, have Regulations been used as the form of legislation in procurement matters. Thus, for example are the relevant EU threshold values revised every two years in a Regulation.[22] The Financial Regulation, which applies to the EU Institutions when awarding contracts will not be addressed in this Thesis.[23] However, the case law from the General Court regarding the EU Institutions' potential breach of the principles derived from the Treaties is a useful tool for interpretation in this Thesis because the EU Institutions must apply the principles of the Treaties when awarding a contract (see section 3.2.1).

3.1.2.2. Directives

The Public Procurement Directives currently consist of three Directives:

The Public Sector Directive (also referred to as Directive 2004/18/EC)	Directive 2004/18/EC of the European Parliament and of the Council of 31 March 2004 on the coordination of procedures for the award of public works contracts, public supply contracts and public service contracts, [2004] OJ L 134/114
The Utilities Directive (also referred to as Directive 2004/17/EC)	Directive 2004/17/EC of the European Parliament and of the Council of 31 March 2004 coordinating the procurement procedures of entities operating in the water, energy, transport and postal services sectors, [2004] OJ L 134/1.

22. The current thresholds are established through Regulation 1251/2011 of 30 November 2011 amending Directives 2004/17/EC, 2004/18/EC and 2009/81/EC of the European Parliament and of the Council in respect of their application thresholds for the procedures for the awards of contract, [2011] OJ L 319/43, which entered into force on January 1, 2012.
23. Regulation 1605/2002 of 25 June 2002 on the Financial Regulation applicable to the general budget of the European Communities, [2002] OJ L 248/1, henceforth 'the Financial Regulation'.

The Defence and Security Directive.	Directive 2009/81/EC of the European Parliament and of the Council of 13 July 2009 on the coordination of procedures for the award of certain works contracts, supply contracts and service contracts by contracting authorities or entities in the fields of defence and security, and amending Directives 2004/17/EC and 2004/18/EC, [2009] OJ L 216/76.

An analysis of the rules in the Procurement Directives falls outside the aim of this Thesis because the three types of contracts are either not covered, or not fully covered, by the Public Sector Directive. Nevertheless, all three Procurement Directives will function as a source for inspiration with main emphasis on the Public Sector Directive. Thus, the starting point in defining the three types of contracts will be taken in the Public Sector Directive. This will also be the case when examining the reasons for not covering the three types of contracts fully by the Procurement Directives.
Three Public Procurement Directives applied before the Public Sector Directive:

The Works Directive	Directive 93/37/EEC of 14 June 1993 concerning the coordination of procedures for the award of public works contracts, [1993] OJ L 199/54.
The Service Directive	Directive 92/50/EEC of 18 June 1992 relating to the coordination of procedures for the award of public service contracts, [1992] OJ L 209/1.
The Supply Directive	Directive 93/36/EEC of 14 June 1993 coordinating procedures for the award of public supply contracts, [1993] OJ L 199/1.

The prior Procurement Directives will be used to a limited extent as grounds for analysing the current state of law, primarily to set the rules in a historic context regarding the definitions of the three types of contracts (see chapters 3-5).

On December 20, 2011, the Commission published three new proposals for new Directives in the field of public procurement:

Proposal to change the Public Sector Directive,[24]
Proposal to change the Utilities Directive,[25] and
Proposal for a Directive concerning concession contracts.[26]

These proposals for new Directives will be illustrative in use here rather than functioning as a means of interpretation because the Directives clearly need to be adopted before they are binding.

Part III of this Thesis addresses enforcement. In this regard, two Remedies Directives exist, both of which were amended in 2007.

The Public Sector Remedies Directive	Directive 89/665/EEC of 21 December 1989 on the coordination of the laws, regulations and administrative provisions relating to the application of review procedures to the award of public supply and public works contracts, [1989] OJ L 395/33.
The Utilities Remedies Directive	Directive 92/13/EEC of 25 February 1992 coordinating the laws, regulations and administrative provisions relating to the application of Community rules on the procurement procedures of entities operating in the water, energy, transport and telecommunications sectors, [1992] OJ L 76/14.
The Amending Remedies Directive (also referred to as Directive 2007/66/EC)	Directive 2007/66/EC of the European Parliament and the Council of 11 December 2007 amending Council Directives 89/665/EEC with regard to improving the effectiveness of review procedures concerning the award of public contracts, [2007] OJ L 335/31.

24. Proposal for a Directive of the European Parliament and the Council on public procurement, COM(2011) 896 final, henceforth the Proposed Procurement Directive.
25. Proposal for a Directive of the European Parliament and the Council on procurement by entities operating in the water, energy, transport and postal services sectors, COM(2011) 895 final, henceforth the Proposed Utilities Directive.
26. Proposal for a Directive of the European Parliament and the Council on the award of concession contracts COM(2011) 897 final, henceforth the Proposed Concessions Directive.

The Thesis will consider only the Public Sector Remedies Directive, because this is the Directive, which applies to contracts covered by the Public Sector Directive, hereunder B-service contracts. Thus, when analysing the enforcement mechanism and remedies available the starting point will be taken in the Public Sector Remedies Directive.

Directives contain Recitals, which expresses the more general reasons as to why the Directives have their precise context. Such Recitals are essential to interpret in order to ensure the Directives are interpreted in accordance with their objectives.

3.1.2.3. The Commission's Interpretative Communications

The aim of Communications from the Commission is to make known the Commission's general approach regarding the application of certain rules. Such Communications represent the Commission's official view of how specific legislation (here, mainly the Treaties and case law from the Court of Justice) must be interpreted. Communications are not a source of law, but a supplement interpretative instrument. The Commission's Communications relevant for this Thesis are:

Interpretative Communication on Concessions	Commission Interpretative Communication on Concessions under Community Law (2000/C121/02).
2006 Communication.	Commission Interpretative Communication on the Community law applicable to contract awards not or not fully subject to the provisions of the Public Procurement Directives (2006/ C179/2).

According to Article 288 TFEU *'Recommendations and opinions shall have no binding force'*. Communications are not mentioned herein, but as they represent the Commission's opinion; Communications do not have binding force. However, Communications can be binding for the Commission itself to some extent and can at least be a useful tool in interpreting the legal rules.[27]

The 2006 Communication stated that infringement procedures: '... will be opened only in cases where this appears appropriate in view of the gravity of the infringement and its impact on the Internal Market'. Thus, the 2006

27. See also Nielsen, Ruth and Tvarnø, Christina *"Retskilder & Retsteorier"* [2011] 3rd Edition, DJØF, p. 133.

Communication can be used for contracting authorities to evaluate the supposed legal status of a procurement action and when one is seeking to establish which types of breaches might be pursued by the Commission when it brings enforcement proceedings against a Member State.

In September 2006, Germany brought an action against the Commission for issuing the 2006 Communication, claiming it should be annulled.[28] Germany asserted that the 2006 Communication was binding because it contained new rules for the award of public contracts that went beyond the obligations pursuant to the existing EU law and produced legal effects for the Member States; hence the Commission had not been competent in adopting such rules.[29] Therefore, according to Germany, the Communication created new rules *de facto* even though the Communication itself stated that it was not legally binding. In May 2010, the General Court dismissed the action as inadmissible. However, the Court did examine the 2006 Communication in order to

'*... determine whether the Communication is designed to produce legal effects which are new as compared with those entailed by the application of the fundamental principles of the EC Treaty.*'[30]

It could be argued that because the Court found that the Communication did not go beyond the obligations, which could be derived from the principles of the Treaties, the 2006 Communication thus possesses a more binding effect.[31] However, as will be analysed in chapters 6 and 7, the General Court was vague in its statements regarding the obligations, which can be derived from the principles of the Treaties. Therefore, the lack of legal certainty remains regarding the content of the obligations derived from the principles of the Treaties.

3.1.3. Other sources

Besides Interpretative Communications, other relevant EU documents can serve as support interpretative sources in analysing the Commission's view on specific matters. Such documents include the Commission's proposals to various legislation, Green Papers such as the Commission's Green Paper on

28. Case T-258/06, Germany v. Commission, [2010] ECR II-2027.
29. Case T-258/06, Germany v. Commission, [2010] ECR II-2027, paragraph 32.
30. Case T-258/06, Germany v. Commission, [2010] ECR II-2027, paragraph 27.
31. See also Petersen, Zsofia *"Below-threshold contract awards under EU primary law: Federal Republic of Germany v. Commission (T-258/06)"* [2010] PPLR n° 6, NA 215-220, who states: '*This inadmissibility decision brings about more legal certainty for the contracting authorities with respect to their obligations concerning the procurement of below-threshold public contracts.*'

Public Procurement Partnerships,[32] and the Green Paper on the modernisation of EU public procurement policy,[33] internal working documents and Impact Assessments. However, the Court of Justice can naturally reject the interpretation of the law set in these documents.

3.2. The Court of Justice

3.2.1. Case law

The case law from the Court of Justice is an essential element when analysing the EU Public Procurement rules. Moreover, the development of the obligations derived from the principles of the Treaties, applicable for contracting authorities when awarding one of the three types of contracts, has been achieved through the case law of the Court of Justice. Therefore, case law from the Court of Justice possesses a high value in the concrete analysis in this Thesis, and is considered the most essential means for interpreting the principles derived from the Treaties.

A significant part of the case law from the Court of Justice concerns contracts falling outside of the Utilities Directive (*Telaustria* was such a case). However, because these cases are ruled on the principles derived from the Treaties, no difference in the assessment between cases outside the Public Sector Directive and outside the Utilities Directive will be made in this Thesis.

Because the EU Institutions are required to follow the principles of the Treaties, case law regarding the European Institutions has also been used in the analysis. Such cases are ruled by the General Court, and will be used as a tool for interpreting the obligations derived from the principles of the Treaties analysed in Part II as well as the applicable remedies available analysed in Part III (mainly in relation to interim measures – see chapter 11).

All language versions from the Court of Justice have the same value.[34] Thus, an analysis of the language versions, the meaning of which sometimes differs, must be taken into consideration. However, French is by custom the working language of the Court of Justice, which perhaps gives this version of the Court's judgments a slightly higher value in interpretation of the cases because all the judges in the case have read this version.

32. Commission's Green Paper on Public Procurement Partnerships, COM (2004)327.
33. Commission's Green Paper on the modernisation of EU public procurement policy Towards a more efficient European Procurement Market, COM (2011)15, henceforth the Green Paper on Modernisation.
34. Case C-283/81, Srl CILFIT and Lanificio di Gavardo SpA v. Ministry of Health, [1982] ECR 3415, paragraph 18.

3.2.2. Interpretation method

According to Article 19 TEU, the Court of Justice shall ensure that the law is observed in the interpretation and application of the Treaties. The legal sources available must be examined when the Court of Justice interprets the legal rules. The Court itself has stated that:

'It must be borne in mind that Community legislation is drafted in several languages and that the different language versions are all equally authentic. An interpretation of a provision of community law thus involves a comparison of the different language versions.'[35]

Thus, when interpreting the law, the Court of Justice will take into consideration the wording of the provision in question, by examining the different language versions. However, the Court also stated in *CILFIT* that:

'Every provision of Community law must be placed in its context and interpreted in the light of the provisions of Community law as a whole, regard being had to the objectives thereof and to its state of evolution at the date on which the provision in question is to be applied.'[36]

Thus, not only is a literal interpretation relevant, the Court also interprets the rules purposive or teleological.[37] Thus, the rationale of the provision, *ratio legis*, or the policy aim underlying the rule will be taken into account.[38] Overall, the Court's interpretation shall ensure that the EU rules are effective.[39] The teleological method plays an important role in many different and complex legal contexts.[40] In procurement context the Court often refers to the

35. Case C-283/81, Srl CILFIT and Lanificio di Gavardo SpA v. Ministry of Health, [1982] ECR 3415, paragraph 18.
36. Case C-283/81, Srl CILFIT and Lanificio di Gavardo SpA v. Ministry of Health, [1982] ECR 3415, paragraph 20.
37. See, for example, Craig, Paul and Búrca, Gráinne de *"EU Law – Text, Cases and Materials"* [2011] 5th Edition, Oxford University Press, p. 64.
38. Hesselink, Martijn W *"A Toolbox for European Judges"* in Neergaard, Ulla, Nielsen, Ruth and Roseberry, Lynn (Eds) *"European Legal Method – Paradoxes and Revitailisation"* [2010] DJØF, p. 204.
39. Nielsen, Ruth & Neergaard, Ulla *"EU Ret"* [2010] 6th Edition, DJØF, p. 116.
40. Neergaard, Ulla & Nielsen, Ruth *"Where Did the Spirit and Its Friends Go? On the European Legal Method(s) and the Interpretation Style of the Court of Justice of the European Union"* in Neergaard, Ulla, Nielsen, Ruth and Roseberry, Lynn (Eds) *"European Legal Method – Paradoxes and Revitailisation"* [2010] DJØF, p. 127.

purpose of a provision or a Directive. For example recently in *Strong Segurança,*[41] the Court stated:

> *'... there is no indication from the wording of the provisions of Directive 2004/18, or **from its spirit and general scheme**, that (...)' [emphasis added].*[42]

Thus, examining the aim of the EU procurement rules is relevant to establishing the correct grounds for interpretation in procurement matters (see chapter 2).

Historical interpretation can also be relevant for the Court.[43] In *Telaustria,* the Court, amongst other aspects, examined the legislative background of the Service Directive and concluded that the legislator did not intend for the Directive to cover these types of contracts (see chapter 3).

The EU legislator had clearly decided not to cover the three types of contracts entirely by the Procurement Directives. Many reasons exist for not covering all situations (here all contracts) through EU legislation. One such reason is to give the Court a margin of discretion regarding the current state of law. However, when the Court found that certain positive obligations nevertheless applied when awarding one of the three types of contracts, the Court can be said to have found inspiration in secondary law to fulfil a gap in primary law.[44] *Treumer* and *Werlauf* call the fact that the Court finds inspiration in secondary law and interprets similar obligations in primary law for the leverage principle.[45] By requiring 'a degree of advertising', for certain contracts

41. Case C-95/10, Strong Segurança SA v. Município de Sintra, Securitas-Serviços e Tecnologia de Segurança, [2011] March 17, 2011, (not yet reported).
42. Case C-95/10, Strong Segurança SA v. Município de Sintra, Securitas-Serviços e Tecnologia de Segurança, [2011] March 17, 2011, (not yet reported), paragraph 31. See also, from the Court's earlier case law, Case C-31/87, Gebroeders Beentjes BV v. the Netherlands, [1988] ECR 04635, paragraph 11, where the Court found that the term 'State' must be interpreted in functional terms. Hereafter the Court emphasised on the aim of the Works Directive and found that the body in question was to be considered as part of the 'State' for the purpose of the procedures in the Directive.
43. Neergaard, Ulla & Nielsen, Ruth *"Where Did the Spirit and Its Friends Go? On the European Legal Method(s) and the Interpretation Style of the Court of Justice of the European Union"* in Neergaard, Ulla, Nielsen, Ruth and Roseberry, Lynn (Eds) *"European Legal Method – Paradoxes and Revitailisation"* [2010] DJØF, p. 127.
44. More on the Court of Justice's 'Gap-filling function' see Tridimas, Takis *"The General Principles of EU Law"* [2006] 2nd Edition, Oxford University Press, p. 17.
45. Treumer, Steen and Werlauff, Erik *"The Leverage Principle: Secondary Law as a Lever for the Development of Primary Community Law"* [2003] ELR n° 1, 28(1) pp. 124-133.

not covered by the Public Procurement Directives, the Court of Justice can be said to have found its inspiration from the Public Procurement Directives themselves.

This aspect is relevant in this Thesis in two ways. First, it can be relevant to find inspiration in the Public Procurement Directives as to which obligations derived from the principles of the Treaties apply outside the Directives, hereunder elements such as whether there exists a duty of prior advertising and which award and selection criteria can be used (chapters 7 and 8). Second, the leverage principle can be relevant when examining the remedies available for the three types of contracts, where the Court of Justice has yet not ruled on the matter,[46] but will likely find inspiration in the Remedies Directives to ensure that the remedies are effective for the three types of contracts (see chapter 11).

3.2.3. Opinions from advocates general

Eight advocates general whose function it is *'to make, in open court, reasoned submissions on cases'*[47] assists the Court of Justice. These opinions are not required in all cases,[48] but if opinions are given, they are produced before the Court makes its decision in a case. The opinions are intended as an advice to the Court. Therefore, the opinions from advocates general are relevant when analysing the current state of law, although these opinions are not binding.[49]

Because no EU legislation exists in the field of the three types of contracts and the obligations analysed in this Thesis have developed through the case law from the Court of Justice, the advocates generals' opinions are useful for interpretation because they illuminate various problems and opinions of the parties. As will be discussed later, the Court of Justice's case law is unclear on which obligations can be derived from the principles of the Treaties. Hence the opinions from the advocates general are useful tools when interpreting the current state of law.

46. Except for Case C-91/08, Wall AG v. La ville de Francfort-sur-le-Main and Frankfurter Entsorgungs- und Service (FES) GmbH, [2010] ECR I-2815, where the Court did not exclude that certain remedies apply (see chapter 11).
47. Article 252 TFEU.
48. See the Rules of Procedure of the Court of Justice of 19 June 1991, last amended by 'Amendments to the Rules of Procedure of the Court of Justice' [2011] OJ L 162/17.
49. For further on the Advocate General's role see, for example, Tridimas, Takis *"The role of the Advocate General in the Development of Community law: Some Reflections"* [1997] CMLR n° 34, pp. 1349-1387.

4. Delimitation

To make the analysis manageable, the research question requires further delimitation before an analysis can be proceed.

First, the EU Procurement rules are rules concerning '*how to enter into a contract*' (procedural rules) and not '*what to buy*' (material rules).[50] This focus persists throughout the Thesis. Thus, material rules such as product requirements and relevant specifications for contracts as well as related contractual aspects such as contract law, labour law, and environmental standards have been omitted.

Second, the Thesis addresses three types of contracts not covered, or not fully covered, by the Public Sector Directive. Thus, other types of excluded contracts have been left out of the Thesis (see section 4.1).

Third, regarding the rules and obligations when entering into one of the three types of contracts focus in this Thesis is laid upon the obligations derived from the principles of the Treaties (and the enforcement of these principles). Even though the TFEU's competition rules, the rules on state aid, and provisions on services of general economic interest (found in Articles 101 to 109 TFEU) are relevant to some extent when addressing public contracts, such considerations will be omitted from the analysis in this Thesis. The same goes general exceptions to the obligations derived from the principles of the Treaties, which are found within the Treaties (see section 4.2).

National legislation (see section 4.3) as well as international agreements such as the Government Procurement Agreement,[51] has been left out of the Thesis.

50. The Green Paper on Modernisation asks whether this focus should be changed. However, the recent proposals for new Procurement Directives have not changed this focus.
51. The Government Procurement Agreement (GPA) is an international agreement relating to public procurement. The current version entered into force on January 1, 1996, and establishes a set of rules, which govern the procurement activities of its parties. With decision of 22 December 1994 concerning the conclusion on behalf of the European Community, as regards matters within its competence, of the agreements reached in the Uruguay Round multilateral negotiations (1986-1994), [1994] OJ L336/1, the EU entered into this agreement. The GPA is currently under revision and on 15 December 2011, negotiators reached a agreement, which was confirmed, on 30 March 2012, by the formal adoption of the Decision on the Outcomes of the Negotiations under Article XXIV:7 of the Agreement on Government Procurement (GPA/113), can be found at: http://www.wto.org/english/tratop_e/gproc_e/gp_gpa_e.htm (last visited May 14, 2012).

Finally, only enforcement of the obligations derived from the principles of the Treaties at national level have been taking into account (see section 4.4).

4.1. The three types of contracts

The Public Sector Directive excludes several types of contracts such as those mentioned in Article 12-18,[52] contracts not concluded in writing,[53] and in-house contracts.[54] To some extent Article 31 of the Directive also excludes certain types of contracts because this provision permits a contracting authority to enter into a contract with negotiation without publishing a contract notice.

52. Directive 2004/18/EC Article 12 concerns the utilities contract (contracts in the water, energy, transport and postal services sectors), Article 13 a specific exclusion in the field of telecommunications, Article 14 secret contracts and contracts requiring special security measures (now covered by the Defence- and Security Directive), Article 15 concerns contracts awarded pursuant to international rules, Article 16 concerns some specific exclusions such as for example employment contracts, Article 17 concerns service concession contracts (which will be covered in this Thesis) and Article 18 concerns service contracts awarded on the basis of an exclusive right.
53. See Case C-532/03, Commission v. Ireland, [2007] ECR I-11353.
54. When a contract is to be considered in-house has been devolped through the case law of the Court of Justice starting with Case C-107/98, Teckal Srl v. Comune di Viano and Azienda Gas-Acqua Consorziale (AGAC) di Reggio Emilia, [1999] ECR I-8121, paragraph 50. These principles have been applied to contract outside the Procurement Directives in for example Case C-458/03, Parking Brixen GmbH v. Gemeinde Brixen and Stadtwerke Brixen AG, [2005] ECR I-8585 and Case C-324/07, Coditel Brabant SA v. Commune d'Uccle and Région de Bruxelles-Capitale, [2008] ECR I-8457. For further on in-house see, for example, Comba, Mario & Treumer, Steen (Eds) *"The In-house Providing in European Law"* [2010] DJØF. See also the Danish Competition and Consumer Authority's guideline on in-house for certain public independent institutions, which mainly concerns B-service contracts. The guideline can be found at: http://www.kfst.dk/index.php?id=28949 (last visited December 30, 2011). For literature covering the most recent case law see Wiggen, Janicke *"Public procurement rules and cooperation between public sector entities: the limits of the in-house doctrine under EU procurement law"* [2011] PPLR n° 5, pp. 157-172; Casalini, Dario *"Beyond EU Law: the new "public house"* in Ølykke, Grith, Hansen, Carina Risvig and Tvarnø, Christina D. *"EU Public Procurement – Modernisation, Growth and Innovation"*, DJØF, July 2012.

    See also a recent Commission Staff Working Paper concerning the application of EU public procurement law to relations between contracting authorities ('public-public cooperation') SEC(2011)1169.

The Thesis covers only the three types of contracts (service concession contracts, contracts below the thresholds and contracts regarding B-services) for several reasons:

First, these types of contracts are presumably the three most relevant types of contracts either not covered, or not fully covered, by the Public Sector Directive because they account for a high value of the overall public expenditure. For many contracting authorities these contracts will be the ones entered into most frequently.

Second, most of the other types of excluded contracts are excluded due to the nature of the contract or the sector in which the procurement are to take place such as for example the defence and utilities sectors.

Contrary, the three types of contracts cover various products and services, and are excluded from the Public Sector Directive for other reasons.[55] Subsequently, a service concession contract can consist of both A- and B-services, contracts below the EU thresholds can be service contracts, and, in theory, also a service concession contract, even though the latter is rare because du service concession contracts often posses a high contract value.

Third, and perhaps the most important aspect, these three types of contracts are covered by the same positive obligations derived from the principles of the Treaties,[56] with the one exception that B-service contracts are covered by the Public Sector Remedies Directive (see chapter 10).

Whether the Treaties will apply to the same extent for other types of excluded contracts, or in situations where the Public Sector Directive contains derogations to the Directive, such as Article 31, is not entirely clear. The Court of Justice has not ruled on the matter thus far. However, Article 31 addresses some concrete situations where awarding a contract without prior publication of a notice is permitted. Thus, in such situations awarding a contract without following the obligations derived from the principles of the Treaties should also be allowed.[57]

55. The reasons for excluding these types of contracts will be further elaborated on in chapters 3-5.
56. *Telaustria*, concerned a service concession contract. For B-services, the Court of Justice found in the Case C-507/03, Commission v. Ireland, [2007] ECR I-9777, that such contracts were also required to follow the principles of the Treaties. Regarding contracts below the thresholds a similar statement can be found in, for example, Case C-412/04, Commission v. Italy, [2008] ECR I-619.
57. This is also the opinion of Advocate General Jacobs in his Opinion in the Case C-525/03 Commission v. Italy, [2005] ECR I-9405, delivered on June 2, 2005 para-

4.2. Exceptions found in the Treaties

A few exceptions apply as to when it is necessary for contracting authorities to follow the obligations derived from the principles of the Treaties when awarding one of the three types of contracts.

In *Coname*[58] the Court of Justice stated that a difference in treatment of undertakings could be justified by objective circumstances. The Court stated:

'*Unless it is justified by objective circumstances, such a difference in treatment, which, by excluding all undertakings located in another Member State, operates mainly to the detriment of the latter undertakings, amounts to indirect discrimination on the basis of nationality, prohibited under Articles 43 EC and 49 EC.*'[59]

Thus, cases where a restriction can be justified by objective circumstances constitute an exception as to when the principles derived from the Treaties apply. Such objective circumstances can, for example, be found in Article 36 TFEU, which allows for restrictions on the free movement rules in certain situations such as if the measure is:

'*justified on grounds of public morality, public policy or public security; the protection of health and life of humans, animals or plants; the protection of national treasures possessing artistic, historic or archaeological value; or the protection of industrial and commercial property*'.[60]

graph 47. See also the Opinion of Advocate General Stix-Hackl in Case C-532/03, Commission v. Ireland, [2007] ECR I-11353 delivered on 14 September 2006, paragraph 111, Also the Commission in the 2006 Communication shares this view. See also Arrowsmith, Sue and Kunzlik, Peter (Edt) *"Social and Environmental Policies in EC Procurement Law"* [2009] Cambridge University press p. 51 who state '*Thus it appears that derogations to advertising under the procurement directives (...) also set the limits to the Treaty's advertising obligations.*'; Petersen, Zsofia *"Below-threshold contract awards under EU primary law: Federal Republic of Germany v. Commission (T-258/06)"* [2010] PPLR n° 6, NA 215-220; Trybus, Martin *"Public Contracts in European Union Internal Market Law: Foundations and Requirements"* in Nogouelleou, Rozen and Stelkens, Ulrich (Eds) *"Comparative Law on Public Contracts"* [2010] Brussels Bruylant, p. 107.

58. Case C-231/03, Consorzio Aziende Metano v. Comune di Cingia de' Botti, [2005] ECR I-7287.
59. Case C-231/03, Consorzio Aziende Metano v. Comune di Cingia de' Botti, [2005] ECR I-7287, paragraph 19. See later on Case C-412/04, Commission v. Italy, [2008] ECR I-619, Case C-507/03, Commission v. Ireland, [2007] ECR I-9777, paragraphs 30 and 31.
60. Article 36 TFEU.

Also the Court's case law contains grounds that can justify indirect discrimination.[61] It is my opinion that these derogations will apply to the three types of contracts and can justify that the principles of the Treaties are not complied with.

This exception will not be dealt with in this Thesis mainly due to the fact that the focus it laid upon; what are the obligations a contracting authority must follow and the enforcement of such obligations, and not on what can justify not following these obligations.[62]

4.3. National rules

Directives require implementation into national law, but leave some choices to Member States regarding how they are implemented.[63] Additionally, some provisions are voluntary for the Member States to implement. This creates different systems in the Member States as to how the Procurement Directives and the Remedies Directives have been implemented.

Regarding the three types of contract, it is only in cases where a contract is *not* of cross-border interest that Member States are entirely free to regulate whether contracting authorities must follow certain rules when entering into one of the three types of contracts. Contrary, if a contract *is* of cross-border interest and national legislation exists in the Member State, the contracting authorities are obliged to follow the principles derived from the Treaties as well as the national rules. Thus, despite the fact that most Member States have national legislation for contracts below the thresholds, contracting authorities must at the same time apply the principles of the Treaties when a given contract is of cross-border interest (see further on cross-border interest in chapter 7).[64]

61. Starting with Case C-120/78, Rewe-Zentral AG v. Bundesmonopolverwaltung für Branntwein, [1979] ECR 649.
62. For further on objective circumstances see, for example, Barnard, Cathrine *"Derogations, Justifications and the Four Freedoms: Is State Interest Really Protected?"* in Barnard, Cathrine & Odudu, Okeoghene (Eds) *"The Outer Limits of European Union Law"* [2009] Hart; Barnard, Cathrine *"The Substantive Law of the EU"* [2010], 3rd Edition, Oxford University Press, mainly chapters 6 and 13.
63. Article 288 TFEU.
64. See in that regard OECD (2010), Support of Improvement of Governance and Management (SIGMA) Paper n° 45 '*Public Procurement in EU Member States: The Regulation of Contract Below the EU Thresholds and in Areas not Covered by the Detailed Rules of the EU Directives (2010)*', or the Commission's Evaluation Report *'Impact and Effectiveness of EU Public Procurement Legislation'*, part 1 SEC(2011) 853 final.

The national rules vary extensively from Member State to Member State. At one end of the spectrum some Member State apply the same rules for below thresholds contracts and B-service contracts as for contracts falling within the Directive. A few Member States provide for guidance on interpreting the principles of the Treaties alone.[65] Some Member States include a detailed set of rules, whereas others simply require advertising. However, generally most Member States provide a more lenient regime for contracts below the thresholds and B-service contracts.[66]

Most Member States have national thresholds where contracts can be awarded directly below these thresholds. The thresholds vary from 1500 euros in Cyprus, to approximately 67.000 euros in Denmark (the latter only covers goods and services).[67] Like the thresholds in the Public Sector Directive, the national thresholds also differentiate between works contracts and contracts for services and goods.[68]

65. Commission's Evaluation Report *'Impact and Effectiveness of EU Public Procurement Legislation'*, part 1 SEC(2011) 853 final states that only Holland, UK and Sweden does not have national legislation. In OECD (2010), Support of Improvement of Governance and Management (SIGMA) Paper n° 45 *'Public Procurement in EU Member States: The Regulation of Contract Below the EU Thresholds and in Areas not Covered by the Detailed Rules of the EU Directives (2010)'*, p. 8 it is stated that only in UK and Ireland is guidance documentation the only exclusive means of instructing contracting entities on their obligations for procurement below the thresholds. Of the above-mentioned Member States Sweden do, however, have legislation regarding contracts below the thresholds and B-services (see Lagen om offentlig upphandling (LOU) (SFS 2007:1091).
66. Commission's Evaluation Report *'Impact and Effectiveness of EU Public Procurement Legislation'*, part 1 SEC(2011) 853 final, states that this simplification '*normally refers to the shortening of the time limits for submission of applications (i. e. requests for participation) and tenders and less demanding rules for publication and for selection of tenders.'*
67. For an overview of the national thresholds see the Commission's evaluation report: *"Impact and Effectiveness of EU Public Procurement Legislation"*, part II, SEC(2011) 853 final, Annex 5.
68. See OECD (2010), Support of Improvement of Governance and Management (SIGMA) Paper n° 45 *'Public Procurement in EU Member States: The Regulation of Contract Below the EU Thresholds and in Areas not Covered by the Detailed Rules of the EU Directives (2010)'*, which states: *'The majority of regulating Member States have two or even three sub-thresholds below the EU thresholds, which normally differ depending on the type of contract: lower for supply and service contracts, higher for works contracts (...).'*

National thresholds can either be only a single set of thresholds or, in some Member States, such as Bulgaria and Malta, up to four sets of national thresholds.[69] If a contract falls under the lowest national thresholds, contracting authorities are often allowed to enter into such a contract without following any publication requirements (according to national law). However, even though national rules exist, following the obligations derived from the principles of the Treaties if the contract is of cross-border interest (see chapter 4 for further on cross-border interest) is still necessary. National law will not be pursued in this Thesis, but selected national law will be used on a limited basis as illustrations. Examples from national legislation are mainly used where Member States have a choice when implementing the rules (the Public Sector Remedies Directive).

4.4. Enforcement

In procurement matters the Court of Justice handles two types of cases: enforcement actions against a Member State[70] and preliminary rulings.[71] Because disputes regarding the three types of contracts are most likely to start in

69. Commission's Evaluation Report '*Impact and Effectiveness of EU Public Procurement Legislation*', part 1 SEC(2011) 853 final, pp. 53-54.
70. The Commission is entitled to bring enforcement proceedings against a Member State in accordance with Article 258 TFEU. Enforcement action can also be taken by another Member State under the procedure in Article 259 TFEU. Directive 2007/66/EC Article 3 contains a corrective mechanism the Commission must use prior to a contract being concluded. For further on enforcement actions in procurement situations see, for example, Bovis, Christopher *"EU public procurement law"* [2007] Elgar European Law, chapter 16. Treumer, Steen *"Enforcement of the EU Public Procurement Rules: The State of Law and Current Issues"* in Treumer, Steen & Lichère Francois (Eds) *"Enforcement of the EU Public Procurement Rules"* [2011] DJØF, p. 20 ff., For enforcement proceedings in general, see Hartley, TC *"The Foundations of European Union Law"* [2010] 7th Edition, Oxford University Press, chapter 10, Craig, Paul and Búrca, Gráinne de *"EU Law – Text, Cases and Materials"* [2011] 5th Edition, Oxford University Press, chapter 12.
71. According to Article 267 TFEU. The Court of Justice will, however, not solve the case. For further on preliminary rulings see, for example, Broberg, Morten *"Preliminary References by Public Administrative Bodies: When Are Public Administrative Bodies Competent to Make Preliminary References to the European Court of Justice?"* [2009] ELR n° 15, pp. 207–22; Hartley, TC *"The Foundations of European Union Law"* [2010] 7th Edition, Oxford University Press, chapter 9, Craig, Paul and Búrca, Gráinne de *"EU Law – Text, Cases and Materials"* [2011] 5th Edition, Oxford University Press, chapter 13.

national courts, this Thesis will only analyse the enforcement mechanism and remedies available at national level (see Part III of the Thesis).

Some Member States have chosen to apply the same rules in their enforcement systems regarding the three types of contracts as for contracts falling under the Public Sector Directive.[72] In other Member States the enforcement system is only available for contracts covered by the Public Sector Directive.[73] Examples from the national systems will only be used as illustration. Therefore, where the information has been available, the analysis will be supplied with examples from the Member States.[74]

Case law from the Member States has been used limitedly, and function here only as illustration. Naturally, language obstacles have also limited the analysis. Consequently, only case law from Member States, language comprehension was possible, has been taken into considerations.

72. According to the Commission's Evaluation Report *'Impact and Effectiveness of EU Public Procurement Legislation'*, part 1 SEC (2011) 853 final, p. 68, for contracts below the thresholds, this goes for: Czech Republic, Estonia, Finland, France, Hungary, Portugal, Slovak Republic, Denmark and Sweden. It can be discussed whether Denmark falls in this category as ineffectiveness is only applicable for contracts falling within the Public Procurement Directives (the Enforcement Act §§16-17, for further on remedies see chapter 11).
73. See the Commission's Evaluation Report *'Impact and Effectiveness of EU Public Procurement Legislation'*, part 1 SEC(2011) 853 final, states that this goes for: Germany, Ireland and United Kingdom.
74. For further on the national review systems in general, see, for example, Treumer, Steen & Lichère Francois (Eds) *"Enforcement of the EU Public Procurement Rules"* [2011] DJØF contains an introduction to selected Member States review systems. See also OECD (2007), *"Public Procurement Review and Remedies Systems in the European Union"*, Sigma Papers, No. 41, OECD Publishing; the Commission's Evaluation Report *'Impact and Effectiveness of EU Public Procurement Legislation'*, part 1 SEC(2011) 853 final; Bianchi, Tiziana & Guidi, Valentina *"The Comparative Survey on the National Public Procurement Systems across the PPN"*.

5. Contracting authorities

A comment should be made as to who are obliged to follow the obligations analysed in this Thesis. It is not apparent that the same types of contracting authorities and contracting entities that fall within the Procurement Directives are also covered by the principles of the Treaties when dealing with one of the three types of contracts. Nevertheless, it seems to be the Commission's opinion that the principles of the Treaties apply to both contracting authorities within the meaning of the Public Sector Directive as well as contracting entities covered by the Utilities Directive.[75]

If a contract falls within one of the Procurement Directives, the contracting authority or entity is obliged to follow the principles of the Treaties when awarding such contracts.[76] Thus, it could on one hand be argued that these contracting authorities and contracting entities are also obliged to follow the principles of the Treaties when awarding one of the three types of contracts. On the other hand, it is also possible that a parallel can be drawn to who are obliged by the provisions of free movement in the TFEU.

Regarding who are obliged to follow the provisions of free movement in the TFEU, it is in that regard Member States which are the ones obliged, but the concept of Member State must be interpreted broadly. Thus, as a minimum the free movement rules are direct applicable vertically.[77] Transferred to the Public Sector Directive, which e.g. applies to contracting *authorities*, covering the State, regional, and local authorities and bodies governed by public law,[78] this will in my view as a minimum cover the State, regional, and local authorities. Whether bodies governed by public law are also covered by the Treaty when dealing with one of the three types of contracts can be discussed. The Court of Justice has had the opportunity several times to clarify

75. See the 2006 Communication which does not make any distinction as to the sector involved, and which states: '*In this Communication the term 'contracting entity' covers both contracting authorities within the meaning of Article 1(9) of Directive 2004/18/EC and contracting entities within the meaning of Article 2 of Directive 2004/17/EC.*'
76. See e.g. the Public Sector Directive Article 2.
77. Nielsen, Ruth and Neergaard, Ulla *"EU Ret"* [2010] 6th Edition, DJØF, p. 282.
78. The Public Sector Directive Article 1(9). The Directive also applies to associations formed by one or several of such authorities or one or several of such bodies governed by public law.

which bodies are covered by the Public Sector Directive,[79] but a detailed analysis of such falls outside the aim of this Thesis.[80]

In *Wall,*[81] the Court found that in order for the principles of the Treaty to apply (mainly the transparency obligation), two conditions must be satisfied. First, the undertaking in question had to be effectively controlled by the State or another public authority. Second, the undertaking should not compete in the market.[82] The Court found that these conditions were not satisfied in the case.[83] *Brown* states that:

'... it seems likely that this two-part test will become the standard formulation for assessing whether or not a particular entity is sufficiently tied to the public sector to be subject to the

79. For case law on who are covered by the Public Procurement Directives see, for example, Case C-31/87, Gebroeders Beentjes BV v. the Netherlands, [1988] ECR 4635; Case C-44/96, Mannesmann Anlagenbau Austria AG v. Strohal Rotationsdruck GesmbH, [1998] ECR I-73; Case C-323/96, Commission v. Belgium, [1998] ECR I-5063; Case C-360/96, Gemeente Arnhem og Gemeente Rheden v. BFI Holding BV, [1998] ECR I-6821; Case C-380/98, The Queen H.M. Treasury v. the University of Cambridge, [2000] ECR I-8035; Joined Cases C-223/99 and C-260/99, Agorà Srl and Excelsior Snc di Pedrotti Bruna & C. v. Ente Autonomo Fiera Internazionale di Milano and Ciftat Soc. coop. arl. [2001] ECR I-3605; Case C-373/00, Adolf Truley GmbH v. Bestattung Wien GmbH, [2003] ECR I-1931; Case C-393/06, Ing. Aigner, Wasser-Wärme-Umwelt GmbH v. Fernwärme Wien GmbH, [2008] ECR I-2339.
80. For further on the subject of contracting authorities falling within the Public Sector Directive see Arrowsmith, Sue *"The entity coverage of the EC procurement directives and UK regulations: a review"* [2004] PPLR n° 2, 59-86; Arrowsmith, Sue *"The Law of Public and Utilities Procurement"* [2005] 2nd Edition, Sweet and Maxwell chapter 5; Trepte, Peter *"Public Procurement in the EU"* [2007] 2nd Edition, Oxford, chapter 2 and 3.
81. Case C-91/08, Wall AG v. La ville de Francfort-sur-le-Main and Frankfurter Entsorgungs- und Service (FES) GmbH, [2010] ECR I-2815.
82. Case C-91/08, Wall AG v. La ville de Francfort-sur-le-Main and Frankfurter Entsorgungs- und Service (FES) GmbH, [2010] ECR I-2815, paragraph 49.
83. Case C-91/08, Wall AG v. La ville de Francfort-sur-le-Main and Frankfurter Entsorgungs- und Service (FES) GmbH, [2010] ECR I-2815, paragraphs 53 and 57. Advocate General Bot had in his opinion to the case contrary applied the full conditions of a body governed by public law, see Opinion of Advocate General Bot delivered on October 27, 2009 in Case C-91/08, Wall AG v. La ville de Francfort-sur-le-Main and Frankfurter Entsorgungs- und Service (FES) GmbH, [2010] ECR I-2815.

Treaty principles and obligations associated with the award of contracts falling outside the procurement Directives'.[84]

Whether the requirement in *Wall* regarding that the body must be *'controlled by the State'* is to be considered as the exact same requirement as in the Public Sector Directive Article 1(9) c, is open for discussion. According to the Public Sector Directive Article 1(9), c, a body governed by public law must either be

'(c) financed, for the most part, by the State, regional or local authorities, or other bodies governed by public law; or subject to management supervision by those bodies; or having an administrative, managerial or supervisory board, more than half of whose members are appointed by the State, regional or local authorities, or by other bodies governed by public law'.

These three conditions are not cumulative. Nevertheless, they all have the pupose of ensuring that a body must in fact be under control or financing before the Directive applies. It is my opinion that if one of the three criteria in Article 1(9) c is fulfilled, the body is 'controlled by the State' in the sense that the principles of the Treaties will apply when awarding one of the three times of contracts.

To conclude regarding contracting authorities covered by the Public Sector Directive all such contracting authorities, which are covered by the Public Sector Directive, must ensure that the Treaties are respected, including bodies governed by public law. For example in *Vestergaard,* [85] the Court found a Danish public housing body (a body governed by public law) to be obliged to follow the Treaty's free movement provision on goods. Also, in the *Commission v. Ireland,*[86] the Court of Justice found a body governed by public law, the 'Irish goods Council,' to be bound by the provision of free movement of goods as the body was under control of the Irish Government.

The fact that a criterion for the Treaty to apply is that the undertaking does not compete on the market will in my opinion have the consequence that certain private utilities will not be obliged to follow the principles of the Treaty, as they will in many situations compete at a given market.

84. Brown, Adrian *"Changing a sub-contractor under a public services concession: Wall AG v. Stadt Frankfurt am Main (C-91/08)"* [2010] PPLR n° 5, pp. 160-166.
85. Case C-59/00, Bent Mousten Vestergaard v. Spøttrup Boligselskab, [2001] ECR I-9505. The Case is further elaborated on in mainly chapters 6 and 8.
86. Case C-249/81, Commission v. Ireland, [1982] ECR 4005.

According to Article 30 of the Utilities Directive, it is possible to get an exemption from the Directive in case where '... *an activity is directly exposed to competition...*'.[87] Thus, in my opinion such undertakings will at the same time be granted an exemption from the principles of the Treaties as the activities have been measured as being exposed to competition and as stated in *Wall* in order for the Treaty to apply the undertaking should not compete in the market.[88] Contrary, if an exception has been ejected there will in my opinion be an assumption that the bodies operating on the market is also covered by the Treaty do to lack of competition.

If a contracting authority is covered by the Public Sector Directive but is involved with activities covered by the Utilities Directive,[89] the rules in the Utilities Directive will apply for these activities and the rules in the Public Sector Directive will apply for all other contracts.[90] For the three types of contracts, the Treaties applies to contracting authorities even if the activity involved concerns one of the activities mentioned in Articles 3-7 of the Utilities Directive.[91] However, a contracting entity, which is not a contracting authority within the meaning of the Public Sector Directive, is presumably not obliged to follow the obligations derived from the principles of the Treaties when awarding one of the three types of contracts.[92]

87. The Utilities Directive Article 30 (2).
88. Case C-91/08, Wall AG v. La ville de Francfort-sur-le-Main and Frankfurter Entsorgungs- und Service (FES) GmbH, [2010] ECR I-2815, paragraph 49.
89. Articles 3-7 of Directive 2004/17/EC list the sectors to which the Directive applies. However, it is possible to get an exemption from the Utilities Directive by application according to Article 30. For these entities it is crucial to know whether they are obliged to follow the principles of the Treaties – even though they are exempt from the Utilities Directive.
90. See Case C-393/06, Ing. Aigner, Wasser-Wärme-Umwelt GmbH v. Fernwärme Wien GmbH, [2008] ECR I-2339, paragraph 33: *'a contracting entity, within the meaning of Directive 2004/17, is required to apply the procedure laid down in that directive only for the award of contracts which relate to activities carried out by that entity in one or more of the sectors listed in Articles 3 to 7 of that directive'.*
91. In line with Szydlo, Marek *"Contracts beyond the scope of the EC procurement Directives – who is bound by the requirement for transparency"* [2009] ELR n° 34(5), pp. 720-737.
92. However, the Commission seems to be of the opinion that the principles of the Treaties applies equally to bodies falling under both Directives, since they are using the term contracting entities throughout the 2006 Communication. Contrary, for example Nielsen, Ruth *"Udbud af offentlige kontrakter"* [1998] 1st Edition, DJØF p. 89; Trepte, Peter *"Public Procurement in the EU"* [2007] 2nd Edition, Oxford University Press, p. 279, who is of the opinion that at least Article 30 TFEU does not apply to private persons or entities. Trybus, Martin *"Public Contracts in European Union Internal Market*

Whether the provisions are direct applicable horizontally, in the way that also private bodies are obliged by the free movement provisions is unclear.[93] In my opinion such bodies are not covered by the Treaty's principles of equal treatment and transparency when awarding one of the three types of contracts, hence neither an undertaking nor an association, organisation or similar, which are not covered by the Public Procurement Directives is covered by the transparency obligation derived from the principles of the Treaty.

Finally, it should be mentioned that the Public Sector Directive also contains specific provisions that can extend the rules in the Directive to certain private parties, such as Article 8, which addresses contracts subsidised by more than 50 percent by contracting authorities. That such rules will apply outside the Directive appears unlikely. The same goes for situations when Member States, in their national legislation, include more bodies than those mentioned in the Public Sector Directive – such bodies will not be obliged to follow the Treaties.

6. Plan and structure of the Thesis

The Thesis will be divided into three parts.

Part I of the Thesis, *'Introduction, Definitions and Foundations'* defines the three types of contracts and set out the foundations regarding awareness of when the obligations derived from the Treaties apply. The aim and principles of the EU procurement rules will be discussed in chapter 2, because it is essential that the right grounds for interpretation of the principles of the Treaties is established.

Furthermore, part I is found necessary to establish whether a contract falls within the Public Sector Directive. The task of defining a service concession contract has proved to be complicated. Thus, analysing what constitutes a service concession contract in order to know which rules a contracting au-

Law: Foundations and Requirements" in Nogouelleou, Rozen and Stelkens, Ulrich (Eds) *"Comparative Law on Public Contracts"* [2010] Brussels Bruylant, p. 90 states *'It is clear that it [the Treaty] applies to the acts of contracting authorites subject to Directives (...). It is not clear whether it applies to private utilities (...).'* For further on the subject of who are obliged to follow the obligations derived from the principles of the Treaties, see Szydlo, Marek *"Contracts beyond the scope of the EC procurement Directives – who is bound by the requirement for transparency"* [2009] ELR n° 34(5), pp. 720-737.

93. Case C-281/98, Roman Angonese v. Cassa di Risparmio di Bolzano SpA, [2000] ECR I-4139, in where the Court applied Art. 45 TFEU to a private body.

thority is required to follow is essential. Therefore, chapter 3 analyses in details what constitutes a service concession contract. Chapter 4 establishes when a contract falls below the thresholds. Chapter 5 concerns B-service contracts and will examine the reasons for having divided services into two categories in the Public Sector Directive.

Because the principles of the Treaties only apply if the contract in question is of 'certain cross-border interest', it is relevant to analyse when a contract is of cross-border interest (chapter 6). The analysis of when a contract is of cross-border interest has been placed in part I of the Thesis because 'cross-border interest' is considered an essential requirement for the principles of the Treaties to apply and not as an obligation that can be derived from the principles of the Treaties.

Part II of the Thesis *'Positive obligations derived from the principles of the Treaties'* includes an analysis of the positive obligations derived from the principles of the Treaties that a contracting authority is required to follow when entering into one of the three types of contract. Chapter 7 addresses the transparency obligation and questions the necessity of advertising the contract beforehand. Chapter 8 analyses the existence of other types of obligations derived from the principles of the Treaties, other than the transparency obligation that a contracting authority must ensure when awarding one of the three types of contracts. Chapter 9 will analyse whether a contracting authority is required to state reasons for its decisions taken when awarding one of the three types of contracts and whether contracting authorities are under a duty to respect a standstill period before a contract can be signed.

Part III of this Thesis *'Enforcement and Remedies'* will analyse how the obligations derived from the principles of the Treaties can be enforced. This part will be divided into two chapters. Chapter 10 relates to the enforcement mechanism, which must be available in the Member States (at the national level), and addresses concerns such as who are entitled to bring proceedings and where proceedings can be brought. Accordingly, the chapter will examine and analyse the rules in the Public Sector Remedies Directive and whether they apply to the three types of contracts or if similar rules apply based on the EU principles.

Chapter 11 will analyse which remedies must be available at the national review bodies. Accordingly, the chapter will analyse and discuss whether remedies in the Public Sector Remedies Directive apply as well as analysing whether there exist remedies that are not to be found in the Directive.

Finally, chapter 12 includes a summary of the findings in this Thesis.

CHAPTER 2

Objectives and principles of the EU Procurement Rules

1. Introduction

This chapter establishes some common grounds for interpreting the obligations derived from the principles of the Treaties (as will be analysed in Part II of the Thesis). The chapter explores and discusses the objectives and principles of the EU Procurement rules.

As explained in chapter 1, the Court of Justice's interpretation method is often teleological. Therefore, in order to lie down the grounds for interpretation, it is important to examine the overall objectives of the EU procurement rules. In order to establish the objectives of the EU procurement rules, the legislative history of the Directives will be explored to examine the EU legislator's intentions of adopting EU procurement rules. To this end, the present chapter examines the Commission's proposal and background documents for the first Works Directive. Furthermore, it also examines the Court of Justice's understanding of the objectives of the EU procurement rules in order to determine the right grounds for interpreting the rules. The aim of this chapter is not to make a comprehensive analysis of the Procurement Rules in historic perspective, but merely to examine the objectives behind the rules.[1]

The principles of the Treaties play a substantial role in EU public procurement. Indeed, Article 2 of the Public Sector Directive now elaborates on the principles, stating that: *'Contracting authorities shall treat economic operators equally and non-discriminatorily and shall act in a transparent way.'* The prior Procurement Directives did not explicitly mention the principles; nonetheless, the Court of Justice interpreted a principle of equal treatment to

1. For further on the historical aspects of the procurement rules, see Trepte, Peter *"Public Procurement in the EU"* [2007] 2nd Edition, Oxford, chapter 1, section C.

lie within the very essence of the first Works Directive. In *Greatbelt*,[2] the Court stated that

> '... *although the directive makes no express mention of the principle of equal treatment of tenderers, the duty to observe that principle lies at the very heart of the directive (...)*'.[3]

Thus, the principles of the procurement rules were already inherent in the rules without the Directives having to state it expressly. This chapter examines whether, in terms of procurement matters, the principles of the Procurement Directives are the same as those of the Treaties. I consider the principle of equal treatment and the principle of transparency to be the most relevant principles for the analysis in Part II of the Thesis. Accordingly, the present chapter examines the origin of these principles, while Part II of the Thesis analyses their substance.

1.1. Outline

The chapter starts by discussing the objectives of the EU procurement rules (section 2). Section 3 examines the principles of the Treaties and their development in relation to procurement situations, with particular focus on the principle of non-discrimination on grounds of nationality and the principle of equal treatment (sections 3.1 and 3.2). The latter section also discusses and examines whether the principle of non-discrimination has an independent function compared to the principle of equal treatment. Section 3.3 explores and discusses the principle of transparency. It explores whether the principle has a 'stand-alone' function, in the sense that the principle can be invoked alone.

2. Objectives of the EU procurement rules

The aim of the first Works Directive[4] was to:

2. Case C-243/89, Commission v. Denmark, [1993] ECR I-3353.
3. Case C-243/89, Commission v. Denmark, [1993] ECR I-3353, paragraph 33. The Court of Justice has since referred to this paragraph in several cases. See, for example, Case C-513/99, Concordia Bus Finland v. Helsingin kaupunki and HKL-Bussiliikenne, [2002] ECR I-7213, paragraph 81 and the case law cited herein.
4. Directive 71/305/EEC of 26 July 1971 concerning the co-ordination of procedures for the award of public works contracts, [1971] OJ L 185/5. Henceforth, the first Works Directive.

'... *remove restrictions on freedom of establishment and freedom to supply services for the benefit of public works contractors*'.[5] As well as: '*To ensure development of effective competition in the field of public contract it is necessary that contract notices drawn up by the authorities (...) be advertised throughout the Community*'.[6]

By requiring contracting authorities to follow certain procedures laid down in the Directives, effective competition would be developed for public works contracts and restrictions of the free movement rules would be removed. Requiring that certain procedures be followed creates transparency for the contracts. On one hand, this ensures that contracts are put out for competition; on the other, it ensures that the procedures are followed. The need for further improvements of transparency over time has also been identified.[7] Opening public contracts for competition will create equal access for economic operators to public contracts, which will help ensure that the interests of economic operators are protected.

Despite the fact that the overall objective of the Procurement Directives was to remove restrictions and ensure the creation of competition for a contract, further objectives have been identified. For example, the Commission's Green Paper from 1996 states:

'*There are, of course, many other, perhaps less obvious, benefits of a more open procurement policy. Fair, non-discriminatory and transparent procurement procedures render perpetration of fraud and corruption in public administration more difficult.*'[8]

Therefore, avoiding corruption has also been identified as one of the procurement rules' objectives. However, the Green Paper also acknowledged that the primary objectives of the EU procurement rules have remained unchanged. These objectives are:

5. See the Explanatory Memorandum to the Commission's Proposal for a first directive of the Council on the co-ordination of procedures for the conclusion of public works contract, Supplement to Bulletin of the European Economic Community No 9/10, 1964/12.
6. See Recital 9 to the first Works Directive.
7. White Paper *'Completing the Internal Market'* [1985] COM(85)310, paragraph 85 of which states: *'In order to stimulate a wider opening up of tendering for public contracts, there is a serious and urgent need for improvement of the Directives to increase transparency further.'*
8. Green Paper *'Public Procurement in the European Union: Exploring the way'*, [1996] COM (1996) 583, p. 4, section 2.4.

'To create the necessary competitive conditions in which public contracts are awarded without discrimination and value for taxpayers' money is achieved through the choice of the best bid submitted; to give suppliers access to a single market (...).'[9]

As can also been seen from this, another objective of the procurement rules is to ensure that the public receives the 'best value for money'. However, it could be argued that elements such as this, as well as avoiding corruption, are not the aims of the procurement rules themselves, but an added benefit gained from the rules.[10] It has also been argued that getting the best value for money is more the aim of the national rules governing procurement,[11] whereas the EU regime has the aim of opening up procurement to trade between Member States.[12]

According to the Court of Justice, in *Beentjes*,[13] the objective of the first Works Directive was

'... to coordinate national procedures for the award of public works contracts concluded in Member States on behalf of the State, regional or local authorities or other legal persons governed by public law.' It was emphasised hereafter that the aim of the Directive is *'to ensure the effective attainment of freedom of establishment and freedom to provide services in respect of public works contracts (...).'*[14]

Here, the Court emphasises the achievement of the Internal Market. Later on, the Court also found that ensuring an effective Internal Market is the objective of the EU Procurement Directives, and that the procurement rules aim to

9. Green Paper '*Public Procurement in the European Union: Exploring the way*', [1996] COM (1996) 583, p. 3, section 2.3.
10. Arrowsmith, Sue and Kunzlik, Peter (Eds) *"Social and Environmental Policies in EC Procurement Law"* [2009] Cambridge University Press, p. 31 state that it is not an objective of neither the Directives or the free movement provisions to ensure that Member States achieve the best value for money.
11. Neumayr, Florian, *"Value for money v. equal treatment: the relationship between the seemingly overriding national rationale for regulating public procurement and the fundamental E.C. principle of equal treatment"* [2002] PPLR n° 4, 215-234, who states: '*In E.C. Member States, obtaining value for money generally plays a key role in regulating public procurement.*'
12. Arrowsmith, Sue *"The Law of Public and Utilities Procurement"* [2005] 2nd Edition, Sweet and Maxwell, p. 73.
13. Case C-31/87, Gebroeders Beentjes BV v. the Netherlands, [1988] ECR 4635.
14. Case C-31/87, Gebroeders Beentjes BV v. the Netherlands, [1988] ECR 4635, paragraph 9.

eliminate barriers to the Internal Market. In *Lianakis,*[15] for example, the Court stated that the objective is to

'... *eliminate barriers to the freedom to provide services and therefore to protect the interests of economic operators established in a Member State who wish to offer services to contracting authorities established in another Member State*'.[16]

Thus, when eliminating barriers to the Internal Market, the interest of undertakings would be protected. In line with the protection of the undertakings' interests, the Court of Justice has also identified ensuring competition as an essential objective of the Directives.[17]

In *Pressetext,*[18] the Court found that the aim of the procurement rules is twofold: to '... *ensure the free movement of services and the opening-up to undistorted competition in all the Member States.*'[19] The Court added that, in order to pursue this two-fold objective,

15. Case C-532/06, Emm. G. Lianakis AE, Sima Anonymi Techniki Etaireia Meleton kai Epivlepseon and Nikolaos Vlachopoulos v. Dimos Alexandroupolis and Others, [2008] ECR I-251.
16. Case C-532/06, Emm. G. Lianakis AE, Sima Anonymi Techniki Etaireia Meleton kai Epivlepseon and Nikolaos Vlachopoulos v. Dimos Alexandroupolis and Others, [2008] ECR I-251, paragraph 39. See also, for example, Case C-380/98, The Queen v. H.M. Treasury, ex parte The University of Cambridge, [2000] ECR I-8035, paragraph 16. Case C-19/00, SIAC Construction, [2001] ECR I-7725, paragraph 32. Case C-92/00, Hospital Ingenieure Krankenhaustechnik Planungs-Gesellschaft mbH (HI) v. Stadt Wien, [2002] ECR I-5553, paragraph 43.
17. See, for example, Case C-95/10, Strong Segurança SA v. Município de Sintra, Securitas-Serviços e Tecnologia de Segurança, [2011] March 17, 2011 (not yet reported), paragraph 37, in which the Court states: '... *whereas effective competition constitutes the essential objective of that directive (...)*'. For more on competition concerns in public procurement, see Graells, Albert Sánchez *"Public Procurement and the EU Competition Rules"* [2011] Hart, chapter 5 and by Ølykke, Grith *"Abnormally low Tenders – with an emphasis on public tenderers"* [2010] DJØF, chapter 2. Ølykke, Grith Skovgaard *"How does the Court of Justice of the European Union pursue competition concerns in a public procurement context?"* [2011] PPLR n° 6, pp. 179-192.
18. Case C-454/06, Pressetext Nachrichtenagentur GmbH v. Austria, APA-OTS Originaltext-Service GmbH and APA Austria Presse Agentur registrierte Genossenschaft mit beschränkter Haftung, [2008] ECR I-4401.
19. Case C-454/06, Pressetext Nachrichtenagentur GmbH v. Austria, APA-OTS Originaltext-Service GmbH and APA Austria Presse Agentur registrierte Genossenschaft mit beschränkter Haftung, [2008] ECR I-4401, paragraph 31.

> *'... Community law applies inter alia the principle of non-discrimination on grounds of nationality, the principle of equal treatment of tenderers and the obligation of transparency resulting therefrom.'*[20]

Thus, it is not only the EU Procurement Directives that aim to ensure equal access to public contracts for economic operators; the principles of the Treaties also have this aim. In *Wall,*[21] the Court also clearly stated that the objectives of the Procurement Directives, as well as those pursued by the principles, derived from the Treaties are identical. More specifically, the Court of Justice found that:

> *'... the principles of equal treatment and non-discrimination on grounds of nationality, and the consequent obligation of transparency,* ***pursue the same objectives as Directive 92/50, in particular the free movement of services and their opening up to undistorted competition in the Member States'*** [emphasis added].[22]

To conclude, the analysis in Part II of this Thesis is based on the assumption that the main objective of the procurement rules found within the principles of the Treaties is to ensure undistorted competition by guaranteeing open and equal access to public contracts.

3. Principles derived from the Treaties

Various principles derived from the Treaties apply when awarding one of the three types of contracts (see part II of the Thesis). Sections 3.1–3.3 will address the origin of the principles.

3.1. The principle of non-discrimination

According to Article 18 TFEU, any discrimination on grounds of nationality shall be prohibited. Thus, a contracting authority shall treat non-domestic economic operators and domestic operators equally.

20. Case C-454/06, Pressetext Nachrichtenagentur GmbH v. Austria, APA-OTS Originaltext-Service GmbH and APA Austria Presse Agentur registrierte Genossenschaft mit beschränkter Haftung, [2008] ECR I-4401, paragraph 32.
21. Case C-91/08, Wall AG v. La ville de Francfort-sur-le-Main and Frankfurter Entsorgungs- und Service (FES) GmbH, [2010] ECR I-2815.
22. Case C-91/08, Wall AG v. La ville de Francfort-sur-le-Main and Frankfurter Entsorgungs- und Service (FES) GmbH, [2010] ECR I-2815, paragraph 48.

Even though the principle of non-discrimination on grounds of nationality can be found directly in the TFEU, the Court has stated that the principle of non-discrimination by reason of nationality is merely an expression of the more general principle of equal treatment. In *Überschär*, for example, the Court of Justice stated that the principle of equal treatment, *'of which the prohibition on discrimination on grounds of nationality is merely a specific enunciation, is one of the fundamental principles of community law'*.[23] Also, in a more recent case, *Land Oberösterreich*, did the Court find that the principle of non-discrimination is: *'... a specific expression of the general principle of equality, which itself is one of the fundamental principles of Community law'*.[24] Therefore, it could be argued that because the principle of non-discrimination on grounds of nationality stems from the principle of equal treatment, the former has no independent function, as the principle of equal treatment would always apply.

Trepte states that the two principles are not to be treated as the same, and that, the principle of non-discrimination is not to be confused with the broader principle of equal treatment.[25] Whilst discrimination in a given context will produce unequal treatment, unequal treatment does not always necessarily give rise to discrimination.[26] The principle of discrimination on the grounds of nationality is described negatively in Article 18 TFEU, which states that '*... any discrimination on grounds of nationality shall be prohibited.*' The principle of equal treatment, on the other hand, is viewed more positively, ensuring that '*comparable situations must not be treated differently and that different situations must not be treated in the same way unless such treatment is objectively justified.*'[27] Even though the two principles are formulated differently, it is submitted that the effect of these two principles in procurement matters is largely the same; this point is explored further in section 3.2.

23. Case C-810/79, Peter Überschär v. Bundesversicherungsanstalt für Angestellte, [1980] ECR 2747, paragraph 16.
24. Case C-115/08, Land Oberösterreich v. ČEZ, [2009] ECR I-10265, paragraph 89.
25. Trepte, Peter *"Public Procurement in the EU"* [2007] 2nd Edition, Oxford, p. 7.
26. Trepte, Peter *"Public Procurement in the EU"* [2007] 2nd Edition, Oxford, p. 14.
27. See, for example, joined cases C-21/03 and C-34/03, Fabricom SA v. Belgian State, [2005] ECR 2005 I-1559, paragraph 27. See also Case T-125/06, Centro Studi Antonio Manieri Srl v. Council of the European Union, [2009] ECR II-69, paragraph 82, and Case C-304/01, Spain v. Commission, [2004] ECR I-7655, paragraph 31.

3.2. The principle of equal treatment

The principle of equal treatment applies regardless of nationality. This has been stated in, for example, *Parking Brixen,*[28] where the Court found that

> '*... the principle of equal treatment of tenderers is to be applied to public service concessions* ***even in the absence of discrimination on grounds of nationality***' [emphasis added].[29]

The Court found that the principle of equal treatment also applied outside the Directive, which means that the principle is to be found directly in the Treaties.

Arrowsmith and Kunzlik considered the approach taken by the Court to be incorrect. They argued that:

> *'There is no authority for such a general principle separate from specific obligations such as non-discrimination on grounds of nationality (...) and the fact that the principle of non-discrimination (...) is one aspect of equal treatment does not entail that all the consequences of the equal treatment principle as manifested in the directives must follow from the Treaty.'*[30]

Arrowsmith and Kunzlik argued that a principle of equal treatment cannot be considered as a general principle of the Treaty,[31] but that the principle can only be found under the Procurement Directives. Thus, the principle of equal

28. Case C-458/03, Parking Brixen GmbH v. Gemeinde Brixen and Stadtwerke Brixen AG, [2005] ECR I-8585.
29. Case C-458/03, Parking Brixen GmbH v. Gemeinde Brixen and Stadtwerke Brixen AG, [2005] ECR I-8585, paragraph 48.
30. Arrowsmith, Sue and Kunzlik, Peter (Eds) *"Social and Environmental Policies in EC Procurement Law"* [2009] Cambridge University Press p. 86. Along the same lines is Krugner, Matthias *"The principles of equal treatment and transparency and the Commissions Interpretative Communication on Concessions"* [2003] PPLR n° 5, pp. 181-207, which submits that the application of the principle of equality is limited to the enunciation of non-discrimination on grounds of nationality. The contrary view is that of Hatzis, Nicholas *"The legality of SME development policies under EC procurement law"* in Arrowsmith, Sue and Kunzlik, Peter (Eds) *"Social and Environmental Policies in EC Procurement Law"* [2009] Cambridge University Press, p. 350.
31. Arrowsmith, Sue and Kunzlik, Peter (Eds) *"Social and Environmental Policies in EC Procurement Law"* [2009] Cambridge University Press, p. 86. See also Krugner, Matthias *"The principles of equal treatment and transparency and the Commissions Interpretative Communication on Concessions"* [2003] PPLR n° 5, pp. 181-207.

treatment would not apply when awarding a contract that falls outside the Directive. In line with this is *Braun*, who argues that '... *the positive effects of the fundamental procurement principles of equality and transparency are embodied in the directives and cannot be imported into the Treaty.*'[32] The above statements can be considered controversial, as other fields of law have accepted that a principle of equal treatment is inherent in the Treaty.[33]

Chapter 6 argues that the principle of transparency and the principle of equal treatment only apply if a contract is of 'certain cross-border interest'. Therefore, if a contract is of cross-border interest, the contracting authority has already found that an undertaking from a Member State other than the contracting authority could potentially be interested in the contract. This means that such an undertaking should not be treated differently than domestic undertakings, either by negative measures (by requiring the non-domestic undertaking to fulfil certain criteria that domestic undertakings should not fulfil) or in positive way (by giving one domestic undertaking an advantage that all the other tenderers do not have). Therefore, it is necessary that a principle of equal treatment apply regardless of nationality. In my view, the Court's approach in *Parking Brixen*[34] was correct. Once cross-border interest is established, the contracting authority must ensure the principle of equal treatment, regardless of who actually choses to tender for the contract. The principle of equal treatment also applies if it turns out that only domestic undertakings are interested in the contract, given that the assessment of whether a contract is of cross-border interest must be made at the time that the contracting authority decides whether to put the contract out for competition. If the contract is put out for competition, the principle of equal treatment applies in all phases of the competition, regardless of the tenderers' nationality (see chapter 6 for more).

The fact that the principle of equal treatment applies regardless of nationality, even outside the Public Sector Directive, was also confirmed later on in the Court's case law. For example, see *ANAV,* where the Court found that

32. Braun, Peter *"A Matter of Principle(s) – The Treatment of Contracts Falling Outside the Scope of the European Procurement Directives"* [2000] PPLR n° 1, pp. 39-49.
33. See Tridimas, Takis *"The General Principles of EU Law"* [2006] 2nd Edition, Oxford University Press, Krugner, Matthias *"The principles of equal treatment and transparency and the Commissions Interpretative Communication on Concessions"* [2003] PPLR n° 5, pp. 181-207.
34. Case C-458/03, Parking Brixen GmbH v. Gemeinde Brixen and Stadtwerke Brixen AG, [2005] ECR I-8585.

'Besides the principle of non-discrimination on grounds of nationality, the principle of equal treatment of tenderers is also to be applied to public service concessions even in the absence of discrimination on grounds of nationality.'[35]

In sum, regardless of the varying points of view,[36] it must now be considered settled case law that a principle of equal treatment follows from the TFEU. Thus, when a contracting authority enters into one of the three types of contracts, the principle of equal treatment must be applied regardless of the tenderers' nationality.[37]

It is difficult to imagine that the principle of non-discrimination would have an independent function in procurement context. In terms of the principle of non-discrimination in relation to the free movement provisions, the Court has frequently emphasised that Article 18 TFEU has a residual character. In that regard, the provision only applies if one of the free movement provisions does not.[38] Perhaps the same could be said to apply in procurement contexts. Therefore, if the principle of equal treatment is not applicable (which, in my opinion, would be the case if the contract is not of cross-border interest), then the principle of non-discrimination could theoretically play a role. In such cases, however, is it most likely that a given situation would instead fall under one of the free movement provisions, which makes the principle of non-discrimination secondary also in procurement cases.

35. Case C-410/04, Associazione Nazionale Autotrasporto Viaggiatori (ANAV) v. Comune di Bari and AMTAB Servizio SpA, [2006] ECR I-3303, paragraph 20. See also Case C-220/06, Asociación Profesional de Empresas de Reparto y Manipulado de Correspondencia v. Administración General del Estado, [2007] ECR I-12175, paragraph 74. Case C-196/08, Acoset SpA v. Conferenza Sindaci e Presidenza Prov. Reg. ATO Idrico Ragusa and Others, [2009] ECR I-9913, paragraph 48.
36. Arrowsmith, Sue (ed.) *"EU Public Procurement Law: An Introduction"* [2010] p. 78 now acknowledges that such a principle must be said to be found within the Treaty. She stated: *'However, recent CJEU jurisprudence accepts the Commission's view that such a general principle exists in the public procurement context.'*
37. In line with Neumayr, Florian *"Value for money v. equal treatment: the relationship between the seemingly overriding national rationale for regulating public procurement and the fundamental E.C. principle of equal treatment"* [2002] PPLR n° 4, 215–234, who stated: *'As a first conclusion, it can be stated that there seems to be nothing to back up the assertion that the ECJ would consider the Basic Principle to originate from the procurement directives alone. On the contrary, the ECJ has repeatedly indicated that this principle stems from the provisions of the E.C. Treaty.'*
38. See, for example, Case C-91/08, Wall AG v. La ville de Francfort-sur-le-Main and Frankfurter Entsorgungs- und Service (FES) GmbH, [2010] ECR I-2815, paragraph 32 with reference to the case law cited therein.

3.3. The principle of transparency

Traditionally, the principle of transparency within the Treaties ensures transparency in terms of access to documents at the EU Institutions or in the context of holdings of meetings in public.[39] Here, the function of the principle of transparency is a control function regarding whether certain rules have been breached.[40] In this context, transparency is generally a measure for ensuring that the EU Institutions act in accordance with the law, and that the public receives information about what takes place at the Institutions. In this way, ensuring transparency provides an image of fairness and frankness at the Institutions.

As will be explained below, the principle of transparency in a procurement context also contains such a control function (the principle of transparency's control function; see section 3.3.1.). However, the principle of transparency in the procurement context also pursues other goals, such as ensuring equal opportunities and competition (the principle of transparency's competition function; see section 3.3.2.).

3.3.1. The principle of transparency's control function

In a procurement context, the principle of transparency is primarily a measure for ensuring equal treatment of tenderers. In that regard, the principle of equal treatment can be characterised as the general principle.[41] However, this does not make the principle of transparency any less important. On the contrary, as argued by Advocate General *Mengozzi*: '... *the fact that it* [the principle of transparency] *is ancillary does not make it subordinate'*.[42] *Mengozzi* also argued that, if there is a lack of transparency, '... *it becomes difficult, if not im-*

39. Article 15(3) TFEU deals with access to documents of the Union's institutions. See also Regulation 1049/2001 of the European Parliament and of the Council of 30 May 2001 regarding public access to European Parliament, Council and Commission documents, [2001] OJ L 145/43. The right of access to documents can also be found in Article 42 of the Charter of Fundamental Rights.
40. For example, the Commission and European Parliament have launched a Transparency Register that aims to create transparency for all those seeking to influence European policy. See http://ec.europa.eu/transparency/. (last visited January 31, 2012)
41. Treumer, Steen *"Ligebehandlingsprincippet i EU's udbudsregler"* [2000] DJØF, p. 25: *'The principle of equal treatment can be characterised as the general principle, since the principle of transparency primarily serves as a measure to ensure the equal treatment of tenderers, which the procurement Directives aims at'* [My translation].
42. Opinion of Advocate General Mengozzi delivered on 29 June 2010 in C-226/09, Commission v. Ireland, [2010] November 18, 2010 (not yet reported), paragraph 35.

possible, to ascertain whether or not it may have failed to fulfil the requirements of equal treatment and non-discrimination'.[43]

Thus, the principle of transparency has a control function that ensures that other principles have been complied with. Consequently, the principle has a high value under the Procurement Directives, where the principle of transparency is mentioned several times.[44] As with the principle of equal treatment, earlier Directives did not mention the principle of transparency. However, the Court in the *Wallonian Bus* case[45] found that the Procurement Directives must be interpreted in accordance with a principle of transparency. The Court stated that:

'The procedure for comparing tenders therefore had to comply at every stage with both the principle of the equal treatment of tenderers and ***the principle of transparency so as to afford equality of opportunity to all tenderers when formulating their tenders****'* [emphasis added].[46]

Thus, the Court talks about the principle of transparency in context of evaluation of tenders where transparency is necessary, in order for tenderers to be assured that their bids are evaluated in accordance with the award criteria as advertised (which they took into account when drafting their tenders). Thus, the principle of transparency also function as a measure to ensure that the specific rules (and, ultimately, the principle of equal treatment) have not been breached. This is what, in the following, is called the principle of transparency's control function.

43. Opinion of Advocate General Mengozzi delivered on 29 June 2010 in Case C-226/09, Commission v. Ireland, [2010] November 18, 2010 (not yet reported), paragraph 35. The case is further discussed in chapter 8. *Arrowsmith* takes the same line in Arrowsmith, Sue *"The Law of Public and Utilities Procurement"* [2005] 2nd Edition, Sweet and Maxwell, p. 191, stating that the aim of transparency is *'... to make it possible to verify compliance with the principle of non-discrimination on grounds of nationality.'* See also Treumer, Steen *"Ligebehandlingsprincippet i EU's udbudsregler"* [2000] DJØF p. 23, who stated that: *'The purpose of the principle of transparency is to make the contract award transparent to reduce the possibility of abuse and ease the control and enforcement of the procurement rules.'* [My translation].
44. See Article 2. See also the Public Sector Directive, Recitals 2, 12, 14, 35, 39 and 46. Furthermore, the Directive's chapter VI bears the title: *'Rules on advertising and transparency'.*
45. Case C-87/94, Commission v. Belgium, [1996] ECR I-2043.
46. Case C-87/94, Commission v. Belgium, [1996] ECR I-2043, paragraph 54.

Regarding contracts outside the Directive, in *RI.SAN*,[47] the Court held that the principle of transparency could be found within the Treaty. The Court stated:

'... [the rules of] *the Treaty on freedom of movement, which impose in particular on the Member States obligations to ensure equal treatment* ***and transparency*** *vis-à-vis economic operators from other Member States, may be relevant*' [emphasis added].[48]

In *Unitron*,[49] the Court of Justice found that the principle of transparency was a consequence of the principle of non-discrimination on grounds of nationality. The Court stated that:

'... ***the principle of non-discrimination on grounds of nationality*** *implies in particular, an obligation of transparency in order to enable the contracting authority to satisfy itself that it has been complied with'* [emphasis added].[50]

The same was stated in *Hospital Ingenieure*,[51] except that the Court used the principle of equal treatment as the foundation for transparency. The Court stated: '*... the principle of equal treatment, (...) implies in particular an obligation of transparency in order to enable verification that it has been complied with'*.[52]

These cases show that the principle of transparency primarily serves the goal of creating transparency to ensure that a breach of the principle of equal treatment does not take place. In this context, the principle of transparency has a control function.

47. Case C-108/98, RI.SAN. Srl v. Comune di Ischia, Italia Lavoro SpA and Ischia Ambiente SpA, [1999] ECR I-5219.
48. Case C-108/98, RI.SAN. Srl v. Comune di Ischia, Italia Lavoro SpA and Ischia Ambiente SpA, [1999] ECR I-5219, paragraph 20.
49. Case C-275/98, Unitron Scandinavia and 3-S, Danske Svineproducenters Serviceselskab v. Ministeriet for Fødevarer, Landbrug og Fiskeri, [1999] ECR I-8291.
50. Case C-275/98, Unitron Scandinavia and 3-S, Danske Svineproducenters Serviceselskab v. Ministeriet for Fødevarer, Landbrug og Fiskeri, [1999] ECR I-8291, paragraph 31.
51. Case C-92/00, Hospital Ingenieure Krankenhaustechnik Planungs-Gesellschaft mbH (HI) v. Stadt Wien, [2002] ECR I-5553.
52. Case C-92/00, Hospital Ingenieure Krankenhaustechnik Planungs-Gesellschaft mbH (HI) v. Stadt Wien, [2002] ECR I-5553, paragraph 45.

3.3.2. The principle of transparency's competition function

The principle of transparency also aims to determine who can participate in a competition for a specific contract and to create competition for the contract. This can be referred to as 'the principle of transparency's competition function'. Advocate General *Mengozzi* argued that:

> *'... observance of the duty of transparency is a vital precondition for guaranteeing that all potential tenderers are properly informed of the tendering procedure, thereby ensuring equality of treatment'.*[53]

Thus, ensuring transparency also aims to create competition among tenderers, since equal treatment (hereunder non-discrimination, section 3.3.1) and competition are mutually interconnected in this field.

Creating transparency in procurement procedures helps open up the public market for more non-domestic suppliers, which will increase competition and, ultimately, mean better value for money.[54]

The fact that the principle of transparency under the Procurement Directives has a competition function was seen in *Pressetext*,[55] where the Court stated that the principle of transparency is ensured for contracts falling under the Directive: *'... by requiring inter alia certain award procedures'.*[56] In *Telaustria*, the Court found that the transparency obligation placing on the contracting authority an obligation to ensure:

53. Opinion of Advocate General Mengozzi delivered on 29 June 2010 in Case C-226/09, Commission v. Ireland, [2010] November 18, 2010 (not yet reported), paragraph 36.
54. However, as pointed out by *Graells* in Graells, Albert Sánchez *"Public Procurement and the EU Competition Rules"* [2011] Hart, p. 107: *'over a certain limit, transparency (...) generates certain risk for the competitive dynamics of the markets (...) as disclosure of excessive information can increase the risk of collusion and other anti-competitive practices. Thus, though transparency ensures equal treatment and competition, it can in some situations lead to certain anti-competitive practices.'*
55. Case C-454/06, Pressetext Nachrichtenagentur GmbH v. Austria, APA-OTS Originaltext-Service GmbH and APA Austria Presse Agentur registrierte Genossenschaft mit beschränkter Haftung, [2008] ECR I-4401.
56. Case C-454/06, Pressetext Nachrichtenagentur GmbH v. Austria, APA-OTS Originaltext-Service GmbH and APA Austria Presse Agentur registrierte Genossenschaft mit beschränkter Haftung, [2008] ECR I-4401, paragraph 33.

*'... **a degree of advertising** sufficient to enable the services market to be opened up to competition and the impartiality of procurement procedures to be reviewed'* [emphasis added].[57]

This emphasises the principle of transparency's competition function by stating that transparency aims to open the contract for competition. As discussed in more detail in chapter 7, this transparency obligation contains a duty for the contracting authority to ensure competition for the contract is created, as well as how to ensure such competition.

3.3.3. Can the principle of transparency be invoked alone?

It is debatable whether the principle of transparency can create obligations of its own without relying upon other principles or rules. *Trepte* submits that transparency is not an objective in itself, but rather a mechanism used to achieve other objectives. *Trepte* therefore considers the principle of transparency as a tool.[58] This is in line with *Dreijber and Stergiou*, who argued that the principle of transparency has not been identified as a 'stand-alone' legal principle.[59] According to *Trybus*: *'... transparency is a vehicle for other principles such as competition, value for money, and non-discrimination rather than a principle in itself'.*[60]

The consequence of the above conclusions is that it would be necessary for another principle or rule to have been breached in order for a breach of the transparency principle to take place. This is true if the contracting authority enters into a contract directly, in which case the contracting authority would have breached both the principle of equal treatment and the principle of transparency. Therefore, it is common for a breach of another principle to have taken place at the same time.

Nevertheless, the transparency's competition function presumably does not require another principle to rely on;[61] for example, advertising a contract

57. Case C-324/98. Telaustria Verlags GmbH and Telefonadress GmbH v. Telekom Austria AG, [2000] ECR I-10745, paragraphs 61–62.
58. Trepte, Peter *"Transparency requirements"* in Treumer, Steen and Nielsen, Ruth (Eds) *"The New EU Public Procurement Directives"* [2005] DJØF, p. 50.
59. Drijber, Jan Berend & Stergiou, Hélène *"Public Procurement Law and Internal Market Law"* [2009] CMLR n° 46, pp. 805-846.
60. Craig, Poul & Trybus, Martin *"England and Wales"* in Noguellou, Rozen & Ulrich, Stelkens (eds.) *"Droit comparé des Contrats – Publics Comparative Law on Public Contracts"* [2010] Brussels Bruylant.
61. It could be argued, to some extent, that the principle of transparency relies here on a principle of competition. However, one could argue whether competition itself is

in a media where the access to the contract is limited. This would not be a breach of the principle of equal treatment, but one could argue that it will not create competition for the contract and, therefore, that the principle of transparency – the competition function of the principle – has been breached.

In *Strong Securanca,*[62] the Court of Justice split the principles of equal treatment and transparency when exploring whether a breach had taken place; this could indicate that the Court will treat the principle of transparency as a stand-alone principle. Therefore, in my opinion, the transparency's competition function can create obligations alone (this is examined and discussed in chapter 7).

4. Summary of findings

The overall aim of the procurement rules found within the principles of the Treaties is to ensure undistorted competition by guaranteeing open, equal access to public contracts.

In order to pursue this aim, contracting authorities must apply the principles of the Treaties when awarding one of the three types of contracts. In this regard, the principle of non-discrimination does not have an independent function. It is submitted that the interpretation of the principles is the same under the Directive as under the Treaties. Therefore, the case law from the Court of Justice, where the ruling is based on the principle of equal treatment and transparency, will most likely apply to the three types of contracts, which are explored and analysed in Part II of this Thesis.

a principle of the Treaty. In Case C-95/10, Strong Segurança SA v. Município de Sintra, Securitas-Serviços e Tecnologia de Segurança, [2011] March 17, 2011 (not yet reported), paragraph 37, the Court found that effective competition was an essential objective of the Directive 2004/18/EC, but despite its importance: '... *it is, cannot lead to an interpretation that is contrary to the clear terms of the directive, (...)*'. Here, the Court refers to competition as an objective rather than a principle of competition.

62. Case C-95/10, Strong Segurança SA v. Município de Sintra, Securitas-Serviços e Tecnologia de Segurança, [2011] March 17, 2011 (not yet reported).

CHAPTER 3

Service Concession Contracts[1]

1. Introduction

This chapter analyses what constitutes a service concession contract.[2] It is often difficult to define a service concession contract, since the definition in the

1. Part of this chapter was presented on Public Procurement Days 2012 (international conference on the modernisation of the EU procurement rules, organised by the Law Department at Copenhagen Business School and the Danish Competition and Consumer Authority, February, 9. -10, 2012).The paper is published as Chapter 9 *'Defining a service concession contract, Will the proposed new definition of service concession contracts increase legal certainty in the field of concessions?'* in Ølykke, Grith, Hansen, Carina Risvig and Tvarnø, Christina D. *"EU Public Procurement – Modernisation, Growth and Innovation"*, DJØF July 2012.
2. Various authors have dealt with the subject of defining a service concession contract in a range of contexts. However, as the Court of Justice has recently elaborated on what defines a concession contract, the older literature is somewhat less useful when defining the concept of concession. For more on concessions see, for example, Arrowsmith, Sue *"Public Private Partnerships and the European Procurement rules: EU Policies in Conflict?"* [2000] CMLR n° 37, pp. 709-737; Neergaard, Ulla *"The Concept of Concessions in EU Public Procurement Law Versus EU Competition Law and National Law"* in Treumer, Steen and Nielsen, Ruth (Eds) *"the New EU Public Procurement Directives"* [2005] DJØF; Neergaard, Ulla in U.2006B.299 *"Pligt til udbud af "koncessionskontrakter om tjenesteydelser" i henhold til EU-retten?"*; Neergaard, Ulla *"Public service concessions and related concepts – the increased pressure from Community law on Member States' use of concessions"* [2007] PPLR n° 6, pp. 387-409; Burnett, Michael *"A new EU Directive on Concessions – the right Approach for PPP?"* [2008] EPPPL n° 3, pp. 107-115; Stergiou, Hélène, *"The Increasing Influence of Primary EU Law on EU Public Procurement Law: Must a Concession to Provide Services of General Economic Interest be Tendered?"* in Van de Gronden, Johan *"EU and WTO law on services: Limits to the realization of general interest policies within the services market"* [2008] Kluwer; and Madell, Tom & Indén, Tobias *"Offentlig-Privat Samverkan"* [2010] Iustus Förlag, chapter 6.

Public Sector Directive is not clear.[3] Indeed, even the Court of Justice has stated that it can be difficult to define a service concession. In *Oymanns,*[4] the Court emphasised that since the definition of a service contract and the definition of a service concession contract have fairly similar characteristics: '... *it is not easy to draw a clear distinction between them in advance*'.[5]

Because the rules for regular service contracts and service concession contracts are not identical, whether a given contract is a service concession contract can lead to legal uncertainty for contracting authorities when awarding a contract. Therefore, it is essential to define the correct nature of a given contract in order to know which rules to follow. Since service concession contracts are excluded from the Public Sector Directive (Public Sector Directive Article 17), a contracting authority is only required to follow the obligations derived from the principles of the Treaties when entering into such a contract.

The Public Sector Directive, on the other hand, covers a regular service contract.[6] Thus, it is important to define the contract correctly due to the potential remedies that might occur if a breach of the procurement rules has taken place. For example, if a service contract is mistaken for a service concession contract, which means that the contracting authority has entered into the contract following only the principles derived from the Treaties, this can have serious consequences such as ineffectiveness of the contract.[7] This is due to the fact that the award of such a contract will most likely be considered a direct award of the contract, given that no contract notice has been published in the OJ. This will even be the situation when the obligations derived from the principles of the Treaties have been complied with. Therefore, it is crucial to

3. The Commission has also recognised the need for further clarification in the area of concessions. On December 20, 2011 a proposal for a new Directive containing rules for service concession contracts and works concession contracts was published (Proposal for a Directive of the European Parliament and the Council on the award of concession contracts COM(2011) 897 final, henceforth 'the proposed Concessions Directive'). The analysis of the current state of law will not take this proposal into account, but some observations regarding the definition of concessions in the proposal are made in section 5. The Directive's proposed rules will be briefly elaborated on in the summary of findings in chapter 12.
4. Case C-300/07, Hans & Christophorus Oymanns GbR, Orthopädie Schuhtechnik v. AOK Rheinland/Hamburg, [2009] ECR I-4779.
5. Case C-300/07, Hans & Christophorus Oymanns GbR, Orthopädie Schuhtechnik v. AOK Rheinland/Hamburg, [2009] ECR I-4779, paragraph 70.
6. Article 1(2)(d) and Article 1(2)(a) of the Public Sector Directive.
7. Article 2(d) of the Public Sector Remedies Directive. For more on ineffectiveness, see chapter 11.

have a clear and precise definition for service concession contracts in order to have legal certainty when awarding a given contract.

1. 1. Outline

Following a brief overview of the foundations for interpretation and the history of concessions in the EU procurement Directives (sections 2 and 3), the analysis of what constitute a service concession contract will take its starting point in the definition of a service concession contract laid down in the Public Sector Directive (section 4). What distinguishes a service concession contract from a regular service contract is the concessionaire's right to exploit the service, hereunder the element of risk. This will be explored and discussed in section 4.3. It will be discussed in section 4.3.1, whether the risk element must be substantial. Section 5 examines the definition of a service concession contract found in the Commission's new proposal for a Directive on concessions.

2. Foundations for interpretation

The fact that the Public Sector Directive does not cover service concession contracts does not mean that these types of contracts are of no relevance to economic operators in Member States other than that of the contracting authority. In fact, these contracts were not excluded from the Public Procurement Directives on the assumption that they lacked cross-border interest, but for other reasons (see section 3). Indeed, the fact that a service concession contract often involves activities related to what are likely to be considered the State's responsibility, and often involve substantial contract value and long contract duration, means that they will be of particular importance to economic operators in other Member States. However, service concession contracts can also involve smaller contracts, such as running a public restaurant or administrating a specific parking lot.

Most of the Court's case law, discussed in this chapter, deals with the concept of a service concession contract falling within the utilities sector. This is probably due to the high use of concessions in these sectors (such as waste, water, gas, electricity).[8] However, since the definition of a service concession

8. According to the Commission's Impact Assessment on Concessions (Impact Assessment of an Initiative on Concessions, accompanying the Proposal for a Directive of the European Parliament and of the Council on the award of concession contracts SEC(2011) 1588 final) p. 12, studies have shown that: '*... concessions are*

contract found in Directive 2004/18/EC is the same as that in Directive 2004/17/EC, the case law regarding the utilities sector will have the same value in relation to setting a definition as the one in the public sector.[9]

It can sometimes be difficult to distinguish a service concession contract from a works concession contract, and a contract will often contain both works and services. For example, building a hospital will be considered as works, whereas running the hospital will be a service. However, works concession contracts fall within the Public Sector Directive[10] and therefore outside the scope of this Thesis. Nonetheless, the analysis in this chapter will also be relevant for defining a works concession contract, since the definition of a works concession contract in the Public Sector Directive has the same characteristics as the definition of a service concession contract. Thus, the case law relating to the definition of a works concession contract is also relevant when defining a service concession contract.

Finally, it should be mentioned that in some specific areas; common EU rules have been adopted, which to some extent cover service concession contracts in this specific area. These rules will not be pursued further in this Thesis.[11]

mostly used in water distribution and treatment, road and rail transport, ports and airports services, motorway maintenance and management, waste management, energy or heating services, leisure facilities and car parks'.

9. Case C-348/10, Norma-A SIA, Dekom SIA v. Latgales plānošanas regions, [2011] November 10, 2011, (not yet reported), paragraph 39, states: *'The fact that the definitions* [in the two Directives] *are substantially similar means that the same considerations are applicable to an interpretation of the concepts of service contract and service concession within the respective spheres of application of those two directives.'* See also Case C-206/08, Wasser- und Abwasserzweckverband Gotha und Landkreisgemeinden v. Eurawasser Aufbereitungs- und Entsorgungsgesellschaft mbH, [2009] ECR I-8377, paragraph 43.
10. Articles 56–61 of the Public Sector Directive.
11. Specific legislation exists regarding the award of contracts for passenger transport services by rail and road (Regulation 1370/2007, OJ L315/1) as well as air transport services (Regulation 1008/2008, OJ L 293/3). For further, see, for example, Kekelekis, Mihalis and Rusu, Ioana Eleonora *"The award of public contacts and the notion of "internal operator" under Regulation 1370/2007 on public passenger transport services by rail and by road"* [2010] PPLR n° 6, pp. 198-216. Ølykke, Grith Skovgaard *"Regulation 1370/2007 on Public Passenger Transport Services"* [2008] PPLR n° 3, NA84. To some extent, Directive 94/22/EC of May, 30, 1994 on the conditions for granting and using authorizations for the prospection, exploration and production of hydrocarbons, OJ L 164/3, also deals with concessions.

Before analysing the definition of a service concession contract (section 4), it is necessary to clarify whether defining concessions are purely an EU matter (section 2.1) and whether the fact that service concession contracts are excluded from the Public Sector Directive means that defining these contracts should be treated as an exception (section 2.2).

2.1. Whether defining service concession contracts is an EU matter?

The Court of Justice has stated that the task of defining a service concession contract falls within EU law. In *Privater Rettungsdienst,*[12] the Court found that:

> *'... the question whether an operation is to be classified as a 'service concession' or a 'public service contract' must be considered exclusively in the light of European Union law.'*[13]

What some Member States refer to in their national legislation, as a concession contract might not constitute a concession contract in the sense of EU law. If Member States could set their own definition for concessions, it would cause inconsistencies in the Member States' systems and therefore it is essential that a common EU definition exist.

The national legislation of some Member States has extended the rules in the Public Sector Directive to include service concession contracts.[14] A definition seems to hold little relevance for such Member States, given that the Directive's rules will also apply when awarding a service concession contract. However, differences may well exist regarding some element such as the legality of the length of the contract period or in matters concerning the

12. Case C-274/09, Privater Rettungsdienst und Krankentransport Stadler v. Zweckverband für Rettungsdienst und Feuerwehralarmierung Passau, [2011] March 10, 2011 (not yet reported).
13. Case C-274/09, Privater Rettungsdienst und Krankentransport Stadler v. Zweckverband für Rettungsdienst und Feuerwehralarmierung Passau, [2011] March 10, 2011 (not yet reported), paragraph 23. See also Case C-348/10, Norma-A SIA, Dekom SIA v. Latgales plānošanas regions, [2011] November 10, 2011, (not yet reported), paragraph 40, Case C-382/05, Commission v. Italy, [2007] ECR I-6657, paragraphs 30-31, and Case C-196/08, Acoset SpA v. Conferenza Sindaci e Presidenza Prov. Reg. ATO Idrico Ragusa and Others, [2009] ECR I-9913, paragraph 38.
14. The Commission's Evaluation Report *'Impact and Effectiveness of EU Public Procurement Legislation'*, part 1 SEC(2011) 853 final, footnote 189, states that this applies to the Czech Republic, Hungary, Italy, Romania, Slovakia and Spain.

field of enforcement and remedies. Therefore, what constitutes a concession will not be entirely irrelevant in such Member States.

Regardless of the national legislation in the field of service concession contracts, it is exclusively up to EU law to define the concept of a concession contract. However, it is up to the national courts to classify a concrete contract as a concession contract (or a service contract).[15]

2.2. Are service concession contracts exceptions to the Directive

Article 17 of the Public Sector Directive states that the Directive does not apply to service concession contracts.[16] It can therefore be discussed whether this means that service concession contracts should be considered as an exception to the Directive or just not covered. Prior Procurement Directives did not include a provision such as Article 17. Service concessions contracts were simply, just not mentioned (see below section 3). Advocate General *Fennelly* argued in *Telaustria* that, since no specific provision was contained in the Public Service Directive, service concession contracts were not excluded, just not covered. She states:

> *'... it is important to bear in mind that "public service concessions" are not covered by Directive 93/38/EEC. I do not therefore accept, (...), that it is necessary to interpret their scope narrowly. They do not constitute derogations from the publicity rules of the Directive but rather a type of 'arrangement' that is not covered by the Directive and thus beyond the remit of those rules.'*[17]

Even though the Public Sector Directive now contains a provision, stating that the Directive does not apply to service concession contracts, I would argue that this provision is merely a clarification of the current state of law and that service concession contracts should not be considered as an exception (a derogation) to the Public Sector Directive. This argument finds support in

15. See, for example, Case C-348/10, Norma-A SIA, Dekom SIA v. Latgales plānošanas regions, [2011] November 10, 2011, (not yet reported), paragraph 40.
16. The Public Sector Directive Article 17 states that: *'Without prejudice to the application of Article 3, this Directive shall not apply to service concessions as defined in Article 1(4).'*
17. See the Opinion of Advocate General Fennelly delivered May 18, 2000 in the Case C-324/98, Telaustria Verlags GmbH and Telefonadress GmbH v. Telekom Austria AG, [2000] ECR I-10745, paragraph 29.

Gotha,[18] where the Court stated that a contracting authority is free to classify the contract as a concession or, using the Court's wording, free *'to ensure the supply of services by way of a concession (...)'*.[19] In that regard, if it is open for a contracting authority to classify a given contract as a concession, the choice of classifying a contract as a concession should not be limited to exceptional situations, but should only depend upon whether the conditions for whether a contract is to be considered as a concession are fulfilled.

Therefore, the definition of when a contract is a service concession contract should not be interpreted limited (so it would only constitute a service concession contract in exceptional situations), as Article 17 should be considered merely a codification of the case law.

3. Concessions in the Procurement Directives

Unlike works concession contracts, service concession contracts were not even mentioned in the prior Procurement Directives until Directive 2004/18/EC.

Works concessions contracts were already mentioned in the first Works Directive, Article 3 of which stated that the Directive did not apply when authorities awarded a concession contract unless the concessionaire was a contracting authority.[20] However, the contracting authority's award of a works concession contract was first covered by a later amendment of the Directive.[21] These rules were carried on in Directive 93/37/EEC as well as in the current Public Sector Directive.[22]

18. Case C-206/08, Wasser- und Abwasserzweckverband Gotha und Landkreisgemeinden v. Eurawasser Aufbereitungs- und Entsorgungsgesellschaft mbH, [2009] ECR I-8377.
19. Case C-206/08, Wasser- und Abwasserzweckverband Gotha und Landkreisgemeinden v. Eurawasser Aufbereitungs- und Entsorgungsgesellschaft mbH, [2009] ECR I-8377, paragraph 74.
20. Article 3 of the first Works Directive also stated that when a contracting authority grants to a concessionaire contracts: *'the concession contract shall stipulate that such concessionaire must observe the principle of non-discrimination on grounds of nationality in respect of contracts awarded to third parties.'*
21. Directive 89/440/EEC of July 18, 1989 amending Directive 71/305/EEC concerning coordination of procedures for the award of public works contracts, OJ L 210/1.
22. Directive 93/37/EEC of June 14, 1993 concerning the coordination of procedures for the award of public works contracts, OJ L 199/54. For further on works concession contract in the prior Works Directives see, for example, Trepte, Peter *"Public Procurement in the EC"* [1993] 1st Edition, CCH Editions Limited, Arrowsmith,

When proposing the Public Service Directive in 1991, the Commission had intended to cover service concession contracts by the Directive. The Commission's proposal for the Public Service Directive[23] contained provisions on public service concessions similar to those for public works concessions in the Works Directive. However, the Council decided not to include service concession contracts by the Service Directive. The reasons for this decision were as follows:

'[T]he differences in established practice between the Member States as to the legal forms used to achieve the delegation of public service provision. This led to a concern that the provisions would not produce a symmetrical impact across the Member States and would, in particular, fall to cover forms of delegated provision of services which rely on administrative decision rather than on concession contracts, (...).'[24]

The Commission regretted the Council's decision, but replied that,

'... although it is not to be disputed that concessions are currently more widely used in some Member States than in others, current trends in the use of concession contracts would ensure that substantial opportunities arise in all Member States.'[25] The Commission also stated that, *'... the concerns expressed, both as to the differential impact of concessions and as to the different forms of delegation used, have to be allayed. For this reason the Commission accepts the deletion of this element in its proposal, it will return to the matter at an opportune time in the light of further investigation.'*[26]

Sue *"The Law of Public and Utilities Procurement"* [1996] 1st Edition, London, Sweet and Maxwell, chapter 8.

23. The original proposal for a Directive relating to the Coordination of Procedures on the award of public service contract COM(90)72 OJ C23/1. Also the Commission's Amended Proposal COM(91)322 final AL, OJ C250/4 contained provisions on service concession contracts.
24. Communication from the Commission to the European Parliament regarding the Council's common position on the proposal for a Directive coordinating the procedures on the award of public service contracts, March 5, 1992, SEC (92) 406 final, paragraph 9. See also Opinion of Advocate General Fennelly delivered on May 18, 2000 in the Case C-324/98, Telaustria Verlags GmbH and Telefonadress GmbH v. Telekom Austria AG, [2000] ECR I-10745, footnote 15, with reference to Council document No 4444-92-ADD-1 of 25 February 1992.
25. Communication from the Commission to the European Parliament regarding the Council's common position on the proposal for a Directive coordinating the procedures on the award of public service contracts, March 5, 1992, SEC (92) 406 Final, paragraph 10.
26. Communication from the Commission to the European Parliament regarding the Council's common position on the proposal for a Directive coordinating the proce-

Hence, the wide differences of national practices in matters of service concessions, and not the assumption that service concession contracts had limited importance for trade, was the reason for not covering these types of contracts by the Directive.[27]

Even though the Public Service Directive did not mention service concession contracts, it had been suggested early on that the Court of Justice might conclude that service concession contracts were actually covered by the Service Directive. *Arrowsmith* stated:

> '*... on a literal reading of the Service Directive Concessions do appear to be covered the definition of a public service contract (...)*' and that: '*It is possible that the European Court could bring concessions within this definition if it wished to do so despite the legislative history, by a wide interpretation of the concept of pecuniary interest.*'[28]

However, this was not the Commission's view. The Commission's Interpretative Communication on Concessions[29] stated: '*However, in the absence of Court case law on this point* [whether service concessions were covered by the Directives] *the Commission has not accepted this interpretation in the actual cases it has had to investigate.*'[30] In *Telaustria*,[31] the Court concluded that: '*... such contracts* [service concession contracts] *are not included in the concept of contracts for pecuniary interest concluded in writing appearing in Article 1(4) of that directive*'.[32]

dures on the award of public service contracts, March 5, 1992, SEC (92) 406 final, paragraph 11.

27. See also Arrowsmith, Sue and Kunzlik, Peter (Eds) *"Social and Environmental Policies in EC Procurement Law"* [2009] Cambridge University Press. p. 83.
28. Arrowsmith, Sue *"The Law of Public and Utilities Procurement"* [1996] 1st Edition, London, Sweet and Maxwell, p. 366, footnote 50. The same view is shared by Nielsen, Ruth *"Udbud af offentlige kontrakter"* [1998] 1st Edition, DJØF, p. 123. However, *Williams* argued, before *Telaustria*, that the Directives did not cover concession contracts. See Williams Rhodri *"The European Commission's interpretative Communication under Community Law"* [2000] PPLR n° 5, NA105-110, who states: '*The only reasonable conclusion to be drawn is that the directives do not cover services concessions.*'
29. Commission Interpretative Communication on Concessions under Community Law (2000/C121/02).
30. See Commission Interpretative Communication on Concessions under Community Law (2000/C121/02), footnote 15.
31. Case C-324/98, Telaustria Verlags GmbH and Telefonadress GmbH v. Telekom Austria AG, [2000] ECR I-10745.
32. Case C-324/98, Telaustria Verlags GmbH and Telefonadress GmbH v. Telekom Austria AG, [2000] ECR I-10745, paragraph 57 (concerning the prior Utilities Di-

The Commission's Communication on Concession is from April 2000, which is before the definition of a service concession contract was included in the Public Sector Directive, and even before *Telaustria*. However, since the definition of a works concession contract remained the same under the Public Sector Directive as it was in the Works Directive, and since the characteristics of service and works concessions: *'are generally the same, regardless of their subject'*,[33] the Communication can still be a useful source when analysing what constitutes a service concession contract.

4. The definition of a service concession contract

This section analyses what constitutes a service concession contract. Section 4.1. examines the definition in the prior and current EU Procurement Directives. Section 4.2. examines whether service concession contracts involve specific types of services. Section 4.3. analyses the concept of 'right to exploit', which is considered the most essential element in defining a service concession contract.

4.1. The definition in the Procurement Directives

The definition of service concession contracts can be found in Article 1(4) of the Public Sector Directive. This definition is very similar to that of a works concession contract found in the first Works Directive. The two definitions are shown below:

First Works Directive Article 1	**Public Sector Directive Article 1(4)**
'A contract of the same type as that indicated in Article 1 [works contract] except for the fact that the consideration for the works to be carried out consist either solely in the right to exploit the construction or in this right together with a payment.'	*'A contract of the same type as a public service contract except for the fact that the consideration for the provision of services consists either solely in the right to exploit the service or in this right together with payment.'*

rective). See also Order of May 2002, Case C-358/00, Buchhändler-Vereinigung GmbH v. Saur Verlag GmbH & Co. KG, Die Deutsche Bibliothek, [2002] ECR I-4685, which came to the same conclusion regarding the Service Directive.

33. See the Commission Interpretative Communication on Concessions under Community Law (2000/C121/02).

Thus, what constitutes a concession contract has remained the same throughout the various Procurement Directives. This indicates that the assessment that must be made in determining what constitutes a concession contract is the same today as it was more than 40 years ago. However, despite the fact that the definition of concessions has remained the same in the Procurement Directives, the Court of Justice has given several rulings over the last 15 years concerning the definition of concession contracts. This might also indicate that the question of categorising the contract as a concession contract has become more important in the recent years. This could be due to increase over the past decade in the use of PPPs in which concession contracts play a great role.[34] The increase in the number of cases before the Court of Justice might also indicate that the enforcement system has become more effective and, thus, more disputes occur. Alternatively, it could be that undertakings after *Telaustria* are now aware of the fact, that certain positive obligations apply when contracting authorities are awarding service concession contracts, and therefore bring proceedings more often (bearing in mind that, before *Telaustria,* it was assumed by the most that the principles of the Treaties only let to certain negative obligations: see chapter 1, section 3.1.1.1).

A closer look at the definition in Article 1(4) of the Public Sector Directive reveals that a service concession contract must be a contract of the same type as a public service contract,[35] but that the definition does not con-

34. See also the Communication from the Commission to the European Parliament, the Council, the European Economic and Social Committee and the Committee of the Regions on public-private partnerships and community law on public procurement and concessions, COM(2005)569, (henceforth 'the 2005-Communication') which, for example, states that: *'In view of the increasing importance of PPPs it was considered necessary to explore the extent to which existing Community rules adequately implement these objectives when it comes to awarding PPP contracts or concessions.'* This indicates the importance of concessions for PPPs. See also Communication from the Commission to the European Parliament, the Council, the Economic and Social Committee of the Regions *"Single Market Act Twelve levers to boost growth and strengthen confidence"* (SEC(2011) 467 final), which states: '*Service concessions represent an important share of economic activity in the EU* [footnote left out] *and are the most common form of public-private partnerships.*'
35. Therefore, it will be relevant to consider, firstly, whether a contract meets the definition of a service contract and, secondly, whether the consideration involves the grant of a right to exploit the work. See, for example, Neergaard, Ulla *"The Concept of Concessions in EU Public Procurement Law Versus EU Competition Law and National Law"* in Treumer, Steen and Nielsen, Ruth *"the New EU Public Procurement Directives"* [2005] DJØF.

tain any requirement regarding the type of service, which is the subject of the contract (see section 4.2). Given that a service concession contract also contains the same elements as a service contract, the distinctive feature of a concession contract lies in the fact that the consideration for the service is different from a regular service contract. The Court of Justice has also stated this in *Norma,* for example (the most recent case regarding concessions) that:

'the difference between a service contract and a service concession lies in the consideration for the provision of services. A service contract involves consideration which is paid directly by the contracting authority to the service provider while, for a service concession, the consideration for the provision of services consists in the right to exploit the service, either alone, or together with payment.'[36]

Instead of direct payment, the consideration for the service consists of the right to exploit the service (analysed below in section 4.3). It is also clear from the definition that the contracting authority is allowed to pay the concessionaire a sum of money as it follows from the provision that the right to exploit can exist either alone or *'together with payment'*.[37] However, this possibility only exists as long as the payment does not eliminate the risk completely (more on the payment, see below section D).[38]

4.2. The type of service to be performed

The Commission's Interpretative Communication on Concessions suggests that concessions normally concern activities that fall within '*the States re-*

36. Case C-348/10, Norma-A SIA, Dekom SIA v. Latgales plānošanas regions, [2011] November 10, 2011, (not yet reported), paragraph 41. See also Case C-274/09, Privater Rettungsdienst und Krankentransport Stadler v. Zweckverband für Rettungsdienst und Feuerwehralarmierung Passau, [2011] March 10, 2011 (not yet reported), paragraph 24, and Case C-206/08, Wasser- und Abwasserzweckverband Gotha und Landkreisgemeinden v. Eurawasser Aufbereitungs- und Entsorgungsgesellschaft GmbH, [2009] ECR I-8377, paragraph 51.
37. Wang, Ping *"Public-Private Partnerships under the EU Public Procurement Rules"* in Tvarnø, Christina (ed.), *"PPP – An international analysis in a legal and economic perspective"*, [2010] Asia Link, p. 134, seems to indicate that this is not possible stating: *'For a concession it is also necessary that the remuneration for providing the services should not come from the contracting authority itself (...).'*
38. See also the Commission Interpretative Communication on Concessions under Community Law (2000/C121/02) (regarding works) which states that: *'the definition of a concession allows the State to make a payment in return for work carried out, provided that this does not eliminate a significant element of the risk inherent in the exploitation'*.

sponsibilities'. Also Advocate General *Pergola* stated in his opinion in *Arnhem*, that:

'... the service that is the subject of a service concession must also be in the general interest, so that a public authority is institutionally responsible for providing it.'[39]

On the other hand, Advocate General *Fennelly* has argued that:

'... there should, in my opinion, be no qualitative bar to the sorts of service that a contracting entity may legitimately seek to award by way of concession, although it is likely that there will be a public interest in most of the services that are awarded in that manner.'[40]

In the *Commission v. Italy,*[41] the Court explicitly stated that: '*The circumstance that the treatment of waste comes within the general interest does not change that conclusion* [that the contract was not a concession].'[42] Therefore, the categorisation of the contract as a service concession contract does not depend on the type of service to be performed, but rather on the contractual relationship between the parties. Thus, the same type of service can, in one situation, be performed in a way that fulfils the conditions for a service concession contract and, in another situation, the contract must be seen as a regular service contract. In *Privater Rettungsdienst,*[43] the contract in the case (a rescue service) was considered a service concession. However, other municipalities had made a regular service contract of the same type of service. Therefore, a concession contract can cover both A- and B-services, which means it is not necessary to classify the type of service further.

Considering that the Member States' systems vary, it would not be the same types of services that were to be considered as *'the State's responsibil-*

39. Opinion of Advocate General Pergola delivered on February 9, 1998 in Case C-360/96, Gemeente Arnhem and Gemeente Rheden v. BFI Holding BV, [1998] ECR I-6821, paragraph 26. Also the literature suggested that concessions should contain a type of service within the generel interest; see, for example, Arrowsmith, Sue *"Public Private Partnerships and the European Procurement rules: EU Policies in Conflict?"* [2000] CMLR n° 37, pp. 709-737.
40. Opinion of General Advocate Fennelly delivered on May 18, 2000 in the Case C-324/98, Telaustria Verlags GmbH and Telefonadress GmbH v. Telekom Austria AG, [2000] ECR I-10745, paragraph 35.
41. Case C-382/05, Commission v. Italy, [2007] ECR I-6657.
42. Case C-382/05, Commission v. Italy, [2007] ECR I-6657, paragraph 43.
43. Case C-274/09, Privater Rettungsdienst und Krankentransport Stadler v. Zweckverband für Rettungsdienst und Feuerwehralarmierung Passau, [2011] March 10, 2011 (not yet reported).

ity', which would make such an assessment difficult.[44] This is also supported by the fact that, as mentioned above, that defining a service concession contract is purely for EU law, which therefore would require a common terminology, of what would be considered as *'the State's responsibility'*.

4.3. The right to exploit

The Public Sector Directive does not clarify what is to be understood by the wording '*the right to exploit*'. A concession contract will often cover a situation where the economic operator, in most cases, does not receive payment for performing the task from the contracting authority. Instead, the concessionaire is allowed to demand payment from those who use the service. Consequently, the concessionaire earns money when it *exploits* the right granted. *Neergaard* states that: *'the exploitation criterion means that most of the operator's payment should come from exploiting the service'*. [my translation][45] However, the payment itself does not categorise a concession contract alone; instead, it is merely one of concessions contract's distinctive features (see section D).

Advocate General *Pergola* noted in *Arnhem*,[46] that exploitation entails that the provider *'assumes the economic risk arising from the provision and management of the services'*.[47] It was also the Commission's view that the economic operator should bear the risk, in order for a contract to be classified as a concession. According to the Communication on Concessions, a contract is to be considered a concession when

> *'... the operator bears the risk involved in operating the service in question (establishing and exploiting the system), obtaining a significant part of revenue from the user ...'*[48]

44. Also the view of Drijber, Jan Berend & Stergiou, Hélène *"Public Procurement Law and Internal Market Law"* [2009] CMLR n° 46, pp. 805-846, p. 809.
45. Neergaard, Ulla in U.2006B.299 *"Pligt til udbud af "koncessionskontrakter om tjenesteydelser" i henhold til EU-retten?"*[the Danish version states: *'Udnyttelseskriteriet indebærer, at størstedelen af den økonomiske vederlag skal hidrøre fra udnyttelsen.'*]
46. Case C-360/96, Gemeente Arnhem and Gemeente Rheden v. BFI Holding BV, [1998] ECR I-6821.
47. Opinion of Advocate General Pergola delivered on February 9, 1998 in Case C-360/96, Gemeente Arnhem and Gemeente Rheden v. BFI Holding BV, [1998] ECR I-6821, paragraph 26.
48. Commission Interpretative Communication on Concessions under Community law, (2000/C 121/02).

This reasoning is in line with Advocate General *Fennelly*, who argued that in order for a contract to constitute a concession, the right to exploit a particular service had to be transferred to the concessionaire: '*as well as the simultaneous transfer of a* ***significant proportion of the risk*** *associated with that transfer to the concessionaire.*' [emphasis added].[49]

In *Commission v. Italy,*[50] the Court of Justice stated that:

> '*... A service concession exists where the agreed method of remuneration consist in the right of the service provider to* ***exploit for payment his own service*** *and means that he* ***assumes the risk connected with operating the services in question.*** ' [emphasis added].[51]

The fact that the economic operator must assume the risk connected with operating the service in question was confirmed in *Norma*, where the Court stated: '*... it also follows from the case-law that the service concession implies that the service supplier takes the risk of operating the services in question.*'[52] Thus, even though the definition of a concession in the Public Sector Directive, does not mention the risk factor, it does seem to be the most important characteristic of a concession contract.

The element of risk can be said to be inherent in the term of '*the right to exploit,*'[53] and is the main element that distinguishes a concession contract

49. Opinion of Advocate General Fennelly delivered on May 18, 2000 in the Case C-324/98, Telaustria Verlags GmbH and Telefonadress GmbH v. Telekom Austria AG, [2000] ECR I-10745, paragraph 37. See also Case C-234/03, Contse and Others, [2005] ECR I-9315, paragraph 22, where the Court did not consider whether the contract in question was a concession, but merely found that since the contracting authority remained liable for all harm suffered on account of the failure of the service, this implied that *'there is no transfer of risks connected with the service concerned, and the fact that the service is paid for by the [contracting authority ed.] support that conclusion.'*
50. Case C-382/05, Commission v. Italy, [2008] ECR I-6657.
51. Case C-382/05, Commission v. Italy, [2008] ECR I-6657, paragraph 34. See also Case C-300/07, Hans & Christophorus Oymanns GbR, Orthopädie Schuhtechnik v. AOK Rheinland/Hamburg, [2009] ECR I-4779, paragraph 72 and Case C-206/08, Wasser- und Abwasserzweckverband Gotha und Landkreisgemeinden v. Eurawasser Aufbereitungs- und Entsorgungsgesellschaft mbH, [2009] ECR I-8377, paragraph 59.
52. Case C-348/10, Norma-A SIA, Dekom SIA v. Latgales plānošanas regions, [2011] November 10, 2011, (not yet reported), paragraph 44.
53. Burnett, Michael *"A new EU Directive on Concessions – the right Approach for PPP?"* [2008] EPPPL n° 3, pp. 107-115, states *'Public contracts and concessions differ only in respect of the extent of risk borne by the private partner i.e. the extent to which payment for the transaction is certain.'*

from a regular service contract. As *Neergaard* stated: *'it is considered determinative that the risk for the exploitation rests with the operator and not the authority.'*[54] Section 4.3.1. below analyses the element of risk.

4.3.1. The element of risk

This section analyses when the economic operator can be said to have taken the risk. It also looks at what types of risk must be present (section 4.3.1.1.) and whether the risk must be substantial in order for the contract to be considered as a concession (section 4.3.1.2).

4.3.1.1. Types of risk

In every contractual relationship, the economic operator will face the risk of not making any profit from the work of the contract. However, it is not the regular contractual risk an economic operator must bear in order for a contract to classify as a concession contract. The risk must lie in the *'risk of operating the services in question.'*[55]

Wang found that the risk:

> *'... arises out of the fact that the service provider bears the cost of providing the service, and obtains income to cover those costs and make a profit only if it is successful in generating revenue by exploiting the services by selling them to the public'.*[56]

Thus, the risk involved in a concession contract must be linked to the exploitation of the transferred right to explore, or in other words; it must be linked to operating the service ('the operating risk').

The fact that the risk must be some sort of operating risk also means that the risk is not linked to the risk of, for example, not being awarded a contract. When a regular service contract is put out for competition, the tenderers can calculate their costs and tender for the contract on that basis. In this situation, the economic operator will have measured its costs and, to some extent, have calculated the chances that it would not be awarded the contract. This is not the type of risk involved when dealing with concessions.

54. Neergaard, Ulla *"Public service concessions and related concepts – the increased pressure from Community law on Member States' use of concessions"* [2007] PPLR n° 6, pp. 387-409.
55. As stated in Case C-348/10, Norma-A SIA, Dekom SIA v. Latgales plānošanas regions, [2011] November 10, 2011, (not yet reported), paragraph 44.
56. Wang, Ping *"Public-Private Partnerships under the EU Public Procurement Rules"* in Tvarnø, Christina (ed.), *"PPP – An international analysis in a legal and economic perspective"*, [2010] Asia Link, p. 133.

Similar to a framework agreement, the risk that arises in such an agreement is that the contracting authority does not need the products or services of the undertaking, which means that the contracting authority will not make use of the framework agreement. The same applies to a framework agreement in which it is necessary to re-open the competition by a mini–competition. In such a case, if the undertaking does not have the most economically advantageous offer the undertaking may never be awarded a concrete contract. The economic risk in a framework agreement is not linked to the performances of the contract, only to the risk of not being awarded a concrete contract; therefore, this is not the type of risk that needs to be present in order to define a concession contract. As *Burnett* has noted *'... there is no conclusive definition of how much risk or* ***what type of risks*** *a private partner must accept for the transaction to be classified as concession as opposed to a public contract.'* [emphasis added].[57]

When establishing whether a specific contract contains a risk linked to the exploitation, it can be relevant to consider elements such as exposure to the vagaries of the market,[58] the risk of changes to legislation,[59] management and use of the facilities,[60] funding, and – perhaps most importantly – the element of payment. It may in that regard be relevant to consider where the payment comes from and whether this can be a sufficient criterion for establishing that a contract is a concession.

Elements that are not considered a risk in order to categorise a contract as a concession include for example, *'bad management or errors of judgment by the economic operator (...).'*[61] The elements that can constitute risk in a service concession contract are discussed below, sections A-E.

57. Burnett, Michael *"A new EU Directive on Concessions – the right Approach for PPP?"* [2008] EPPPL n° 3, pp. 107-115.
58. See to that effect, Case C-206/08, Wasser- und Abwasserzweckverband Gotha und Landkreisgemeinden v. Eurawasser Aufbereitungs- und Entsorgungsgesellschaft mbH, [2009] ECR I-8377, paragraphs 66 and 67. See also Case C-348/10, Norma-A SIA, Dekom SIA v. Latgales plānošanas regions, [2011] November 10, 2011, (not yet reported), paragraph 48.
59. Mentioned in the Commission Interpretative Communication on Concessions under Community Law (2000/C121/02).
60. Mentioned in the Commission Interpretative Communication on Concessions under Community Law (2000/C121/02).
61. Case C-274/09, Privater Rettungsdienst und Krankentransport Stadler v. Zweckverband für Rettungsdienst und Feuerwehralarmierung Passau, [2011] March 10, 2011 (not yet reported), paragraph 38. See also Case C-348/10, Norma-A SIA,

A. Exposure to the vagaries of the market

One element in the risk assessment is to examine whether the concessionaire is exposed to the vagaries of the market. In *Norma*, the Court stated: '*The risk linked to such an operation must be understood as the risk of exposure to the vagaries of the market.*'[62] This implies that the concessionaire must be exposed to some sort of risk, which is derived from the market; this risk could consist of various elements, such as:

> *'... competition from other operators,*
> *the risk that supply of the services will not match demand,*
> *the risk that those liable will be unable to pay for the services provided, the risk that the costs of operating the services will not fully be met by revenue or for example also*
> *the risk of liability for harm or damage resulting from an inadequacy of the service.*'[63]

In this context, it is relevant that the concessionaire enjoys a degree of economic freedom in order to compete with other economic operators. This was stated in *Oymanns*, where the Court found that the trader in the case did not '*... enjoy the degree of economic freedom which would distinguish a concession*'.[64]

In order to examine whether an economic operator is exposed to the vagaries of the market, it can be relevant to consider whether the service is actually being used. *Arrowsmith* calls this the 'demand risk', which means '*... the risk concerning the extent to which parties will choose to use the service.*'[65] In some cases users are obliged to use the service (and the price for

Dekom SIA v. Latgales plānošanas regions, [2011] November 10, 2011, (not yet reported), paragraph 49.

62. Case C-348/10, Norma-A SIA, Dekom SIA v. Latgales plānošanas regions, [2011] November 10, 2011, (not yet reported), paragraph 48. See also Case C-206/08, Wasser- und Abwasserzweckverband Gotha und Landkreisgemeinden v. Eurawasser Aufbereitungs- und Entsorgungsgesellschaft GmbH, [2009] ECR I-8377, paragraph 67.
63. Case C-274/09, Privater Rettungsdienst und Krankentransport Stadler v. Zweckverband für Rettungsdienst und Feuerwehralarmierung Passau, [2011] March 10, 2011 (not yet reported), paragraph 37. See also Case C-234/03, Contse and Others, [2005] ECR I-9315, paragraph 22, and Case C-300/07, Hans & Christophorus Oymanns GbR, Orthopädie Schuhtechnik v. AOK Rheinland/Hamburg, [2009] ECR I-4779, paragraph 74.
64. Case C-300/07, Hans & Christophorus Oymanns GbR, Orthopädie Schuhtechnik v. AOK Rheinland/Hamburg, [2009] ECR I-4779, paragraph 73.
65. Arrowsmith, Sue *"The Law of Public and Utilities Procurement"* [2005] 2nd Edition, Sweet and Maxwell, p. 324.

the use can be fixed), which will eliminate the risk to some extent, since it is possible to calculate the income from the service and hereby measure the costs involved. In other situations, the users will not be obliged to use the service and the concessionaire can be exposed to competition from other economic operators operating on the market.

Also in *Oymanns*,[66] the Court emphasised the amount of use of the service. The case concerned a preliminary question regarding whether the supply of orthopaedic shoes was to be regarded as a service concession contract or a framework agreement within the meaning of the provisions of Directive 2004/18. The contract in the case was concluded between a statutory sickness insurance fund and a trader. According to the contract, the trader undertook an obligation to serve insured persons who came to him. The prices for the various services were fixed in the contract, as was the duration of the contract. The quantities of the various services were not fixed. The statutory sickness insurance fund alone paid the remuneration of the provider. The Court found that even though the trader was exposed to certain risk, in that insured persons might not avail themselves of its products and services, that risk was limited. What was important was that:

> '*The trader is spared the risk connected with recovery of payment and the insolvency of the other party to the individual contract (...), it does not have to incur considerable advance expenditure (...)* [and] *the number of insured persons (...) is known in advance, with the result that a reasonable forecast can be made as to the number of customers.*'[67]

The Court concluded that the contract in question was a regular framework agreement and not a concession contract.

In *Norma*,[68] a contract in which the economic operator was guaranteed to recoup its losses was, according to the Court of Justice, a regular service contract. In that regard, the economic operator was not exposed to the market, as regardless of what would occur, the economic operator would be guaranteed its payment.

Exposure to the vagaries of the market can also take place when a contracting authority grants a concession to more than one economic operator.

66. Case C-300/07, Hans & Christophorus Oymanns GbR, Orthopädie Schuhtechnik v. AOK Rheinland/Hamburg, [2009] ECR I-4779.
67. Case C-300/07, Hans & Christophorus Oymanns GbR, Orthopädie Schuhtechnik v. AOK Rheinland/Hamburg, [2009] ECR I-4779, paragraph 74.
68. Case C-348/10, Norma-A SIA, Dekom SIA v. Latgales plānošanas regions, [2011] November 10, 2011, (not yet reported).

However, such situations are not to be mistaken with licences,[69] which are granted to an undertaking if it meets certain criteria. A concession contract, on the other hand, is used for something the contracting authority wishes to be performed and grants a right to one or more undertakings to perform the task.[70]

It is also possible that several economic operators may be granted the same type of concession. This situation occurred in *Commission v. Italy,* (the horse betting case),[71] where the contracting authority had granted 329 concessions on horse betting without advertising to a limited number of economic operators. The more economic operators the contracting authority grants the right to exploit a certain task, the greater the risk will (most likely) be, since the economic operator then will be exposed to competition from other concessionaries.

B. Management and use of facilities/equipment

Another element in the risk assessment is whether the concessionaire bears any risk in relation to management of the service or in relation to the use of facilities. The fact that this element can be relevant in the risk assessment can be seen from the Commission's Communication on Concessions, which states that:

> *'Moreover, the concessionaire bears not only the usual risks inherent in any construction – he also bears much of the risk inherent in the management and use of the facilities. It follows, that the risk inherent are transferred to the concessionaire.'*

However, the utilisation of facilities is not so frequently an issue in a service concession contract, since it will often not be necessary for the concessionaire to invest in expensive equipment in order to perform the service.

69. See also Proposed Concessions Directive, Recital 6, which states: '*... certain State acts such as authorisations or licences whereby the State or a public authority establishes the conditions for the exercise of an economic activity, should not qualify as a concession.'*
70. However, even though a licence is not a concession, such a licence may not be granted without following the principles of the Treaties. See also Brown, Adrian *"The grant of concessions to operate casinos in Austria without competitive tendering"* [2011] PPLR n° 2, NA13-16, which states: '*... The obligation of transparency must be met before a Member State awards licences to operate casinos, irrespective of the method of selecting operators, because the effects of such awards on potentially interested undertakings established in other Member States are the same as those of a service concession contract.'*
71. Case C-260/04, Commission v. Italy, [2007] ECR I-7083.

Setting up a large construction like building a bridge or a highway (which would typically be works), will often contain a risk element in itself since such a construction can be highly expensive and it can be difficult to measure whether there will be a profit. However, the type of risk inherent in a service concession contract will typically not relate to expensive equipment, but will lie in the management and use of such facilities/constructions. Therefore, even though the element should be taken into consideration in the assessment of the risk factor, it will most likely only occur in mix-concessions contracts (and PPPs), where the economic operator is going to build for example, a hospital (works) and then be responsible for running and maintaining it (service). In such a situation, the risk will be higher as it will be costly to build the hospital as well as to run and maintain the hospital afterwards.

In the above-mentioned *Oymanns* case, in which the Court found that a (simple) contract for the supply of orthopaedic shoes should be regarded as a service contract, the Court of Justice also emphasised that there was no risk in relation to the equipment. The Court stated that: *'although the trader must be sufficiently equipped to provide its services, it does not have to incur considerable advance expenditure...'*.[72] Thus, the less expenses the concessionaire have the less likely it is that there is a risk involved in the performance of the contract.

C. Funding

In most cases, a concessionaire will be the party supplying the funding; hence, the risk contained in a concession contract will often relate to the funding.[73]

However, in line with the comments in section B regarding investment in equipment, it can be difficult to establish that there is a risk involved in relation to the funding in many service concession contracts. There is often no substantial funding issue as performing the task does not require an investment in expensive equipment. However, this clearly is an element to be taken into consideration and, as stated in the 2005 Communication, *'... private capital involvement is considered to be one of the key incentives for public authorities to enter into PPPs.'*

72. Case C-300/07, Hans & Christophorus Oymanns GbR, Orthopädie Schuhtechnik v. AOK Rheinland/Hamburg, [2009] ECR I-4779, paragraph 74.
73. In line with the 2005-Communication, which states: *'The main difference to public procurement is the risk inherent in such exploitation, which the concessionaire, usually providing the funding of at least parts of the relevant project has to bear.'*

The length of the contract may also influence whether the contract is to be categorised as a concession. If most of the investment takes place during the first years of the contract period, then the longer the contract will run, the more likely it is that the economic operator will profit from the contract, which reduces the likelihood that the contract involves a risk. However, the Commission's Communication on Concessions states that *'... the duration of concessions makes these risk more likely to occur, and makes them relatively greater.'*[74] An example of this is risk arising from changes in legislation during the life of the contract. The Commission seems to indicate that risk is more likely to occur in contracts with a long duration. However, a contract with a long duration cannot be a sufficient argument in order to categorise a contract as a service concession. In *Commission v. Italy*,[75] the Court stated:

> *'... the length of the agreements at issue and the significant initial investment which the operator must make in performing them are not conclusive either for the purpose of classifying those agreements, as such characteristics may be present both in public contracts and in service concessions'.*[76]

Thus, it will be necessary to examine the concrete contract in order to determine whether there is a risk involved.

D. Security of payment

Perhaps the most important element to consider when examining whether an economic operator bears a risk relates to where the payment comes from and how insecure it is.[77] The greater risk the contracting authority bears in relation to the payment, the less likely it is to categorise the contract as a concession contract. Thus, in a situation where the contracting authority pays the economic operator for a given service and the price is fixed beforehand, it can be difficult to see a risk involved.

This was also the case in *Arnhem*,[78] which involved a public limited company (ARA) being entrusted with a series of tasks from two municipalities in

74. Commission Interpretative Communication on Concessions under Community Law (2000/C121/02).
75. Case C-382/05, Commission v. Italy, [2008] ECR I-6657.
76. Case C-382/05, Commission v. Italy, [2008] ECR I-6657, paragraph 42.
77. See also the Commission Interpretative Communication on Concessions under Community Law, (2000/C 121/02): *'... the way in which the operator is remunerated is a factor which helps to determine who bears the exploitation risk'.*
78. Case C-360/96, Gemeente Arnhem and Gemeente Rheden v. BFI Holding BV, [1998] ECR I-6821.

the field of waste collection. The municipalities paid the company either in advance as a fixed price per unit or afterwards, where the payment would constitute the expenses the company had upheld. The Court found that this type of payment *'... comprises only a price and not the right to operate the service'*.[79] Therefore, the risk was not transferred in the case, since the municipality would ultimately pay the company's expenses, which made it a regular service contract.

A similar situation occurred in *Commission and Italy,*[80] with the economic operator's payment consisting of a royalty being paid by the contracting authority. The amount was fixed by agreements as Euros per ton of waste transferred to the operator by the municipalities. Therefore, the provider in the case was guaranteed payment and did not obtain any risk involved in the execution of the contract. The Court found

> *'... the method of remuneration for which the agreements at issue provide does not consist in the right to exploit for payment the services in question, nor does it involve the assumption by the operator of the risk connected with operating them'*.[81]

In *Norma*, the contracting authority compensated the economic operator for the losses related to the provision of transport services and the Court found that such a contract would be a regular service contract.[82]

On the basis of the above-cases, it may be concluded that if the payment is secured (in other words, guaranteed) in advance, the contract will not be a concession contract.[83]

E. Payment method

As the security of the payment is often linked to the source of the payment, it is not surprising that most concession contracts involve payment from the users of the service. However, it could be questioned whether the payment

79. Case C-360/96, Gemeente Arnhem and Gemeente Rheden v. BFI Holding BV, [1998] ECR I-6821, paragraph 25.
80. Case C-382/05, Commission v. Italy, [2008] ECR I-6657.
81. Case C-382/05, Commission v. Italy, [2008] ECR I-6657, paragraph 35.
82. Case C-348/10, Norma-A SIA, Dekom SIA v. Latgales plānošanas regions, [2011] November 10, 2011, (not yet reported), paragraph 58.
83. In line with Burnett, Michael *"A new EU Directive on Concessions – the right Approach for PPP?"* [2008] EPPPL n° 3, pp. 107-115, who states: *'Public contracts and concessions differ only in respect of the extent of risk borne by the private partner i.e. the extent to which payment for the transaction is certain.'*

method could be a risk factor sufficient to establish that the contract is a concession.

In *Parking Brixen*,[84] the economic operator was given the right to run a parking area with payment consisting of users' fee. The Court found that:

'*... That method of remuneration means that the provider takes the risk of operating the services in question and is thus characteristic of a public service concession.*'[85]

It could be argued that, by referring to '*that method of remuneration,*' the Court meant to state that when users are paying the economic operator, the contract would always constitute a concession. However, the concessionaire in the case also had to pay the municipality a sum of money for the use of the area and was obliged to have a weekly market on the facilities. These two obligations, together with the users' payment, constituted a risk for the economic operator and thus a concession contract. Thus, I would argue that the Court's reference to *'that method of remuneration'* only indicates that, in most cases, when users pay for the use of the service, this will be a concession contract, but the risk must also be transferred to the concessionaire.[86] This view was later confirmed in *Gotha,* where the Court found that:

'the fact that the service provider is remunerated by payments from third parties, in this case from users of the service in question, ***is one means of exercising the right,*** *granted to the provider, to exploit the service.'* [emphasis added].[87]

84. Case C-458/03, Parking Brixen GmbH v. Gemeinde Brixen and Stadtwerke Brixen AG, [2005] ECR I-8585.
85. Case C-458/03, Parking Brixen GmbH v. Gemeinde Brixen and Stadtwerke Brixen AG, [2005] ECR I-8585, paragraph 40.
86. This is also the Commission's view, where the Communication on Concessions states: *'the way in which the operator is remunerated is a factor which helps to determine who bears the exploitation risk'*. And furthermore: *'Even though the origin of the resources – directly paid by the user of the construction – is, in most cases a significant factor, it is the existence of exploitation risk, involved in investment (...) which is the determining factor.'*
87. Case C-206/08, Wasser- und Abwasserzweckverband Gotha und Landkreisgemeinden v. Eurawasser Aufbereitungs- und Entsorgungsgesellschaft mbH, [2009] ECR I-8377 paragraph 53. See also Case C-348/10, Norma-A SIA, Dekom SIA v. Latgales plānošanas regions, [2011] November 10, 2011, (not yet reported), paragraph 44. See also Case C-274/09, Privater Rettungsdienst und Krankentransport Stadler v. Zweckverband für Rettungsdienst und Feuerwehralarmierung Passau, [2011] March 10, 2011 (not yet reported), paragraph 28. However, this does not seem to be the view of Advocate General *Mazak*, who in paragraph 39 of in his

Thus, the fact that all the payment derives from the users is not sufficient to categorise a contract as a concession; it is still necessary to establish whether the economic operator assumes the risk of operating the service in question.[88] This also means that it is possible to categorise a contract as a concession in cases where the contracting authority collects the payments from the users and passes it on to the economic operator.[89]

However, the question of whether a contract should be classified as a concession contract still depends on the risk element. Risk can exist even when all of the payment comes from the contracting authority; however, it is more likely to occur when no payment comes from the contracting authority. In a situation where the provider is guaranteed a specific amount that will cover its expenses and guarantee some profit, the agreement will not be a concession.[90] Therefore, I would argue that the method of payment can be used as a criterion to determine the nature of the contract, but cannot itself define a contract.

4.3.1.2. Must the risk be substantial/principal?

Having established that the economic operator bears some risk in the operation of the service, the next question is whether a limited risk can be transferred to the concessionaire or whether the risk must be something more substantial in order for the contract to be categorised as a concession contract. Advocate General *Fennelly* took the view that although not all the risk needs to be transferred, the transferred risk must be significant. *Fennelly* stated;

opinion delivered on September 9, 2010, in Privater Rettungsdienst, stated: *'The lack of direct remuneration of the service provider by the public authority which assigned to it the service in question constitutes a sufficient criterion for the purposes of classifying a contract as a service concession.'*

88. See also Arrowsmith, Sue *"The Law of Public and Utilities Procurement"* [2005] 2nd Edition, Sweet and Maxwell, p. 326 where she argues that a concession can exist '*even when the user is not the source of payment'*.
89. Contrary, Arrowsmith, Sue *"Public Private Partnerships and the European Procurement rules: EU Policies in Conflict?"* [2000] CMLR n° 37, pp. 709-737, who states that such a situation will not be a concession. She argues that: '*... a concession arguably does not cover the situation where payments are made to the provider from the Authorities funds based on public use'*.
90. In line with Arrowsmith, Sue *"Public Private Partnerships and the European Procurement rules: EU Policies in Conflict?"* [2000] CMLR n° 37, pp. 709-737.

'... the mere fact that there is a likelihood that the concessionaire will be able to beneficially to exploit the concession would not suffice to permit a national court or a tribunal to conclude that there is no economic risk'.[91]

The Court did not elaborate on this element in *Telaustria.*

In *Oymanns,* the Court stated that the contract did not constitute a concession contract because:

'... the trader in the present case does ***not bear the principal burden of the risk*** *connected with the carrying on of the activities in question (...)'.* [emphasis added].[92] Therefore, the contract was not a concession contract because the economic operator was not *'... exposed to a* ***significant*** *risk connected with the services it provides'.* [emphasis added].[93]

This seems to indicate that the concessionaire must assume the principal burden of the risk, which is also in line with *Commission v. Italy,*[94] where the Court stated that the contract in question was a works contract, as the contracting authority paid 60 percent of the contract expenses, with only 40 percent of the expenses originating from another operator who should use the work; this meant that the risk was not substantial. Regarding the Court's judgment in *Commission v. Italy, Brown* stated that the case:

'... underlines that a contractual arrangement can only be categorized as a true concession, for the purpose of Community procurement law, if the private partner will bear real and ***significant*** *economic risk'.* [emphasis added].[95]

Burnett also indicates that a substantial risk must be present, arguing that

'... clearly, if the extent of the guaranteed amount were to exceed, say, 50% of the total expected income of the private partner, this would raise questions about the extent to which the private partner was accepting risk'.[96]

91. Opinion of Advocate General Fennelly delivered on May 18, 2000 in Case C-324/98, Telaustria Verlags GmbH and Telefonadress GmbH v. Telekom Austria AG, [2000] ECR I-10745, paragraph 40.
92. Case C-300/07, Hans & Christophorus Oymanns GbR, Orthopädie Schuhtechnik v. AOK Rheinland/Hamburg, [2009] ECR I-4779, paragraph 75.
93. Case C-300/07, Hans & Christophorus Oymanns GbR, Orthopädie Schuhtechnik v. AOK Rheinland/Hamburg, [2009] ECR I-4779, paragraph 73.
94. Case C-437/07, Commission v. Italy, [2008] ECR I-153.
95. Brown, Adrian *"Incorrect categorisation of a tramway contract as a works concession by an Italian municipality: Commission v. Italy (C-437/07)"* [2009] PPLR n° 2, NA55-58.

In recent case law from the Court of Justice, the Court seems to have changed its view that the risk must be substantial, indicating that the risk does not always have to be substantial itself, only that the transferred risk must be substantial. Therefore, if a given market has no risk of loss, the contracting authority would not be in a condition to transfer any risk. According to the Court of Justice, such a situation can still constitute a concession contract.

In *Gotha*,[97] the Court found that a very limited risk would be sufficient to categorise a contract as a concession. The contract at issue concerned a 20-year-long contract for the distribution of drinking water. The service provider only received payment from the users, not from the contracting authority. The Commission, who intervened in the case, had argued, that it was necessary for the supplier to assume the financial risk of operating the service in question and that the risk in operating the service had to be significant. According to the Commission a service contract in which the financial risk was reduced to a minimum by the public authorities could not be categorised as a service concession.[98] The supply of the services in question in *Gotha* involved very limited financial risks, even for the contracting authority if it performed the service in-house. This was mainly due to the rules governing the sector of activity concerned. Despite the limited risk, the Court held that such a contract could constitute a concession if: *'... the contracting authority transfer to the concession holder all, or at least a significant share, of the operating risk which it faces (...)'*.[99] The Court's reasoning for this was that, in some sectors, it is not unusual for the activity involved to be *'... subject to rules which may*

96. Burnett, Michael *"A new EU Directive on Concessions – the right Approach for PPP?"* [2008] EPPPL n° 3, pp. 107-115, p. 110.
97. Case C-206/08, Wasser- und Abwasserzweckverband Gotha und Landkreisgemeinden v. Eurawasser Aufbereitungs- und Entsorgungsgesellschaft mbH, [2009] ECR I-8377.
98. Case C-206/08, Wasser- und Abwasserzweckverband Gotha und Landkreisgemeinden v. Eurawasser Aufbereitungs- und Entsorgungsgesellschaft mbH, [2009] ECR I-8377 paragraph 48 and 65.
99. Case C-206/08, Wasser- und Abwasserzweckverband Gotha und Landkreisgemeinden v. Eurawasser Aufbereitungs- und Entsorgungsgesellschaft mbH, [2009] ECR I-8377, paragraph 77. Also confirmed in Case C-274/09, Privater Rettungsdienst und Krankentransport Stadler v. Zweckverband für Rettungsdienst und Feuerwehralarmierung Passau, [2011] March 10, 2011 (not yet reported), paragraph 29.

have the effect of limiting the financial risks entailed'.[100] In such a situation, the detailed rules of public law, which govern the service:

'... facilitate the supervision of how that service is operated, and scale down the factors which may threaten transparency and distort competition'.[101]

The above statement is somewhat peculiar, and in my opinion, the question of whether a given contract is a concession should not depend on the need for transparency and competition, since these are factors that should be taken into consideration once the nature of the contract has been established. First then will the contracting authority know whether the principles of the Treaties apply (hence transparency and equal treatment must be ensured) or whether the Procurement Directives applies. Furthermore, it is not clear in which sectors such an assessment could take place. Because the national legislations vary, introducing such a possibility would create inconsistency in the Member States regarding when a contract is a concession (due to national legislation). As the Court has held several times, it is exclusively up to EU law to determine the concept of a concession.[102] If a sector is regulated and it is not possible for the contracting authority to transfer a lot of risk because it does not have any risk to transfer in the first place (because the market itself lack's competition due to regulation), there can be no requirement that the risk be 'invented'. Therefore, I find the approach taken by the Court to be unfortunate; defining a concession should not depend on the type of market.

Apart from emphasising the type of sector involved, the Court also found that:

*'it must remain open to the contracting authorities, **acting in all good faith**, to ensure the supply of services by way of a concession, if they consider that to be the best method of en-*

100. Case C-206/08, Wasser- und Abwasserzweckverband Gotha und Landkreisgemeinden v. Eurawasser Aufbereitungs- und Entsorgungsgesellschaft mbH, [2009] ECR I-8377, paragraph 72. See also Case C-348/10, Norma-A SIA, Dekom SIA v. Latgales plānošanas regions, [2011] November 10, 2011, (not yet reported), paragraph 46.
101. Case C-206/08, Wasser- und Abwasserzweckverband Gotha und Landkreisgemeinden v. Eurawasser Aufbereitungs- und Entsorgungsgesellschaft mbH, [2009] ECR I-8377, paragraph 73. See also Case C-348/10, Norma-A SIA, Dekom SIA v. Latgales plānošanas regions, [2011] November 10, 2011, (not yet reported), paragraph 46.
102. See section 2.1.

suring the public service in question, even if the risk linked to such an operation is limited'. [emphasis added].[103]

The fact that the Court in *Gotha* underlined that the contracting authority should act in good faith, when classifying its contract, indicates that the Court will only accept a limited operational risk in situations where the risk is already limited due to specific legislation in the sector. It is problematic that defining a contract as a concession can depend on whether a contracting authority is acting in good faith. It is my opinion that an analysis of whether a contract is a concession should only depend on facts relating to the concrete contract. Therefore, the elements that define a service concession contract should be based on objective criteria, which will make it clearer when a contract is considered as a concession.

Finally, the Court in *Gotha* stated that

'... it would not be reasonable to expect a public authority granting a concession to create conditions which were more competitive and involved greater financial risk than those which, on account of the rules governing the sector in question, exist in that sector'.[104]

This statement is peculiar because it is clear that the contracting authority should not invent a risk that does not exist; however, this should, in my opinion not be an element when classifying a contract, but the classification should depend on objective criteria.

The Court's ruling in *Gotha* does not seem to be in line with previous case law. *Kotsonis* argue that the conclusion in the case is 'unsatisfactory',[105] and I agree. The case does not clarify when a contract is a concession and it seems to introduce more elements that need to be taken into account as well as introducing exceptions to when a contract is a concession; that a limited risk can be sufficient in some situations. In my view, what distinguishes a regular service contract from a concession contract should only depend on the risk

103. Case C-206/08, Wasser- und Abwasserzweckverband Gotha und Landkreisgemeinden v. Eurawasser Aufbereitungs- und Entsorgungsgesellschaft mbH, [2009] ECR I-8377, paragraph 74.
104. Case C-206/08, Wasser- und Abwasserzweckverband Gotha und Landkreisgemeinden v. Eurawasser Aufbereitungs- und Entsorgungsgesellschaft mbH, [2009] ECR I-8377, paragraphs 73-75.
105. Kotsonis, Totis *"The role of risk in defining a services concession contract: Wasser- und Ab- wasserzweckverband Gotha und Landkreisgemeinden (WAZV Gotha) v. Eurawasser Aufbereitungs- und Entsorgungsgesellschaft mbH (C-206/08) (WAZV)",* [2010] PPLR n° 1, NA4-12.

factor inherent in the 'right to exploit'. This would require that the risk must be substantial in order to measure whether it has been transferred otherwise, the contract might as well constitute a service contract.

To conclude, the Court in Gotha, found that the risk the contracting authority had in the first place must be: 'transfer[ed] to the concession holder all, or at least a significant share, of the operating risk which it faces in order for a service concession to be found to exist.'[106] The fact, that a very limited risk can be sufficient for a contract to be categorised as a concession, was repeated in Privater Rettungsdienst.[107] Also, in Norma, the Court repeated the findings from Gotha and Privater Rettungsdienst, but nevertheless found that the contract in question did not constitute a concession because the economic operator was guaranteed payment. In that regard, the Court stated that a contract

> *'... by which a contracting party, pursuant to the rules of public law and the terms of the contract which govern the provision of the services in question,* ***does not bear a significant share of the risk run by the contracting authority*** *is to be regarded as a 'service contract'(...)'.* [emphasis added].[108]

Therefore, the Court seems to imply in *Norma* that the economic operator must bear significant part of the risk, which the contracting authority has. This means that the contracting authority cannot guarantee an economic operator to cover its loses and still have the contract qualify as a concession. This approach is reasonable and takes us back to objective criteria instead of elements such as good faith and sectorial rules (which the Court, however, also referred to without commenting on the substance).

Even though the risk element in a concession can be very limited based on the Court's recent case law, it is essential that the risk is *transferred*. This had also been stated before *Gotha*, in *Helmut Müller*,[109] where the Court found

106. Case C-206/08, Wasser- und Abwasserzweckverband Gotha und Landkreisgemeinden v. Eurawasser Aufbereitungs- und Entsorgungsgesellschaft mbH, [2009] ECR I-8377, paragraph 77.
107. Case C-274/09, Privater Rettungsdienst und Krankentransport Stadler v. Zweckverband für Rettungsdienst und Feuerwehralarmierung Passau, [2011] March 10, 2011 (not yet reported), paragraph 34.
108. Case C-348/10, Norma-A SIA, Dekom SIA v. Latgales plānošanas regions, [2011] November 10, 2011, (not yet reported), paragraph 59.
109. Case C-451/08, Helmut Müller GmbH v. Bundesanstalt für Immobilienaufgaben, [2010] not yet reported.

that a right to exploit a task that the contracting authority already possesses must be transferred to the concessionaire:

'In order for a contracting authority to be able to transfer to the other contracting party the right to exploit a work within the terms of that provision, ***that contracting authority must be in a position to exploit that work.****'* [emphasis added].[110]

Therefore, if the contracting authority does not have the ability to exploit a task, it is not possible to transfer a right for others to do so (in the case, the contracting authority did not own the land in question.)

It could be argued that emphasising the risk element in concession contracts is not the right way to define a concession. It is noteworthy that in jurisdictions other than EU, the risk factor is not of great importance in order to categorise a contract relationship as a concession.[111] As *Tvarnø* mentions:

'The parties are the best placed to negotiate the risk and the value of this risk. If the public party in the tender notice already sets up the distribution of the risk as demanded by the public procurement law, the project cannot create the best value for money'.[112]

Thus, it could be argued that other (objective elements) would be better for determining what constitutes a concession contract. As long as service concession contracts are not regulated, it is essential that contracting authorities cannot circumvent the Public Sector Directive by simply *choosing* to classify a contract as a concession. Consequently, it is my opinion that the element of risk in the contract constitutes an objective element, and should therefore be

110. Case C-451/08, Helmut Müller GmbH v. Bundesanstalt für Immobilienaufgaben, [2010] not yet reported, paragraph 72. The case is commented by Brown, Adrian *"Helmut Muller GmbH v. Bundesanstalt fur Immobilienaufgaben (C-451/08): clarification on the application of the EU procurement rules to land sales and development agreement"* [2010] PPLR n° 4, NA125-130.
111. Fugou Cao *"PPP in China"* in Tvarnø, Christina (ed.) *"PPP – An international analysis in a legal and economic perspective"*, [2010], Asia Link, p. 192 taking about concessions in China: '*Therefore the role of the project risk in determining a concession project remains to be seen.*' Nor the World Bank elaborate on the risk element. In that regard, a concession is a private sector arrangement whereby asset ownership remains in public hands, but where the private operator is responsible for new investments as well as operating and maintaining existing assets (see the World Banks guidelines '*Procurement of Goods, Works, and Non-Consulting Services, under IBRD Loans and IDA Credits & Grants*').
112. Tvarnø, Christina *"PPPs in an international legal, economic and political perspective"* in Tvarnø, Christina (ed.), *"PPP – An international analysis in a legal and economic perspective"*, [2010], Asia Link p. 240.

the decisive factor. However, it is unfortunate that the case law from the Court of Justice does not seem to be consistent in this field and it is most likely that only new legislation will create legal certainty in this regard.

5. The Commission's proposal for a new Directive on Concessions

A proposal from the Commission to create rules in the field of concessions has long been awaited.[113] In 2010 the Commission launched a consultation that aimed to assess the need for and impact of an initiative on concessions. The consultation shows that the Member States' opinions are divided on the subject.[114]

On December 20, 2011, the Commission published a new proposal for a Directive regarding concession contracts.[115] The purpose of creating secondary legislation in the field of concession contracts is that:

'An adequate legal framework for the award of concessions would ensure effective and non-discriminatory access to the market to all Union economic operators and legal certainty, favouring public investments in infrastructures and strategic services to the citizen.'[116]

The proposal contains a more precise definition of concession contracts with reference to the notion of operational risk. It clarifies the types of risk that are

113. See, for example, the Commission's Green Paper on public-private partnerships and Community law on public contracts and concessions, (COM(2004)327); "the 2005-Communication" (Communication from the Commission to the European Parliament, the Council, the European Economic and Social Committee and the Committee of the Regions (COM(2005)569)). See also Communication from the Commission to the European Parliament, the Council, the Economic and Social Committee of the Regions *"Single Market Act –Twelve levers to boost growth and strengthen confidence"* (SEC(2011) 467 final), section 2.12.
114. For further information in that regard, see: http://ec.europa.eu/internal_market/publicprocurement/modernising_rules/consultations/index_en.htm (last visited January 13, 2012).
115. Commission's proposal for a Directive of the European Parliament and the Council on the award of concession contracts COM(2011)897 final, henceforth 'The Proposed Concessions Directive'.
116. Recital 1 of the Proposed Concessions Directive

to be considered operational and how to define significant risk.[117] The proposed definition is examined below in section 5.1.

5.1. The proposed new definition

The Proposed Concessions Directive provides a new definition of concessions. According to the definition found in Article 2(1) (7) of the proposal, a service concession is:

'... a contract for pecuniary interest concluded in writing between one or more economic operators and one or more contracting authorities or contracting entities and having as their object the provision of services other than those referred to in points 2 and 4 where the consideration for the services to be provided consists either solely in the right to exploit the services that are subject of the contract or in that right together with payment.'

So far, this definition appears to be in line with the current definition on service concession contracts found in the Public Sector Directive Article 1(4). However, the proposal further adds to the definition; namely that the right to exploit the service shall:

'... imply the transfer to the concessionaire of the substantial operating risk. The concessionaire shall be deemed to assume the substantial operating risk where it is not guaranteed to recoup the investments made or the costs incurred in operating the works or the services which are the subject-matter of the concession.'[118]

Thus, the new definition explicitly states that the contracting authority must transfer the substantial operating risk. Emphasising on the substantial operating risk seems to indicate that the Court of Justice case law, which as elaborated on above has stated that under some situations a limited risk will be sufficient (see above section 4.3.1.2) has been reverted. This is also the conclusion to be made by looking at the Commission's non-paper from February 17, 2012 wherein it is stated that the Commission concludes on the basis of the Court of Justice's case law that the transfer of the operating risk:

'... is a necessary and sufficient criterion for distinction. Although the case law is not clear on the level of the required risk, several of these judgments refer implicitly or explicitly to a possibility of loss. The Commission considered that, in the light of difficulty to assess the

117. Explanatory memorandum to the Proposed Concessions Directive ', p. 5.
118. Article 2(2) of the Proposed Concessions Directive.

substantial character of the risk transferred, reference to the lack of guarantee of "breaking even" is the only way to ensure a certain level of legal certainty.'[119]

This reasoning is in my view rational. By requiring that the risk must be substantial and that this also requires that the concessionaires will not be guaranteed to recoup their investment will make for a more suitable way of defining a concession contract as the current state of law. As a consequence of this proposed definition it would not be possible to transfer a limited risk. Hence, if only a limited risk is transferred, such a contract will constitute a regular service contract. This will also be the case if the sector concerned does not contain any risk for the contracting authority. Thus, without stating specifically that the *Gotha* case law has been abandoned, Recital 8[120] also argues that sector-specific regulation may not limit the risk. The same can be seen in Recital 7, which states that:

'*The main feature of a concession, the right to exploit the works or services, always implies the transfer to the concessionaire of an economic risk involving the possibility that it will not recoup the investments made and the costs incurred in operating the works or services awarded.*'

Thus, it will always be necessary to assess whether economic risk is indeed transferred to the concessionaire. In my view, this is the correct way forward given that the case law has made the definition of a service concession contract uncertain and dependent upon elements such as whether the contracting authority acts in good faith.

The proposal further clarifies what should be understood by the economic risk stating that such a risk may consist of either of the following:

'*(a) the risk related to the use of the works or the demand for the provision of the service; or*

119. See p. 5 of the non-paper on the proposal issued by the Commission, which can be found at: http://register.consilium.europa.eu/pdf/en/12/st06/st06626.en12.pdf. Another paper can be found at: http://register.consilium.europa.eu/pdf/en/12/st08/st08075.en12.pdf.
120. Recital 8 states: '*Where sector specific regulation provides for a guarantee to the concessionaire on breaking even on investments and costs incurred for operating the contract, such contract should not qualify as a concession within the meaning of this Directive.*'

(b) the risk related to the availability of the infrastructure provided by the concessionaire or used for the provision of services to users.'[121]

The Commission's non-paper explains that as a consequence of only referring to the demand and availability risk above:

'It is therefore clear that certain risks such as a purely financial risk (related to increase of the cost of the capital borrowed), regulatory risks (related to changes in the regulatory environment), construction risks (common to public works contract), management risks (bad management or errors of judgment by the economic operator) can not be considered as "operating risk".'

To sum up, it is necessary for the contracting authority to make a concrete evaluation of the contract in question and measure whether a substantial risk is inherent in the contract in question, and my doing so emphasis should be laid upon the operating risk meaning that the risk must lie in the demand or availability risk. If these elements show that the concessionaire is not guaranteed to recoup its investment the contract is a concession contract. I find the definition more useful and it will create legal certainty in more cases. However, as it can be difficult to assess whether risk is in fact substantial there will still be border cases where defining a contract can be difficult.

6. Summary of findings

The above analysis of the definition of a service concession contract shows that it is difficult to define a service concession contract. As the case law stands, the definition is not particularly functional,[122] in that it is not accurate and leaves many unresolved questions. Therefore, the Commission's proposal to change the definition is highly welcome.

The analysis has shown that the following elements must exist in order for a contract to be defined as a concession contract:

Firstly, the contract must contain a service that has the same features as under a regular service contract: –the nature of the task does not define a concession. Secondly, the difference between a regular service contract and a

121. Article 2(2) of the Proposed Concessions Directive.
122. In line with Neergaard, Ulla *"Public service concessions and related concepts – the increased pressure from Community law on Member States' use of concessions"* [2007] PPLR n° 6, pp. 387-409, who states: *'No doubt, these various criteria are not very operational at the practical level in their present shape.'*

service concession contracts is that the consideration consists of the right to exploit the service. Hence, the economic operator must bear the risk of profiting from the contract by being exposed to elements such as competition from the market, financing and whether he is guaranteed payment. Thirdly, the risk arising from operating the service must be substantial. However, the risk can be limited in cases where due to legislation in a specific sector (most likely only in the utilities sector), the contracting authority does not have a risk if the service were to be provided in-house. In these cases, the *transferred* risk must still be significant, which means that the risk that is present despite the legislation in the area must be transferred. Fourthly, the way in which the economic operator is remunerated is only one of several elements that must be considered – it cannot in itself decisively define a concession. When the above elements are taken into consideration, it is necessary make a concrete case-by-case evaluation of whether the contract in question should be considered as a service concession contract.

CHAPTER 4

Contracts Below the Thresholds

1. Introduction

This chapter examines contracts with a value below the thresholds set in the Public Procurement Directives. It also discusses the reasons for setting thresholds in the Procurement Directives, which resulted in some contracts being excluded by the detailed rules of the Procurement Directives.

Despite their relatively minor value, the amount of contracts below the thresholds are significant. The value of contracts below the threshold has been estimated to 12 percent of the total government and utility expenditure on works, goods and services.[1] Therefore, it is not surprising that most Member States regulate contracts below the thresholds.[2] These contracts present significant opportunities for businesses in the Internal Market, particularly for SMEs and start-up companies.[3]

The Court of Justice has handled a few cases regarding contracts below the thresholds.[4] For example, in *Commission v. Italy*,[5] the Court found that contracts below the thresholds had to apply the principles of the Treaties once the contract was of cross-border interest. Thus, the obligations derived from

1. Commission's Evaluation Report *'Impact and Effectiveness of EU Public Procurement Legislation'*, part 1 SEC(2011) 853 final, p. 35.
2. See chapter 1, section 4.3.
3. The 2006 Communication. For further on the importance of SMEs, see, for example, 'European Code of Best Practices facilitating access by SME's to Public Procurement Contracts', SEC(2008)2193.
4. See, for example, Case C-59/00, Bent Mousten Vestergaard v. Spøttrup Boligselskab, [2001] ECR I-9505; see also Case C-264/03, Commission v. France, [2005] ECR I-8831; Joined Cases C-147 and C-148/06, SECAP SpA and Santorso Soc. coop. arl v. Comune di Torino, [2008] ECR I-3565.
5. Case C-412/04, Commission v. Italy, [2008] ECR I-619. See also Case C-264/03, Commission v. France, [2005] ECR I-8831, paragraph 32.

the principles of the Treaties (analysed in part II of the Thesis) apply to these contracts.

1.1. Outline

Section 2 of this chapter examines contracts below the EU thresholds and addresses the various thresholds set in the Public Sector Directive. Section 3 addresses the EU legislator's reasons for setting thresholds and section 4 addresses the modernisation of the EU procurement rules in relation to contracts below the thresholds.

2. The thresholds in the Public Sector Directive

The thresholds for public contracts can be found in Article 7 of the Public Sector Directive. The thresholds for works, services and goods vary depending on which type of contracting authority is awarding a contract. Therefore, sub-central contracting authorities are subject to a higher threshold than central government authorities.

The current thresholds are applicable until December 31, 2013.[6] For works, services and supplies in the public sector, the thresholds are as follows:[7]

	Works	**A-services**	**B-services**	**Supplies**
Central Government authorities	5,000,000 EUR	130,000 EUR	200,000 EUR	125,000 EUR
Sub-central contracting authorities	5,000,000 EUR	200,000 EUR	200,000 EUR	200,000 EUR

6. The relevant threshold values are revised every two years. The current thresholds are established through Regulation 1251/2011 of 30 November 2011 amending Directives 2004/17/EC, 2004/18/EC and 2009/81/EC of the European Parliament and of the Council in respect of their application thresholds for the procedures for the awarding of contracts, [2011] OJ L 319/43, which entered into force on January 1, 2012.
7. According to Article 7(1) of the Public Sector Directive, the contract's estimated value excluding VAT must be taken into account when determining the value of the contract.

There are various methods for calculating the thresholds,[8] which reflect the different ways in which a contracting authority remunerates the economic operator.[9]

A contract will often cover more than one type of public contract. Therefore, the Public Sector Directive also contains various rules for categorising a contract. These rules are relevant for determining which of the above thresholds apply. For example, when a contract involves the supply of products as well as a service to be performed, the contract in question is considered a supply contract if the supply of the product is the main object of the contract.[10] This could be the case when the contracting authority wants an elevator; here, the main object would be the elevator itself, even though the installation of the elevator also will have a high value.

When dealing with a contract concerning both products and services, and where both types are considered the purpose of the contract, the contract will be a service contract if the value of the service exceeds the value of the product.[11] With regard to a contract concerning both services and works, the main purpose of the contracts will be decisive.[12]

Chapter 5, section 5 examines some elements relating to classifying the contract in the correct manner, hereunder who will bear the burden of proof that a contract is below the thresholds.

3. Purpose of setting thresholds in the Public Sector Directive

The Commission's proposal for the first Works Directive stated that thresholds were necessary since works contracts below these thresholds:

8. See Article 9 of the Public Sector Directive.
9. See, for example, the Commission's amended proposal to the Service Directive, [1991] OJ C250/4, which states: *'Given that the way in which service providers are remunerated may vary, additional provisions are made relating to calculation of the contract value.'*
10. Article 1(2)(c)(2) of the Public Sector Directive.
11. Article 1(2)(d)(2) of the Public Sector Directive.
12. Article 1(2)(d)(2) of the Public Sector Directive. See also Case C-412/04, Commission v. Italy, [2008] ECR I-619, paragraph 47.

'... ***seem unlikely to attract competition at Common Market level****, and it is therefore reasonable that the provisions for co-ordination should not apply to them*' [emphasis added].[13]

However, the proposal also mentioned that there were practical reasons for setting the thresholds: *'Whereas for practical reasons, Community-wide publicity cannot apply to all contracts subject to the provisions for co-ordination.'*[14]

The Recital for the adopted Works Directive stated that contracts below the thresholds can:

'For the moment, be exempted from competition as provided for under this Directive, and it is appropriate to provide for their exemption from co-ordination measures (...) the Commission will at a later date submit to the Council a new proposal for a Directive whose aim is to lower the threshold.'[15]

The threshold was set at one million Euro,[16] but with the intention that the thresholds should be reduced at a later stage. However, the Commission's proposal to the Directive had suggested that the Directive reduce the thresholds gradually over the years, but the adopted Directive only contained one threshold.[17]

The idea behind the thresholds in the first Works Directive was that competition was not necessary below these thresholds as it was assumed that such contracts were not likely to be of cross-border interest and, for practical rea-

13. Recital to the proposal for a first directive of the Council on the co-ordination of procedures for the conclusion of public works contracts, Supplement to Bulletin of the European Economic Community No 9/19, 1964, p.12.
14. Recital to the proposal for a first directive of the Council on the co-ordination of procedures for the conclusion of public works contracts, Supplement to Bulletin of the European Economic Community No 9/19, 1964, p.12.
15. Directive 71/305/EEC of 26 July 1971 concerning the co-ordination of procedures for the award of public works contracts, [1971] OJ L 185/5.
16. See Article 7(1) of the first Works Directive. At that time, the thresholds were set in "Units of Account". Later on, the thresholds were set in ECU and finally in Euros. For further om the currency terminology and history, see, for example, http://ec.europa.eu/economy_finance/emu_history/legalaspects/part_c_1.htm (last visited January 18, 2012).
17. See Recital to the Proposal for a first directive of the Council on the co-ordination of procedures for the conclusion of public works contracts, Supplement to Bulletin of the European Economic Community No 9/19, 1964, p.12, which stated: '... *and it is advisable to fix for a transitional period degressive limits of 1 million, 600 000 and 300 000 units of account*'.

sons, contracting authorities should not need to follow the detailed rules in the Directive for every contract. Therefore, it was a policy choice by the EU legislature when excluding contracts below the thresholds from the first Works Directive. It is peculiar that, even though the Recital for the first Works Directive had stated its intention to reduce the thresholds at a later stage, the thresholds were raised significantly with Directive 89/440/EEC.[18] The reason for doing so was:

> '... *the rise in the cost of construction work and the interest of small and medium-sized firms in bidding for medium-sized contracts, this threshold should now be set at ECU 5 million'*.[19]

The value of this threshold was kept in the later Directive 93/37EEC.[20]

Regarding the setting of thresholds, the first Supply Directive, Directive 77/62,[21] stated that supply contracts below a given threshold: *'can be exempted, inasmuch as* ***their impact on competition is limited****'*. [emphasis added].[22] Thus, the threshold in the Supply Directive was set on the assumption that the impact on competition was limited below the threshold, which would mean that the contract would not be of interest to many undertakings. Directive 80/767 amended the first Supply Directive.[23] At that time, the Agreement on

18. Directive 89/440/EEC of 18 July 1989 amending Directive 71/305/EEC concerning the coordination of procedures for the award of public works contracts, [1989] OJ L 210/1. See Article 4a, where the thresholds were set at 5 million ECU (5 million Euro).
19. See the Recital to Directive 89/440/EEC of 18 July 1989 amending Directive 71/305/EEC concerning coordination of procedures for the award of public works contracts, [1989] OJ L 210/1.
20. Directive 93/37/EEC of 14 June 1993 concerning the coordination of procedures for the award of public works contracts, [1993] OJ L 199/54. Regarding the setting of the thresholds, the Recital to the Directive stated that works contract below the thresholds '... *may be exempted from competition as provided for under this Directive and it is appropriate to provide for their exemption from coordination measures'*.
21. Directive 77/62/EEC of 21 December 1976 coordinating procedures for the award of public supply contracts, [1977] OJ L13/1.
22. Recital to Directive 77/62/EEC of 21 December 1976 coordinating procedures for the award of public supply contracts, [1977] OJ L13/1. The thresholds were sat at a value equivalent to 200,000 Euro.
23. Directive 80/767/EEC of 22 July 1980 adapting and supplementing in respect of certain contracting authorities Directive 77/62/EEC coordinating procedures for the award of public supply contracts, [1980] OJ L 215/1.

Government Procurement (GPA) had been adopted,[24] which meant that the thresholds had to be adjusted to ensure the EU fulfilled this international agreement.[25] Article 3(2) of the Directive stated:

'... the Commission shall decide on any adjustments to be made to the latter value on the basis of the procedures adopted for determining the value in European units of account of the amount given in Article 1 (1) (b) of the Agreement'.

Thus, the Directive also gave the Commission the competence to adjust the thresholds to ensure the fulfilment of the GPA.

The first Service Directive, Directive 92/50/EEC,[26] stated that the threshold had been set *'... **in order to avoid unnecessary formalities**; whereas this threshold may in principle be the same as that for public supply contracts (...)'* [emphasis added].[27] Thus, the thresholds were set to the same as for supply contracts in order to avoid unnecessary formalities.

From this brief examination of the reasoning behind the thresholds, it can be concluded that the thresholds serve two main purposes. Firstly, it is assumed that a contract below the threshold is not of cross-border interest. Secondly, the thresholds are set to ensure the EU's compliance with the GPA.[28]

The Court of Justice has emphasised that it was a policy choice to set the thresholds. In *Commission v. Italy*, the Court found that

24. With Council Decision of 10 December 1979 concerning the conclusion of the Multilateral Agreements resulting from the 1973 to 1979 trade negotiations, 80/271/EEC [1980] OJ L 71/1.
25. The value of 200,000 European units of account laid down in Article 5 (1) (a) of Directive 77/62/EEC was replaced by 140,000 European units of account. See Article 3 of Directive 80/767/EEC of 22 July 1980 adapting and supplementing in respect of certain contracting authorities, Directive 77/62/EEC coordinating procedures for the award of public supply contracts, [1980] OJ L 215/1.
26. Directive 92/50/EEC of 18 June 1992 relating to the coordination of procedures for the award of public service contracts, [1992] OJ L 209/1.
27. Recital to Directive 92/50/EEC of 18 June 1992 relating to the coordination of procedures for the award of public service contracts, [1992] OJ L 209/1.
28. See the Public Sector Directive Recital 17, which states that: '... *while at the same time ensuring compliance with the thresholds provided for by the Agreement which are expressed in special drawing rights (...)*'.

'... the Community legislature expressly made a policy choice to exclude contracts under a certain threshold from the advertising regime which it introduced and therefore did not impose any specific obligation with respect to them'.[29]

Advocate-General *Colomer*, in his Opinion in *SECAP*, expressed this policy choice as:

'The setting of a financial threshold (...) is based on a single premise, namely that contracts of small value do not attract operators established outside national borders; (...) However, that rebuttable presumption is open to evidence to the contrary ...'[30]

Thus, despite the assumption that contracts below the thresholds are not of cross-border interest, as the Court's case law also shows, it is necessary to make a concrete evaluation of the contract in order to determine whether the contract is of cross-border interest and should be noted when the principles derived from the Treaties are applicable (see chapter 6 for cross-border interest).

4. Modernisation of the EU Procurement rules

On January 27, 2011, the Commission issued a Green Paper on the modernisation of EU public procurement policy towards a more efficient European Procurement Market.[31] The Green Paper on Modernisation reflected a large number of ideas regarding how various objectives could be better achieved, also in relation contracts below the thresholds.

According to the Green Paper, some stakeholders felt the thresholds were too low and had asked for them to be raised. However, at the same time, the Green Paper noted that:

'Any increase in the applicable thresholds in the EU would automatically involve a corresponding increase in all the agreements concluded by the EU (meaning not only in the

29. Case C-412/04, Commission v. Italy, [2008] ECR I-619, paragraph 65.
30. Opinion of Advocate General, Ruiz Jarabo Colomer delivered on 27 November 2007 in Joined Cases C-147/06 and C-148/06 SECAP SpA v. Comune di Torino and Santorso Soc. coop. arl v. Comune di Torino, [2008] ECR 1-3565 paragraph 23.
31. The Commission's Green Paper on the modernisation of EU public procurement policy Towards a more efficient European Procurement Market, COM (2011)15, henceforth the Green Paper on Modernisation

> *GPA, but also in all other international agreements). This situation could in turn trigger requests for compensation from our partners. These requests could be quite significant.'*[32]

Therefore, it is not surprising that the Commission's proposal for a new Procurement Directive has kept the same thresholds as in the Public Sector Directive.[33] Many Member States, as well as members of the Parliament, have, however, expressed the view that the thresholds should be raised despite this being contrary to the GPA. Thus, it is still possible that the thresholds will be raised in the adopted Directive.

Regarding contracts below the EU thresholds, the Commission asked whether the current Communication from the Commission was sufficient or whether further guidance was needed. The Commission also expressed the view that

> *'Even though contracts below the thresholds would most probably not be covered by a future legislative proposal, further guidance could be considered to help contracting authorities in assessing the existence or not of a certain cross-border interest in specific cases.'*

Thus, it is possible that the Commission will issue further guidance on contracts below the thresholds in the future.

5. Summary

It can be concluded that there were two reasons for excluding contracts below the EU thresholds from the procedural rules in the Public Sector Directive. Firstly, it is assumed that contracts below the threshold are not of cross-border interest. Secondly, the thresholds are set to ensure that the EU complies with the GPA.

32. The Commission's Green Paper on the modernisation of EU public procurement policy Towards a more efficient European Procurement Market, COM (2011)15, p. 9.
33. The Proposed Procurement Directive Article 4.

CHAPTER 5

B-service Contracts

1. Introduction

This chapter examines what constitutes a B-service contract as well as its characteristics. It also examines why the Procurement Directives did not fully cover these types of contracts, which has led to them to being excluded from the procedural rules of the Directive.

Section 2 shows that B-services can cover a range of different types of services. Certain sectors that involve B-services, such as education, health and social services, has been estimated to amount to 36 percent of the total government and utility expenditure on works, goods and services.[1] Therefore, these contracts as with contracts below the thresholds also present significant opportunities for businesses in the Internal Market.

The Commission has acknowledged the relevance of certain B-service contracts for economic operators. In its proposal for a new Procurement Directive, it proposes to abolish the distinction between A-services and B-services from the Directive (see section 6).

The Court of Justice has handled a few cases regarding B-service contracts.[2] For example, in *Commission v. Ireland*,[3] the Court found that B-service contracts had to apply the principles of the Treaties once the contract was of cross-border interest. Therefore, the obligations derived from the principles of the Treaties apply to these contracts.

1. Commission's Evaluation Report *'Impact and Effectiveness of EU Public Procurement Legislation'*, part 1 SEC(2011) 853 final, p. 35, bearing in mind that the estimate also covers goods and works in these sectors.
2. See, for example, Case C-226/09, Commission v. Ireland, [2010] November 18, 2010 (not yet reported). Case C-95/10, Strong Segurança SA v. Município de Sintra, Securitas-Serviços e Tecnologia de Segurança, [2011] March 17, 2011 (not yet reported).
3. Case C-507/03, Commission v. Ireland, [2007] ECR I-9777.

1.1. Outline

Section 2 explores the subject of B-service contracts and what distinguishes these types of contracts from A-service contracts. Section 3 examines the reasons why the Public Procurement Directives only partially cover these types of contracts. Section 4 addresses the rules in the Public Sector Directive that contracting authorities must apply when awarding a B-service contract. Section 5 makes some observations regarding the classification of a contract, including the question of who bears the burden of proof that a correct classification of the contract has been conducted. These observations will also be relevant for contracts below the thresholds and service concession contracts. Finally, section 6 will explore the Commission's proposal for a new Procurement Directive.

2. B-services

The first Public Procurement Directive to cover services was Directive 92/50/EC.[4] Like the current Public Sector Directive, the Service Directive contained two categories of services. Therefore, a service can be considered either as an Annex II A service or Annex II B service. Annex II B currently contains the following categories (which have not been changed since the Service Directive):

Category No	**Subject**
17	Hotel and restaurant services
18	Rail transport services
19	Water transport services
20	Supporting and auxiliary transport services
21	Legal services
22	Personnel placement and supply service
23	Investigation and security services, except armoured car services
24	Education and vocational education services
25	Health and social services
26	Recreational, cultural and sporting services
27	Other services

4. Directive 92/50/EEC of 18 June 1992 relating to the coordination of procedures for the award of public service contracts, OJ L 209/1, henceforth the first Service Directive.

A contract frequently contains both types of services, in which case the value of the service is decisive for the categorisation of the contract. For example, if the estimated value of the B-service is higher than the A-service, then the contract is to be considered a B-service contract.[5]

The fact that the value is decisive also means that a service contract can be covered fully by the Public Sector Directive, even if the A-service itself does not exceed the thresholds. This will be the case if the value of the A-service is higher than the B-service and, potentially, vice-versa. Thus, if the A-service exceeds the thresholds, this can be considered a B-service contract if the value of the B-service is higher than that of the A-service.

3. Reasons why the Public Sector Directive does not fully cover B-services

According to Recital 21 of the first Service Directive, the application of the Directive's provisions in full had to be limited, for a transitional period, to contracts for services in which its provisions will:

*'... **enable the full potential for increased cross-frontier** trade to be realized; whereas contracts for other services need to be monitored for a certain period before a decision is taken on the full application of this Directive'.* [emphasis added].[6]

This indicates that B-services were excluded from the first Service Directive because of their lack of cross-border interest. This can also be seen in the Commission's Communication to the Parliament regarding the Council's position to the proposal for the Service Directive, where with regard to the choice of having two categories, the Communication stated that:

*'The full system is applied to services identified as being of priority interest because **of their potential in cross-frontier operations**. The other categories of services are only subject to minimum retrospective transparency requirements'.* [emphasis added].[7]

Directive 2004/18/EC retained the two categories of services, with the same purpose why B-services were not fully covered by the Directive.[8]

5. Article 22 of the Public Sector Directive.
6. Recital 21 of the first Service Directive.
7. Communication from the Commission to the European Parliament regarding the Council's common position on the proposal for a Directive coordinating the procedures on the award of public service contracts, [1992] SEC (92) 406.

The Court of Justice has also stressed upon why the Directive did not fully cover B-services. In *Strong Segurança,*[9] the Court found that

'*... the European Union legislature based itself on the assumption that contracts for the services referred to in Annex I B to Directive 92/50 are, in principle, in the light of their specific nature,* ***not of sufficient cross-border interest*** *to justify their award being subject to the conclusion of a tendering procedure intended to enable undertakings from other Member States to examine the contract notice and submit a tender'.* [emphasis added].[10]

Therefore, the main reason that the Directive did not fully cover B-services was the assumption that these types of services, at the time of setting the categories, were not of sufficient cross-border interest to require the detailed procedural rules in the Directive to apply. However, despite this assumption, it is still necessary to determine whether the concrete contract is of cross-border interest in order for the principles of the Treaties to apply (see chapter 6).

4. Applicable rules in the Public Sector Directive

According to Article 21 of the Public Sector Directive, '*Contracts which have as their object services listed in Annex II B shall be subject solely to Article 23 and 35(4).*' Therefore, two provisions in the Directive are applicable for B-service contracts.

The first of these is Article 23, which relates to the technical specifications that must be ensured in order to afford equal access for tenderers to the contract and not to create unjustified obstacles to the opening-up of public procurement to competition.[11] This also means that the contract must be described either in reference to technical specifications or in terms of performance or functional requirements.[12]

8. See Recital 19 of the Public Sector Directive.
9. Case C-95/10, Strong Segurança SA v. Município de Sintra, Securitas-Serviços e Tecnologia de Segurança, [2011] March 17, 2011 (not yet reported).
10. Case C-95/10, Strong Segurança SA v. Município de Sintra, Securitas-Serviços e Tecnologia de Segurança, [2011] March 17, 2011 (not yet reported), paragraph 35. See also Case C-507/03, Commission v. Ireland, [2007] ECR I-9777, paragraph 25.
11. Article 23(2) of the Public Sector Directive.
12. For further on Article 23, see, for example, Arrowsmith, Sue *'The Law of Public and Utilities Procurement'* [2005] 2nd Edition, Sweet and Maxwell, chapter 17. Trepte, Peter *"Public Procurement in the EU"* [2007] 2nd Edition, Oxford, chapter 5, section A.

Secondly, Article 35(4) refers to the contracting authorities' obligations to give notice of the results of the contract award procedure. Thus, a contracting authority, having awarded a contract regarding a B-service, shall send *'a notice of the results of the award procedure no later than 48 days after the award of the contract (...)'*.[13]

The reason for requiring contracting authorities to send a contract award notice when awarding a B-service contract, is for monitoring purposes.[14] However, the contracting authority can choose not to have the contract award noticed published, in which case the contracting authority must state this in the notice.

5. Classifying the contract

It is important that the contracting authority classifies the contract correctly in order to determine whether the rules in the Public Sector Directive apply or whether only the obligations derived from the principles of the Treaties must be ensured. Thus, the contracting authority must assess a range of aspects, such as the type of contract and whether the value of the contract is above or below the thresholds. This classification of the contract will often be a difficult task to perform.[15] Nevertheless, it is important to classify the contract correctly because a contract that has been classified incorrectly to fall outside the Directive can later on be declared ineffective[16] if the contract has been entered into without following the rules in the Public Sector Directive.

The difficulty involved in correctly classifying a B-service contract can be seen from a recent report from DG Markt performed by Rambøll on cross-border procurement above the thresholds. This report stated that 38 percent of all awards on B-services between 2007 and 2009 were classified as '*other services*' (category 27). However, a manual check of the awards performed by Rambøll showed that 9 percent of these contracts were actually contracts concerning works or supply, 25 percent of the contracts covered A-services and 8 percent were another type of B-service.[17]

13. Article 35(4) of the Public Sector Directive.
14. See especially Recital 21 for the Service Directive.
15. See, for example, chapter 3 regarding the difficulties of defining a service concession contract.
16. See chapter 11 for more on ineffectiveness.
17. Report from DG Markt prepared by Rambøll *'Final Report Cross-border Procurement above EU Thresholds'*, p. 61.

Contracts that contain more than one element, such as if both services and goods are involved, is an example of a contract which are difficult to classify. In *Hotel Loutraki*,[18] the disputed contract involved such a 'mix-contract'. The case concerned a situation in which the contracting authority had decided to privatise a casino that was fully owned by the Greek State. The contract involved four different elements, including the transfer of 49 percent of the shares as well as entrusting the management to the private party. The Court found that the main purpose of the contract was the sale of the shares; hence, the Directive did not cover the contract.[19] Consequently, the Court applied the same rules for classification of a contract falling outside the Directive as for those falling within the Directive. This is perhaps unsurprising given that, in order to know whether a contract falls within the Directive, the contracting authority needs to make an assessment according to the provisions in the Public Sector Directive, and it would not be meaningful to have different calculations rules, classification rules, etc. for contracts outside the Public Sector Directive. Thus, the same rules apply in order to make a correct assessment of the nature of the contract.

5.1. The burden of proof of a correct classification

It is up to the contracting authority to determine the classification of a contract, although the subject is open for review by the national courts.[20] In this regard, it can be discussed whether it is the contracting authority who must bear the burden of proof that the contract has been classified correctly, or whether the burden of proof should be laid upon the party claiming that the classification of the contract has not been done correctly.

18. Joined Cases C-145/08 and C-149/08, Club Hotel Loutraki AE, Athinaïki Techniki AE, Evangelos Marinakis v. Ethniko Simvoulio Radiotileorasis, Ipourgos Epikratias (C-145/08) and Aktor Anonimi Tekhniki Etairia (Aktor ATE) v. Ethniko Simvoulio Radiotileorasis (C-149/08), [2010] ECR I-4165.
19. The Court of Justice, nevertheless, found that the contracting authority had to comply with the principles of the Treaty. See Joined Cases C-145/08 and C-149/08, Club Hotel Loutraki AE, Athinaïki Techniki AE, Evangelos Marinakis v. Ethniko Simvoulio Radiotileorasis, Ipourgos Epikratias (C-145/08) and Aktor Anonimi Tekhniki Etairia (Aktor ATE) v. Ethniko Simvoulio Radiotileorasis (C-149/08), [2010] ECR I-4165, paragraph 63. The case is commented on by McGowan, David, *'Consortia member rights and classification of mixed contracts: a note on Club Hotel Loutraki (C-145/08 and C-149/08)'* [2010] PPLR n° 5, N174-179.
20. Case C-411/00, Felix Swoboda GmbH v. Österreichische Nationalbank, [2002] ECR I-10567, paragraph 62. See further on enforcement in Part III of this Thesis.

In *Commission v. Italy,*[21] the Commission claimed that a specific contract was above the threshold. The Court found that it was the Commission's responsibility to prove all elements of the alleged infringement, without relying on any presumptions, and that the Commission had not provided any proof of the value of the contracts concluded under the framework agreement. Consequently, the Commission had failed to establish a violation of the Service Directive. The case was an enforcement proceeding, in which case it is generally up to the Commission to prove a breach.[22] However, this does not mean that it will always be up to the claimant in the national courts to prove that the value of a contract exceeds the thresholds.[23] In my view, the contracting authority is closest to bearing this burden. This is mainly because it will be the contracting authority that knows what it wishes to procure, which means it will be best to measure what type of contract is involved and the value of such a contract.[24]

In Denmark, the burden of proof for whether a contract is above the threshold has been placed on the contracting authority, as stated by the Danish Complaints Board for Public Procurement on more than one occasion.[25] Also, in cases regarding the type of contract, has the Board found that the burden of proof that a contract has been classified in a correct manner lies

21. Case C-119/ 06, Commission v. Italy, [2007] ECR I-168.
22. See also Case C-96/81 Commission v. Netherlands, [1982] ECR 1791, paragraph 6, Case C-434/01, Commission v. United Kingdom, [2003] ECR I-13239, paragraph 21. Case C-117/02, Commission v. Portugal, [2004] ECR I-5517, paragraph 80.
23. See also Case C-241/06, Lämmerzahl GmbH v. Freie Hansestadt Bremen, [2007] ECR I-8415, where the Court found that a tenderer could not be expected to be aware of the fact that the contract was above the thresholds. The case is further dealt with in relation to time limits for review. See chapter 10.
24. In line with *Brown*, who states that it is debatable whether the Court in the *Commission v. Italy* had struck the right balance on this issue. See Brown, Adrian, *'Application of the directives to contracts with not-for-profit organisations and transparency under the EC Treaty: a note on Case C-119/06 Commission v. Italy'* [2008] PPLR n° 3, NA96-99, who states: *'... it is the contracting authority which has first-hand knowledge of the estimated value which it attributes to a particular contract and of the prices which bidders in fact offer. It is not clear how the Commission (or, for that matter, a private complainant in a national court) is expected positively to prove that value'.*
25. Decision of June 7, 2010, Play Tech Limited v. Danske Spil, where the Board concluded that a considerable degree of uncertainty as to whether the contract should be tendered according to the Directive, should lead to a requirement to follow the Procurement Directives. See also decision of July 27, 2009, Alfa Laval Nordic A/S v. Odense Vandselskab A/S.

with the contracting authority.[26] For example, in *P. Jensen og Sønner Outrup ApS v. Blaabjerg Kommune,*[27] the Board found that the contracting authority's decision, that the contract fell outside the Public Sector Directive based on the value of the contract, was incorrect. The Board found that it was up to the contracting authority to make a decision regarding which rules applies, and that the contracting authority in that regard is required beforehand to ensure an adequate basis for making this decision. The Board emphasised that the authority did not provide documents showing the basis upon which the assessment of not to follow the Public Sector Directive had been made, nor did it provide a statement for its consideration in that regard; it only referred to a statement from the technical advisor. Thus, the Board concluded that the decision to follow the Danish national rules instead of the Public Sector Directive was a violation of the Directive.

6. Modernisation of the EU Procurement rules

The before-mentioned Green Paper on modernisation, issued by the Commission in January 2012 reflects a large number of ideas regarding how various objectives could be better achieved, also in relation to B-services.

Regarding B-services, the Commission asked in the Green Paper whether it was still appropriate to divide services into two categories. The Commission noted that the reason for dividing services into two categories in the first place was that B-services did not have the same cross-border interest as A-services. However, the Commission expressed the following view in the Green Paper on modernisation:

'For some of the services explicitly mentioned in the "B" list, such as water transport services, hotel services, personnel placement and supply services or security services, it does

26. For example, in the decision of January 7, 2011, Scan-Plast v. Silkeborg Kommune regarding a pre-manufactured toilet building, the contract was found to be a works contract and not a supply contract as the contracting authority had classified it. See also decision of September 23, 2010, Getinge Danmark A/S v. Region Midtjylland, where the Board considered a contract to be a supply contract in a situation where the contracting authority had found it was a works contract; since the thresholds for works contracts are higher than those for service contracts, the contract in question had been entered into directly.
27. Decision of January 19, 2007, P. Jensen og Sønner Outrup ApS v. Blaabjerg Kommune.

indeed appear difficult to assume that they represent a lesser cross-border interest than the services in the "A" list.'

Thus, it is not surprising that the Commission's proposal for a new Public Sector Directive[28] suggest covering only one category of services.[29] This means that a future Directive might fully cover B-services. As mentioned above, the Directive only covered B-services in order to monitor whether it would, at a later stage, be appropriate to regulate this type of service. Regulating these services now seems to be the Commission's view that this is necessary. However, at the same time that it is suggested to delete the distinction between A- and B-services a special regime for social services is proposed.[30] According to the proposal, such services:

'continue by their very nature to have a limited cross-border dimension, namely what are known as services to the person, such as certain social, health and educational services'.[31]

Thus, the proposal suggest that contracting authorities awarding such contracts shall publish a contract notice, make the result of the procedure known, and leave it up to the Member States to implement appropriate procedures for the award of the contract. This national procedure must comply with the principles of transparency and equal treatment (the proposal is elaborated further on in chapter 12).

Two compromise proposals regarding the proposed 'light regime' has been suggested by the Danish Presidency. [32] As can be seen from both proposals they seek to make the suggested social regime even 'lighter' as well as more services that are currently B-services have been suggested to be removed to the new light regime.

28. Proposal for a Directive of the European Parliament and the Council on public procurement, COM(2011) 896 final.
29. According to the Explanatory Memorandum to the Proposed Procurement Directive, the Commission's evaluation of the rules had shown that it is: '... *no longer justified to restrict the full application of procurement law to a limited group of services. However, it became also clear that the regular procurement regime is not adapted to social services which need a specific set of rules (see below).'*
30. See the Proposed Procurement Directive Articles 74-76.
31. Recital 11 of the Proposed Procurement Directive.
32. The first was issued on March 16, 2012 (can be found at: http://register.consilium.europa.eu/pdf/en/12/st07/st07457.en12.pdf) and the second was issued on April 18, 2012 (and can be found at: http://register.consilium.europa.eu/pdf/en/12/st08/st08765.en12.pdf)

7. Summary

It can be concluded that B-service contracts were excluded from the procedural rules in the Public Sector Directive on the assumption that these types of contracts were not of cross-border interest.

The contracting authority bears the burden of proof that the contract in question has been classified correctly. If the contracting authority is mistaken and it turns out that the contract falls within the Public Sector Directive, it is possible that a review body could declare the contract as ineffective (see chapter 11).

CHAPTER 6

Cross-border Interest

1. Introduction

Part II of this Thesis will analyse and discuss which obligations can be derived from the principles of the Treaties when contracting authorities enter into one of the three types of contracts. However, these obligations derived from the principles of the Treaties only apply if the contract in question is of certain cross-border interest.[1]

The purpose of this chapter is to analyse when a contract is of certain cross-border interest. In that regard, the chapter examines and analyses various aspects of the concept. Even though the subject is highly practical and important in order for contracting authorities to know which rules and obligations apply, it has not been explored in great detail, either in the literature or jurisprudence.[2]

One reason why a contract must be of cross-border interest in order for the principles of the Treaties to apply is that if no undertakings in other Member States would have an interest in a given contract,

1. For service concession contracts, some sort of cross-border interest was mentioned in Case C-231/03, Consorzio Aziende Metano v. Comune di Cingia de' Botti, [2005] ECR I-7287. For below-threshold contracts, see, for example, Case C-412/04, Commission v. Italy, [2008] ECR I-619. For B-service contracts, cross-border interest was stated in the Case C-507/03, Commission v. Ireland, [2007] ECR I-9777.
2. The topic has been touched upon briefly. See, for example, Brown, Adrian *"EU primary law requirements in practice: advertising, procedures and remedies for public contracts outside the procurement directives"* [2010] PPLR n° 5, pp. 169-181 or Drijber, Jan Berend & Stergiou, Hélène *"Public Procurement Law and Internal Market Law"* [2009] CMLR n° 46, pp. 805-846.

'... the effects on the fundamental freedoms concerned should therefore be regarded as too uncertain and indirect to warrant the conclusion that they may have been infringed'.[3]

In such a situation, therefore, it is legitimate to award a contract without following the obligations derived from the principles of the Treaties.

The obligations derived from the principles of the Treaties apply *once* a contract is of certain cross-border interest. Thus, cross-border interest of a contract should in my view not be interpreted in the sense that the Treaty will apply *unless* the contract is not of cross-border interest. It can be argued that (at least in relation to B-services), that since these contracts were excluded on the assumption that they lack cross-border interest, it will be the main rule that such contracts is not of cross-border interest and only in cases where it can be proved otherwise will these contract be of cross-border interest. This will in theory have the consequence that as a main rule the principles of the Treaties do not apply to these contracts. On the other hand, since the Treaties are primary law it could also be interpreted in the sense that as the main rule the Treaties do in fact apply to all contracts. Thus, it is the assumption that contracts do have cross-border interest, and hence only if otherwise can be supported will the contract not be of cross-border interest. In the *Commission v. Ireland*, the Court of Justice seems to apply that cross-border interest of a contract is a prerequisite for the use of the Treaties. The Court of Justice stated that even though B-services were excluded from the advertising arrangements in the Public Sector Directive, this could not

'... be interpreted as precluding application of the principles resulting from Articles 43 EC and 49 EC, ***in the event that such contracts nevertheless*** *are of certain cross-border interest'* [emphasis added].[4]

This statement supports the view that the Treaties apply once a contract is of cross-border interest. This means, that it is neither a main rule nor an exception, which a given contract is of cross-border interest. The requirement of cross-border interest has been developed by the case law of the Court of Justice. Thus, cross-border interest is a EU concept and must be interpreted in accordance with EU law.

3. Case C-231/03, Consorzio Aziende Metano v. Comune di Cingia de' Botti, [2005] ECR I-7287, paragraph 20. See also Case T-258/06, Germany v. Commission, [2010] ECR II-2027, paragraph 88.
4. Case C-507/03, Commission v. Ireland, [2007] ECR I-9777, paragraph 29.

1.1. Outline

Section 2 offers some observations regarding the subject of cross-border interest in relation to contracts falling within the Public Sector Directive. This shows that cross-border interest is not necessary to determine when a contract falls within the Directive. Section 3 examines the Court of Justice's development on cross-border interest regarding the three types of contracts. Section 4 analyses, which elements can lead to a contract being of cross-border interest. Section 5 explores the *assessment* of cross-border interest, particularly whether it is a hypothetical assessment or whether an undertaking must be interested in the contract *de facto*. The section also addresses the time, which such an assessment must be made as well as discusses the Court of Justice's requirement of the cross-border interest being *certain*. Section 6 examines which principles of the Treaties will apply when the contract is of cross-border interest. Section 7 examines who bears the burden of proof that the contract is categorised correctly so as not to be of cross-border interest. Section 8 discusses whether perspectives can be drawn to the Treaties' provisions of free movement in relation to internal situations, or to the *de minimis* rules in competition law and state aid.

2. Cross-border interest and the Public Sector Directive

As elaborated further in chapter 2, the objective of the Public Sector Directive is to ensure undistorted competition by guaranteeing open, equal access to public contracts. It could be said that it is within the very nature of the Public Sector Directive that a contracting authority must provide undertakings in other Member States with the opportunity to tender for a contract in order to eliminate barriers to the freedom to provide services and to facilitate free movement of goods. Therefore, it should not be necessary for contracting authorities to make an assessment of whether a contract is of cross-border interest. However, a contract that falls within the Public Sector Directive must ensure that the Directive and the Treaties are applied, regardless of whether the specific contract is of cross-border interest.

Therefore, the Public Sector Directive will also apply in a situation where only domestic undertakings have submitted a tender. This was seen in the *Wallonian Bus* case,[5] in which Belgium claimed that the principle of equal treatment had not been breached by taking into account amendments in a ten-

5. Case C-87/94, Commission v. Belgium, [1996] ECR I-2043.

der that had been made after the opening of all the bids. Belgium argued that such a situation did not constitute a breach of the principle of equal treatment due to the fact that all of the tenderers were Belgium undertakings; according to Belgium, this meant that '*the case concerned a purely internal situation to which Community law did not apply.*'[6] Nevertheless, the Court of Justice stated that

> '*... the Directive is not subject to any condition concerning the nationality or seat of tenderers (...) it is always possible that undertakings established in other Member States may be concerned directly or indirectly by the award of a contract*'.[7]

Therefore, to ensure the market is open to potential competitors, all contracts falling within the Directive must follow the Directive's procedures when a contracting authority awards such contracts. *Trepte* described the contracts covered by the Procurement Directives as those that are most *'clearly capable of having impact on competition and of effecting trade between Member States'*.[8] Therefore, it could be argued that the principles of the Treaties apply to these contracts because they are indeed of cross-border interest. However, it will often be the case that only domestic undertakings are interested in the contract in question, which means that the contract is not, in itself, of cross-border interest.

Regardless of whether a contract is of cross-border interest, most contracts end up being awarded to undertakings within the same Member State as the Member State of the contracting authority. For example, statistics from 2007–2009 show that only 1.6 percent of all contracts falling within the scope of the Public Sector Directive were awarded to an undertaking located in a Member State other than that of the contracting authority.[9] This does not mean that the awarded contracts are not of cross-border interest. Other reasons, such as the

6. Case C-87/94, Commission v. Belgium, [1996] ECR I-2043, paragraph 31. For further on internal situations, see section 8.2.
7. Case C-87/94, Commission v. Belgium, [1996] ECR I-2043, paragraph 34.
8. Trepte, Peter *"Public Procurement in the EU"* [2007] 2nd Edition, Oxford University Press, p. 20.
9. See *'Final Report Cross-border Procurement above EU Thresholds'*, p. 36, which also estimates the indirect cross-border activity from 2007–2009 to 29.1 percent. The number is slightly higher if looking at cross-border interest in terms of value, where 3.5 percent in terms of total contract value was awarded as 'direct cross-border procurement', which could be a small indication that the higher the value of the contract, the greater the interest the contract will have for non-domestic undertakings to bid for.

contracting authorities preferences and competition in the market, clearly also play a role in whether contracts end up being awarded to non-domestic undertakings. Despite this, the low number of direct cross-border procurement indicates that cross-border procurement is still relatively low, even under the Procurement Directives. It might also indicate that competition for contracts should be increased, which could be done by making it easier for non-domestic undertakings to bid for cross-border contracts. According to the Proposed Procurement Directive one of the two objectives to propose a new Directive is to:

'Increase the efficiency of public spending to ensure the best possible procurement outcomes in terms of value for money. This implies in particular a simplification and flexibilisation of the existing public procurement rules. Streamlined, more efficient procedures will benefit all economic operators ***and facilitate the participation of SMEs and cross-border bidders****.'* [emphasis added][10]

Thus, by seeking to establish a more flexible and simpler procurement regime, it is the assumption that this will create more cross-border competition; hence it is the intention with the proposal that cross-border competition should be increased. However, simpler rules are only one way to facilitate more cross-border competition.[11]

If it was in fact always necessary to make an assessment of whether a specific contract is of cross-border interest, this would make it uncertain whether contracting authorities would actually follow the rules in the Directive, and would presumably create different practices in the Member States.

To conclude, the Treaties and the Public Sector Directive apply in all cases when a contract falls within the Directive and contracting authorities do not need to make an assessment of whether the contract is of cross-border interest, but must apply the rules in the Directive for all contracts falling within the Directive.

10. Explanatory note to the Proposed Procurement Directive, p. 2.
11. For further on the topic see, for example, Sánchez Graells, Albert *"Are the Procurement Rules a Barrier for Cross-border Trade within the European Market? – A view on proposals to lower that barrier and spur growth"* in Ølykke, Grith, Hansen, Carina Risvig and Tvarnø, Christina D. *"EU Public Procurement – Modernisation, Growth and Innovation"*, DJØF, July 2012.

3. The Court of Justice's development of cross-border interest for the three types of contract

The first case from the Court of Justice to emphasise that the obligations derived from the principle of transparency (as will be analysed in chapter 7) only apply if some sort of cross-border interest is involved, was *Coname*.[12]

A few months after *Coname*, in *Parking Brixen*,[13] the contracting authority tried to argue that the situation in the case was to be regarded as purely internal for the Member State, given that all of the undertakings were based in the same Member State (Italy).[14] It was the same argument Belgium had tried to invoke in the *Wallonian bus* case in relation to a procedure falling within the Public Sector Directive (see above section 2). However, the Court of Justice dismissed this argument, even though the contract in question was a service concession contract and therefore fell outside the Directive. The Court stated:

'... It is possible that, in the main proceedings, undertakings established in Member States other than the Italian Republic might have been interested in providing the services concerned (...)'.[15]

Failure to follow the transparency obligation could potentially constitute indirect discrimination against undertakings in Member States other than the Member State of the contracting authority.

In *Commission v. Ireland*[16] the Court of Justice stated that even though B-services were excluded from the advertising arrangements in the Directive, this could not

'... be interpreted as precluding application of the principles resulting from Articles 43 EC and 49 EC, in the event that such contracts nevertheless are of ***certain cross-border interest****'* [emphasis added].[17]

12. Case C-231/03, Consorzio Aziende Metano v. Comune di Cingia de' Botti, [2005] ECR I-7287. See paragraph 20.
13. Case C-458/03, Parking Brixen GmbH v. Gemeinde Brixen and Stadtwerke Brixen AG, [2005] ECR I-8585.
14. Case C-458/03, Parking Brixen GmbH v. Gemeinde Brixen and Stadtwerke Brixen AG, [2005] ECR I-8585, paragraph 54.
15. Case C-458/03, Parking Brixen GmbH v. Gemeinde Brixen and Stadtwerke Brixen AG, [2005] ECR I-8585, paragraph 55.
16. Case C-507/03, Commission v. Ireland, [2007] ECR I-9777.

Thus, with this case, the requirement that the cross-border interest of a given contract must be certain in order for the Treaties to apply was introduced. However, the conclusion in the case leaves the following questions unanswered:

1. When is a contract of cross-border interest? (section 4)
2. Is the assessment of cross-border interest hypothetical or de facto, and what does it mean that the cross-border interest must be *certain*? (section 5)
3. At what time should the assessment of whether a contract is of cross-border interest be made? (section 5)
4. Which principles of the Treaties apply when the contract is of cross-border interest? (section 6)
5. Who bears the burden of proof of a correct assessment of a contract not to be of cross-border interest? (section 7)

4. When is a contract of cross-border interest?

In order to answer the question of when a contract should be considered as being of cross-border interest, it is relevant to analyse for whom must the contract be of interest (section 4.1) as well as the elements that can lead to a contract being of cross-border interest (section 4.2).

4.1. For whom must the contract be of interest? Direct or indirect cross-border interest

When talking about cross-border interest, the contract should clearly be of interest for a non-domestic undertaking. However, it is open to discussion whether this means that the contract must be of *direct* cross-border interest (in the sense that undertakings operating from their home market would be interested in a specific contract in another Member State), or if it is sufficient to have *indirect* cross-border interest (such as where a domestic undertaking wishes to supply a non-domestic product or if a non-domestic undertaking has an affiliate in the Member State of the contracting authority).

17. Case C-507/03, Commission v. Ireland, [2007] ECR I-9777, paragraph 29. The statement has been repeated in later case law, see, for example, Case C-412/04, Commission v. Italy, [2008] ECR I-619, paragraph 66, Case T-258/06, Germany v. Commission, [2010] ECR II-2027, paragraph 80.

Once a contract has been put out for open competition, all interested undertakings which fulfils the criteria set by the contracting authority, can submit a tender, regardless of their nationality. This enables both direct and indirect cross-border procurement to take place.[18] At the time the contract has been put out for open competition, it is not relevant to examine either direct or indirect cross-border interest. It is only in relation to establishing which rules and obligations to follow that the question of what constitutes 'certain cross-border interest' becomes relevant. Only in such situations is it relevant for the contracting authority to make an assessment of whether a given contract is of cross-border interest (henceforth 'the cross-border assessment'). In order to know for the contracting authority what to include in this cross-border assessment it is relevant to examine whether the cross-border assessment must include undertakings that are indirectly interested in the contract, or if the assessment can focus on whether undertakings are directly interested in the contract.

I would argue that the-cross-border-assessment should only be based upon whether there are undertakings directly interested in the contract. Indirect cross-border interest should not be a part of the cross-border assessment since it is too difficult to determine this with any certainty. It should not be for the contracting authority to show (or know) that an affiliate is not domestic or whether an undertaking has the potential to perform the contract by creating a consortium or by using sub-contractors.

It is always possible for undertakings to use the free movement rights, such as the right of establishment, or the right to supply products or services in another Member State. Thus, it can be argued that undertakings rights are already secured through the possibility of using these rules. Naturally, a domestic undertaking that intends to supply a foreign product will always be allowed to supply such products, but the undertaking supplying the products will often not have an interest in the potential contract without a domestic

18. The *'Final Report Cross-border Procurement above EU Thresholds'* states regarding indirect cross-border procurement (not cross-border *interest*) that this arises when *'firms bid for contracts through subsidiaries, i.e. when their foreign affiliates bid for tenders launched by authorities of a country different from the home country where the firm has its headquarters or where the parent company is located, domestic bidders (prime contractor) include foreign subcontractors, foreign bidders submit offers in consortia with local firms in order to participate in competitive procurement, a domestic firm imports goods in order to supply them to a contracting authority or entity.'* This terminology for cross-border procurement has been used as inspiration to determine what constitute direct and indirect cross-border interest.

middleman. Thus, the cross-border assessment should only rely on whether a direct cross-border interest is present.

Arrowsmith seems to indicate that indirect cross-border interest is sufficient in the cross-border interest assessment. She states:

'... it may be that it is not necessary to advertise contracts of interest to purely local suppliers. However, this argument is unlikely to succeed since locally established suppliers (...) ***may wish to supply foreign products***' [emphasis added].[19]

However, at the time of her statement, the Court had not yet ruled that the contract should be of *certain* cross-border interest, and it is possible that she only considered that it should be allowed to supply non-domestic products, as was the case in *Vestergaard.*[20] Thus, a contract will often have a cross-border element; in my view, this is not the same as the contract being of certain cross-border interest (see section 7.1).

The cross-border interest assessment would be even more difficult for contracting authorities if they also had to include indirect cross-border interest. It would also mean an expansion of when the principles of the Treaties applies, since it would cover even more situations and a contract could be considered as not being of cross-border interest only in very limited situations. Another relevant argument in that regard is that it should not be up to the contracting authority to make an EU-wide assessment of whether certain undertakings might wish to exercise their free movement rights. Therefore, I argue that in the Cross-border assessment, the contracting authority should only take into consideration whether there is a direct cross-border interest in the contract.

4.2. Elements that can lead to a contract being of cross-border interest

The question of whether a contract is of cross-border interest depends on many factors and will always require a concrete examination of the contract in question. Thus, it is argued that it could in fact be helpful if national law contain criteria to be taken into account in determining whether a given contract is of cross-border interest. That it is permitted to set national criteria was

19. Arrowsmith, Sue *"The Law of Public and Utilities Procurement"* [2005] 2nd Edition, Sweet and Maxwell, p. 193.
20. Case C-59/00, Bent Mousten Vestergaard v. Spøttrup Boligselskab, [2001] ECR I-9505. The case is dealt with in more detail in section 8.1 and chapter 8.

also stated by the Court of Justice in *SECAP*.[21] In this case the Court found that Member States are allowed to set up national legislation, such as national thresholds. The Court stated:

> '*... it is permissible, however, for legislation to lay down objective criteria, at national or local level, indicating that there is certain cross-border interest'*.[22]

Nonetheless, national criteria are only indicators of when the Member State in question considers a contract to be of cross-border interest; hence, such national criteria cannot be read alone. Nevertheless, despite the fact that in the end it is for the contracting authority to bear the risk of whether the cross-border interest assessment was correctly, national criteria will function as a practical tool when a contracting authority must determine whether a specific contract is of cross-border interest.

There is little guidance regarding the exact elements that can lead to a contract being of certain cross-border interest. In *SECAP*, the Court found that the value and place of performance of the contract could be taken into consideration.[23] Furthermore, the 2006 Communication contains the following elements that, according to the Commission, must be taken into consideration when making an assessment of whether the contract is of cross-border interest:

- The subject matter of the contract
- The estimated value of the contract
- The specifics of the sector concerned
- The geographic location of the place of performance.

These elements will be the starting point in the analysis of when a contract is to be considered as being of cross-border interest. However, other elements are examined in section 4.2.5.

21. Joined cases C-147 and C-148/06, SECAP SpA and Santorso Soc. coop. arl v. Comune di Torino, [2008] ECR I-3565.
22. Joined cases C-147 and C-148/06, SECAP SpA and Santorso Soc. coop. arl v. Comune di Torino, [2008] ECR I-3565, paragraph 31.
23. Joined Cases, C-147 and C-148/06, SECAP SpA and Santorso Soc. coop. arl v. Comune di Torino, [2008] ECR I-3565, paragraph 31.See also Case T-258/06, Germany v. Commission, [2010] ECR II-2027, paragraphs 93 and 94.

4.2.1. The subject matter of the contract

Whether a contract is of certain cross-border interest naturally depends on what the contracting authority wishes to buy; that is, the subject matter of a contract. Some types of products are likely to be of higher cross-border interest than others. The same goes for the type of service to be performed or the works to be executed.

Some elements that could make the cross-border interest less certain include requirements that a specific language must be spoken or similar (section 4.2.1.1), as well as specific national legal requirements, hereunder whether an economic operator needs to have knowledge of national law (section 4.2.1.2).

4.2.1.1. Language

Language can be an obstacle to a contract being of cross-border interest. If an economic operator cannot speak the domestic language, some types of contracts can be difficult (if not impossible) to perform, as it will be difficult to tender for a given contract. Indeed,

> *'Higher levels of cross-border procurement can be observed between Member States with common or similar languages. Language barriers are one of the main obstacles for bidding cross-border in businesses' view.'*[24]

Language can be relevant in relation to the performance of the contract (section A) as well as when tendering for a contract (section B).

A. Language barriers in the performance of a contract

In most situations, a contracting authority can require an economic operator to speak the domestic language, as long as the principle of proportionality is still satisfied. For example, it could be relevant to require personnel to speak the domestic language in a case concerning healthcare in homes for the elderly; in such a situation, it is likely that the persons receiving the service only speak the local language and it is essential to understand the economic operator.

Requiring an economic operator to speak the domestic language in the performance of the contract could lead to a contract not being of interest for an economic operator in another Member State and, as a result, the contract

24. See *'Final Report Cross-border Procurement above EU Thresholds'*, p. 90. See also p. 46, which shows that 85 percent of all contracts awarded to a non-domestic undertaking in Austria were awarded to a German undertaking.

not being of cross-border interest. This will particularly be the case if the contracting authority is from one of the smaller Member States whose domestic language is not often spoken outside that Member State. However, since it is always possible for a non-domestic undertaking to hire local employees, the contracting authority's requirement for a specific language cannot, in itself, be sufficient to conclude that the contract is not of certain cross-border interest.

Some contracts concerning the delivery of products require specific guidance for the use of the product to be written in the domestic language. This could also be an indicator of the contract is not of cross-border interest. However, as it is possible for the economic operator to have the guidance translated, a language requirement cannot in itself lead to the conclusion that such a contract will never be of cross-border interest.

B. Language barriers in the tender phase

There are no requirements in the tender phase for the contracting authority to advertise (or conduct a competition) in a specific language. While a contract notice published in the OJ is automatically translated into the other EU languages, this will not be the case when advertising other places. Although advertising in a specific language is not prohibited, it will clearly have an impact on which non-domestic undertakings will tender for the contract. Nevertheless, the choice of language of a publication is entirely up to the contracting authority.

The contracting authority can require that applications and tenders be submitted in a specific language. Indeed, the contracting authority can even reject a tenderer on the grounds that a tender was submitted in a language other than the one required, as such a tender is to be considered unconditional. This has been the situation in recent cases before the Danish Complaints Board for Public Procurement. In one case, *Logica Danmark A/S v. Danmarks Miljøportal*, the contracting authority rejected an applicant who submitted certain insurance documents in English (when they should have been submitted in Danish). The Complaints Board found that the contracting authority had been justified in not considering the applicant.[25] In another case, *Axiell v. Aalborg Kommune*,[26] the contracting authority had required that tenders had to be submitted in Danish. The Complaints Board found that the

25. See decision of September 16, 2011, Logica Danmark A/S v. Danmarks Miljøportal.
26. Decision of April 14, 2011, Axiell v. Aalborg Kommune. See also decision of August 3, 2011, Isoplus v. Guldborgsund Varme.

contracting authority would had been justified in not considering a tender in which some annexes were submitted in English. However, the contracting authority was not obliged to dismiss such an application.

Even though a contracting authority is justified in not considering tenders where annexes and similar have been submitted in another language, such an approach can lead to a high level of discretion for the contracting authority to reject a tender on grounds that seem very formalistic. Rejecting such tenderers will limit the competition for the contract. This could lead to foreign undertakings refraining from bidding for contracts due the cost of translating documents that have no influence on the tender itself but only function as documentation of the undertaking's ability to perform the contract.

In many cases, there seem to be no reasons for requiring documents to be submitted in a certain language. Nevertheless, a requirement of specific language for certain documents or similar is not sufficient to conclude that a contract is not of cross-border interest.

4.2.1.2. Legal requirements

If it is necessary to have certain knowledge of national legal requirements or if a special licence for the performance of a certain task is required, this could also indicate that the contract will not be of cross-border interest since not many non-domestic economic operators would be qualified to perform the contract.

Legal requirements can be many things, and regarding legal services themselves (which are B-services), it is interesting to note that 21.2 percent of the value of all legal services was awarded to undertakings outside the territory of the Member State of the contracting authority.[27] This suggests that legal services themselves often seem to be of cross-border interest. However, legal services convers a range of contracts and it is difficult to see that all types of legal services would be of interest to non-domestic undertakings. For example, the type of service which require a lawyer who are qualified to go to trial such a service will rarely be of cross-border interest. Contrary, a contract that contains advice or legal support in relation to a given international contract might be of interest for non-domestic undertakings.

Another element that can be relevant in order for a contract to be of cross-border interest is the type of contract the contracting authority wishes to create. If the contract places substantial risk on the undertaking, this could indi-

27. See the *'Final Report Cross-border Procurement above EU Thresholds'*, p. 62. The numbers are based on 2007-2009.

cate that even though the service to be performed could be of interest for an undertaking in another Member State, the contract is too complex for a non-domestic undertaking to be interested in it, as it may require certain knowledge of national legal requirements, national contract law and so on.

4.2.2. The estimated value of the contract

The fact that the contract has a low value is not sufficient to rule out the possibility that the contract is not of interest to undertakings in other Member States. Nevertheless, a very low contract value will indicate that the contract will be of less (or even no) interest for undertakings in other Member States. This was stated in *Coname*, where the Court held that

> *'... because of special circumstances, such as a very modest economic interest at stake it could reasonably be maintained that an undertaking located in a Member State other than that of the Comune di Cingia de' Botti would have no interest in the concession at issue (...)'.*[28]

A low-value contract can be considered not to be of cross-border interest particularly because of factors such as costs of transportation or investments when establishing a business, or the costs of hiring new employees in the Member State in question to perform parts of the contract, etc. Nevertheless, if a contract concerns a simple delivery of goods, it is difficult to see how such a contract would not be of interest to undertakings in other Member States unless some sort of after-sales services are required or if there are significant costs of transportation.

The value of the contract cannot be read alone and must be seen in light of the complexity of the contract.[29] If a contract has a value close to the EU thresholds, it is easier to assume that the contract is of cross-border interest. However, a contract that is technically complex (for example, if it requires fulfilment of specific national legislation), might not be of any interest to undertakings in other Member States.

Many Member States have set new national thresholds in order to apply the national rules, which vary considerably across the Member States.[30] The-

28. Case C-231/03, Consorzio Aziende Metano v. Comune di Cingia de' Botti, [2005] ECR I-7287, paragraph 20.
29. See also Joined Cases, C-147 and C-148/06, SECAP SpA and Santorso Soc. coop. arl v. Comune di Torino, [2008] I-3565, paragraph 24, where the Court stated, *'estimated value in conjunction with its technical complexity'*. See also Case T-258/06, Germany v. Commission, [2010] ECR II-2027, paragraph 88.
30. See chapter 1, section 4.3.

se national thresholds can indicate that if the value of a contract falls below this national threshold, the Member State considers the contract not to be of cross-border interest. However, it is not sufficient that a contract falls below the national thresholds, as the contracting authority must always consider the concrete contract in question. The General Court has also stated that whether a breach of the fundamental freedoms had taken place, *'... cannot be based solely on the fact that the value of the contract in question does not exceed a certain threshold'.*[31] Therefore, national thresholds will only function as guidelines as to when a contract is of cross-border interest.

4.2.3. The specifics of the sector concerned

In some sectors, undertakings are more exposed to competition from other undertakings. Thus, it can be relevant for the contracting authority to consider the specifics of a given sector when assessing whether the contract is of cross-border interest. For example, studies have shown that in most Member States the share of direct cross-border procurement in the utilities sector is higher than in the public sector.[32]

If a market has few domestic undertakings, the contract will be more attractive for undertakings in other Member States due to the minimal national competition. However, the presence of many undertakings in the domestic market cannot lead to the contract not being of interest to foreign undertakings in itself; this will depend on other factors. If a Member State does not have expertise in a given field, a contract is more likely to be of cross-border interest.[33]

In her opinion to Pressetext, Advocate General Kokott suggested that the following considerations could be taken into account: *'The fact that a number of news agencies are internationally active suggests that there may be a*

31. Case T-258/06, Germany v. Commission, [2010] ECR II-2027, paragraph 88. See also Joined Cases, C-147 and C-148/06, SECAP SpA and Santorso Soc. coop. arl v. Comune di Torino, [2008] I-3565, paragraph 25.
32. See the *'Final Report Cross-border Procurement above EU Thresholds'*, p. 60.
33. In line with Stergiou, Hélène *"Public Procurement Law and Health Care: From Theory to Practice"* Research chapters in law 2/2010. Can be found at www.coleurop.be, which, regarding cross-border interest for operations, states: *'Whether a health care service is of "certain cross-border interest" will highly depend on the size and estimated value of the contract. Further, the complexity of the contractual obligation, requiring a high degree of expertise unlikely to be found at the local level, would justify interest from other Member States (...)'.*

cross-border interest'.[34] This indicates that if the service to be performed concerns an activity for which suppliers are already known to operate internationally, this could indicate that the service is of cross-border interest. In such a situation, it is possible that an undertaking wishes to strengthen its involvement on the market.

Kokott also stated that what argues against a cross-border interest is:

'... the fact that a large part of the services required by the Austrian federal authorities display specific references to Austria and also to regional events in that country'.[35]

Thus, if the service to be provided is highly orientated towards the domestic market, it might lead to a contract not being of cross-border interest. However, many types of services are related to the public – the citizens – in a Member State. This is not to say that the service is orientated at a particular domestic market, which is only the case if it relates to specific circumstances particular to that Member State.

4.2.4. Place of performance of the contract

The specific place where the contract is to be performed will also have influence on whether a contract is of cross-border interest. If the location is close to a border, the contract is more likely to be of cross-border interest than if it is located far from a border, it can lead to the opposite conclusion.

In *SECAP*, the Court of Justice also emphasised where a given works contract was to be performed and whether this place was *'a place which is likely to attract the interest of foreign operators'*.[36] However, the Court did not elaborate on the aspects to be taken into consideration when determining whether a place is *'likely to attract the interest of foreign operators'*. Instead, it merely stated that:

34. Opinion of Advocate General Kokott delivered on March 13, 2008 in Case C-454/06, Pressetext Nachrichtenagentur GmbH v. Austria, APA-OTS Originaltext-Service GmbH and APA Austria Presse Agentur registrierte Genossenschaft mit beschränkter Haftung, [2008] ECR I-4401, paragraph 114.
35. Opinion of Advocate General Kokott delivered on March 13, 2008 in Case C-454/06, pressetext Nachrichtenagentur GmbH v. Austria, APA-OTS Originaltext-Service GmbH and APA Austria Presse Agentur registrierte Genossenschaft mit beschränkter Haftung, [2008] ECR I-4401, paragraph 114.
36. Joined Cases C-147 and C-148/06, SECAP SpA and Santorso Soc. coop. arl v. Comune di Torino, [2008] ECR I-3565, paragraph 24.

'account must be taken of the fact that the borders straddle conurbations which are situated in the territory of different Member States and that, in those circumstances, even low-value contracts may be of certain cross-border interest'.[37]

It could be argued that a service to be performed in Luxembourg is more likely to have cross-border interest than a contract regarding a service in northern Denmark, Finland or Sweden, for example, since Luxembourg is a small Member State located in the middle of Europe. That smaller Member States have a high number of cross-border procurement has also been confirmed by the before mentioned "cross-border procurement report". Member States such as Cyprus, Luxembourg, Malta and Slovakia have a share of value of direct cross-border procurement of over 15 percent.[38] Such high numbers of direct cross-border procurement could indicate that the cross-border interest in these Member States is significant. Thus, because these countries are all small Member States it is likely that they do not have national undertakings in all sectors, or at least that the competition from domestic undertakings there could be smaller due to the size of the country.

If the performance of the contract needs to be established in a specific location, such as when a contracting authority needs hotel rooms for a specific event or the like,[39] this could also indicate that there is no cross-border interest.[40] This was also the conclusion in a case before the Danish Complaints Board for Public Procurement *Smørum Kraftvarme AmbA v. Energinet.dk*,[41] regarding a contract that fell outside the Utilities Directive. The Complaints Board found that it was not necessary to follow the obligations derived from the principles of the Treaties since it was essential that the utility was physically located in a specific place in order to perform the task. Thus, there was

37. Joined Cases C-147 and C-148/06, SECAP SpA and Santorso Soc. coop. arl v. Comune di Torino, [2008] I-3565, paragraph 31.
38. Commission's Evaluation Report *'Impact and Effectiveness of EU Public Procurement Legislation'*, part 1 SEC(2011) 853 final, p. 137. The overall average of direct cross-border procurement is estimated at 1.6 percent.
39. These services are listed in category 17 in Annex II B.
40. Nonetheless, according to the Commission's Evaluation Report *'Impact and Effectiveness of EU Public Procurement Legislation'*, part 1 SEC(2011) 853 final, p. 136, hotel services account for 39.1 percent (in value) of indirect cross-border procurement, which probably means that many hotels are owned by foreign companies (hotel chains).
41. Decision of December 23, 2010, Smørum Kraftvarme AmbA v. Energinet.dk. The same contract was disputed by another complainant in the decision of September 8, 2011, Østermose BioEnergi A/S v. Energinet.dk, where the Complaints Board reached the same conclusion.

no assumption that the contract would be of direct interest for undertakings in other Member States.

In a case before the Danish Competition and Consumer Authority,[42] the Authority concluded that a contract concerning eye operations to be performed locally in the north of mainland Denmark was not of cross-border interest. It was essential that the operations were performed locally due to the fact that most of the people having the operations were elderly (and faced greater transportation difficulties), but also as the value of the contract was so insignificant that it would not be in the interests of undertakings to establish a new business there. Together, these elements let the Authority to conclude that the contract in question was not of cross-border interest.

4.2.5. Other elements that can influence cross-border interest

The *'Cross-border procurement Report'* indicates that there are four main obstacles for cross-border bidding (above the thresholds). These are the lack of undertakings that have experience doing business abroad, language barriers, strong competition from national bidders, and legal requirements leading to market entry barriers in the awarding Member State (special permits or procedures necessary for offering services abroad).[43] The only factor that a contracting authority can influence in that regard is language, but it is obvious that the contracting authority can set as few requirements as possible. This will make it easier to gain access to the competition and, therefore, more likely that the contract will be of cross-border interest. Accordingly, the way in which the contracting authority puts out a contract for competition can also affect the cross-border interest.

The length of the contract could also have an impact on whether a contract is of cross-border interest. If the duration of the contract is very long, this could lead to a cross-border interest as an undertaking would have better opportunities to establish itself on the domestic market. A very short contract period could indicate the opposite. Elements such as the type of procedure and contract can also have an impact on whether the contract will be of interest for non-domestic undertakings.[44]

42. Danish Competition and Consumer Authority, July 7, 2007, *'Klage over manglende udbud af sundhedsydelser og aflysning af udbud af grå stær operationer'*.
43. The *'Final Report Cross-border Procurement above EU Thresholds'*, p. 91.
44. The *'Final Report Cross-border Procurement above EU Thresholds'* states that higher direct cross-border procurement occurs when the negotiated procedure is used.

To conclude, cross-border interest depends on many factors and must, in all cases, be subject to a concrete evaluation where the above elements can be taken into consideration.

5. The cross-border interest assessment

The first assessment of whether a specific contract is of cross-border interest must be for the contracting authority to determine. This was stated by the Court of Justice in *SECAP,* which found:

'It is in principle for the contracting authority concerned to assess whether there may be cross-border interest in a contract whose estimated value is below the threshold (...), it being understood that that assessment may be subject to judicial review.'[45]

Also, the Commission's 2006 Communication stated that it was up to the contracting authority to make a cross-border interest assessment. In *Germany v. Commission,*[46] Germany had disputed also this part in the 2006 Communication, and argued that:

'... by requiring the contracting authorities to evaluate in each case the relevance of a public contract to the internal market (...), the Communication creates a new obligation and thus produces binding legal effects.'

However, the General Court found that the case law already required contracting entities to

'... carry out an evaluation (...) of the particular features of the contract at issue in the light of the appropriateness of the detailed arrangements for putting it out to competitive tender'.[47]

Therefore, according to the General Court, this obligation did not create *de facto* new legislation.

Consequently, the contracting authority must assess whether the contract is of cross-border interest, at the same time as assessing other aspects in relation to the contract, such as the value and the type of service the contract is

45. Joined Cases C-147 and C-148/06, SECAP SpA and Santorso Soc. coop. arl v. Comune di Torino, [2008] ECR I-3565, paragraph 30.
46. Case T-258/06, Germany v. Commission, [2010] ECR II-2027.
47. Case T-258/06, Germany v. Commission, [2010] ECR II-2027, paragraphs 90–91.

concerned with. If the contracting authority's assess that the contract in question is not of cross-border interest, this assessment can be challenged in national courts, as it will constitute a decision within the meaning of the Public Sector Remedies Directive Article 2(1), litra b., Thus, the contracting authority's decision to determine whether a contract is of a cross-border interest must, as stated in *SECAP*, be the subject of review.[48] Hereafter, it is for the national complaints bodies (or courts) to determine whether the cross-border assessment was correct (see also section 7 for a discussion of who bears the burden of proof that a given contract is of cross-border interest).

5.1. A hypothetical or de facto cross-border interest assessment?

A question for discussion is whether the concept of cross-border interest only includes situations where an undertaking in another Member State is actually interested in the contract *de facto*, or whether it is sufficient for the cross-border interest to be hypothetical, in the sense that undertakings located in Member States other than the contracting authority would, in theory, be interested in the contract. The question is relevant to answer as this can influence a national courts decision as to whether the cross-border assessment made by the contracting authority was correct.

If taking a look at *Coname*, the Court stated that the contract *'may be of interest to undertakings located in other Member States'*.[49] This seems to indicate that the cross-border interest must be hypothetical as it is uncertain whether any undertakings were interested in the contract. Thus, it could not be ruled out that potentially undertakings in other Member States would have been interested in the contract. In some of the later cases, the Court has merely found that the contract was of cross-border interest and referred to the fact that the contracting authority had made a publication in OJ.[50] This indicates that, in these cases, the Court is of the opinion that the contracting authority had found the contract in question to be of cross-border interest.

48. See joined Cases C-147 and C-148/06, SECAP SpA and Santorso Soc. coop. arl v. Comune di Torino, [2008] ECR I-3565, paragraph 30. Chapter 11 elaborates further on what constitutes a decision within the Public Sector Remedies Directive.
49. Case C-231/03, Consorzio Aziende Metano v. Comune di Cingia de' Botti, [2005] ECR I-7287, paragraph 19. The same statement is used in Parking Brixen, Case C-458/03, Parking Brixen GmbH v. Gemeinde Brixen and Stadtwerke Brixen AG, [2005] ECR I-8585, paragraph 55.
50. Case C-91/08, Wall AG v. La ville de Francfort-sur-le-Main and Frankfurter Entsorgungs- und Service (FES) GmbH, [2010] ECR I-2815, paragraph 35. Case C-95/10, Strong Segurança SA v. Município de Sintra, Securitas-Serviços e Tecnologia de Segurança, [2011] March 17, 2011 (not yet reported), paragraph 38.

In *Commission v. Ireland*[51] *(translation services)*, the Court emphasised the fact that the contracting authority had made a publication, and also that undertakings were interested in the contract. The Court found that the contract at issue:

'... may have been of interest to undertakings located in a Member State other than Ireland is apparent both from the publication of a notice for that contract in the Official Journal of the European Union and from the fact that three of the tenderers were undertakings established in a Member State other than Ireland'.[52]

Thus, the case could indicate a sort of *de facto* analysis, as the Court emphasised the fact that three of the tendering undertakings were located in other Member States. The media in which the contracting authority had advertised could be an indicator that the contracting authority had considered the contract at issue to be of cross-border interest. However, the above cases place no emphasis on whether the cross-border interest could also have been established based on a hypothetical assumption, or on how the case would have turned out if such a notice had not been published.

I submit that the cross-border assessment is a hypothetical assessment.[53] This is mainly because, at the time the contracting authority makes its assessment of cross-border interest, it cannot be sure whether non-domestic undertakings will bid for the contract, which means it would not know if the contract is of a *de facto* cross-border interest. If it were in fact a *de facto* analysis, any non-domestic undertakings would, in theory, only need to launch a proceeding against the contracting authority, claiming that the undertaking would have been interested in the contract. This will not be sufficient, as is supported by the *Commission v. Ireland (An-Post)*, where the Court also found:

51. Case C-226/09, Commission v. Ireland, [2010] November, 18, 2010 (not yet reported).
52. Case C-226/09, Commission v. Ireland, [2010] November, 18, 2010 (not yet reported), paragraph 33.
53. *Stergio*, on the other hand, suggested that there must be '*a real interest of an undertaking from another Member State (...). In other words, an undertaking would have been interested in fulfilling the contract if the undertaking would have been informed in advance*'. This indicates that the cross-border assessment is a de facto one.. See Stergoiu, Hélène, *"The Increasing Influence of Primary EU Law on EU Public Procurement Law: Must a Concession to Provide Services of General Economic Interest be Tendered?"* in Gronden, Johan van de *"EU and WTO law on services: Limits to the realization of general interest policies within the services market"* [2008] Kluwer.

'... A mere statement by it that a complaint was made to it in relation to the contract in question is not sufficient to establish that the contract was of certain cross-border interest (...)'.[54]

It is difficult to imagine that a contract would not always hypothetically be of interest to an undertaking in another Member State, since there may always be another undertaking interested in the contract. Therefore, the requirement for *certain* plays a great role in the assessment, as discussed in section 5.2.

5.2. 'Certain' – cross-border interest

In *Commission v. Ireland*, the Court of Justice ruled that the cross-border interest must be *certain.*[55] The Court of Justice has not elaborated further on what *certain* means.

According to *Brown*, the Court's use of certain, 'seemed to suggest that there needed to be a high degree of certainty surrounding the existence of interest from suppliers located in other EU Member States.'[56] Drijber and Stergiou argued that certain means that: *'... on the basis of the features and value of the market involve, there is a* ***clear likelihood*** *that non-domestic parties could reasonably have an interest in taking part in the bidding process'.* [emphasis added].[57]

In a case from the UK, *Chandler, R v. Secretary of State for Children, Schools and Families*,[58] the Court of Appeal noted that there was no authori-

54. Case C-507/03, Commission v. Ireland, [2007] ECR I-9777, paragraph 34.
55. Case C-507/03, Commission v. Ireland, [2007] ECR I-9777, paragraph 29. The requirement for *certain* was repeated in Joined Cases C-147 and C-148/06, SECAP SpA and Santorso Soc. coop. arl v. Comune di Torino, [2008] I-3565. Case C-119/06, Commission v. Italy, [2007] ECR I-168. Case C-274/09, Privater Rettungsdienst und Krankentransport Stadler v. Zweckverband für Rettungsdienst und Feuerwehralarmierung Passau, [2011] [2011] March 10, 2011 (not yet reported), paragraph 49, Case C-95/10, Strong Segurança SA v. Município de Sintra, Securitas-Serviços e Tecnologia de Segurança, [2011] March 17, 2011, (not yet reported), paragraph 35.
56. Brown, Adrian *"EU primary law requirements in practice: advertising, procedures and remedies for public contracts outside the procurement directives"* [2010] PPLR n° 5, pp. 169-181.
57. Drijber, Jan Berend & Stergiou, Hélène *"Public Procurement Law and Internal Market Law"* [2009] CMLR n° 46, pp. 805-846.
58. The Court of Appeal in R. (on the application of Chandler) v. Secretary of State for Children, Schools and Families, Court of Appeal (Civil Division), October 9, 2009.

tative guidance provided as to *how* cross-border interest should be applied and stated:

'We doubt whether the Court of Justice intended to hold that cross-border interest had been shown beyond reasonable doubt (...). Clearly there must ***be a realistic prospect*** *of cross-border interest. It may be that, in the interests of protecting contracting authorities,* ***a higher test than reasonable prospect applies*** *so that the contracting authority would only be bound to follow the general principles in the Treaty if it* ***was likely*** *that there was cross-border interest. (...). We will proceed on the basis most favourable to the appellant that* ***if there is a realistic prospect of cross-border interest****, the principles of the Treaty are engaged. (...)'.* [emphasis added.][59]

In the specific situation, the Court of Appeal found that there was no certain cross-border interest since the only potential sponsor from outside the United Kingdom had not shown an interest in the contract and no other potential tenderer brought proceedings. The case is commented on by *Henty*[60] who argue that in order for a contract to be of cross-border interest, *'There must be demonstrated by the claimant an interest of a provider from another Member State in the contract being tendered. It must be shown that that provider would have been interested in tendering had the opportunity been put out to tender'.*

In line with the above-mentioned authors, and the Chandler case, I would argue that the requirement for a contract to be of *certain* cross-border interest requires something further than the fact that a contract might potentially be of interest to non-domestic undertakings. Consequently, there must be something to indicate that other undertakings would have an interest in the contract. This would require the contracting authority to make a concrete assessment of the case, taking into consideration the elements discussed in section 4. If, for example, an undertaking has previously shown interest in a similar contract or is operating on the domestic market already, this could indicate cross-border interest. The requirement of *certain* will mainly play a role in a concrete situation before a review body regarding the burden of proof (see section 7).

59. The Court of Appeal in R. (on the application of Chandler) v. Secretary of State for Children, Schools and Families, Court of Appeal (Civil Division), October 9, 2009, paragraph 30.
60. Henty, Paul *"Chandler in the Court of Appeal: public procurement issues – R. (on the application of Chandler) v. Secretary of State for Children, Schools and Families"* [2010] PPLR n° 2, NA64-67.

5.2.1. 'Certain' – service concession contracts – a difference in the assessment?

In *Wall AG*,[61] the Court of Justice did not use the term *certain*, but stated instead that the concession in question *'... may be of interest to an undertaking located in a Member State other that in which the concession is awarded'*.[62] It can be argued that since the Court of Justice used the term *'may be of interest'* instead of *'certain cross-border interest'*, there could be a difference in the assessment of cross-border interest depending on whether the contract is a service concession contract, a B-service contract or a contract below the thresholds.

Service concession contracts were not excluded by the Public Sector Directive based on the assumption that they were not of cross-border interest.[63] The Commission's Communication on Concessions from 2000[64] makes no reference to cross-border interest. Nonetheless, the Communication was issued before the Court of Justice's ruling in *Coname* and the following cases. Therefore, it is not safe to assume that just because the Commission did not expressly provide a reference to cross-border interest (as it did in the later 2006-Communication covering B-services and below thresholds contracts) that such an interest should not be present.

Also, in *Gotha*,[65] the Court of Justice stated, without any references to the case law on cross-border interest, that if a contract were to be categorised as a service concession contract, the Treaties' principles would apply. However, in the later *Privater Rettungsdienst*,[66] the Court stated that the obligations derived from the principles of the Treaty applied when *'... the contract con-*

61. Case C-91/08, Wall AG v. La ville de Francfort-sur-le-Main and Frankfurter Entsorgungs- und Service (FES) GmbH, Wall AG, [2010] ECR I-2815.
62. Case C-91/08, Wall AG v. La ville de Francfort-sur-le-Main and Frankfurter Entsorgungs- und Service (FES) GmbH, [2010] ECR I-2815, paragraph 34.
63. See chapter 3.
64. Commission Interpretative Communication on Concessions under Community Law (2000/C121/02).
65. Case C-206/08, Wasser- und Abwasserzweckverband Gotha und v. Eurawasser Aufbereitungs- und Entsorgungsgesellschaft mbH, [2009] ECR I-8377. The case is further dealt with in chapter 3.
66. Case C-274/09, Privater Rettungsdienst und Krankentransport Stadler v. Zweckverband für Rettungsdienst und Feuerwehralarmierung Passau, [2011] March 10, 2011 (not yet reported).

cerned has a ***certain transnational dimension*** *'* [emphasis added].[67] Despite the fact that the Court did not use the term cross-border in the English version, the Italian, French, German and Danish version remains the same as in *Commission v. Ireland*,[68] consequently, no difference should be made regarding the 'new' English wording.

Based on the above arguments it is concluded that there is no difference in the assessment of cross-border interest regarding the three types of contracts. Nevertheless, it is possible that service concession contracts will be of cross-border interest more often than B-services and contracts below the thresholds due to the characteristics of these types of contracts, mainly their high contract value and duration of the contract.

6. Applicable principles derived from the Treaties

Once it has been established that a contract is of cross-border interest, the question is which principles of the Treaties apply and what these principle means. The latter will be elaborated on in Part II of this Thesis.

Regarding which principles apply, I would argue that the transparency obligation (which will be analysed in chapter 7), as well as the principle of equal treatment, need a contract to be of certain cross-border interest in order for these principles to apply when a contracting authority is awarding one of the three types of contracts.[69]

In most of the cases discussed in this chapter, the dispute has been whether the transparency obligation had been infringed. In *SECAP*, however, the dispute concerned whether Italian national legislation in the evaluation phase (national legislation, which automatically excluded abnormally low tenders). The Court found that such legislation was not allowed according to the Treaty if the contract had a certain cross-border interest.[70] Thus, if a contract is of certain cross-border interest, the contracting authority must not only follow

67. Case C-274/09, Privater Rettungsdienst und Krankentransport Stadler v. Zweckverband für Rettungsdienst und Feuerwehralarmierung Passau, [2011] March 10, 2011 (not yet reported), paragraph 49.
68. Case C-507/03, Commission v. Ireland, [2007] ECR I-9777.
69. As elaborated on in chapter 2, it is my opinion that the principle of non-discrimination in procurement matters does not have an independent function. Thus, the applicable principle can be reduced to the principle of equal treatment.
70. Joined Cases, C-147 and C-148/06, SECAP Spa and Santorso Soc. coop. arl v. Comune di Torino, [2008] I-3565, and paragraph 24.

the transparency obligation and ensure *'a degree of advertisement'*, but also follow the principles of the Treaties when, for example, evaluating the tenders submitted. Thus, it is also relevant to for a contract to be of certain cross-border interest when applying national rules (for example, in the award phase) and whether such rules are in accordance with the principles of equal treatment and transparency.

The applicability of these principles when a contract is of cross-border interest can be seen in *Germany v. Commission,*[71] where the General Court found, regarding cross-border interest, that B-services and contracts below the thresholds had to be of a *certain* cross-border interest. The General Court stated:

'... the obligations under primary law ***concerning equal treatment and transparency*** *apply automatically to contracts – albeit outside the scope of the Public Procurement Directives – which are of certain cross-border interest'* [emphasis added].[72]

Thus, the General Court referred to both principles, as did the Court of Justice in *Commission v. Ireland.*[73] Here, the Court stated:

'... therefore, of the requirements designed to ensure transparency of procedures and ***equal treatment of tenderers*** [apply]*'* [emphasis added].[74]

Also in *Strong Segurança,*[75] the Court referred to both principles and stated:

'However, the Court has held that even such contracts, where they have a certain cross-border interest, are subject ***to the general principles of transparency and equal treatment*** *resulting from Articles 49 TFEU and 56 TFEU'* [emphasis added].[76]

Consequently, it can be concluded that the principle of equal treatment and the principle of transparency apply once a contract has a cross-border interest,

71. Case T-258/06, Germany v. Commission, [2010] ECR II-2027.
72. Case T-258/06, Germany v. Commission, [2010] ECR II-2027, paragraph 80.
73. Case C-226/09, Commission v. Ireland, [2010] November 18, 2010 (not yet reported).
74. Case C-226/09, Commission v. Ireland, [2010] November 18, 2010 (not yet reported), paragraph 31
75. Case C-95/10, Strong Segurança SA v. Município de Sintra, Securitas-Serviços e Tecnologia de Segurança, [2011] March 17, 2011 (not yet reported).
76. Case C-95/10, Strong Segurança SA v. Município de Sintra, Securitas-Serviços e Tecnologia de Segurança, [2011] March 17, 2011 (not yet reported), paragraph 35.

as will be argued below section 8 some provisions in the Treaty apply regardless of whether a contract is of cross-border interest or not.

7. Burden of proof of the contract being of cross-border interest

When a question is put before a national review body regarding whether a contracting authority has breached the principles of the Treaties, it is relevant for the review body to decide who bears the burden of proof as to whether the assessment made by the contracting authority was justified. It will most likely only be in situations where the contracting authority has decided not to follow the principles of the Treaties that the contracting authority needs to justify that such action was appropriate. It is difficult to imagine a situation where an undertaking would challenge the fact that the contracting authority *did* put out a contract for competition, given that the contracting authority would always be permitted to do so. However, the dispute could, in principle, occur the other way around such as for example in relation to the principle of equal treatment where the contracting authority could argue that even though the contract had been put out for competition, it was not required to ensure equal treatment as the contract was not of cross-border interest.

It is up to the Commission to bear the burden of proof in enforcement cases before the Court of Justice. In *Commission v. Ireland*,[77] the Court of Justice stated that it was up to the Commission to establish that the contract was of certain cross-border interest. In that regard, when the Commission brings a proceeding before the Court of Justice, it is *'the Commission's responsibility to provide the Court with the evidence necessary to enable it to establish that an obligation has not been fulfilled (...)'*.[78]

Nevertheless, I would argue that the fact that it is up to the Commission to bear the burden of proof when bringing enforcement proceedings cannot lead to the conclusion that the burden of proof in national courts would lie on the complainant. In this regard, the contracting authority is the most appropriate party to bear this burden of proof. Therefore, I would argue that it should be up to the contracting authority to bear the burden of proof of a contract not being of cross-border interest. This is primarily since cross-border interest is a requirement that must be fulfilled before the principles of the Treaties apply.

77. Case C-507/03, Commission v. Ireland, [2007] ECR I-9777.
78. Case C-507/03, Commission v. Ireland, [2007] ECR I-9777, paragraph 33. See also chapter 5, section 5.

Thus, it is up to the contacting authority to show that the requirement was not fulfilled (that the contract was in fact not of cross-border interest). On the other hand, it could be argued that a complainant will be most likely to know its competitors in a market and will therefore be more likely to provide information about whether the contract is of interest to other undertakings in other Member States (including themselves).

It is my opinion that even though the contracting authority is not required to make a wide market assessment beforehand, it must be able to prove that it did explore the potential of the market. If the contracting authority wishes to invoke that the principles of the Treaties does not apply, it must make sure that some sort of market assessment has been made and must bear the burden of proof that the assessment is correct. *Drijber and Stergiou* argued to the contrary, stating: '*... the burden of proof should be on the private complainant, who argues that the obligation of transparency has been violated'*.[79]

In Denmark, the Complaints Board for Public Procurement has found that it is up to the contracting authority to prove elements such as whether the contract in question falls outside the Public Sector Directive (see chapter 5, section 5). I see no reason why it should not be up to the contracting authority to justify that its assessment of whether a contract has a cross-border interest was correct. In a Scottish case[80] concerning a contract below the thresholds, the Scottish court found:

> *'The assessment as to whether there may cross-border interests in a below threshold* ***contract is one for the Council [the contracting authority]*** *to make'* [emphasis added].[81]

Thus, it is up to the party that wishes to invoke that the Treaties principles do not apply to prove that the contract is not of cross-border interest. *Drijber and Stergiou* referred to a Dutch case in which the complainant had not made it sufficiently plausible that the contract at stake was of cross-border interest.[82] The examples above appear to show that the national review bodies have differing practices of placing the burden of proof. Therefore, it would indeed be

79. Drijber, Jan Berend & Stergiou, Héléne *"Public Procurement Law and Internal Market Law"* [2009] CMLR n° 46, pp. 805-846.
80. Sidey Ltd v. Clackmannanshire Council [2010] CSIH 37 IH (1 Div).
81. Sidey Ltd v. Clackmannanshire Council [2010] CSIH 37 IH (1 Div), paragraph 30 furthermore states: *'First of all it was for the contracting authority (or anyone else claiming an interest) to rebut the presumption that Community principles were not engaged.'*
82. Drijber, Jan Berend & Stergiou, Hélène *"Public Procurement Law and Internal Market Law"* [2009] CMLR n° 46, pp. 805-846, p. 815 footnote 44.

welcomed if the Court of Justice would clarify this point rather than leaving it for the courts to determine whether the contract is of certain cross-border interest,[83] but also give the national review bodies some sort of guidelines to use in their assessment.

8. The 'relationship' with the free movement provisions

Section 8.1 shows that the free movement provisions in the TFEU apply regardless of cross-border interest because no *de minimis* rule exists. That section discusses whether a *de minimis* rule could be established in relation to the principles derived from the Treaties when awarding one of the three types of contracts.

The free movement provisions also contain a situation that is very similar to cross-border interest; namely, that if the situation concerns an internal situation, the free movement provisions cannot be invoked. Internal situations are discussed in section 8.2 in order to see whether a parallel can be drawn to cross-border interest.

8.1. Whether cross-border interest can be considered as a *de minimis* rule

In *Coname*, the Court found that in some situations,

'the effects on the fundamental freedoms concerned should be regarded as too uncertain and too indirect to warrant the conclusion that they may have been infringed'.[84]

Trepte has argued, that this statement could indicate *'... a specific de minimis rule in the context of procurement but does not assist particularly in determining what it is'.*[85]

The concept of *'de minimis'* is known from, for example, EU competition law. Under EU competition law, some agreements that infringe Article 101(1) TFEU are considered to be *'de minimis'* and therefore accepted. The

83. See, for example, Case C-376/08, Serrantoni Srl and Consorzio stabile edili Scrl v. Comune di Milano, [2009] ECR I-12169, paragraph 25, *'it is none the less for the referring court to ascertain whether the contract in question involves certain cross-border interest'.*
84. Case T-258/06, Germany v. Commission, [2010] ECR II-2027, paragraph 88.
85. Trepte, Peter, *'Public Procurement in the EU'* [2007] 2nd Edition, Oxford University Press, p. 23.

idea behind such a rule is that even though the agreement is not permitted, it does not have a significant impact on the market and should therefore be allowed.[86] The Commission shares this view and has issued a notice indicating when it is the Commission's view that an agreement is likely to be considered to be of minor importance. This is the case, for example, regarding agreements between undertakings, where the aggregate market share held by the parties to the agreement does not exceed 10 percent on any of the relevant markets affected by the agreement.[87] A *de minimis* rule also be said to apply in relation to state aid.[88]

A similar 'exception' has not been accepted regarding free movement provisions. Case law from the Court of Justice[89] has found that a national measure does not fall outside the scope of the prohibitions in the free movement provisions, simply because the hindrance it creates is minor; in other words, there is no *de minimis* rule in order for the TFEU's free movement rules to apply.[90] This means that even though the restriction only has a very limited impact on the market, the rules on free movement will apply. Advocate General *Jacobs* has suggested that a *de minimis* rule should be construed, arguing:

86. See, for example, Case C-5/69, Franz Völk v. S.P.R.L. Ets J. Vervaecke, [1969] ECR 295, where the Court found that an agreement falls outside the prohibition in what is currently Article 101(1) TFEU when it only has an insignificant effect on the market.
87. See Commission Notice on agreements of minor importance that do not appreciably restrict competition under Article 81(1) of the Treaty establishing the European Community (de minimis), [2001] OJ C 368/13.
88. See Regulation 1998/2006 of 15 December 2006 on the application of Articles 87 and 88 of the Treaty to de minimis aid, [2006] OJ L 379/5.
89. See, for example, joined cases C-177/82 and C-178/82, Van de Haar [1984] ECR 1797, paragraph 13 states: *'if a national measure is capable of hindering imports it must be regarded as a measure having an effect equivalent to a quantitative restriction, even though the hindrance is slight and even though it is possible for imported products to be marketed in other ways'*. See also Case C-269/83, Commission v. France, [1985] ECR 837, Case C-103/84, Commission v. Italy [1986] ECR 1759, Case C-67/97 Bluhme [1998] ECR I-8033.
90. See also Trybus, Martin *"Public Contracts in European Union Internal Market Law: Foundations and Requirements"* in Nogouelleou, Rozen and Stelkens, Ulrich (eds) *"Comparative Law on Public Contracts Treatise"* [2010] Brussels Bruylant, p. 90, which states: *'There is no de minimis rule whereby an act would be so insignificant that it would fall outside the prohibition.'* Arrowsmith, Sue *"The Law of Public and Utilities Procurement"* [2005] 2nd Edition, Sweet and Maxwell, p. 184. Drijber, Jan Berend & Stergiou, Hélène *"Public Procurement Law and Internal Market Law"* [2009] CMLR n° 46, pp. 805-846, p. 815.

'... *the Court has accepted that some* ***restrictions may be so uncertain and indirect in their effects as not to be regarded as capable of hindering trade****. I would suggest that they may also be so slight and so ephemeral as to fall into the same category. It would seem for example out of the question that a brief delay to traffic on a road occasionally used for intra-Community transport could in any way fall within the scope of Article 28. A longer interruption on a major transit route may none the less call for a different assessment'* [emphasis added].[91]

However, in this case the Court did not find that there was a breach of the rules of free movement of goods.[92] Therefore, no *dè minimis* rule exists in relation to the free movement rules. This means that, regardless of whether a contract is of cross-border interest, the contracting authority must ensure the free movement provisions are applied and cannot require an undertaking to supply a specific domestic product. This was seen in the *Vestergaard* case.[93]

The *Vestergaard* case concerned a situation where a Danish social housing company had put out a works contract for competition. The estimated value of the entire contract was 9,643,000 DKK (approximately 1.2 million Euro). The value of the contract meant that the contract fell below the EU threshold of 5 million Euro. Vestergaard had won parts of the contract, but had made a reservation concerning the provision of windows of the make 'Hvidbjerg Vinduet' (a Danish make), since he had calculated his tender on the basis of providing windows of 'Trokal' (a German make). If the Danish windows were used, the additional price would be DKK 23,743 excluding VAT (approximately 3100 Euro). The work was then carried out using the domestic type of windows as required, but Vestergaard maintained his claim for payment of DKK 23,743.

The case was brought before the Danish Complaints Board, which had reached the conclusion that since the contract was below the thresholds in the Procurement Directive such contracts would not have interest in EU procurement situations and it would be *'disproportionately costly for contracting authorities to follow the rules in the Procurement Directive regarding tech-*

91. Opinion of Advocate General Jacobs delivered on 11 July 2002 in Case C-112/00, Eugen Schmidberger, Internationale Transporte und Planzüge v. Austria, [2003] ECR I-5659, paragraph 65.
92. Case C-112/00, Eugen Schmidberger, Internationale Transporte und Planzüge v. Austria [2003] ECR I-5659, paragraph 94.
93. Case C-59/00, Bent Mousten Vestergaard, [2001] ECR I-9505. The case is also dealt with in chapter 8.

nical specifications' [my translation].[94] In other words, the Complaint Boards seemed to argue that a sort of *de minimis* rule should apply based on what it would cost the contracting authority to follow the rules in the Directive. The Board hence concluded that the contracting authority was not according the Treaty required to add the wording 'or similar' when referring to a make. The case was appealed to a Danish court, which asked the Court of Justice for a preliminary ruling on the matter.

In a reasoned order, the Court of Justice handled the case since the Court found that the answer to the question was clear based on its previous ruling in *UNIX*.[95] The Court concluded that even though the contract did not exceed the thresholds, it was clear from the case law that:

'Article 30 of the Treaty precludes a contracting authority from including in the contract documents for that contract a clause requiring the use in carrying out the contract of a product of a specified make, without adding the words "or equivalent".'[96]

Thus, the Court found that the Treaty's free movement rules also apply below the thresholds.

The case shows that even when the contract has a very small value, the TFEU's free movement rules must be ensured if the contract has a cross-border *element*. However, it is my opinion that a cross-border *element* in a given contract is not the same, as the contract is of cross-border *interest*. Only when a contract is of cross-border *interest* is the contracting authority required to follow the Treaties' principles of equal treatment and transparency. However, this assessment does not address the question of when a contract potentially has a cross-border element. A contract will often have a cross-border element, and there are, presumably, only a few situations in which it is possible to exclude beforehand the possibility that a contract will not have a cross-border element.[97]

In my opinion, the contract in *Vestergaard* was not of cross-border interest, mainly due to the low value of the contract itself, but also the fact that the value of the windows was very low. Furthermore, the fact that a German pro-

94. See decision of November 11, 1998, Tømrermester Bent Mousten Vestergaard v. Spøttrup boligselskab.
95. Case C-359/93, Commission v. Netherlands, [1995] ECR 1-157.
96. Case C-59/00, Bent Mousten Vestergaard v. Spøttrup Boligselskab, [2001] ECR I-9505, paragraph 24.
97. See also Steinicke, Michael *"Varernes frie bevægeligthed og offentlige indkøb"* [2001] DJØF, p. 128, who discussed cross-border element in procurement situations and divides the discussion into potential v. concrete situations.

ducer was indirectly involved is not sufficient to establish cross-border interest (see section 4.1). The order came after *Telaustria* but before *Coname*, which was before the Court had introduced the requirement of certain cross-border interest. As elaborated on in section 4.1, the concept of certain cross-border interest, in my view, only covers the situation in which an undertaking itself wishes to tender for a contract (direct cross-border interest). Therefore, the fact that the contractor wished to use a German product in the performance of the contract (which was located in Denmark) does not lead to the main contract being of cross-border interest. Furthermore, the value of the windows was so insignificant that the German producer would (most likely) not have tendered for the main contract itself. Nevertheless, even if a contract is not of cross-border interest, the contract cannot be entered into in breach of the free movement provisions since no *de minimis* rule exists in this field.

In my view, cross-border interest cannot be considered as a *de minimis* rule.[98] Arguing that cross-border interest was to be considered as a *de minimis* rule would require stating when a contract was so insignificant that it would have no relevance for undertakings in other Member States, which could be difficult to assess. On the other hand, there is no doubt that a *de minimis* rule would be helpful for contracting authorities, although it would be difficult to measure when a contract is so insignificant that it is of no interest to undertakings in other Member States. Since the Public Sector Directive, by setting thresholds, did not constitute a *de minimis* in itself, it is doubtful whether it would ever be possible to construe such a rule. *Graells* submits that: *'... as regards compliance with the principles of equality, transparency and competition, no de minimis exception should be construed in the field of public procurement'.*[99] *Steinicke* argued that one substantial problem with creating a *de minimis* rule in relation to the freedom to provide goods is that there is no objective measure similar to that for the competition rules. Therefore, it makes no sense to talk about market shares or similar.[100] It is doubtful whether setting a lower threshold or creating a new category of B-services would change the fact that one cannot be sure that the Court would not rule

98. Drijber, Jan Berend & Stergiou, Hélène *"Public Procurement Law and Internal Market Law"* [2009] CMLR n° 46, pp. 805-846, p. 814 are of the opinion that no *de minimis* rule exist and that the Court's use of *'... certain should not be equated to any kind of De Minimis rule.'*
99. Graells, Albert Sánchez *"Public Procurement and the EU Competition Rules"* [2011] Hart, p. 211.
100. Steinicke, Michael *"Varernes frie bevægeligthed og offentlige indkøb"* [2001] DJØF p. 139.

that the principles of the Treaties would apply (as it has already done for the contracts that currently fall outside the Directive).

8.2. Internal situations

The requirement for some sort of cross-border interest in *Coname* was perhaps not so surprising given that the Court of Justice has also accepted that the TFEU's free movement rules do not apply to situations that are purely internal in the Member States. However, it is my opinion that internal situations in relation to the free movement rules are not the same as cross-border interest (as will be argued in this section).

Regarding the free movement provisions, it should be recalled that various provisions in the TFEU seek to prohibit restrictions that hinder the access to the Internal Market, such as Article 34 TFEU, which concerns free movement of goods, or Article 54 TFEU concerning free movement of services. However, the free movement provisions cannot be invoked in situations that are considered to be purely internal in the Member State.[101] This means that if an undertaking wishes to invoke the provisions, some sort of cross-border activity must take place. Such an approach can lead to reverse discrimination in the sense that domestic suppliers are more heavily burdened by the law than non-domestic suppliers.[102]

Taking the provisions of free movement of goods as an example, Article 34 TFEU applies to the purchase of goods in public contracts, which also covers individual decisions taken by a contracting authority.[103] The provision

101. See, for example, Case C-41/90, Klaus Höfner and Fritz Elser v. Macrotron GmbH, [1991] ECR I-1979. For further on internal situations, see, for example, Tryfonidou, Alina *"The Outer Limits of Article 28 EC: Purely Internal Situations and the Development of the Court's Approach through the Years"* in Barnard, Cathrine & Odudu, Okeoghene (Eds) *"The Outer Limits of European Union Law"* [2009] Hart.
102. See, for example, Monti, Giorgio & Davies, Gareth & Chalmers, Damian *"European Union Law"*, [2010] Cambridge University Press, p. 755 and Tryfonidou, Alina *"The Outer Limits of Article 28 EC: Purely Internal Situations and the Development of the Court's Approach through the Years"* in Barnard, Cathrine & Odudu, Okeoghene (Eds) *"The Outer Limits of European Union Law"* [2009] Hart.
103. See, for example, Case C-3/88, Commission v. Italy, [1989] ECR 4035, Case C-243/89, Commission v. Denmark, [1993] ECR I-3353, Case C-359/93, Commission v. Netherlands, [1995] ECR 1-157. Case C-59/00, Bent Mousten Vestergaard v. Spøttrup Boligselskab, [2001] ECR I-9505. *Arrowsmith* and *Kunzlik* have questioned whether this is correct; see Arrowsmith, Sue and Kunzlik, Peter (Eds) *"Social and Environmental Policies in EC Procurement Law"* [2009] Cambridge University Press, p. 57.

prohibits restrictions on import, as well as measures having equivalent effect. The latter means that measures that have the effect of market restrictions are also prohibited. In that regard, a measure can discriminate against imported goods directly,[104] as well as indirectly; that is, even though the measure looks neutral, the effect is that it discriminates against foreign products.[105] The lack of transparency in the form of '*a degree of advertisement*' will constitute an indirect discrimination.[106] Finally, a measure can be neither directly nor indirectly discriminating, but still hinder imports in other ways; such measures are also prohibited.

The Court has stated several times that it is not possible to invoke the free movement provisions if the dispute is internal. A few of these cases will be mentioned here.

In *Oeosthoeck*,[107] the Court of Justice found that Dutch legislation on sales in Holland of lexica produced in Holland did not relate to import or export, which meant it was an internal dispute.[108] In *Guimont*,[109] the dispute concerned whether the use of the word 'Emmentaler' was permitted. In France the word could only be used for cheese with a crust. France argued that the ban on using 'Emmentaler' only applied to domestic undertakings, but the rule was so generally formulated that the Court held that it was an import restriction. In the specific case, the complainant was a French producer, so the Court considered the dispute to constitute an internal situation.[110] In *Höfner*,[111] a dispute between a German employment consultancy and a German company regarding the hiring of a German national, the TFEU could not be invoked, even though there was a theoretical possibility that other citizens in other Member States would apply for the position.

104. As seen in Case C-243/89, Commission v. Denmark, [1993] ECR I-3353, where the contracting authority had required that Danish workers and material should be used.
105. See, for example, Case C-45/87, Commission v. Ireland, [1988] ECR 4929.
106. See Case C-412/04, Commission v. Italy, [2008] ECR I-619, paragraph 65.
107. Case C-286/81, Oosthoek's Uitgeversmaatschappij BV, [1982] ECR 4575.
108. Case C-286/81, Oosthoek's Uitgeversmaatschappij BV, [1982] ECR 4575.
109. Case C-448/98, Jean-Pierre Guimont, [2000] ECR I-10663.
110. Case C-448/98, Jean-Pierre Guimont, [2000] ECR I-10663.
111. Case C-41/90, Klaus Höfner and Fritz Elser v. Macrotron GmbH, [1991] ECR I-1979.

However, in *Pistre*,[112] the Court found the free movement of goods provision to be applicable in a case concerning French producers in France. In France, the use of the word 'montagne' was restricted by French legislation. In a criminal proceeding before a French court, the question was raised whether labels with the word 'montagne' could be used. Even though the dispute only concerned French manufacturers, the Court found:

'Article 30 [Article 34TFEU] cannot be considered inapplicable simply because all the facts of the specific case before the national court are confined to a single Member State.'[113]

This case shows that the Court will sometimes rule on a matter even when all parties are from the same Member State.

RI.SAN[114] concerned a situation where an Italian contracting authority had awarded a service concession contract. The undertaking that had challenged the legality of the award of the concession was located in Italy. The Court found that since

'all the facts are confined to within a single Member State and which does not therefore have any connecting link with one of the situations envisaged by Community law in the area of the freedom of movement for persons and freedom to provide services'.[115]

As seen above, the case law on what constitutes an internal situation is not consistent. In recent years, very few situations have been qualified as completely internal situations and, in procurement cases, the requirement seems to have disappeared.[116] To my knowledge, it has not been ruled on since *RI.SAN*, even though the contracting authority in, for example, *Parking Brix-*

112. Joined Cases C-321/94, C-322/94, C-323/94 and C-324/94, Criminal proceedings against Jacques Pistre, Michèle Barthes, Yves Milhau and Didier Oberti, [1997] ECR I-2343.
113. Joined Cases C-321/94, C-322/94, C-323/94 and C-324/94, Criminal proceedings against Jacques Pistre, Michèle Barthes, Yves Milhau and Didier Oberti, [1997] ECR I-2343, paragraph 44.
114. Case C-108/98, RI.SAN. Srl v. Comune di Ischia, Italia Lavoro SpA and Ischia Ambiente SpA, [1999] ECR I-5219.
115. Case C-108/98, RI.SAN. Srl v. Comune di Ischia, Italia Lavoro SpA and Ischia Ambiente SpA, [1999] ECR I-5219. paragraph 23.
116. Drijber, Jan Berend & Stergiou, Hélène *"Public Procurement Law and Internal Market Law"* [2009] CMLR n° 46, pp. 805-846, p.816.

en[117] tried to invoke it. Instead, the concept of 'certain cross-border interest' seems to have taken over for contracts outside the Public Sector Directive.

As seen above, the case law on internal situations depends on who can invoke the free movement rules. This means it is more a variation of cross-border interest. In cases where the requirement for a contract to be of cross-border interest is a necessity with regard to whether the rules apply, it can be argued that the case law on internal situation is a question of who can invoke the rules. However, I would argue that as the principle of equal treatment is inherent in the Treaties, the question of who can invoke that a contract is of certain cross-border interest will be different that in relation to the case law on internal situations. An example could be that a Danish undertaking should be able to take a Danish contracting authority before the complaints board if the latter has breached the principles of the Treaties. This is due to the fact that if the contract is of cross-border interest, no discrimination must take place between neither national nor non-national tenderers. If a domestic tenderer feels discriminated, it should also be possible for that undertaking to bring the contracting authority before the courts. This does not appear to be possible based on the case law on free movement in relation to internal situations.

Also, if a contract has a cross-border interest but the contracting authority has entered into the contract directly, neither domestic nor non-domestic undertakings had a chance to compete for the contract. In my opinion such a national undertaking should be able to bring proceedings for lack of transparency. Therefore, the case law of internal situation does not function here in order to protect the rights of undertakings. Thus, cross-border interest should not be confused with the case law of internal situations.

9. Summary of findings

A contract must be of certain cross-border interest before the principle of equal treatment and the principle of transparency, hereunder the transparency obligation applies.

What constitutes a certain cross-border interest depends on the specific contract in question and will only cover the situation where a non-domestic undertaking wishes to tender directly for the contract; therefore, only direct

117. Case C-458/03, Parking Brixen GmbH v. Gemeinde Brixen and Stadtwerke Brixen AG, [2005] ECR I-8585, paragraph 55.

cross-border interest is necessary. In all cases, the contracting authority must make a concrete assessment by including elements such as the value of the contract, language elements, the complexity of the works or services to be performed, the location for the performance of the contract, national legal requirements, the type of contract and the duration of the contract. Whether a contract is of certain cross-border interest is up to the contracting authority to determine, based on a hypothetical analysis of the market and the contract in question. The Member States can set guidelines regarding what can lead to a contract being of certain cross-border interest. Ultimately, however, it is up to EU law, hence the Court of Justice, to determine whether a contract is of cross-border interest.

The contracting authority's decision on whether a given contract is of cross-border interest must be open for review. In such a situation, it is most likely that the contracting authority must bear the burden of proof regarding whether the cross-border assessment was correct when a procedure takes place in the national courts.

Despite the fact that cross-border interest has similar characteristics as the concept of internal situations in relation to the free movement provisions the two situations are not identical and it is important to separate the two issues. The chapter also concludes that no *de-minimis* rule exist in relation to determining whether the principles of the Treaties are applicable. Thus, it will always be the subject of a concrete assessment whether a given contract is of cross-border interest bearing in mind the difference between the contract having a cross-border element and being of interest to non-domestic undertakings.

PART II

‘Positive obligations derived from the principles of the Treaties’

CHAPTER 7

The Transparency Obligation[1]

1. Introduction

This chapter (as well as chapters 8 and 9) analyses which positive obligations derived from the principles of the Treaties can be imposed upon contracting authorities when awarding one of the three types of contracts.[2] The subject is not new; in fact, it has been debated in legal literature since the Court of Justice in *Telaustria* stated that although service concession contracts were excluded from secondary law, contracting authorities entering into such contracts are bound by

'the fundamental rules of the Treaty, in general, and the principle of non-discrimination on grounds of nationality, in particular'.[3]

More importantly, the Court found that the principle of non-discrimination implies an obligation of transparency on the contracting authority in order to ensure:

'... ***a degree of advertising*** *sufficient to enable the services market to be opened up to competition and the impartiality of procurement procedures to be reviewed'* [emphasis added].[4]

1. I have examined the subject previously: Hansen, Carina Risvig *"Practical requirements arising from the Treaty principles: Advertising, procedures and remedies"*, paper for the Conference 'Global Revolution IV', Copenhagen, September 2010, and Hansen, Carina Risvig *"Chapter 8, Treaty requirements for contracts 'outside' the procurement Directives"* in Trybus, Martin, Caranta, Roberto & Edelstam, Gunille (Eds) *"EU Law and Public Contracts"* [2012] Bruylant Brussels, forthcoming. However, the subject is further developed in the present chapter.
2. When such a contract is of certain cross-border interest as analysed in chapter 6.
3. Case C-324/98, Telaustria Verlags GmbH and Telefonadress GmbH v. Telekom Austria AG, [2000] ECR I-10745, paragraph 60.

The Court's findings in the case have subsequently been confirmed and developed further in several cases; they are perhaps among the most important steps that the Court of Justice has taken in EU procurement law.

The rules in the Public Sector Directive are based on the following principles: 'Prohibition of technical specifications that have a discriminatory effect, adequate advertising of contracts, [and] the fixing of objective criteria for participating (...)'.[5] In line with these principles, the Public Sector Directive requires that contracting authorities publish a contract notice in the OJ. This chapter will analyse and discuss whether EU law also contains a duty to advertise the three types of contracts, and if such a duty exists, where a contract notice or similar should be advertised.

However, *Telaustria* was not the first time the Court of Justice had the chance to rule on a matter regarding contracts falling outside the Directive.[6] Therefore, this chapter will also make some observations as to why the Court came to its conclusions.

1.1. Outline

Firstly, the chapter examines the Court's ruling in *Telaustria* and the background of the case (section 2). Section 3 examines the case law post *Telaustria.* Section 4 will make some observations as to why the Court in *Telaustria* required certain positive obligations deriving from the principles of the Treaties. Section 5 discusses the means of competition, which can be used before awarding one of the three types of contracts.

4. Case C-324/98. Telaustria Verlags GmbH and Telefonadress GmbH v. Telekom Austria AG, [2000] ECR I-10745, paragraphs 61-62.
5. See Recital 3 to Directive 71/305/EEC of 26 July 1971 concerning the co-ordination of procedures for the award of public works contracts, [1971] OJ L 185/5.
6. See, for example, Case C-360/96, Gemeente Arnhem and Gemeente Rheden v. BFI Holding BV, [1998] ECR I-6821. Case C-108/98, RI.SAN. Srl v. Comune di Ischia, Italia Lavoro SpA and Ischia Ambiente SpA, [1999] ECR I-5219. See also chapter 1, section 3.1.1.2. wherein it is elaborated on that it was not the general assumption that the Treaty contained positive obligations when awarding a contract outside the scope of the Procurement Directives.

2. Telaustria

2.1. Background – the reference for a preliminary ruling

The reference for a preliminary ruling in *Telaustria* did not contain any questions about whether obligations derived from the principles of the Treaties existed. The Austrian review body simply asked the Court of Justice for a preliminary ruling as to whether service concession contracts fell within the Service Directive (which the Court found they did not; see chapter 3). Nor did any of the intervening Member States[7] submit that any of the free movement provisions had been breached. Only the Commission, which intervened in the case, had submitted that contracting authorities were bound by an obligation to ensure transparency.

In the Green Paper from 1996, the Commission expressed the view that contracting authorities when awarding service concession contracts:

'must respect the provisions of the EC Treaty, in particular the rules governing free movement of goods and services as well as fundamental principles such as non-discrimination, equality of treatment, transparency and mutual recognition'. Furthermore: *'the principle of non-discrimination on grounds of nationality, implies that there is* ***an obligation to be transparent*** *so that the contracting authority will be able to ensure it is adhered to'*. [emphasis added].[8]

The Commission's opinion that some sort of positive obligation could be derived from the principle of transparency was also stated in the Interpretative Communication on Concessions. The Communication is from 2000, which is prior to the Court of Justice's ruling in *Telaustria.* Regarding the principle of transparency, the Communication also stated that:

'... Transparency can be ensured by any appropriate means, including advertising depending on, and to allow account to be taken of, the particularities of the relevant sector.'

Therefore, it seemed early on that the Commission's opinion was that transparency was necessary, and that advertising could ensure that transparency was complied with.

7. Austria, Denmark, France, and the Netherlands intervened in the case.
8. Green Paper *'Public Procurement in the European Union: Exploring the way forward'*, [1996] COM (1996) 583, p.12. The latter statement was repeated in the Interpretative Communication on Concessions.

In its arguments before the Court, in *Telaustria*, the Commission had argued that *Unitron*[9] supported its view.[10] In this case, the Court had previously held that the principle of non-discrimination on grounds of nationality implies '*... in particular, an obligation of transparency in order to enable the contracting authority to satisfy itself that it has been complied with*' [emphasis added].[11] Therefore, despite being asked by the Austrian review body, the Advocate General in *Telaustria*, *Fennelly*, found it necessary to answer the following question:

'*... If the relevant advertising rules of the Community procurement directives are not applicable, what, if any, publicity requirements would flow from the application of general Treaty principles?*'[12]

Also, the Court decided to elaborate on whether obligations could be derived from the principles of the Treaty. The Court stated that the fact that such a question had not been asked did not:

'*... preclude the Court from helping the national court (...). To that end, the Court may take into consideration other factors in making an interpretation which may assist the determination of the main proceedings.*'[13]

Therefore, the Court decided to answer the question of whether obligations could be derived from the principles of the Treaties.

9. Case C-275/98, Unitron Scandinavia and 3-S, Danske Svineproducenters Serviceselskab v. Ministeriet for Fødevarer, Landbrug og Fiskeri, [1999] ECR I-8291.
10. See Opinion of Advocate General Fennelly delivered on May 18, 2000 in the Case C-324/98, Telaustria Verlags GmbH and Telefonadress GmbH v. Telekom Austria AG, [2000] ECR I-10745, paragraph 42.
11. Case C-275/98, Unitron Scandinavia and 3-S, Danske Svineproducenters Serviceselskab v. Ministeriet for Fødevarer, Landbrug og Fiskeri, [1999] ECR I-8291, paragraph 31.
12. Opinion of Advocate General Fennelly delivered on May 18, 2000 in the Case C-324/98, Telaustria Verlags GmbH and Telefonadress GmbH v. Telekom Austria AG, [2000] ECR I-10745.
13. Case C-324/98, Telaustria Verlags GmbH and Telefonadress GmbH v. Telekom Austria AG, [2000] ECR I-10745, paragraph 59.

2.2. The Court's ruling

In *Telaustria,* the Court found that although service concession contracts were excluded from secondary law, contracting authorities entering in to such contracts are bound by

'the fundamental rules of the Treaty, in general, and the principle of non-discrimination on grounds of nationality, in particular'.[14]

More importantly, the Court found that the principle of non-discrimination implies an obligation of transparency on the contracting authority in order to ensure:

*'... **a degree of advertising** sufficient to enable the services market to be opened up to competition and the impartiality of procurement procedures to be reviewed'.* [emphasis added].[15]

This statement can be called the transparency obligation; section 3 will examine whether the transparency obligation requires prior advertising.

The different language versions of the Court's statement of '... *a degree of advertising*' are somewhat contradictory, as not all language versions use the wording similar to advertising. A look at five different language versions can be seen below:

Language	**Phrase**
English version	*'... a degree of advertising'*
German version	*'... einen angemessenen Grad von Öffentlichkeit sicherstellen'*
French version	*'... un degré de publicité'*
Italian version	*'... un adeguato livello di pubblicità'*
Danish version	*'... en passende grad af offentlighed'*

In her opinion on the case *Commission v. Finland*, Advocate General *Sharpston* stated that the different language versions

14. Case C-324/98, Telaustria Verlags GmbH and Telefonadress GmbH v. Telekom Austria AG, [2000] ECR I-10745, paragraph 60.
15. Case C-324/98. Telaustria Verlags GmbH and Telefonadress GmbH v. Telekom Austria AG, [2000] ECR I-10745, paragraphs 61-62.

> *'... are more akin to "publicity" in English.* ***In my view, "publicity" does not necessarily imply an obligation to publish.*** *It does, however, imply an obligation to do more than simply contacting a single potential tenderer and awarding the contract to that undertaking'.* [emphasis added].[16]

The language versions all indicate that the meaning of a *'degree of advertising'* should more likely imply a *'degree of publicity'*. The question is whether publicity leads to a requirement to advertise a contract beforehand; *Sharpston* (quoted above) did not find that it did. The answer requires a further examination of the case, and the cases following after, as *Telaustria* was not clear on the matter (see section 3).

Going back to Telaustria, the Court of Justice also stated that 'a degree of advertising' should be '*sufficient to enable the services market to be opened up to competition and the impartiality of procurement procedures to be reviewed.*' A closer look at this statement in the various language versions shows that also this statement, specifically the wording 'service market', also has different meanings in the various language versions of the case.

An overview of five language versions can be seen below:

Language	**Phrase:**
English	'... *the services market*'
Danish	'... *markedet for tjenesteydelser*'
Italian	'... *appalto*'
German	'... *Dienstleistungsmarkt*'
French	'... *marché des services*'

Some versions are more akin to 'contract' rather than service market. The Court's later quoting of the phrase uses the word 'concessions'. For example, in *Parking Brixen* it is stated: *'a degree of advertising sufficient to enable the* ***service concession*** *to be opened up to competition'* [emphasis added].[17] Thus, it can only be assumed that the Court meant to state that the concession (or the contract)[18] must be opened to competition.

16. Opinion of Advocate general Sharpston, delivered on 18 January 2007, in Case C-195/04, Commission v. Finland, [2007] ECR I-3351, paragraph 82.
17. Case C-458/03, Parking Brixen GmbH v. Gemeinde Brixen and Stadtwerke Brixen AG, [2005] ECR I-8585, paragraph 49.
18. In line with Brown, Adrian *"Seeing Through Transparency: the Requirement to Advertise Public Contracts and Concessions Under the EC Treaty"* [2007] PPLR n° 1, pp. 1-21, see mainly footnote 14.

In my opinion, the Court's statement in *Telaustria* implies two aspects. The first is that competition is created for the contract (the transparency's competition function). The second aspect is that it is possible for the procurement procedures to be reviewed (the transparency's control function). Below, I will examine the cases from the Court of Justice (in chronological order), as well as some opinions from advocates generals and discuss whether, based on these cases, the transparency's obligations can lead to a duty to advertise one of the three types of contracts.

3. Is advertising necessary?

3.1. Post-*Telaustria* case law

In her opinion to *Telaustria,* Advocate General *Fennelly* stated that: *'the principle of non-discrimination on grounds of nationality requires that the award of concessions respect a minimum degree of publicity and transparency'.*[19] However, she also argued that:

> *'... publicity should not necessarily be equated with publication. (...) Transparency, in this context, is therefore concerned with ensuring the fundamental fairness and openness of the award procedures, particularly as regards potential tenderers who are not established in the Member State of the awarding authority'.*[20]

By referring to the openness of the award procedures, *Fennelly* emphasised that the principle of transparency contains aims other than the control function.

A few years after *Telaustria*, in *Coname*,[21] the Court of Justice confirmed the transparency obligation. The importance of *Coname* can be seen from the fact that the Court's ruling was given by the Grand Chamber consisting of 11 judges. Four Member States,[22] as well as the Commission, intervened in the case.

19. Opinion of Advocate General Fennelly delivered on May 18, 2000 in the Case C-324/98, Telaustria Verlags GmbH and Telefonadress GmbH v. Telekom Austria AG, [2000] ECR I-10745, paragraph 43.
20. Opinion of Advocate General Fennelly delivered on May 18, 2000 in the Case C-324/98, Telaustria Verlags GmbH and Telefonadress GmbH v. Telekom Austria AG, [2000] ECR I-10745, paragraph 43.
21. Case C-231/03, Consorzio Aziende Metano v. Comune di Cingia de' Botti, [2005] ECR I-7287.
22. Austria, Italy, the Netherlands and Finland.

The question in the case was whether direct awarding of a concession contract was permitted. The Court elaborated on the transparency obligation and found that doing so did not *'... imply an obligation to hold an invitation to tender'*.[23] This statement supports the view that it is not necessary to advertise the contract beforehand. The Court found that the potential tenderers must:

> *'... have access to appropriate information regarding that concession before it is awarded, so that, if that undertaking had so wished, it would have been in a position to express its interest in obtaining that concession'.*[24]

The Court of Justice argued that in *'the absence of any transparency, the latter undertaking has no real opportunity of expressing its interest in obtaining that concession'.*[25] The argument that lack of transparency means that undertakings cannot express interest in the contract could lead to the conclusion that the purpose of transparency is for undertakings to be able to express their interest in obtaining such a contract. This does not necessarily mean advertising, provided that the contracting authority can make undertakings express their interest by other means. However, it was still left to explore how this should be done.

Only a few months after the Court of Justice's Grand Chamber decision in *Coname*, the Court of Justices' first Chamber gave a ruling in the case of *Parking Brixen.*[26] This case also concerned a service concession contract. The Court of Justice stated that a:

> *'... **complete lack of any call for competition** in the case of the award of a public service concession (...) does not comply with the requirements of (...) transparency'* [emphasis added].[27]

It is not entirely clear whether it was the intention of the Court of Justice to state that a contracting authority has a duty to advertise prior to the award of a

23. Case C-231/03, Consorzio Aziende Metano v. Comune di Cingia de' Botti, [2005] ECR I-7287, paragraph 21.
24. Case C-231/03, Consorzio Aziende Metano v. Comune di Cingia de' Botti, [2005] ECR I-7287, paragraph 21.
25. Case C-231/03, Consorzio Aziende Metano v. Comune di Cingia de' Botti, [2005] ECR I-7287, paragraph 18.
26. Case C-458/03, Parking Brixen GmbH v. Gemeinde Brixen and Stadtwerke Brixen AG, [2005] ECR I-8585. The same Member States, which had intervened in Coname (except for Finland), had intervened in the case.
27. Case C-458/03, Parking Brixen GmbH v. Gemeinde Brixen and Stadtwerke Brixen AG, Parking Brixen, [2005] ECR I-8585, paragraph 50.

public contract, given that only a few months earlier in *Coname,* the Court of Justice had explicitly stated that transparency does not: *'necessarily imply* [edt.] *an obligation to hold an invitation to tender'.*[28] However, in *Parking Brixen*, the Court also found that it was

'for the concession-granting public authority to evaluate (...) the appropriateness of the detailed arrangements of ***the call for competition*** *to the particularities of the public service concession in question'* [emphasis added].[29]

This emphasises the requirement for competition. As seen in chapter 2, the objective of the EU procurement rules, found within the principles of the Treaties, is to ensure undistorted competition by guaranteeing open, equal access to public contracts. This objective is also in line with the fact that the Court found that transparency consists of ensuring *'for the benefit of any potential tenderer a degree of advertisement'.*[30]

Therefore, in order for a tenderer to benefit from the transparency obligation, equal access to the contracts be granted to ensure undistorted competition. In my opinion, the transparency obligation could be said to imply an obligation to create competition for the contract. By creating competition for a contract, the risk of discrimination will be reduced. In that regard, a contracting authority needs to make various undertakings aware of the possibility of obtaining the contract, thereby creating transparency.

Coname and *Parking Brixen* were handed down in late 2005. In April 2006, in *ANAV,*[31] regarding a service concession contract, the Court confirmed the *Parking Brixen* requirement that a complete lack of any call for competition in the case of the award of a public service concession does not comply with the transparency obligation.[32]

28. Case C-231/03, Consorzio Aziende Metano v. Comune di Cingia de' Botti, [2005] ECR I-7287, paragraph 21.
29. Case 458/03, Parking Brixen GmbH v. Gemeinde Brixen and Stadtwerke Brixen AG [2005], ECR I-8585, paragraph 50.
30. Case C-458/03, Parking Brixen GmbH v. Gemeinde Brixen and Stadtwerke Brixen AG, [2005] ECR I-8585, paragraph 49.
31. Case C-410/04, Associazione Nazionale Autotrasporto Viaggiatori (ANAV) v. Comune di Bari and AMTAB Servizio SpA, [2006] ECR I-3303.
32. Case C-410/04, Associazione Nazionale Autotrasporto Viaggiatori (ANAV) v. Comune di Bari and AMTAB Servizio SpA, [2006] ECR I-3303, paragraph 22.

In *Commission v. Italy*,[33] the Court of Justice again had the opportunity to explore the principle of transparency. In this case, the Court noted that:

'... the complete failure to ***invite competing*** *bids (...) infringes the general principle of transparency and the obligation to ensure a sufficient degree of advertising'* [emphasis added].[34]

In my view, the wording '*failure to invite competing bids*' can also be read as the failure to contact other possible tenderers. It is also clear that an invitation does not necessarily imply a duty to advertise the contract. Thus, supporting the view that advertising is not always necessary.

Telaustria, *Coname*, *Parking Brixen*, and *ANAV* were all preliminary rulings, but in *Commission v. Italy*, the Commission had brought an enforcement proceeding against Italy. The Commission later brought proceedings against other Member States as well, such as Ireland, Finland and France, for lack of transparency by not advertising certain types of contracts.[35]

In August 2006, the Commission issued its 2006 Communication,[36] regarding its interpretation of the principles of the Treaties that contracting authorities should follow when entering into a contract below the thresholds or a B-service contract. At the time that the 2006 Communication was issued, the Court of Justice had not yet ruled on whether the principles did in fact apply to these situations, as all the above-mentioned cases concerned service concession contracts (in September 2006, Germany brought an action against the Commission for issuing the Communication and claimed it should be annulled; see below). Going back to the Communication, it can be seen that it was the Commission's opinion that:

'the practice of contacting a number of potential tenderers would not be sufficient in this respect, even if the contracting entity includes undertakings from other Member States or attempts to reach all potential suppliers. Such a selective approach cannot exclude dis-

33. Case C-260/04, Commission v. Italy, [2007] ECR I-7083. Denmark and Spain intervened in the case in support for Italy.
34. Case C-260/04, Commission v. Italy, [2007] ECR I-7083, paragraph 25.
35. See Commission Press release IP/03/266, Brussels, July 17, 2003 'Public procurement: Commission acts against six Member States'.
36. Commission Interpretative Communication on the Community law applicable to contract awards not or not fully subject to the provisions of the Public Procurement Directives, (2006/C179/2).

crimination against potential tenderers from other Member States, in particular new entrants to the market'.[37]

Therefore, the Commission concluded that,

'*the only way that the requirements laid down by the ECJ can be met is* ***by publication of a sufficiently accessible advertisement prior to the award of the contract***' [emphasis added].

Thus, it was the Commission's view that advertising was necessary.

In January 2007, Advocate General *Sharpston* submitted her opinion in *Commission v. Finland*, concerning a contract below the thresholds.[38] *Sharpston* stated that:

'*... the appropriate degree of publicity is to be determined by reference to the potential market for* that *contract. The contracting authority must ensure a degree of publicity* ***sufficient to open up that market to competition*** *and to permit the impartiality of the procurement procedure to be reviewed.'* [emphasis added].[39]

Thus, even though the case came after the 2006 Communication, *Sharpston* did not find that a requirement for advertising existed in such a case.

In November 2007, in Commission v. Ireland,[40] the Court found that it was up to the Commission to prove that an 'undertaking was unable to express its interest in that contract because it did not have access to adequate information before the contract was awarded.'[41] The Court only refers to lack of transparency, not to what is required according to the transparency obliga-

37. The 2006 Communication, which furthermore states: *'The same applies to all forms of 'passive' publicity where a contracting entity abstains from active advertising but replies to requests for information from applicants who found out by their own means about the intended contract award. A simple reference to media reports, parliamentary or political debates or events such as congresses for information would likewise not constitute adequate advertising.'*
38. Opinion of Advocate General Sharpston delivered on January 18, 2007, in Case C-195/04, Commission v. Finland, [2007] ECR I-3351. The Court, however, dismissed the action as inadmissible.
39. Opinion of Advocate General Sharpston delivered on January 18, 2007, in Case C-195/04, Commission v. Finland, [2007] ECR I-3351, paragraph 83. *Sharpston* also argued that a publicity requirements for contracts below the thresholds would be contrary to, among other things, the principle of subsidiarity as publicity in EU law would disregard part of the legislative intention behind the Procurement Directives.
40. Case C-507/03, Commission v. Ireland, [2007] ECR I-9777.
41. Case C-507/03, Commission v. Ireland, [2007] ECR I-9777, paragraph 32.

tion.[42] Based on the above statement, it can be argued that an undertaking should only have access to information before the contract is awarded, which does not always require advertising.

In December 2007, in *Correos,*[43] the Court repeated its finding in *Parking Brixen* and stated that the transparency obligation consists of ensuring, for '*the benefit of any potential tenderer, a degree of advertising sufficient to enable the public service contract to be opened up to competition and the impartiality of procurement procedures to be reviewed.*'[44] Furthermore:

> '*a complete lack of any call for competition in the case of the award of a public service contract like that at issue in the main proceedings does not comply with the requirements of Articles 43 EC and 49 EC any more than with the principles of equal treatment, non-discrimination and transparency*'.[45]

Thus, nothing new was added to the picture that could clarify the extent of the transparency obligation.

In April 2008, in her opinion to *Pressetext*, Advocate General *Kokott* stated:

> '*What precise requirements flow from that rule* [the transparency obligation edt.] *is currently unclear. **It is certain only that the transparency rule does not necessarily entail a duty to call for tenders***' [emphasis added].[46]

Thus, despite the 2006 Communication, it was still the opinion of many that transparency did not in all cases require a duty to call for tenders or prior advertising.

In May 2010, the General Court ruled in *Germany v. Commission.*[47] In September 2006, Germany had brought an action against the Commission for

42. Case C-507/03, Commission v. Ireland, [2007] ECR I-9777, paragraph 30.
43. Case C-220/06, Asociación Profesional de Empresas de Reparto y Manipulado de Correspondencia v. Administración General del Estado, [2007] ECR I-12175.
44. Case C-220/06, Asociación Profesional de Empresas de Reparto y Manipulado de Correspondencia v. Administración General del Estado, [2007] ECR I-12175, paragraph 75.
45. Case C-220/06, Asociación Profesional de Empresas de Reparto y Manipulado de Correspondencia v. Administración General del Estado, [2007] ECR I-12175, paragraph 76.
46. Opinion Advocate General Kokott delivered on 13 March 2008 in Case C-454/06, Pressetext Nachrichtenagentur GmbH v. Austria,,APA-OTS Originaltext-Service GmbH and APA Austria Presse Agentur registrierte Genossenschaft mit beschränkter Haftung, [2008] ECR I-4401, paragraph 117.

issuing the 2006 Communication and claimed it should be annulled. According to Germany, the Communication was a binding act containing new rules for the award of public contracts that extended beyond the obligations pursuant to the existing EU law. Therefore, even though the Interpretative Communication itself stated that it was not legally binding,[48] Germany argued that it created *de facto* new rules.

Several Member States,[49] as well as the European Parliament, intervened in the case in support of Germany. The General Court dismissed the action as inadmissible, but decided to examine the Communication in order to:

> *'... determine whether the Communication is designed to produce legal effects which are new as compared with those entailed by the application of the fundamental principles of the EC Treaty'.*[50]

Germany had argued that the case law from the Court of Justice regarding service concession contracts[51] could not be transferred to apply for contracts below the thresholds and B-services as well.[52] Therefore, the Communication introduced a basic obligation for all Member States to advertise all future contracts before they were awarded; this constituted a new obligation.[53] Considering the long time it had taken for the Court to handle the case, the ruling came after the Court of Justice had already clarified that the obligations derived from the principles of the Treaties applied to contracts below the

47. Case T-258/06, Germany v. Commission, [2010] ECR II-2027.
48. The 2006 Communication itself states that: *'This communication does not create any new legislative rules. It should be noted that, in any event, interpretation of Community law is ultimately the role of the Court of Justice.'*
49. United Kingdom, Greece, Austria, France, Poland and the Netherlands.
50. Case T-258/06, Germany v. Commission, [2010] ECR II-2027, paragraph 29.
51. At the time of the publication of the Communication the following cases had been given: Case C-324/98, Telaustria Verlags GmbH and Telefonadress GmbH v. Telekom Austria AG, [2000] ECR I-10745, Case C-231/03, Consorzio Aziende Metano v. Comune di Cingia de' Botti, [2005] ECR I-7287 and Case C-458/03, Parking Brixen GmbH v. Gemeinde Brixen and Stadtwerke Brixen AG, [2005] ECR I-8585.
52. Case T-258/06, Germany v. Commission, [2010] ECR II-2027, paragraphs 36-37 and paragraph 40.
53. Case T-258/06, Germany v. Commission, [2010] ECR II-2027, paragraph 68. Besides the advertisement requirement Germany's complaint also concerned other issues in the Communication, which is dealt with in chapter 6.

thresholds.[54] At the time of the General Court's ruling, therefore, it could be argued that there was no longer any dispute that the principles of the Treaties were also applicable for contracts below the thresholds and B-service contracts. Therefore, the outcome of the case that the principles of the Treaties also applied to these contracts was no longer as surprising as it could have been if the case had been ruled upon earlier.

Regarding the transparency obligation, the General Court found that the transparency obligation '*presupposes a **form of advertising** that takes place before the award of the public contract in question: in other words, prior publication of an advertisement*' [emphasis added].[55] Accordingly, the General Court concluded that the Communication did not create new obligations for Member States,[56] which means that the Communication did not go beyond the fundamental principles of the Treaty as interpreted by the Court of Justice.

The fact that the General Court supported the 2006 Communication could imply that the Court interprets the case law in such a way that it requires advertising. However, regarding the potential for a contracting authority to contact a number of potential tenderers, the General Court found that this is not ruled out by the Communication. The Court stated:

> '*... the contracting authorities may limit, to an appropriate level, the number of applicants invited to submit an offer*'.[57]

Therefore, it seems to be the General Court's view that, as a rule, the principles of the Treaties leads to a duty of prior advertising, although there will be situations where this will not be necessary.

In November 2010, in *Commission v. Ireland*,[58] the Court stated:

> '*... even though contracting authorities which conclude contracts listed in Annex II B to the Directive are not subject to the rules laid down in the Directive relating to the require-*

54. Case C-412/04, Commission v. Italy, [2008] ECR I-619 and Case C-507/03, Commission v. Ireland, [2007] ECR I-9777, paragraph 29.
55. Case T-258/06, Germany v. Commission, [2010] ECR II-2027, paragraph 79.
56. Case T-258/06, Germany v. Commission, [2010] ECR II-2027, paragraph 79.
57. Case T-258/06, Germany v. Commission, [2010] ECR II-2027, paragraphs 99-100.
58. Case C-226/09, Commission v. Ireland, [2010] November, 18 2010 (not yet reported).

ments to put contracts out to competition by means of prior advertising, they nevertheless remain subject to the fundamental rules of the European Union.'[59]

It could be argued that, by referring to the fact that B-services are not covered by the Public Sector Directive's requirement for prior advertising, such a requirement cannot be found in the Treaties. Therefore, the statement supports the view that B-service contracts do not have to put out to competition by 'means of prior advertising'. However, the Court did not need to rule on whether an infringement of the transparency obligation had taken place as the contract had already been advertised in the OJ beforehand.[60]

The same applied in March 2011 in *Strong Segurança*,[61] where the Court did not elaborate on the transparency obligation, again perhaps because the contract in question had been published in the OJ. However, the Court stated that:

'It should be observed, moreover, that the application of Articles 23 and 35(4) of Directive 2004/18 during the contract award procedures relating to such 'non-priority' services is also intended to ensure ***the degree of transparency*** *that corresponds to the specific nature of those contracts'* [emphasis added].[62]

This suggests that, to some degree, the rules in the Directive already ensure the proper amount of transparency, which means that no further obligations could be laid upon contracting authorities awarding B-services (the case is analysed in chapter 8, section 2).

In another case from March 2011, *Privater Rettungsdienst*,[63] the Court was asked to consider whether a given contract constituted a service conces-

59. Case C-226/09, Commission v. Ireland, [2010] November, 18 2010 (not yet reported), paragraph 29.
60. Case C-226/09, Commission v. Ireland, [2010] November 18, 2010 (not yet reported), referred in paragraph 31 to the obligation of transparency without stating the precise content of such an obligation. It stated: *'The obligation of transparency applies where the contract for the provision of services in question may be of interest to an undertaking located in a Member State other than that in which the contract is to be awarded.'*
61. Case C-95/10, Strong Segurança SA v. Município de Sintra, Securitas-Serviços e Tecnologia de Segurança, [2011] March 17, 2011, (not yet reported).
62. Case C-95/10, Strong Segurança SA v. Município de Sintra, Securitas-Serviços e Tecnologia de Segurança, [2011] March 17, 2011, (not yet reported), paragraph 39.
63. Case C-274/09, Privater Rettungsdienst und Krankentransport Stadler v. Zweckverband für Rettungsdienst und Feuerwehralarmierung Passau, [2011] March 10, 2011 (not yet reported).

sion contract. Having concluded that the contract was indeed a concession (see chapter 3), the Court stated that the contracting authorities:

> *'... are bound to comply with the fundamental rules of the Treaty on the Functioning of the European Union, including Articles 49 TFEU and 56 TFEU, and with the consequent obligation of transparency. (...)'.*[64]

Accordingly, the Court only referred to the transparency obligation, without emphasising on the content of that obligation.[65]

It could be argued that the later cases does not elaborate on whether the transparency obligation leads to an obligation to advertise because the contracting authorities have already assumed that advertisement was needed, or it could also indicate that national law[66] now contains a duty for contracting authorities to advertise beforehand – making the question less important. In recent years, the literature has been divided regarding whether it is necessary to advertise beforehand, although most authors seem to be of the opinion that some sort of advertising is required.[67] However, I submit that, based on the

64. Case C-274/09, Privater Rettungsdienst und Krankentransport Stadler v. Zweckverband für Rettungsdienst und Feuerwehralarmierung Passau, [2011] March 10, 2011 (not yet reported), paragraph 49.
65. The Court referred in that regard to Case C-91/08, Wall AG v. La ville de Francfort-sur-le-Main and Frankfurter Entsorgungs- und Service (FES) GmbH, [2010] ECR I-2815, paragraphs 33 and 34, wherein it is merely stated that a transparency obligation apply to service concession contracts.
66. See chapter 1, section 4.3.
67. See, for example, Trybus, Martin *"Public Contracts in European Union Internal Market Law: Foundations and Requirements"* in Nogouelleou, Rozen and Stelkens, Ulrich (Eds) *"Comparative Law on Public Contracts"* [2010] Brussels Bruylant, p. 103 who states: *'The requirement of advertising is already a positive requirement.'* and p. 105: *'publicity would be compromised if a practise of contacted tenderers instead would be allowed.'*, Arrowsmith, Sue *"The Law of Public and Utilities Procurement"* [2005] 2nd Edition, Sweet and Maxwell, p. 192 *'at least some form of advertising is needed'*. Brown, Adrian *"EU primary law requirements in practice: advertising, procedures and remedies for public contracts outside the procurement directives"* [2010] PPLR n° 5, pp. 169-181, where the purpose of his article is to assess the practical question of how to comply with the transparency obligation. However, *Brown* also finds that *'it ought to be sufficient for an authority to reach out to a known set of suppliers in certain circumstances'*, Treumer, Steen and Werlauff, Erik *"The Leverage Principle: Secondary Law as a Lever for the Development of Primary Community Law"* [2003] ELR n° 1, 28(1) pp. 124-133, state: *'Some kind of tendering procedure'*. Thus, not referring to advertising but moreover, tender procedure.

case law discussed above, it cannot be concluded that contracting authorities are under a general duty to advertise a contract. However, I believe that the transparency obligation does lead to an obligation to create competition for the contract, and that such a duty does not always require advertising. See section 5 for the means of competition.

4. Why introduce a transparency obligation?

Telaustria (and the following cases) has certainly led to legal uncertainty in the field for contracts not covered by the Directives. It has also been argued that the judgment

'... exceeds the bounds of acceptable judicial interpretation and amounts to legislative activity that undermines the proper division of responsibility between legislative and judicial branches of the EU'.[68]

Furthermore, *Braun* is of the opinion that the case created new legislation, and that this:

'... legislatory strategy, which goes well beyond a mere interpretative guidance, is irreconcilable with the substantial procedural requirements of a due legislative process as laid down in the E.C. Treaty (...) It deprives the Council and the European Parliament of their rights of being consulted in the course of a proper legislative procedure'.[69] *Treumer* stated that *Telaustria* was not: *'... a question of logic but of creation of new law without a clear legal basis'.*[70]

The Court has been seeking to fulfil gaps the EU legislator has not been able to close.[71] Thus, *Telaustria* can be seen as such a situation. Thus, even though service concession contracts were excluded from the Directives, the Court (and the Commission) found it necessary to ensure that some sort of competition was created for these types of contract. As seen in chapter 3, the decision to exclude service concession contracts from the Directives was primarily po-

68. Arrowsmith, Sue (Eds) *"EU Public Procurement Law: An Introduction"* [2010].
69. Braun, Peter *"A Matter of Principle(s) – The Treatment of Contracts Falling Outside the Scope of the European Procurement Directives"* [2000] PPLR n° 1, pp. 39-49.
70. Treumer, Steen *"The discretionary powers of contracting entities – towards a flexible approach in the recent case law of the European Court of Justice?"* [2006] PPLR n° 3, pp. 71-85.
71. See chapter 1 regarding the interpretations methods of the Court of Justice.

litical and the Commission had first proposed to cover them when proposing the Service Directive. Therefore, it could be argued that, since these contracts will often attract more than one undertaking if put out for competition, it was perhaps not overly surprising that the first time the Court stated that certain positive obligations could be derived from the principles of the Treaties was for these contracts. As *Cahill* argued:

'this [requiring a degree of advertising] is an example of where the Court wishes to support the Internal Market in Public Services rather than shielding them from competition based in other Member States'.[72]

Therefore, even though a clear legal basis could not be found in the Directives, and even though the EU legislator explicitly did not cover these contracts by the procurement Directives, the Court found it necessary to require certain obligations for these types of contracts, which has led to a high degree of legal uncertainty in this field. However, as *Treumer* argued, even though the case led to legal uncertainty:

'... It must, however, be admitted that a more dynamic approach would be difficult due to the legality principle, which requires a legal basis for the imposition of obligations. The vaguer the legal basis, the vaguer will the outlined obligation tend to be. (...) It would nevertheless have been preferable if the Court had taken the last step and had specified the material content of the transparency obligation in further detail'.[73]

In my opinion, it is unlikely that the Court will provide further guidance on the transparency obligation. By introducing the requirement for '... *ensuring a degree of advertising*', the Court has to some extent placed the burden of clarifying what this transparency obligation means on the Member States. Thus, the legislation of most Member States includes some sort of obligation to advertise the three types of contracts in most situations.[74]

72. Cahill, Dermot *"The Ebb and Flow, the Doldrums and the Raging Tide: Single Market Law's EBB and Flow over Services of General Economic Interest, the Legal Doldrums over Services of General Interest, and the Raging Tide of Article 106(2) (ex Art 86(2)) over State Aid & Public Procurement"* [2010] EBLR, pp. 629-662.
73. Treumer, Steen *"The discretionary powers of contracting entities – towards a flexible approach in the recent case law of the European Court of Justice?"* [2006] PPLR n° 3, pp. 71-85.
74. See chapter 1, section 4.3.

5. Means of competition

Advertising often creates transparency (depending on where the advertising has been done), but it does not always create competition. Competition depends on many other elements, such as whether undertakings are interested in the contract, the language of a given notice, the market, etc.

A contract can be put out for competition if a contracting authority invites a certain number of potential tenderers (five, for example) to compete for the contract. In that regard, these five undertakings will compete for the contract. However, it could be argued that such a practice could exclude new undertakings from gaining access to the domestic market. Under the Public Sector Directive, it is permissible to limit the number of candidates to be prequalified in, for example, the restricted procedure. However, this is only permitted if a contract notice has already been published in the OJ. When limiting the number of candidates the Directive requires that *'In any event the number of candidates invited shall be sufficient to ensure genuine competition'*.[75] Here, the Public Sector Directive still requires the contracting authority to create competition, even in situations where a contract notice has already been published. Thus, it can be argued that it is not sufficient just to advertise; the contracting authority must also ensure competition for the contract.

I submit that some sort of competition must be present beforehand, and one way to create competition would be to advertise the contract, although such advertising will not be necessary in all cases. The essential factor in the transparency obligation is that competition is created for the contract.

A contracting authority can choose to advertise a contract beforehand. Advertising can be done in many places and one place does not exclude the other. At one end of the spectrum, a contracting authority could advertise in the OJ, national or international websites, newspapers and journals; at the other end of the spectrum is the option of contacting potential tenderers directly.

Where a contracting authority should advertise the contract in order to create competition will depend on the contract in question. According to the 2006 Communication, the contracting authorities choice of where to advertise:

'... should be guided by an assessment of the relevance of the contract to the Internal Market, in particular in view of its subject-matter and value and of the customary practices in the relevant sector'.

75. Article 44(3) of the Public Sector Directive.

The more that the contract is of interest to potential tenderers from other Member States, the wider the coverage should be.

5.1. Advertising: Official Journal, websites, journals and newspapers

On the European level, it is possible to publish a contract in the OJ for the three types of contract like it is possible for contracts that fall within the Public Sector Directive. Advertising broadly to as many tenderers as possible would be in line with the intention of the Directive, where according to the Directive:

> *'To ensure development of effective competition in the field of public contracts, it is necessary that contract notices drawn up by the contracting authorities of Member States be advertised throughout the Community.'*[76]

Therefore, advertising in the OJ would clearly fulfil the transparency obligation, which was also stated by Advocate General *Sharpston*: *'There can be no doubt that the transparency obligation is satisfied by publishing a contract notice in the Official Journal of the EU for a contract to be awarded under a restricted procedure.'*[77] However, advertising in OJ alone might not always be the best solution for the contracting authority, considering the contract in question. In many cases, especially those involving low-value contracts, such contracts might be interesting for small undertakings, which might not normally look in the OJ for contract opportunities.

The Commission seems to be of the opinion that contracts for B-services that exceed the thresholds in the Public Sector Directive *'require publication in a medium with wide coverage'.*[78] In my view, the Commission's statement is too general and requiring advertising in a medium with wide coverage for all contracts above the thresholds will definitely not always be necessary; it will depend upon the type of contract. If B-services always require publication in a medium with wide coverage (even when the value of the contract is above the thresholds), they should have been covered fully by the Public Sector Directive in the first place. Such contracts are often of cross-border interest only to undertakings in neighbouring countries, which means that the me-

76. Recital 36 of Directive 2004/18/EC.
77. Opinion of Advocate General Sharpston, delivered on January 18, 2007, in the Case C-195/04, Commission v. Finland, [2007] ECR I-3351, paragraph 59.
78. Commission Interpretative Communication on the Community law applicable to contract awards not or not fully subject to the provisions of the Public Procurement Directives, [2006] OJ C179/2.

dium of advertising does not necessarily have to have a wide coverage for these types of contracts. In order to ensure competition for the contract, it will often be sufficient to advertise the contract on the contracting authorities' own website. In theory, a website would be a medium with wide coverage, given that everyone has the possibility to access the website. Nevertheless, since a contracting authority usually has its own website in its domestic language, it will often not have wide coverage.[79]

Another form of advertising is the possibility for the contracting authority to establish a form of supplier lists. Such a possibility already exists under the Utilities Directive,[80] and makes it possible for the contracting authority to create a supplier list, which it intends to use (often for repetitive purchases) and suppliers can access the list in all cases once qualified to supply the task.

In some situations, in order to ensure competition, it could arguably be necessary to advertise a contract in more languages than in the domestic ones, bearing in mind that a specific language is not necessary.[81] However, if there is only limited competition at the local level, it might be necessary for the contract to advertise broadly to ensure competition. In many Member States, it is not a question of whether a duty to advertise exists since national legislation requires it. Some Member States even have a common platform on which to advertise contracts.[82]

5.2. Inviting tenderers

In order to create competition for a contract, it will often be sufficient to invite potential tenderers. This will especially be the case in situations where the contracting authority has a good knowledge of a given market. In such situations, where the contracting authority already knows the suppliers in a market, the authority should be allowed to contact these suppliers directly. In

79. Arnould, Joel *"Procedures for awarding low-value contracts in France: the Region Nord-Pas-de-Calais case"* [2006] PPLR, n° 2, NA66-69, elaborates on a French case where the Council of State (French Supreme Administrative Court) had found that advertisement of a works contract below the thresholds on the contracting authority's own website and in a regional newspaper had not been a sufficient form of advertisement (and thus annulled the procedure).
80. See the Utilities Directive Article 41.
81. For further on language barriers see chapter 6, section 4.2.1.1.
82. For example Finland, www.hankintailmoitukset.fi, UK http://www.contractsfinder.businesslink.gov.uk/ Also Norway has a platform: www.doffin.no. Denmark introduced on April 1, 2012 a platform and at the same time making it mandatory to publish certain types of contracts at the platform. The new platform: www.udbud.dk

many situations, a contracting authority would receive the best offers by directly contacting undertakings that it already knows can perform the task or deliver the goods. For example, if a specific EU licence is required and not many undertakings hold such a license, the contracting authority will know in advance which undertakings can perform the contract and can contact those that hold a licence and invite them to participate in a competition.

It could be argued that contacting potential tenderers would restrict new undertakings from gaining access to a market (or unknown bidders). In the former case, however, this not a sufficient argument for requiring advertising, since the Public Sector Directive also permits the exclusion of undertakings as it is permitted to award a contract based on previous experience or setting financial requirements to an undertakings turnover, for example.[83]

Advocate General *Fennelly* argued in *Telaustria*:

> '*... if the awarding entity addresses itself directly to a number of potential tenderers, and assuming the latter are not all or nearly all undertakings having the same nationality as that entity, the requirement of transparency would, in my view, be respected*'.[84]

In order for the principles of the Treaties to be applicable, the contract in question must be of cross-border interest. This would mean that the contracting authority has already made an assessment that the contract would be relevant for undertakings in other Member States. Therefore, in my opinion, it will also be necessary to invite such undertakings. On the contrary, however, the choice of tenderers should not depend on the nationality, but on creating the best competition for the contract in question, which does not depend on where the tenderers are from.

In a Danish case before the Complaints Board for Public Procurement, *Thomas Borgå v. the Municipality of Skive*,[85] the Board found that inviting six undertakings to participate in a competition for a contract regarding a B-service (healthcare for employees) was not a breach of any procurement rules. However, negotiating with only one of the undertakings was a breach. In that regard, the contracting authority was obliged to ensure equal opportu-

83. See also Brown, Adrian *"EU primary law requierements in practice: advertising, procedures and remedies for public contracts outside the procurement directives"* [2010] PPLR n° 5, pp. 169-181.
84. Opinion of Advocate General Fennelly delivered on May 18, 2000 in the Case C-324/98, Telaustria Verlags GmbH and Telefonadress GmbH v. Telekom Austria AG, [2000] ECR I-10745, paragraph 43. See also Bovis, Christopher *"EU public procurement law"* [2007] Elgar European Law, p. 164.
85. Decision of December 14, 2007, Thomas Borgå v. the Municipality of Skive.

nities for tenderers when inviting them, which required that the contracting authority precisely and exhaustively describe the service it wants in its invitation. In this particular case, the contracting authority did not do so.

5.3. A mix of advertising and inviting tenderers

A contracting authority will often need to contact potential tenderers directly in order to make them tender for a specific contract. Otherwise, they will, in many cases, not be aware of the contract opportunity. Clearly, this does not rule out the option of advertising. However, it is important that the contracting authority does not give certain undertakings an advantage by contacting them and not others. Thus, it would not be permitted, for example, to advertise a contract in a place where not many undertakings would see the notice and, at the same time, only making one tenderer aware of the notice.

Nor is it permitted to make a tenderer aware of the fact that a notice will be published beforehand and then state very short time limits for submitting tenders. This would also breach the principle of equal treatment. Therefore, when a contracting authority chooses to advertise and at the same time contact potential bidders, the authority must be careful not to give one tenderer an advantage over other tenderers, as this could potentially breach the principle of equal treatment.

In a Danish case, *VKAREN v. Odense Kommune*,[86] the contracting authority had annulled a tender procedure concerning a B-service contract. The Authority had announced to the tenderers that it intended to put the contract out for competition again, thereby creating a new procedure, and that it would give the tenderers notice when doing so. Four months later, the contracting authority issued a new call for competition by a contract notice on its own website. Due to a mistake made by the contracting authority, one of tenderers from the previous procedure had not been informed about the new contract opportunity. The tenderer brought a complaint to the Complaints Board, stating that the missing notice was contrary to the principle of equal treatment. The Complaints Board found that it was not a breach of either the principle of equal treatment or the Danish national rules.[87] In my opinion, this decision was incorrect. It follows from the principle of equal treatment that some tenderers should not be given information that other tenderers do not receive.

86. Decision of February 2, 2010, VKaren v. Odense Kommune.
87. Also in the decision of February 11, 2010, Einar J. Jensen A/S v. Guldborgsund Kommune did the Board find that there is not a duty to contact the same undertakings that have submitted tenders under a cancelled invitation to participate for a new tender procedure.

This must also apply regardless of the fact that the information in this case only concerned information the contracting authority's announcement of a new procedure. However, given that the undertaking in question had a clear expectation that it would be informed about the new tender procedure, it is my opinion that the contracting authority was obliged to inform the tenderer about it.

5.4. Following the rules in the Public Sector Directive voluntarily

For various reasons, a contracting authority might wish to apply the rules stated in the Public Sector Directive without being obliged to do so. In fact, the Commission's Evaluation report shows that a high number of contracts in which a contract notice has been published in the OJ, fall below the thresholds. For works contracts, this was the case for approximately 70 percent of all published contract notices.[88]

Even though the contracting authority is not obliged to follow the procedural rules in the Public Sector Directive when entering into one of the three types of contracts, it can choose to apply the rules anyhow and may publish a contract notice in the OJ. This was stated in the *Commission v. Ireland*,[89] where the Court found that:

> *'... the fact that Ireland requested the publication of the relevant notice in the Official Journal of the European Union, as permitted under Article 36 of the Directive, does not mean that that Member State is under any obligation to award that contract in accordance with the provisions of the Directive'.*[90]

Therefore, publishing such a contract notice does not also lead to an obligation to follow the procedural rules in the Public Sector Directive. On one hand, the Court's approach is reasonable, as it should not mean that just be-

88. Commission's Evaluation Report *'Impact and Effectiveness of EU Public Procurement Legislation'*, part 1 SEC(2011) 853 final, p. 117. However, this does not mean that the Public Sector Directive covers the award of the contract, the contract can be a part of an aggregated contract for which the combined value is above the thresholds or similar.
89. Case C-226/09, Commission v. Ireland, [2009] November 28, 2010, (not yet reported).
90. See Case C-226/09, Commission v. Ireland, [2009] November 28, 2010, (not yet reported), paragraph 40. The same was concluded in Case C-45/87, Commission v. Ireland, [1988] ECR 4929, where the Commission had tried to argue that since Ireland had published a contract notice it also had to apply the rules in the first Works Directive, despite the contract not falling under the Directive (utilities), the Court, however, rejected such argument.

cause the contracting authority choses to advertise a contract broadly should lead to stricter obligations (to be covered by the full procurement regime) as a consequence hereof. However, a contract where the value is close to the thresholds or similar can make it difficult for the tenderers to be aware of whether the contract is covered by the Directive or whether the contract falls outside the Directive. Therefore, it should be possible in some exceptional situations that the contracting authority would be obliged to follow the rules in the Directive as a consequence of potentially having misled the tenderers to think that the Directive covers the contract in question. This could be the situation if the contracting authority has stated in the contract notice that it intends to follow the Directive's rules.

6. Summary of findings

In the recent proposal for a Directive on Concessions, the Commission stated that:

'Moreover, both the definition of concessions ***and the precise content of the obligations of transparency*** *and non-discrimination arising from the Treaty remain unclear'* [emphasis added].[91]

Thus, the Commission indicates that it is also of the opinion that it remains unclear what the precise content of the transparency obligation is. In my opinion, the current state of law, based on the above analysis, leads to the fact that the transparency obligation requires the contracting authority to ensure that a contract has been put out for some sort of competition before entering into the contract. This is necessary in order to ensure competition for the contract and to ensure that equal treatment of undertakings takes place, which is the overall aim of the EU public procurement rules.

In some cases, it will be necessary to advertise a contract beforehand, if it is not possible for the contracting authority to create sufficient amount of competition for the contract by other means. This is particularly important in cases where the contracting authority is not aware of what exists on the market. However, it is my opinion that it cannot be derived from the case law that a contracting authority is under a general duty to advertise the three types of contracts beforehand. In my view, creating sufficient competition will be the first obligation and it will sometimes be necessary to open such a competition

91. The explanatory note to the Proposed Concessions Directive.

to everyone, in which case the contracting authority must advertise beforehand. Thus, the amount of publicity for the contract depends on the specific contract and the market in the Member States.

CHAPTER 8

Other Positive Obligations[1]

1. Introduction

This chapter analyses and discusses whether other obligations derived from the principles of the Treaties (in addition to the transparency obligation analysed in chapter 7) apply when contracting authorities are entering into one of the three types of contracts.

As seen in chapter 6, if the contract is of 'certain cross-border interest', a contracting authority must ensure in all cases that the Treaties' principles of equal treatment and transparency are observed throughout all phases of the competition.

The application of the principles of the Treaties might lead to obligations similar to those required under the Public Sector Directive because many of the provisions in the Procurement Directives are merely expressions of the principles. Thus, some of the requirements in the Public Sector Directive may be 'transferred' to apply when entering into one of the three types of contracts, or the Court of Justice may find inspiration in the Procurement Directives as to which requirements apply when interpreting the principles of the Treaties.[2] However, even though a few cases have appeared before the Court of Justice on specific matters,[3] whether obligations similar to those in the

1. A small part of this chapter will be published in Hansen, Carina Risvig *"Chapter 8, Treaty requirements for contracts 'outside' the procurement Directives"* in Trybus, Martin, Caranta, Roberto & Edelstam Gunille (Eds) *"EU Law and Public Contracts"* Bruylant Brussels [2012] – forthcoming.
2. Called the leverage principle by Treumer, Steen and Werlauff, Erik *"The Leverage Principle: Secondary Law as a Lever for the Development of Primary Community Law"* [2003] ELR n° 1, 28(1) pp. 124-133.
3. Joined Cases, C-147 and C-148/06, SECAP Spa and Santorso Soc. coop. arl v. Comune di Torino, [2008] ECR I-3565, Case C-226/09, Commission v. Ireland, [2009] November 18, 2011, (not yet reported), Case C-95/10, Strong Segurança SA

Public Sector Directive will apply when awarding one of the three types of contracts remains to be seen.

This chapter examines some specific issues relevant to awarding a contract that falls within the Public Sector Directive and analyses whether similar obligations as under the Public Sector Directive can be said to derive from the principles of the Treaties; therefore, making them applicable when awarding one of the three types of contracts.

1.1. Outline

Section 2 makes some general observations as to whether the rules in the Public Sector Directive are transferrable. Section 3 analyses whether certain requirements apply when a contracting authority describes the contract. Section 4 analyses the procurement procedures, whether they allow for negotiations and whether specific time limits are necessary. Section 5 concerns selection and award criteria. Section 6 analyses whether the Court of Justice's case law on ex post amendments of a contract also apply when amending one of the three types of contracts.

2. Are the rules of the Public Sector Directive transferrable?

As explored in chapters 3–5, for various reasons the Public Sector Directive does not cover the three types of contracts. Therefore, the most logical conclusion is that the rules of the Public Sector Directive do not apply for such types of contracts. On the other hand, arguably many of the provisions in the Directive are merely expressions of the principles of the Treaties; therefore, they would also apply when awarding one of the three types of contracts.

Advocate General *Fennelly* argued in her opinion to *Telaustria* that the transparency obligation does not

> *'... require the awarding entity to apply by analogy the provisions of the most relevant of the Community procurement directives'.*[4]

v. Município de Sintra, Securitas-Serviços e Tecnologia de Segurança, [2011] March 17, 2011, (not yet reported).

4. Opinion of Advocate General Fennelly delivered on May 18, 2000 in Case C-324/98, Telaustria Verlags GmbH and Telefonadress GmbH v. Telekom Austria AG, [2000] ECR I-10745, paragraph 43.

Others have suggested that some requirements could '... *be imported into the Treaty, also, through the Treaty's transparency obligation.*'[5] Thus, the Court may find inspiration in secondary law (here, the Public Procurement Directives) to apply similar obligations under primary law (here, the principles of the Treaties). *Treumer* and *Werlauf* call this use of secondary law the leverage principle.[6]

The question of whether some rules in the Public Sector Directive apply has been the subject of a few cases on specific matters before the Court of Justice. In *Commission* v. *Ireland,*[7] the question of weighting award criteria for a B-service contract was being disputed, and the Court of Justice stated in that regard that

> '... *it would be necessary for the specific rule governing the prior weighting of the award criteria for a contract falling within the ambit of Annex II A to the Directive to be regarded as constituting a* ***direct consequence of the fact that the rities are required to comply with the principle of equal treatment and the consequent obligation of transparency***' [emphasis added].[8]

Thus, emphasising that the rules could not apply as a consequence of the Directive, but must be found within the Treaties (which the Court found that it did not; see section 5.2.4).

5. Arrowsmith, Sue *"The Law of Public and Utilities Procurement"* [2005] 2nd Edition, Sweet and Maxwell, p. 194. Also Brown argues that some requirements from the Directives might apply outside the Directives, see Brown, Adrian *"Seeing through transparency: the requirement to advertise public contracts and concessions under the EC treaty"* [2007] PPLR n° 1, pp. 1-21. See also Treumer, Steen *"The discretionary powers of contracting entities – towards a flexible approach in the recent case law of the European Court of Justice?"* [2006] PPLR, n° 3, pp. 71-85, who states: *'In the concrete case [Telaustria edt], the transparency obligation, based on the Treaty principle of non-discrimination on the ground of nationality, is likely to be developed on the basis of the Public Procurement Directives.'*
6. Treumer, Steen and Werlauff, Erik *"The Leverage Principle: Secondary Law as a Lever for the Development of Primary Community Law"* [2003] ELR n° 1, 28(1) pp. 124-133.
7. Case C-226/09, Commission v. Ireland, [2009] November 18, 2010 (not yet reported).
8. Case C-226/09, Commission v. Ireland, [2009] November 18, 2010 (not yet reported), paragraph 41.

Another recent case *Strong Segurança SA*,[9] addressed whether Article 47(2) of the Public Sector Directive applied when entering into a B-service contract. In the case, the undertaking Strong Segurança SA had submitted a tender and based its financial standings on a third undertaking. According to Article 47(2) of the Public Sector Directive, this action is permissible for contracts falling within the Directive as long as the economic operator can prove '*that it will have at its disposal the resources necessary, (...)*'.[10] Portugal had not provided for the use of Article 47(2) in its national legislation for B-services (which was not required).

Regarding whether the provision was applicable for B-services as a consequence of the Directive, the Court stated that

> '... *there is no indication* ***from the wording of the provisions*** *of Directive 2004/18,* ***or from its spirit and general scheme****, that the subdivision of the services into two categories is based on a distinction between the "substantive" and "procedural" provisions of that directive*' [emphasis added].[11]

Thus, according to the Court, neither the wording nor the spirit of the Directive required that Article 47(2) apply to B-services.

Therefore, the relevance of the debate on the applicability of other provisions in the Public Sector Directive could be questioned because the Court clearly stated that the provisions of the Public Sector Directive do not apply to B-services. However, even though the Court found that the Directive did not apply, it went on to examine whether the principles of transparency and equal treatment could consequently result in the application of Article 47(2) to the case (if the contract was of 'certain cross-border interest'). Thus, the Court acknowledges the possibility that requirements similar to the rules in the Directive apply as a consequence of the principles of the Treaties.

Regarding the principle of transparency, the Court found that

9. Case C-95/10, Strong Segurança SA v. Município de Sintra, Securitas-Serviços e Tecnologia de Segurança, [2011] March 17, 2011, (not yet reported). The case is commented by Smith, Susie *"No obligation to apply specific provisions in the Public Sector Directive to contracts for Annex II B services: Strong Seguranca SA v. Municipio de Sintra (C-95/10)"* [2011] PPLR n° 4, NA 125-127.
10. Article 47(2) of the Public Sector Directive.
11. Case C-95/10, Strong Segurança SA v. Município de Sintra, Securitas-Serviços e Tecnologia de Segurança, [2011] March 17, 2011, (not yet reported), paragraph 31.

> *'... the fact that an economic operator cannot rely on the economic and financial capacities of other entities* ***has no connection with the transparency*** *of the contract award procedure'* [emphasis added].[12]

Thus, relying on another undertaking for economic and financial capacity could not be derived from the principle of transparency and

> *'... application of Articles 23 and 35(4) of Directive 2004/18 during the contract award procedures relating to such "non-priority" services is* ***also intended to ensure the degree of transparency that corresponds to the specific nature of those contracts****'* [emphasis added].[13]

By stating that the Directive already decided the amount of transparency for B-services, it is doubtful that the Court will interpret other provisions in the Procurement Directives to apply as a consequence of the principle of transparency. However, at the same time, the Court did not make any reference to the transparency obligation (as this was already complied with; see chapter 7). Therefore, it can be argued that the Court might not have ruled out exhaustively that some rules in the Directive could apply as a consequence of the principle of transparency.

Regarding the principle of equal treatment, the Court found that not applying Article 47(2) could not give rise *'... to any discrimination, direct or indirect, on the basis of nationality or place of establishment'*.[14] The Court found that if Article 47(2) could be interpreted to derive from the principle of equal treatment, such interpretation could result in other obligations in the Public Sector Directive applying, such as *'... the qualitative criteria for the selection of candidates (Articles 45 to 52) as well as the contract award criteria (Articles 53 to 55)'*.[15] Moreover, the Court found that such obligations would risk making ineffective the distinction between A-services and B-services laid down in the Directive.[16] Thus, the Court found that Article 47(2) was not a consequence of the principle of equal treatment.

12. Case C-95/10, Strong Segurança SA v. Município de Sintra, Securitas-Serviços e Tecnologia de Segurança, [2011] March 17, 2011, (not yet reported), paragraph 39.
13. Case C-95/10, Strong Segurança SA v. Município de Sintra, Securitas-Serviços e Tecnologia de Segurança, [2011] March 17, 2011, (not yet reported), paragraph 39.
14. Case C-95/10, Strong Segurança SA v. Município de Sintra, Securitas-Serviços e Tecnologia de Segurança, [2011] March 17, 2011, (not yet reported), paragraph 41.
15. Case C-95/10, Strong Segurança SA v. Município de Sintra, Securitas-Serviços e Tecnologia de Segurança, [2011] March 17, 2011, (not yet reported), paragraph 42.
16. Case C-95/10, Strong Segurança SA v. Município de Sintra, Securitas-Serviços e Tecnologia de Segurança, [2011] March 17, 2011, (not yet reported), paragraph 42.

The Court of Justice seems to conclude that since services are divided into two categories, the rules in the Public Sector Directive are not applicable to B-services since the EU legislator has decided not to cover these contracts by the Directive. Nevertheless, the Court still indicates that the principles of transparency and equal treatment could in certain cases lead to some obligations. However, for the rules of the Directive to apply, the rules must be a concrete consequence of the principles of equal treatment and transparency; furthermore, the Court doubted that selection and award criteria could be such a consequence.

With respect to the result, I find the Court's approach in the case to be correct. Article 47(2) is a precise provision that does not leave much discretion in its interpretation; therefore, such a provision cannot be derived from the principles of the Treaties. However, had the Court come to the opposite conclusion; this would perhaps not have been surprising, as the Court was already willing to impose a transparency obligation when awarding such contracts. Therefore, the Court might have concluded differently regarding other requirements of the Directive. Even though the question is highly relevant, the Court ruled without an opinion from an Advocate General.

The Court of Justice's ruling could be interpreted as its way to stop the development of a secondary regime for contracts outside the Directive. After *Telaustria,*[17] many criticised the Court for creating obligations that were not found within secondary legislation.[18] Thus, *Strong Segurança SA* can be said to show that the Court has sought to stop the development of placing obligations on contracting authorities when awarding a contract that does not fall within the Directive.

Nevertheless, despite the above cases, the question remains as to whether some of the elements contained in the Directive are already a consequence of the principles of the Treaties. For example, in *SECAP,*[19] the Court of Justice could be said to have found inspiration in its case law and the rules of the Public Sector Directive.

17. Case C-324/98, Telaustria Verlags GmbH and Telefonadress GmbH v. Telekom Austria AG, [2000] ECR I-10745.
18. See chapter 1, section 3.1.1.1.
19. Joined Cases C-147 and C-148/06, SECAP SpA and Santorso Soc. coop. arl v. Comune di Torino, [2008] ECR I-3565. The case is commented by Ølykke, Grith *"Abnormally low Tenders – with an emphasis on public tenderers"* [2010] DJØF p. 201. See also Graells, Albert Sánchez *"Public Procurement and the EU Competition Rules"* [2011] Hart, p. 323.

In the case, an Italian court asked the Court of Justice whether the principles of the Directive's provision on abnormally low tenderers also applied to a contract that fell below the thresholds. According to Article 55 of the Public Sector Directive, a contracting authority can reject a tender that appears abnormally low, but not until the tender has been verified to be abnormally low. Thus, before rejecting the tender, the contracting authority is required to request explanations from the tenderers as to why the tender appears low.[20] National Italian legislation stated that a contracting authority was obliged to reject tenderers identified as abnormally low on the basis of a certain mathematical threshold. Despite the fact that there can be many reasons why a contracting authority wishes not to award a contract to a tenderer, which has submitted a tender, which is abnormally low (such as for example the risk of non-performance if the tenderer is bankrupt or similar), the contracting authority had in the case not rejected such a tenderer. The Court of Justice found that even though the contract fell below the thresholds, if a contract is of certain cross-border interest, the contracting authority was not permitted to exclude the apparently abnormally low tender based on a

> *'... mathematical criterion laid down by the national legislation without allowing those contracting authorities any possibility of verifying the constituent elements of those tenders by requesting the tenderers concerned to provide details of those'.*[21]

The Court based its ruling on the fundamental rules of the Treaty on freedom of establishment and freedom to provide services and the general principle of non-discrimination and, thus, not on the rules of the Public Sector Directive. Even though the ruling was based on the Treaty's principles, that the Court found inspiration in the case law applicable to contracts falling within Directive 2004/18/EC could be argued.

The Directive does not allow the rejection of a tender that appears abnormally low before verifying the reason for the tender being low. Thus, the Court 'transferred' this situation to outside the Directive, meaning that the Court does not rule out that Member States are not allowed to have national rules regarding the exclusion of abnormally low tenders in their national system, but only that the contracting authority must conduct a verification pro-

20. Article 55 (1) of the Directive 2004/18/EC. See Ølykke, Grith *"Abnormally low Tenders – with an emphasis on public tenderers"* [2010] DJØF.
21. Joined Cases C-147 and C-148/06, SECAP SpA and Santorso Soc. coop. arl v. Comune di Torino, [2008] ECR I-3565, paragraph 35.

cess before a tender can be rejected. Thus, the Court also found that similar requirements under the Public Sector Directive apply outside the Directive.

However, that the detailed rules in the Directive can be considered expressions of the Treaties' principles is doubtful.[22] The Directives are built on the principles of the Treaties;[23] therefore, many Court of Justice cases are ruled upon using these principles. Thus, that some of the case law can be applicable to the three types of contracts is possible. Sections 3-6 discuss and examine some of the case law for which the Court of Justice ruled on the grounds of the provisions in the Treaties.

3. Specifications and description of the contract

The principles of transparency and equal treatment imply that tenderers must know what they are competing for and how the procedure will be conducted.[24] Thus, information on the subject matter of and the conditions related to the contract must be clear from the outset. As with contracts falling under the Procurement Directives, the amount of details depends on the type of contract; hence making general statements on the minimum amount of information that must be provided to potential tenderers is difficult. Contracting authorities have a wide discretion in describing the subject matter of a contract, regardless of whether described in functional or technical terms.

To ensure equal treatment of tenderers and to create transparency, the information provided must be sufficient to convey the intent of the contract and how it will be awarded. In other words, what the contracting authority seeks to buy and how an undertaking will be awarded the contract must be transparent. Thus, tenderers must be given sufficient knowledge of the contract to allow them to submit a competitive tender.

22. In line with Arrowsmith, Sue *"The Law of Public and Utilities Procurement"* [2005] 2nd Edition, Sweet and Maxwell, p.194, footnote 65, who argues: *'Obviously some of the more detailed rules regulating discretion would not be imported in the same form – for example, the rules limiting selection criteria in the public sector directives'.*
23. See also Case C-243/89, Commission v. Denmark, [1993] ECR I-3353, paragraph 33 wherein it was stated that the principle of equal treatment lies within the heart of the Directive.
24. In line with the 2006 Communication, which states that the participants must *'be able to know the applicable rules in advance and must have the certainty that these rules apply to everybody in the same way'.*

A contracting authority is obliged to follow its own requirements, as stipulated at the outset of the competition, throughout the procedure to ensure transparency and equal treatment of tenderers.[25] Furthermore, as the General Court has found the invitation to tender must specify clearly

'*the subject-matter and the conditions of the tendering procedure, and to comply strictly with the conditions laid down, so as to afford equality of opportunity to all tenderers when formulating their tenders.*'[26]

Thus, the manner in which the tender procedure will be conducted must be clear from the outset.

The contract must be described in an objective manner to ensure equal treatment of tenderers[27] and to avoid potential discrimination and preferences for a domestic undertaking. Furthermore, the contracting authority may not include requirements contrary to the TFEU's provisions on free movement, such as a requirement that the tenderers should have an office at a specific location before submitting tenders,[28] or referring to a specific type of make (see section 3.1). Furthermore, the contracting authority must accept certain types of documentation otherwise it would make participation in the competition for the contract more difficult for non-domestic tenderers (see section 3.2 for the principle of mutual recognition).

25. In line with the opinion of Advocate General Stix-Hackl delivered on April 12, 2005, in Case C-231/03, Consorzio Aziende Metano v. Comune di Cingia de' Botti, [2005] ECR I-7287, paragraph 86, who states '*... the requirements stipulated at the outset of the award procedure must be met and must be applied in the same manner to all candidates*'.
26. Joined Cases T-191/96 and T-106/97, CAS Succhi di Frutta v. Commission, [1999] ECR II-3181, paragraph 73. See also Case T-203/96, Embassy Limousines & Services v. European Parliament, [1998] ECR II-4239, paragraph 85, and Case T-125/06, Centro Studi Antonio Manieri Srl v. the Council, [2009] ECR II-69, paragraph 87, where it was stated that the principle of transparency: '*... implies an obligation upon the contracting authority to publish all precise information concerning the conduct of the entire procedure*'.
27. This is also the Commission's view. See the 2006 Communication, which states that contracting authorities are required to have a: '*non-discriminatory description of the subject matter of the contract*'. Also the Commission Interpretative Communication on Concessions under Community Law (2000/C121/02) states the choice of candidates must be made on basis of objective criteria and that the award procedure must be conduction in accordance with the procedural rules originally set.
28. Case C-234/03, Contse and Others, [2005] ECR I-9315, paragraph 43.

3.1. Reference to a make or similar

In the contracting authority's description of the contract regarding the technical specifications it is not allowed to refer to a specific make, source or particular process unless the subject matter of the contract justifies such a reference and is accompanied by the words 'or equivalent.' This has been stated in *Vestergaard*[29] for contracts below the threshold.[30]

In *Vestergaard,* the Court found that the contracting authority was not allowed to state in the contract notice that the windows to be used in the works contract should be of a specific Danish make, '*Hvidbjerg Vinduet.*' The Court of Justice found that even though the contract fell below the thresholds,

'the lawfulness of a clause (...) must be assessed by reference to the fundamental rules of the Treaty, which include the free movement of goods set out in Article 30 of the Treaty.'[31] Hereafter, the Court concluded that *'Article 30 of the Treaty precludes a contracting authority from including in the contract documents for that contract a clause requiring the use in carrying out the contract of a product of a specified make, without adding the words "or equivalent".'*[32]

In *UNIX,*[33] a case prior to *Vestergaard* concerning a contract coming under Directive 77/62, the contracting authority required that the UNIX operating system should be used for supply and maintenance of a weather station. The Court of Justice held that

'... the fact that the term UNIX was not followed by the words "or equivalent" (...), may also impede the flow of imports in intra-Community trade, contrary to Article 30 of the Treaty, (...)'.[34] Therefore, the Court found that *'the contracting authority should have add-*

29. Case C-59/00, Bent Mousten Vestergaard v. Spøttrup Boligselskab, [2001] ECR I-9505.
30. A related question concerns the subject of labels, which can be highly relevant when the contracting authority wishes to lay down environmental characteristics in terms of performance or functional requirements. In such a case they may use the technical specifications behind such a label under certain conditions stated Article 23(6) of the Public Sector Directive. However, referring to the label itself is not permitted, see also Case C-368/10, Commission v. The Netherlands, [2012] May 12, 2012 (not yet reported) and the Opinion of Advocate General Kokott in the case delivered on December 15, 2011. Article 42 of the Proposed Procurement Directive suggests widening the scope for labels my making it permissible to refer to such.
31. Case C-59/00, Bent Mousten Vestergaard v. Spøttrup Boligselskab, [2001] ECR I-9505, paragraph 21.
32. Case C-59/00, Bent Mousten Vestergaard, [2001] ECR I-9505, paragraph 24.
33. Case C-359/93, Commission v. Netherlands, [1995] ECR 1-157.
34. Case C-359/93, Commission v. Netherlands, [1995] ECR 1-157, paragraph 27.

ed the words "or equivalent" after the term UNIX, as required by Article 7(6) of Directive 77/62'.[35]

Whereas the Court of Justice in *Vestergaard* referred only to the Treaty, in *UNIX* the Court also referred to Article 7(6) of Directive 77/62, which expressly required that the wording 'or equivalent' should be stated. Thus, a difference in the scope of the prohibition may exist for contracting authorities to state a certain make under the Public Sector Directive for contracts falling outside the Directive.

The following is a comparison of the current provision in the Public Sector Directive with the previous similar provision in the Works – and Supply Directives.

Directive 93/37/EEC Article 10(6) – A similar provision was found within Directive 93/36/EEC, Article 8(6)	**The current Public Sector Directive Article 23(8)**
Unless such specifications are justified by the subject of the contract, Member States shall prohibit the introduction into contractual clauses relating to a given contract of technical specifications which mention products of a specific make or source or of a particular process (...). However, if such indication is accompanied by the words 'or equivalent', it shall be authorized in cases where the contracting authorities are unable to give a description of the subject of the contract using specifications which are sufficiently precise and intelligible to all parties concerned.	Unless justified by the subject-matter of the contract, technical specifications shall not refer to a specific make or source, (...) Such reference shall be permitted on an exceptional basis, where a sufficiently precise and intelligible description of the subject-matter of the contract pursuant to paragraphs 3 and 4 is not possible; such reference shall be accompanied by the words 'or equivalent.'

In the current Public Sector Directive, reference to a make is only permitted on an *'exceptional basis'*, whereas the prior Works Directive and Supply Directive allowed for such a reference if contracting authorities *'are unable to give a description of the subject of the contract'*. Thus, arguably, the Public

35. Case C-359/93, Commission v. Netherlands, [1995] ECR 1-157, paragraph 28. The case was in line with Case C-45/87, Commission v. Ireland, [1988] ECR 4929. In this case, the Court had found that stating in the specifications that certain pipes for a contract regarding construction of a water main, should comply with an Irish standard infringed Article 28 EC [Article 34 TFEU]. Thus, the contracting authority should have allowed for 'equivalent products'.

Sector Directive has limited the scope for referring to makes because doing so is now only permitted on an exceptional basis.

It is the technical specifications, which may not refer to a specific make. The Court has recently stated that the MAX HAVELAAR label, which are used when showing that a product is fair trade does not correspond to the definition of technical specification (as defined in Article a(b) of Annex VI to Directive 2004/18), given that the definition applies exclusively to the characteristics of the products themselves.[36] Compliance with the criteria, which an undertaking should have before being able to obtain the label, fell instead within Article 26 regarding conditions for performance of a contract.[37]

None of the before-mentioned cases from the Court of Justice elaborated on *when* making a reference to a make is permitted, and in all three cases in which the dispute arose the contracting authority would not accept alternative products. *Arrowsmith* indicated that in *UNIX* the Court only allowed for the phrase 'or equivalent' because this was the only way to describe the authorities' requirement.[38] Thus, stating a make is only allowed if describing the contract in other terms (including in functional terms) is not possible; furthermore, because stating a make is only allowed on an exceptional basis, the possibility should be interpreted as limited.

Clearly, under either Article 34 TFEU or the Directive, contracting authorities cannot state in a given contract that a specific make is required to be used if the contracting authority is able to describe the contract. However, in my opinion this requirement should not be interpreted as limited under the Treaty. Under the Treaty it might be easier to justify that it is permitted to state a make, as long as it is always followed by the words 'or similar/equivalent'.[39]

Several cases before the Danish Complaints Board of Public Procurement deal with whether stating a make is permitted.

Brøndum A/S v. Ringgården[40] concerned a framework agreement under the Public Sector Directive regarding plumbing equipment in various apart-

36. Case C-368/10, Commission v. the Netherlands, [2012] May 12, 2012 (not yet reported), paragraph 74.
37. Case C-368/10, Commission v. the Netherlands, [2012] May 12, 2012 (not yet reported), paragraph 75.
38. Arrowsmith, Sue *"The Law of Public and Utilities Procurement"* [2005] 2nd Edition, Sweet and Maxwell, p. 1131.
39. In line with Dethlefsen, Peter & Pedersen, Claus, Kaare *"Tilbudsloven: Bygge & Anlæg"* [2002] Thomson, p. 75. See also Poulsen, Sune U.2008B.41 *"Om henvisning til varemærker ved udbud af offentlige kontrakter"*.
40. Decision of November 5, 2008, Brøndum A/S v. Ringgården.

ments. The contracting authority argued that the reference to a specific make was made because it wished to maintain, to the greatest possible extent, the same appearance for the plumbing elements, which the Complaints Board found to be a valid reason. This case is an exception and is to date the only case in which the Board found stating a make justified under the Directive. The case indicates that stating a make can be permitted in situations in which the contracting authorities want to supply an already exiting contract with something similar. The Complaints Board has found that if the contract can be described using technical specifications[41] or in functional terms,[42] then referring to a specific make is not permitted. The Board even goes so far as to require the contracting authority to seek technical assistance if it does not have the competence to describe the contract itself.[43]

Regarding contracts outside the Public Sector Directive, the Complaints Board takes a more practical point of view. In *Scan-Plast v. Herning Kommune*,[44] which concerned a works contract below the thresholds, the contracting authority stated that the exterior cladding should be *'as larch'*. The Complaints Board found this statement justified since it only indicated that the type of tree should have the same properties as larch. In the decision; *Dansk Glas v. Christians Sogns Menighedsråd*, which concerned a works contract below the thresholds, only two undertakings were invited to submit a tender. The Board found that in such a case, stating a reference that the windows to be used were a specific make (also followed by 'or similar') was justified.[45]

41. Decision of March 12, 2009, Lyreco v. Varde Kommune, the Board found it to be prohibited to state a make in relation to a supply contract falling under the Public Sector Directive since it was possible to describe the contract. Decision of May 19, 2009, Anker Hansen v. Rudersdal Kommune, the Board found that it was prohibited to state make in relation to a works contract under Directive 2004/18/EC, the technical requirements could have been described. Same reasoning applied in decision of October 14, 2009, Frederik Petersen v. Viborg Kommune, and decision of June 21, 2011, Hørkram v. Roskilde Kommune.
42. Decision of August 5, 2003, Georg Berg A/S v. Køge Kommune, where the Board found that it was not permitted to state a make since the function could be described.
43. Decision of March 1, 1999, Enemærke & Petersen A/S v. Fællesorganisationens Boligforening Slagelse, where the Board found that stating a make was not justified by the contract in question as the contracting authority could have used technical assistance when specifying the contract.
44. Decision of September 20, 2010, Scan-Plast v. Herning Kommune.
45. Decision of February 16, 2011, Dansk Glas v. Christians Sogns Menighedsråd.

Thus, the Danish Complaints Board also seems to interpret the TFEU and the Directive as being different in how they permit stating a make for contracts falling within the Directive and for contracts outside the Directive.

3.2. Mutual recognition of diplomas and similar

Contracting authorities must accept the products and services supplied by economic operators in other Member States if these products and services are similar to those in the domestic Member State. This is based on the principle of mutual recognition that, according to the Court of Justice, leads to the assumption that once a certain product is legal in one Member State it will also fulfil the criteria for legality in other Member States.[46] Thus, a contracting authority must accept non-domestic tenderers' diplomas or certificates, or other evidence of the tenderer being qualified, when evidence of a particular qualification is required for participation in a procurement procedure.[47] Naturally, the principle of mutual recognition also applies when awarding one of the three types of contracts because it is found within the Treaty.

In *Medicap,*[48] the Court of Justice ruled on a specific matter regarding a contract for medical devices and whether the contracting authority was permitted to reject a tender as technically unacceptable if such products bear the CE marking. The disputed contract concerned a contract below the thresholds. The Court found that the harmonisation of CE certificates in the field of medical products required contracting authorities to follow the procedures in this specific harmonisation Directive when seeking to reject a tenderer. This Directive harmonises the essential requirements to be met by medical devices that fall within its scope of application. Once those devices comply with the

46. See Case C-120/78, Rewe-Zentral AG v. Bundesmonopolverwaltung für Branntwein, [1979] ECR 649. See also, for example, Case C-340/89, Irène Vlassopoulou v. Ministerium für Justiz, Bundes- und Europaangelegenheiten Baden-Württemberg, [1991] ECR I-2357 and Case C-76/90, Manfred Säger v. Dennemeyer & Co. Ltd., [1991] ECR I-4221.
47. See, for example, also the Communication on Concessions, which states: '... *the Member State in which the service is provided must accept the technical specifications, checks, diplomas, certificates and qualifications required in another Member State if they are recognised as equivalent to those required by the Member State in which the service is provided'.*
48. Case C-6/05, Medipac-Kazantzidis AE v. Venizeleio-Pananeio, [2007] ECR I-4557. The Case is commented by Brown, Adrian *"The Overlap between EC procurement principles and the safeguard procedures laid down in Directive 93/42/EC concerning medical devices: a note on C-6/05 Medipac-Kazandazidis AE v. Venizelio-Pananio"* [2007] PPLR n° 6, NA 159-162, who finds that the outcome of the case was not surprising.

harmonised standards and are certified in accordance with the procedures provided for by that directive, they *'must be presumed to comply with those essential requirements and therefore be deemed to be appropriate for the use for which they are intended'*.[49] If a contracting authority assumes that a product does not meet this standard, the Directive lays down a procedure for ascertaining whether this is actually the case. The contracting authority did not follow this procedure; thus, according to the Court of Justice, not only did the contracting authority breach the Directive that harmonised these products, it also breached the principle of equal treatment and the obligation of transparency. According to the Court, these breaches precluded a contracting authority that specified that certain products should bear a given CE marking

> *'from rejecting, directly and without following the safeguard procedure provided for in Articles 8 and 18 of Directive 93/42, on grounds of protection of public health, the materials proposed, if they comply with the stated technical requirement'*.[50]

Thus, also for cases in which the contract falls outside the Directive, if a product bears a CE make, it must be allowed for use.

4. Procedures

Chapter 7 concluded that the contracting authority must ensure that genuine competition for the contract has taken place, which sometimes creates an obligation to advertise the contract beforehand. The question is whether an obligation to advertise also means an obligation to follow one of the procedures laid down in the Public Sector Directive. In my opinion, it does not, because no such requirement can be found to be a consequence of the principles of the Treaties.[51] A contracting authority is only required to ensure that competition is created for the contract. In that regard, the contracting authorities can

49. Case C-6/05, Medipac-Kazantzidis AE v. Venizeleio-Pananeio, [2007] ECR I-4557, paragraph 42.
50. Case C-6/05, Medipac-Kazantzidis AE v. Venizeleio-Pananeio, [2007] ECR I-4557, paragraph 54.
51. Also in line with Krugner, Matthias *"The principles of equal treatment and transparency and the Commissions Interpretative Communication on Concessions"* [2003] PPLR n° 5, pp. 181-207, which states regarding service concession contract *'There is no need to stick to the procedures prescribed in the procurement Directives.'* See also chapter 7, section 5.4 regarding the choice for contracting authorities to voluntarily follow the rules in the procurement Directives.

choose to follow one of the procedures in the Public Sector Directive, combine the procedures or create their own procedure that fits the needs of the specific contract as long as it ensures that competition is created for the contract (see chapter 7).[52]

Changing the procedure along the way is not allowed for contracts falling within the Public Sector Directive. This was seen in the *Wallonian Bus* case.[53] In that case, Belgium claimed that since it was not obliged to award the contract through an open procedure, it could have chosen a negotiated procedure and thereby no breach would have taken place.[54] However, the Court rejected such an argument and found that even though the negotiated procedure could have been used,

> *'... once they have issued an invitation to tender under one particular procedure, they are required to observe the rules applicable to it, until the contract has been finally awarded'.*[55]

Thus, once a contracting authority has stated that a certain procedure will be followed, the contracting authority must ensure that the procedure is in fact applied. To ensure transparency and equal treatment, this also applies when awarding one of the three types of contracts. However, making amendments such as changing the time limits, certain minimum criteria and conditions for participating along the way when dealing with one of the three types of contracts should be possible to a greater extent than under the Procurement Directives. However, as the starting point in the absence of a specific required procedure, stipulating from the outset how a procedure will be conducted is necessary.

4.1. Negotiation

Whether the contracting authority is allowed to negotiate with tenderers during a competition for one of the three types of contract is a topic for discussion. Negotiating can be particularly relevant in complex contracts that require a certain dialogue with the tenderers and flexibility to ensure that the

52. Krugner, Matthias *"The principles of equal treatment and transparency and the Commissions Interpretative Communication on Concessions"* [2003] PPLR n° 5, pp. 181-207, states: *'The only requirement contracting authorities have to meet is that the procedure chosen does not constitute a restrain on the market access opportunities'.*
53. Case C-87/94, Commission v. Belgium, [1996] I-2043.
54. Case C-87/94, Commission v. Belgium, [1996] I-2043, paragraph 34.
55. Case C-87/94, Commission v. Belgium, [1996] I-2043, paragraph 35.

contracting authority gets the best value for its money. Contrary, for very small contracts of a standard type of good, it will be a costly affair for economic operators to tender for the contract if it is necessary to spend many resources on conducting negotiations. This, will be particular a disadvantageous for SME's. Furthermore, negotiating can have a negative impact on the competition because it creates the risk that the principle of equal treatment will be breached. Thus, guaranteeing effective competition is one reason to conclude that negotiating should not always be allowed[56] when entering into one of the three types of contracts.

Under the first Works Directive, the Council and the Commission issued a common statement regarding negotiations in connection with the open and restricted procedure.[57] According to the Council and the Commission, negotiations with candidates and tenderers in the restricted and open procedure:

> *'... on fundamental aspects of contracts, variations in which are likely to distort competition, and in particular on prices, shall be ruled out. However, discussions with candidates or tenderers may be held, but only for the purpose of clarifying or supplementing the content of their tenders of the requirements of the contracting authorities and provided this does not involve discrimination'.*

The statement is linked to the Procurement Directives, but as these Directives do not explicitly ban negotiation, the statement has greatly influenced the content of the ban on negotiation.[58] The extent to which this statement is a direct consequence of the principle of equal treatment determines whether the content of the statement also applies to the three types of contracts. In my view, the principles of the Treaties do not permit negotiation *per se*.[59] Nego-

56. Graells, Albert Sánchez *"Public Procurement and the EU Competition Rules"* [2011] Hart, p. 340.
57. Statement concerning Article 7 (4) of Council Directive 93/37/EEC of 14 June 1993 concerning the coordination of procedures for the award of public works contracts, [1994] OJ L111/114. A similar statement exists in relation to Article 20 of the Utilities Directive (Statement regarding Article 20 of Council Directive 93/38/EEC of 14 June 1993 coordinating the procurement procedures of entities operating in the water, energy, transport and telecommunications sectors, [1994] OJ L111/114).
58. Treumer, Steen *"Ligebehandlingsprincippet"*, DJØF 2000, p. 146 for critism of the statement as a legal source.
59. In line with Nielsen, Ruth *"Udbud af offentlige kontrakter"* [2010] 4th Edition DJØF, pp. 82-83. See also Berg, Henrik *"Udbud med forhandling – og hvordan forhandler man?"* in Hagel-Sørensen, Karsten (Ed.) *"Aktuel Udbudsret"* [2011]

tiation can create the *risk* of breaching the principle of equal treatment, but this possibility is not sufficient to rule out permitting negotiation. This view is also in line with contracts falling under the Utilities Directive, which always allows the use of a negotiated procedure when a contracting authority has published a call for competition in the OJ.[60] Thus, it can be argued that at least if one of the three types of contracts has been put out for open competition, negotiating with the tenderers afterwards would also permitted. Negotiation is also permitted under the Defence Directive because, as stated in Recital 47

'... the contracts covered by this Directive are characterised by specific requirements in terms of complexity, security of information or security of supply. Extensive negotiation is often required to satisfy these requirements when awarding contracts'.[61]

Thus, the principle of equal treatment does not lead to a ban on negotiation in these sectors, neither should negotiation be ruled out regarding the three types of contracts.[62] This has also been the conclusion before the Danish Complaints Board for Public Procurement.[63] In my opinion, it is also possibly, that the more complex a contract, the easier it is to justify that negotiation take place.[64]

Nevertheless, if negotiation takes place, the contracting authority must provide the tenderers with the same information (principle of equal treatment). Furthermore, that contracting authorities are allowed to negotiate does not mean that substantial parts of the contract are always up for negotiating.

DJØF, who does not discuss the subject but merely assumes that negotiation in relation to B-service contracts are permitted, see p. 134.

60. Article 40 (2) and Article 1(9) litra c of the Utilities Directive.
61. See Recital 47 of the Defence Directive. .
62. This also seems to be the General Court's view, where in Case T-258/06, Germany v. Commission, [2010] ECR II-2027, paragraph 129, it is stated that *'This is particularly relevant to procedures providing for negotiation with shortlisted tenderers. Such negotiations should be organised in a way that gives all tenderers access to the same amount of information and excludes any unjustified advantages for a specific tenderer'*. Thus, indicating that it is permissible to conduct a procedure with negotiation.
63. See decision of July 29, 2011, Social-Medicinsk Tolkeservice v. Region Hovedstaden where the Board found that it is allowed to negotiate when entering into a contract regarding a B-service.
64. The Proposed Procurement Directive suggest in Article 24 to widening the use of the competitive dialouge and a new procedure making the access for contracting authority to negotiate more available.

Such a situation could result in a change in the contract, which would require a new 'competition' because other potential tenderers may have been interested in the contract if these conditions had been known beforehand.

A review of the above-mentioned statement from the Commission and the Council shows that the subject can concentrate on two aspects: negotiations on fundamental aspects and clarifying or supplementing the content of a tender. The latter will always be permitted as long as the contracting authority allows for all tenderers to correct the same types of mistakes.

The statement indicates that price and other fundamental aspects of the contract that are likely to distort the competition may not be negotiated, indicating that once a tender has been submitted, negotiation could lead to the tenderer changing parts of its tender, which may restrict the competition. The case law from the Court of Justice provided little guidance on what may be considered fundamental aspects of a contract. In *Adia*,[65] a case before the General Court, a tenderer made a calculation error in price in its tender and was of the opinion that the Commission had breached the principle of equal treatment by refraining from contacting it to ensure that it could correct the mistake. The General Court found that the Commission had acted correctly by not asking the tenderer to correct the error. The Commission's approach was in accordance with the principle of equal treatment, since contacting the tenderer allowed it to correct elements other than price in the tender.[66] In that regard, the Court emphasised that the calculation error was not particularly obvious, and stated that,

> *'Any contact made by the Commission with the applicant in order to seek out jointly with it the exact nature and cause of the systematic calculation error would have involved a risk that other factors taken into account in order to establish its tender price'.*[67]

The Court of Justice has so far not ruled upon what can be the subject of negotiations when dealing with one of the three types of contracts, but in my opinion it is very likely that the Court would take a similar approach as under with negotiations under the Directive, as this approach is a consequence of the principles of equal treatment and transparency and hence not all elements may be the subject of negotiations.

65. Case T-19/95, Adia Interim SA v. Commission, [1996] ECR II-321.
66. Case T-19/95, Adia Interim SA v. Commission, [1996] ECR II-321, paragraph 51.
67. Case T-19/95, Adia Interim SA v. Commission, [1996] ECR II-321, paragraph 46-47.

4.2. Time limits

The Public Sector Directive contains different time limits depending on the type of procedure and the amount of transparency provided for by the contracting authority. These time limits have been set to ensure equal treatment of tenderers and to give them sufficient time to prepare and submit a tender. In my view, that a particular time limit will apply cannot be derived from the principle of equal treatment. Giving tenderers the same information regarding the procedure and equally applying the time limit to all tenderers concerned is sufficient for fulfilling the principle of equal treatment.

According to the 2006 Communication, contracting authorities awarding a contract regarding a B-service or a contract below the thresholds must apply *'appropriate time-limits'*, and such time limits should *'be long enough to allow undertakings from other Member States to make a meaningful assessment and prepare their offer'*.[68] Thus, the communication does not state that a particular time limit applies.

Some Member States have stated different time limits in their national legislation, whereas other let the contracting authorities impose appropriate time limits.[69] Often, time limits in the national legislation are shorter than the time limits in the Public Sector Directive, and they tend to range from 10 to 15 days for applications and from 10 to 25 days for the submission of tenders. They may often be shortened in the case of electronic submission.[70]

The principle of equal treatment requires the contracting authority not to change substantially the time limits once the procedure begins. Changing a time limit for submission of tenders could have the effect of discriminating against potential tenderers that restrained from bidding on a contract because of a short time limit – at least in situations in which the prolongation is sub-

68. See the 2006 Communication, section 2.2.1. According to the General Court in Case T-258/06, Germany v. Commission, [2010] ECR II-2027, paragraph 123, this part of the Communication *'... which seeks to prevent a contracting authority from excluding, through the time-limits granted to tenderers, the participation of an economic operator established in another Member State, flows from the principles of the EC Treaty, which means that this part of the Communication does not introduce a new obligation either'*.
69. OECD (2010), Support of Improvement of Governance and Management (SIGMA) Paper n° 45 *'Public Procurement in EU Member States: The Regulation of Contract Below the EU Thresholds and in Areas not Covered by the Detailed Rules of the EU Directives (2010)'*, section 1.4, p. 16.
70. Ibid., p. 16. Reduction of time limits can also be reduced under the current Public Sector Directive when using electronic means. See Article 38 of Directive 2004/18/EC.

stantial. In a recent case before the General Court, *Evropaïki Dynamiki v. Commission*,[71] the question of time limits for prolongation arose. The Commission prolonged a time limit by 35 days because it wanted to change the financial requirement of tenderers' turnover to make the contract available to additional tenderers. The Financial Regulation did not contain requirements related to a precise time limit for such a prolongation. The General Court found that the time limit must be extended

'long enough to allow interested parties a reasonable and appropriate period to prepare and submit their tenders (...) A time-limit which is reasonable and appropriate is a matter to be determined in the light of the circumstances of the individual case.'[72]

The Court found that a 35-day extension was sufficient and that the tenderers would have time to submit a bid.

The length of the time limit depends on the type of contract. A complex contract may require a longer time limit compared with a contract concerning simple delivery of goods. The Proposed Concessions Directive suggests setting a time limit of 52 days[73] (as the current Public Sector Directive). At the same time, the Proposal Procurement Directives suggests reducing the time limits in the public sector to 40 days.[74] According to the proposal on Concessions, *'It has been decided to provide for concessions a longer deadline than in case of public contracts, given that concession contracts are usually more complex.'*[75] In my view, the authorities should decide on whether a longer time limit is necessary for concession contracts because such contracts may not always be complicated and may not require a longer time limit. In this regard, the contracting authority and tenderers may possibly agree on a given time limit, which is permitted under the Utilities Directive.[76]

71. Case T-232/06, Evropaïki Dynamiki – Proigmena Systimata Tilepikoinonion Pliroforikis kai Tilematikis AE v. Commission, [2011] September 9, 2011, (not yet reported), paragraph 42. The case has been appealed (Case C-597/11 P).
72. Case T-232/06, Evropaïki Dynamiki – Proigmena Systimata Tilepikoinonion Pliroforikis kai Tilematikis AE v. Commission, [2011] September 9, 2011, (not yet reported), paragraph 41.
73. See Article 37 and 38 of the Proposed Concessions Directive.
74. See Article 45 of the Proposal for a Directive of the European Parliament and the Council on public procurement, COM (2011) 896 final.
75. See the Explanatory memorandum, to the Proposed Concessions Directive, p. 7.
76. See Article 45(3), litra b of the Utilities Directive. The option has also been suggested as possibility for sub central authorities in the Proposal Procurement Directive Article 26(4).

5. Award and selection criteria

The award and selection criteria to be used and how these must be weighted and disclosed is a subject of utmost importance and relevance for contracts covered by the Public Sector Directive, as well as for contracts outside the Directive. Selection and award criteria are essential to procurement matters and are often the subject of complaints by economic operators that believe that procedures were not conducted properly. Selection and award criteria must be in line with the principles of the Treaties to ensure equal treatment and transparency, and '*to afford fair conditions of competition to all economic operators interested in the contract.*'[77]

Thus, it is submitted that when awarding one of the three types of contracts, the contracting authority must use selection and award criteria, but whether the authority needs to follow the same rules as in the Public Sector Directive is questionable. To recall, the Court found in *Strong Segurança* that if Article 47(2) of the Public Sector Directive could be interpreted to constitute a consequence of the principle of equal treatment, this interpretation could cause other obligations in the Public Sector Directive to apply, such as '*... the qualitative criteria for the selection of candidates (Articles 45 to 52) as well as the contract award criteria (Articles 53 to 55)*'.[78] Additionally, according to the Court, such obligations would risk making ineffective the distinction between A-services and B-services as noted in the Directive.[79] Thus, whether other provisions apply outside the Directive must be determined solely based on the principles of the Treaties. Section 5.1 discusses selection criteria and section 5.2 discusses award criteria.

5.1. Selection criteria

Selection criteria relates to requirements for the undertaking that the contracting authority wishes to engage in a contract with. In that regard contracting authorities may establish conditions for participation relating to an undertaking's suitability to perform the task, the economic and financial standing of the undertaking or other conditions such as the technical and professional ability. Selection criteria are a measure to ensure that the economic operator being awarded the contract is actually qualified to perform the task.

77. The 2006 Communication.
78. Case C-95/10, Strong Segurança SA v. Município de Sintra, Securitas-Serviços e Tecnologia de Segurança, [2011] March 17, 2011, (not yet reported), paragraph 42.
79. Case C-95/10, Strong Segurança SA v. Município de Sintra, Securitas-Serviços e Tecnologia de Segurança, [2011] March 17, 2011, (not yet reported), paragraph 42.

Selection criteria are not a requirement for the contracting authority to use when awarding one of the three types of contracts, but when doing so these criteria must be objective and must apply equally to all undertakings. For example, setting selection criteria is not relevant when inviting only certain economic operators to tender for a contract. In such a situation, the contracting authority is assumed to invite only economic operators that it considers qualified.

A contracting authority cannot state requirements that restrict the free movement provisions, such as the requirement to have an office at a specific location before the submission of tenders,[80] or imposing other requirements that non-domestic undertakings will have more difficulty fulfilling.[81]

The principles of transparency and equal treatment call for candidates to be selected on the basis of known objective criteria. Thus, if the contracting authority wishes to use selection criteria, it must state the criteria in the tender documents. Otherwise it will make it impossible for undertakings to know whether they should bid for a given contract.

The Public Sector Directive contains provisions on exclusion of tenders and selection criteria. Some of these requirements are mandatory for the contracting authority whereas others are voluntary. Other provisions contain general requirements on the economic operators' ability to perform the contract in question.

Mandatory grounds for excluding tenderers are found in Article 45(1) of the Public Sector Directive. According to the provision, a contracting authority must exclude an economic operator under certain conditions, such as if the economic operator participated in criminal activities including corruption, fraud and money laundering. Even though the provision is relevant for obvious reasons, in my opinion the requirement cannot be found to be a consequence of the principles of the Treaties. Thus, for the contracting authority to apply requirements similar to those in Article 45(1) when awarding one of the three types of contracts will not be mandatory.

Article 45(2) of the Public Sector Directive addresses voluntary grounds for exclusion. According to this provision, the contracting authority can exclude an economic operator for several reasons, such as if the operator is

80. Case C-234/03, Contse and Others, [2005] ECR I-9315, paragraph 43.
81. In line with the 2006 Communications, which states: *'Contracting entities should not impose conditions causing direct or indirect discrimination against potential tenderers in other Member States, such as the requirement that undertakings interested in the contract must be established in the same Member State or region as the contracting entity.'*

bankrupt, is being wound up or has been found guilty of grave professional misconduct. The Court of Justice has stated that the previous Article 29 in the Service Directive, which is equivalent to Article 45(2), addresses the only limits to the power of the Member States in the sense that they cannot provide for grounds for exclusion other than those mentioned therein, and that power of the Member States is also limited by the *'... general principles of transparency and equal treatment'.*[82] Thus, because the Court refers to the principles of the Treaties, it is arguably only permitted to apply the grounds for exclusion stated in Article 45(2). Thus, in relation to the three types of contracts, the only grounds for exclusion based on the economic operator must be those set in Articles 45(1) and 45(2),[83] and it is submitted that contracting authorities are free to apply these grounds for exclusion because they do not go beyond the principles of the Treaties.[84]

5.1.1. Allowable selection criteria

Articles 46-48 of the Public Sector Directive contain voluntary selection criteria that are linked to the technical or economic capacity of an economic operator. The contracting authority is free to apply these criteria, but other criteria may also apply. When setting criteria, the principle of proportionality, which requires that criteria are disproportionate to the subject of the contract, must be observed.

82. Joined cases C-226/04 and C-228/04, La Cascina Soc. coop. arl and Zilch Srl v. Ministero della Difesa and Others (C-226/04) and Consorzio G. f. M. v. Ministero della Difesa and La Cascina Soc. coop. arl (C-228/04), [2006], ECR I-1347, paragraph 22.
83. However, a few exceptions can be found. See, for example, Joined cases C-21/03 and C-34/03, Fabricom SA v. Belgian State, [2005] ECR 2005 I-1559, where it according to the principle of equal treatment was possible to exclude an undertaking for reasons of conflict of interest. See also Case C-213/07, Michaniki AE v. Ethniko Symvoulio Radiotileorasis and Ypourgos Epikrateias, [2008] ECR I-9999, paragraph 24 where it was stated that Member States are not precluded from *'... providing for further exclusionary measures designed to ensure observance of the principles of equal treatment of tenderers and of transparency, provided that such measures do not go beyond what is necessary to achieve that objective'.*
84. See also Case C-95/10, Strong Segurança SA v. Município de Sintra, Securitas-Serviços e Tecnologia de Segurança, [2011] March 17, 2011, (not yet reported), paragraph 46, which stated that, the Directive does not preclude Member States: *'and, possibly, contracting authorities from providing for such application in, respectively, their legislation and the documents relating to the contract'.*

In *Serrantoni,*[85] the Court of Justice found that the national Italian legislation that automatically excluded members of a permanent consortium from participating in a tender procedure was not valid since it constituted *'... discrimination against that form of consortium, and does not therefore comply with the principle of equal treatment'.*[86] Thus, when a contracting authority sets selection criteria, these cannot discriminate against undertakings that have organised themselves in a certain way.

When selecting candidates, the contracting authority can require that the economic operator has a certain authorisation or similar qualifications. Nevertheless, when setting such a requirement, the free movement rules must be ensured. For example, requiring that a non-domestic operator must be a member of a domestic association is not permitted.[87]

Excluding a tenderer on the grounds that it did not submit the required documents and information to the contracting authority is possible. According to the Court of Justice, in *Greatbelt,*

> *'the principle of equal treatment of tenderers requires that all the tenders comply with the tender conditions so as to ensure an objective comparison of the tenders submitted by the various tenderers'.*[88]

Thus, if a tender has not complied with the stated conditions, for example, lack of submitting certain documents, it is possible to exclude such an undertaking.

The topic of excluding tenderers has been the subject of quite a few cases in Denmark – also in relation to B-services and contracts below the thresholds. For example, in *Keto Vikar ApS v. Københavns Kommune*[89] (regarding a

85. Case C-376/08, Serrantoni Srl and Consorzio stabile edili Scrl v. Comune di Milano, [2009] ECR I-12169.
86. Case C-376/08, Serrantoni Srl and Consorzio stabile edili Scrl v. Comune di Milano, [2009] ECR I-12169, paragraph 37.
87. See Case C-76/81, SA Transporoute et travaux v. Minister of Public Works, [1982] ECR 417, paragraphs 14-15.
88. Case C-243/89, Commission v. Denmark, [1993] ECR I-3353, paragraph 37. Paragraph 40 furthermore states: *'That requirement would not be satisfied if tenderers were allowed to depart from the basic terms of the tender conditions by means of reservations, except where those terms expressly allow them to do so.'*
89. Decision of April 22, 2010, Keto Vikar ApS v. Københavns Kommune. See also decision of March 10, 2010, Manova A/S v. Undervisningsminsteriet, where the Board found that since the contracting authority had asked certain tenderers to submit missing documents regarding their turnover, after the deadline for submis-

B-service contract), the Board found that the contracting authority had a duty to reject an application from an economic operator that did not submit a certain declaration, which was required in the tender material. If the contracting authority had accepted such a tender, the authority would, according to the Complaints Board, have acted contrary to the principle of equal treatment.

5.1.2. Shortlisting

According to the Public Sector Directive Article 44(3) when using a restricted procedure, negotiated procedure with publication of a contract notice or the competitive dialogue procedure the contracting authorities may limit the number of suitable candidates they will invite to tender, to negotiate or to conduct a dialogue with. However, when doing so, it shall be indicated in the contract notice which objective and non-discriminatory criteria or rules they intend to apply, as well as the minimum number of candidates they intend to invite and, where appropriate, the maximum number of candidates. The question is whether a similar rule can be found regarding the three types of contracts requiring the contracting authority to state from the outset which criteria will be used when reducing the number of economic operators to participate in the competition.

On the one hand it can be argued that contracting authorities are not required to use any form of procedure and therefore it should be more flexible if the contracting authority do in fact choose to create a competition for the contract by way of a procedure with prequalification, hence it should be more flexible for the contracting authority to state the conditions for short listing and perhaps also that the conditions are stated at a later stage. On the other hand, it is my opinion that it follows from the principle of transparency that tenders must know beforehand how they can be awarded the contract, which will also require knowing how an undertaking can be taken into consideration.[90] Thus, it is relevant for the contracting authority to state from the outset how undertakings will be selected and how a potential shortlisting will be done.

According to the Public Sector Directive

sion of applications, the contracting authority had in fact acted in breach of the principle of equal treatment.

90. See also the 2006 Communication which states that when limiting the number of applicants '*the contracting entity should provide adequate information on the mechanisms applied to select the applicants shortlisted.*'

'In the restricted procedure the minimum shall be five. In the negotiated procedure with publication of a contract notice and the competitive dialogue procedure the minimum shall be three. In any event the number of candidates invited shall be sufficient to ensure genuine competition.'[91]

Thus, a minimum of applicants must be pre-qualified. Such a minimum cannot be transferred to the three types of contracts, and hence is not necessary regarding the three types of contracts.[92] Thus, it will always be a concrete evaluation how many applicants are necessary to prequalify to ensure competition for the contract (see also chapter 7).

Concerning the permissible conditions regarding shortlisting, the Directive is silent regarding the choice of criteria to be used. Article 44(3) only requires that the criteria must be objective and non-discriminatory. Thus, it is possible to shortlist in many ways such as for example, choosing economic operator based on their general financial and technical position, hence using references, economic turnover etc. It is also possible to select different types of economic operators and chose some large undertakings and some small undertakings or start-ups.[93]

The question here is whether there is room for more flexible criteria to short list when dealing with the award of a contract outside the Directive. The Court of Justice has not yet rules on whether the criteria for shortlisting outside the Directive must also be criteria, which are objective and non-discriminatory, but according to the 2006 Communication they must be.

5.2. Award Criteria

5.2.1. Allowable award criteria

According to the Public Sector Directive, when awarding a contract the criterion *'lowest price'* or *'most economical advantageous tender'* must be used.[94]

91. Article 44(3).
92. In line with the 2006 Communication, which merely state 'In any event, the number of applicants shortlisted shall take account of the need to ensure adequate competition.'
93. For further on the topis see, for example, Arrowsmith, Sue (Ed.) *"EU Public Procurement Law: An Introduction"* [2010] Asia Link Project, p. 156 ff. Treumer, Steen *"The Selection of Qualified Firms to be Invited to Tender under the E.C. Procurement Directives"* [1998] PPLR n° 6, pp. 147-154.
94. Article 53 of Directive 2004/18/EC. The Proposal for a Directive of the European Parliament and the Council on public procurement, COM(2011) 896 final, suggest changing the criteria lowest price to lowest costs. See Article 66 of the proposal.

However, that only these two award criteria were found appropriate for contracts under the Public Sector Directive (as well as the Utilities Directive) does not mean that other award criteria could not satisfy the principles of the Treaties when awarding one of the three types of contracts. Neither the principle of equal treatment nor the principle of transparency requires that one of the two criteria stated in the Public Sector Directive to be used. Nonetheless, the award criterion must be objective. Therefore, in my opinion it is possible for the contracting authority to use award criterion such as 'most environmentally best tender' or only use quality as an award criterion.[95] Thus, in my view the overall award criterion does not need to be *'lowest price'* or *'most economical advantageous tender'*.

Once a contracting authority has stated the overall award criteria, using several sub-criteria is possible. Article 53 of the Public Sector Directive lists a set of criteria to be used when awarding a contract falling within the Directive. The list is not exhaustive.[96] When setting sub-criteria under the Public Sector Directive, the criterion must aim to identify the economically most advantageous tender.[97] However, this will not inevitably be the case for the three types of contracts because price is not required to be a criterion.

95. This is also the choice the Danish legislator has chosen regarding B-services and contracts below the thresholds concerning goods and services where no specific award criteria is requiered. See *"Lovbekendtgørelse om indhentning af tilbud på visse offentlige og offentligt støttede kontrakter nr 1410 af 7. December 2007"* § 15. [The Tender Act § 15], and confirmed in decision of January 30, 2012 Maja Consulting smba v. VisitNordsjælland F.M.B.A. Also a Scottish case, Sidey Ltd v. Clackmannanshire Council [2010] Court of Session (Inner House, First Division) March 5, 2010, paragraph 23, was it found that when awarding below-threshold contracts a public body is free to apply the *'best value'* criterion, as opposed to the most economically advantageous or lowest price criteria specified in the Directive. The case is commented by Henty, Poul *"A note on Sidey v. Clackmannanshire Council and Pyramid Joinery and Construction Limited"* [2010] PPLR n° 6, NA237-241.
96. See, for example, Case C-19/00, SIAC Construction Ltd v. County Council of the County of Mayo, [2001] ECR I-7725, paragraph 35.
97. Case C-31/87, Gebroeders Beentjes BV v. the Netherlands, [1988] ECR 04635, paragraph 19. See also Case C-513/99, Concordia Bus Finland Oy Ab v. Helsingin kaupunki and HKL-Bussiliikenne, [2002] ECR I-7213, paragraph 59, Case C-532/06, Emm. G. Lianakis AE, Sima Anonymi Techniki Etaireia Meleton kai Epivlepseon and Nikolaos Vlachopoulos v. Dimos Alexandroupolis and Others, [2008] ECR I-251, paragraph 29.

The Court of Justice held in *Concordia*[98] that environmental criteria were permitted if they fulfilled four conditions. Firstly, they must be linked to the subject matter of the contract (section 5.2.2). Secondly, they do not confer an unrestricted freedom of choice on the authority (section 5.2.4). Thirdly, they must be expressly mentioned in the contract documents or the tender notice (section 5.2.3). Fourthly, they must comply with all of the fundamental principles of EU law, in particular the principle of non-discrimination.[99] The final criterion, which requires that the principles must comply with the fundamental principles of the Treaty, will naturally apply for the three types of contracts.[100] It is submitted that these four principles will apply when awarding one of the three types of contracts, which will be discussed below.

5.2.2. Linked to the subject matter of the contract

According to case law from the Court of Justice for contracts falling within the Directive, award criteria must *'be linked to the subject-matter of the contract'*.[101]

Even though the Court bases this requirement on the fact that this is due to the criteria 'most economically advantageous tender',[102] it is my opinion that also when awarding one of the three types of contracts it is necessary that a sub-criterion must be linked to the subject matter. The Court stated in *Concordia* that

98. Case C-513/99, Concordia Bus Finland Oy Ab v. Helsingin kaupunki and HKL-Bussiliikenne, [2002] ECR I-7213.
99. Case C-513/99, Concordia Bus Finland Oy Ab v. Helsingin kaupunki and HKL-Bussiliikenne, [2002] ECR I-7213, paragraph 64.
100. See also Case C-234/03, Contse and Others, [2005] ECR I-9315, paragraph 49, where the Court found that evaluation criteria: *'... like any national measures, must comply with the principle of non-discrimination as derived from the provisions of the Treaty relating to the freedom to provide services'*.
101. Case C-513/99, Concordia Bus Finland Oy Ab v. Helsingin kaupunki and HKL-Bussiliikenne, [2002] ECR I-7213, paragraph 59.
102. See also Article 53 (1) (a) which is a codification of the case law and which states: *'... when the award is made to the tender most economically advantageous from the point of view of the contracting authority, various criteria linked to the subject-matter of the public contract in question.'*

> *'... Since a tender necessarily relates to the subject-matter of the contract, it follows that the award criteria which may be applied in accordance with that provision must themselves also be linked to the subject-matter of the contract.'*[103]

This will also apply to the three types of contracts, because a contract must be awarded on the basis of the subject of the contract and not on the basis of who will perform the contract. For tenderers to compete on something other than the contract makes little sense. Thus, I submit that award criteria for the three types of contract must be *'linked to the subject matter of the contract.'* However, certain criteria, such as environmental and social criteria, can possible be used to a further extent than under the Directive,[104] primarily because elements such as price do not need to be a part of the assessment, making room for other criteria such as experience, environmental and social consideration to be used instead. However, according to the *EVN* case,[105] the principle of equal treatment requires that contracting authorities effectively verify whether tenders meet the award criteria.[106] Thus, setting some requirements on the criteria to be used as verification becomes important to guarantee the award is transparent and non-discriminatory.

Under the Public Sector Directive, in all cases the contracting authority must ensure that a selection phase and an award phase take place. An evaluation of the two phases can take place simultaneously, but *'... the two procedures are nevertheless distinct and are governed by different rules'.*[107] The selection phase concerns the tenderers' suitability to perform a given task,

103. Case C-513/99, Concordia Bus Finland Oy Ab v. Helsingin kaupunki and HKL-Bussiliikenne, [2002] ECR I-7213, paragraph 59.
104. In line with Krugner, Matthias *"The principles of equal treatment and transparency and the Commissions Interpretative Communication on Concessions"* [2003] PPLR n° 5, pp. 181-207. For further on environmental consideration in Public Procurement see, for example, Caranta Roberto & Trybus, Martin (Eds) *"The law of green and social procurement in Europe"* [2010] DJØF, Arrowsmith Sue & Kunzlik Peter (Eds) *"Social and environmental policies in EC procurement law"* [2009] Cambridge University Press.
105. Case C-448/01, EVN AG and Wienstrom GmbH v. Austria, [2003] ECR I-14527.
106. Case C-448/01, EVN AG and Wienstrom GmbH v. Austria, [2003] ECR I-14527, paragraph 42 ff.
107. See in relation to works contracts, Case C-31/87, Gebroeders Beentjes BV v. the Netherlands, [1988] ECR 4635, paragraphs 15 and 16. Case C-532/06, Emm. G. Lianakis AE, Sima Anonymi Techniki Etaireia Meleton kai Epivlepseon and Nikolaos Vlachopoulos v. Dimos Alexandroupolis and Others, [2008] ECR I-251, paragraph 26 regarding services. Case C-199/07, Commission v. Greece [2009] ECR I-1669, paragraph 51.

whereas the award phase is an evaluation of the tender submitted for the specific contract in question. A highly relevant (and debated) question is whether elements linked to the suitability of a tenderer, such as tenderers' previous experience with the type of contract in question, is allowed during the award phase.[108]

This question arose in *Lianakis*,[109] in which the Court found that a contracting authority could not use as an award criterion the tenderers' previous experience and manpower. Such elements could only be used during the selection phase. The Court based its ruling in *Lianakis* on the fact that the criterion should be *'linked to the subject matter'*, which in my opinion also applies outside the Directive. Thus, arguably the Court could come to the conclusion that evaluating experience should not be permitted when awarding one of the three types of contracts. Contrary, having only one phase is permitted when awarding one of the three types of contracts. Therefore, experience could arguably be used as a criterion since no distinct selection and award phases exist. Thus, experience could in my opinion be more frequently used outside the Directive.[110]

If a contracting authority wishes to use previous experience as an award criterion, it must be linked to the subject matter of the contract. Therefore, for a simple contract concerning goods, tenderers' experience is not linked to the contract; thus, such criterion cannot be used. For certain service and works contracts, taking 'experience' into consideration is often relevant. In that regard it can be relevant that the contract are performed by persons that has previous experience and not just that the undertaking has experience. Thus, it can be relevant to make an evaluation of which persons the tenderer suggest should perform the actual contract. Thus, whether drawing a strict distinction

108. See, for example, the special issue of Public Procurement Law Review [2009] n° 3, pp. 103-164. In this issue case law from Germany, Italy, Belgium, Norway and Denmark are analysed in the context of before and after Lianakis.

109. Case C-532/06, Emm. G. Lianakis AE, Sima Anonymi Techniki Etaireia Meleton kai Epivlepseon and Nikolaos Vlachopoulos v. Dimos Alexandroupolis and Others, [2008] ECR I-251. See also Case C-199/07, Commission v. Greece [2009] ECR I- 1669, Case T-39/08, Evropaiki Dynamiki v. Commission, [2011] December 8, 2011 (not yet reported).

110. This is also the line the Danish Complaints Board for Public Procurement has taken. See decision of January 30, 2012 Maja Consulting smba v. VisitNordsjælland F.M.B.A, where the Board found that when dealing with a procurement below the thresholds or a B-service the contracting authority are more free to determine which sub-criteria to use and consequently experience was not permitted as a consequense of the principle of transparency.

between selection and award criteria can apply under the Treaties is doubtful.[111] In its new proposal for a Directive, the Commission has suggested that contracting authorities be able to use experience in certain situations.[112]

5.2.3. Whether award criteria must be mentioned beforehand

In theory, a lack of knowledge of the award criteria beforehand is equally true for all tenderers. However, not knowing the criteria beforehand also gives the contracting authority wide discretion that can lead to a more random choice and an unsuitable, non-transparent situation. Thus, it is submitted that award criteria must be present before the submission of tenders.[113] The award criteria need not be stated in the contract notice and can be disclosed at a later stage, provided that all tenderers receive the same information beforehand. In *SIAC*,[114] the Court found that

'... the award criteria must be formulated, in the contract documents or the contract notice, in such a way as to allow all reasonably well-informed and normally diligent tenderers to interpret them in the same way'.[115]

In *Universal Bau*,[116] the Court explicitly found that tenderers must have knowledge of the award criteria, and that this requirement follows from the principles of transparency and equal treatment. Thus, it is submitted that the principle of equal treatment and transparency provides legal basis for the requirement to disclose the award criteria. Setting a sole criterion such as 'the

111. In line with Brown, Adrian *"EU primary law requirements in practice: advertising, procedures and remedies for public contracts outside the procurement directives"* [2010] PPLR n° 5, pp.169-181.
112. See Article 66(2) of the Proposal. See also Recital 41, which states that *'For service contracts and for contracts involving the design of works, contracting authorities should also be allowed to use as an award criterion the organisation, qualification and experience of the staff assigned to performing the contract in question, as this may affect the quality of contract performance and, as a result, the economic value of the tender.'*
113. According to the Commission's 2006 Communication: *'All participants must be able to know the applicable rules in advance and must have certainty that these rules apply to everybody in the same way.'*
114. Case C-19/00, SIAC Construction Ltd v. County Council of the County of Mayo [2001] ECR I-7725.
115. Case C-19/00, SIAC Construction Ltd v. County Council of the County of Mayo [2001] ECR I-7725, paragraph 45.
116. Case C-470/99, Universale-Bau AG, v. Entsorgungsbetriebe Simmering GmbH, [2002] ECR I-11617.

economically most advantageous tender' will not make tenderers aware of what the contracting authority are emphasising. Thus, award criteria must be stated.[117]

Whether a contracting authority is required to publish its sub-criteria is a subject for discussion.[118] On the one hand, the principle of transparency requires that the sub-criteria describing the grounds on which a contract is to be awarded be stated.

Brown states that since full disclosure of elements is build on the principle of equal treatment and transparency, the Court of Justice

'... can be expected to find that the same duty of full disclosure applies equally to procurement procedures conducted under the Treaty'.[119]

I agree with this statement. The principles of transparency and equal treatment require the contracting authority to state the grounds for the award of the contract, which will allow the undertakings to be aware of what they are competing for. However, this does not mean that all elements must be described in the contract notice, and it is also likely that the Court will be more flexible when it comes to disclosure of sub criteria to award criteria when dealing with one of the three types of contracts.

5.2.4. Weighting of award criteria

Under the Public Sector Directive, a main rule is that the contracting authority weights the award criteria it intends to use, unless weighting the criteria can be justified as not possible. In the latter situation, listing the criteria in descending order is necessary.[120]

A requirement that calls for stating the weighting of the criteria cannot be found to be a consequence of the principles of the Treaties. Neither the prin-

117. In decision of April 8, 2010, KPI Communications A/S v. IT- & Telestyrelsen (regarding a B-service), the contracting authority had not stated any sub criterion to *'most economical advantageous tender'*, which the Board found was a breach. Thus, the contracting authority had to state sub-criteria as well.
118. See decision of July 20, 2011, Kijana v. Jysk Fællesindkøb, where the Board found that the contracting authority did not have a duty to publish sub criteria beforehand regarding a B-service contract. However, it was necessary that the contracting authority state sub-criteria, if he wishes to use such.
119. Brown, Adrian *"EU primary law requirements in practice: advertising, procedures and remedies for public contracts outside the procurement directives"* [2010] PPLR n° 5, pp. 169-181.
120. See the Public Sector Directive Article 53(2).

ciple of equal treatment nor the principle of transparency requires such a concrete assessment, which is also in line with the prior Procurement Directives that considered a list of the criteria in priority order as sufficient.[121]

In *Commission* v. *Ireland*,[122] the question of weighting award criteria for a contract regarding a B-service was disputed. In the case, the contracting authority set up seven sub-criteria for awarding the contract without stating the weighting of those criteria.[123] However, the contract notice stated that 'the award criteria should not be construed as being listed in descending order of importance'.[124] On the day of the submission of tenders, the members of the evaluation committee received an evaluation matrix suggesting specific relative weightings. The Court found that

> '... *the reference to the weighting of the award criteria in the case of a contract that is not subject to a provision such as Article 53(2) of the Directive does not constitute an obligation for the contracting authority*'.[125]

The Court found that the contracting authority's failure to give tenderers access to the weighting of the award criteria before the date of submission of the tenders was not a breach of the principle of transparency. However, the principles of equal treatment and transparency imply an obligation for the contracting authorities to interpret the award criteria in the same way throughout the procedure.[126] Thus, the contracting authority was not permitted to change the weighting *after* the opening of the tenders.

In *Intramed A/S v. Region Nordjylland*,[127] a Danish case before the Complaints Board of Public Procurement, the Board came to the opposite conclusion. Even though the decision came after the decision in *Commission v. Ireland*, the latter is not mentioned in the Complaints Board's decision. *Intramed A/S v. Region Nordjylland* concerned a contract below the thresholds

121. Case C-234/03, Contse and Others, [2005] ECR I-9315, paragraph 68.
122. Case C-226/09, Commission v. Ireland, [2009] November 18, 2010 (not yet reported).
123. Case C-226/09, Commission v. Ireland, [2009] November, 18 2010 (not yet reported), paragraph 14.
124. Case C-226/09, Commission v. Ireland, [2009] November 18, 2010 (not yet reported), paragraph 38.
125. Case C-226/09, Commission v. Ireland, [2009] November 18, 2010 (not yet reported), paragraph 43.
126. Case C-226/09, Commission v. Ireland, [2009] November 18, 2010 (not yet reported), paragraph 59.
127. Decision of February 4, 2011, Intramed A/S v. Region Nordjylland.

for an IT quality assurance system for registration of diabetes treatment. Regarding the award criteria, the contract notice stated that the contract would be awarded based on price, quality and the technical solution. Even though the criterion price was listed first, this criterion had the lowest weight. However, the contract notice did not state that it would be listed first. By having listed the criteria, the Complaints Board found that the contracting authority gave the tenderers the assumption that the criteria were listed in order of importance, which the Board found to be contrary to the principle of equal treatment and transparency. In the above-mentioned *Commission v. Ireland*, the contract notice stated that the award criteria should not be construed as being listed in descending order of importance, but the various criteria were numbered 1 through 7. Thus, a small difference existed in the two cases.

In my view, whether the result in the Danish case would have turned out differently had the contract notice stated that the criteria were not listed in prioritised order is not entirely clear. *Mengozzi* also argues in his Opinion to the *Commission v. Ireland* that the only reason for changing the criteria was because it was stipulated from the outset that the criteria were not listed in descending order.[128]

I do not find the Court's approach correct. A closer look at the principle of transparency shows that tenderers must be made aware of the criteria used when awarding a contract to ensure competition and compliance with the principle of equal treatment. This is especially the case when a certain criterion has more weight than other criteria. Otherwise, competition would be irrelevant, as tenderers would not know on which grounds they are competing. Nevertheless, as it stands, the Court of Justice case law seems to allow for the weighting of the criteria not to be stated and for the criteria not to be stated by priority as long as the contract notice states that the criteria are not listed.

6. Ex post contract amendments

Whether a contracting authority and the contractor are permitted to make amendments to the contract after the contract has been signed has gained focus, since in recent cases[129] the Court of Justice has dealt with this subject.[130]

128. Opinion of Advocate General Mengozzi delivered on June 29, 2010, in Case C-226/09, Commission v. Ireland, [2010] November 18, 2010 (not yet reported), paragraph 49.
129. Case C-454/06, Pressetext Nachrichtenagentur GmbH v. Republik Österreich (Bund), APA-OTS Originaltext-Service GmbH and APA Austria Presse Agentur

In every contractual relationship, making adjustments is necessary, but certain amendments can create a new duty that obliges the contracting authority to follow the procurement rules.

In *Pressetext*,[131] the Court of Justice found that amendments to a contract could constitute

> '... *a new award of a contract within the meaning of Directive 92/50 when they are materially different in character from the original contract and, therefore, such as to demonstrate the intention of the parties to renegotiate the essential terms of that contract'*.[132]

Thus, if after amendments a contract is considered materially different from the original contract, the contracting authority may be required to create a new competition for the contract. The Court of Justice repeated the statement from *Pressetext* in *Wall*[133] without emphasising the fact that *Wall* concerned a concession contract. Thus, the Court does not seem to indicate any difference in the treatment of amendments for a contract outside the Directive.[134] In fact, the Court found in *Wall* that,

registrierte Genossenschaft mit beschränkter Haftung, [2008] ECR I-4401, Case C-91/08, Wall AG v. La ville de Francfort-sur-le-Main and Frankfurter Entsorgungs- und Service (FES) GmbH, [2010] ECR I-2815, Case C-423/07, Commission v. Spain, [2011] May 19, 2011 (not yet reported).

130. See for example Brown, Adrian *"When do changes to an existing public contract amount to the award of a new contract for the purposes of the EU procurement rules? Guidance at last in Case C-454/06"* [2008] PPLR n° 6, NA253-267; Brown, Adrian *"Changing a sub-contractor under a public services concession: Wall AG v. Stadt Frankfurt am Main (C-91/08)"* [2010] PPLR n° 5, p. 160-166; Wahl, Morten Liljenbøl *"Ændringer i bestående kontraktforhold – udbudsretlige udfordringer i Offentlig-Private Partnerskaber (OPP)"* in TBB2010.15; Hartlev, Kristian & Liljenbøl, Morten Wahl *"Ændringer af udbudte kontrakter"* in Hagel-Sørensen, Karsten (Ed.) *"Aktuel Udbudsret"* [2011] DJØF.

131. Case C-454/06, Pressetext Nachrichtenagentur GmbH v. Republik Österreich (Bund), APA-OTS Originaltext-Service GmbH and APA Austria Presse Agentur registrierte Genossenschaft mit beschränkter Haftung, [2008] ECR I-4401.

132. Case C-454/06, Pressetext Nachrichtenagentur GmbH v. Republik Österreich (Bund), APA-OTS Originaltext-Service GmbH and APA Austria Presse Agentur registrierte Genossenschaft mit beschränkter Haftung, [2008] ECR I-4401, paragraph 34.

133. Case C-91/08, Wall AG v. La ville de Francfort-sur-le-Main and Frankfurter Entsorgungs- und Service (FES) GmbH, [2010] ECR I-2815.

134. See Brown, Adrian *"Seeing Through Transparency: the Requirement to Advertise Public Contracts and Concessions Under the EC Treaty"* [2007] PPLR n° 1, pp. 1-

*'In **order to ensure transparency of procedures and equal treatment of tenderers**, substantial amendments to essential provisions of a service concession contract could in certain cases require the award of a new concession contract (...)'* [emphasis added].[135]

Thus, the principles of equal treatment and transparency require that a contract not be amended to a degree that makes it materially different from the original contract. Moreover, when dealing with one of the three types of contracts, being aware of amendments to the original contract is necessary, as such amendments may result in the contracting authority being obligated to create a new competition for the contract.[136] However, whether contracting authorities have a greater room for amendments when dealing with amendments to one of the three types of contracts is a point for discussion. On the one hand, contracting authorities are under the same obligation to calculate the contract value and classify the contract,[137] thus requiring the contracting authority to know what it wants to buy and indicating that amendments should be treated in the same way outside the Directive. On the other hand, because service concession contracts are most often long term in nature, adopting certain changes during the life of the contract is likely; therefore, amendments should be possible. However, it is submitted that the assessment can be no different for the three types of contracts as for contracts falling under the Directive.

For example, according to the Court of Justice, a contract is considered materially different from the original contract when it introduces conditions that would have allowed for the admission of tenderers other than those initially admitted had they been part of the initial award procedure, or would have allowed for the acceptance of a tender other than the one initially ac-

21, who states: *'Even though the Pressetext principles were laid down in the context of changes to contracts within the procurement Directives, the Court simply assumed that those principles applied equally to public service concessions under the Treaty.'*

135. Case C-91/08, Wall AG v. La ville de Francfort-sur-le-Main and Frankfurter Entsorgungs- und Service (FES) GmbH, [2010] ECR I-2815, paragraph 37.
136. In line with Brown, Adrian *"Changing a sub-contractor under a public services concession: Wall AG v. Stadt Frankfurt am Main (C-91/08)"* [2010] PPLR n° 5, p. 160-166, who states that the Courts finding: *'would presumably be exactly the same whether the change of sub-contractor occurred under a 'contract within the procurement Directives or under a services concession falling outside the Directives.'*
137. See chapter 5, section 5.

cepted.[138] The contract may also be materially different if the amendment considerably extends the scope of the contract to encompass services not initially covered.[139] This situation is of particular importance for the three types of contracts because the nature of the contract can change, possibly leading to the application of the Public Sector Directive if, for example, the contract is above the thresholds. A modified contract can also be considered materially different if its economic balance changes in favor of the contractor in a manner not provided for in the terms of the initial contract.[140]

Furthermore, the Court found in *Wall* that,

'A change of subcontractor, (...), may in exceptional cases constitute such an amendment to one of the essential provisions of a concession contract where the use of one subcontractor rather than another was, in view of the particular characteristics of the services concerned, a decisive factor in concluding the contract, which is in any event for the referring court to ascertain.'[141]

Thus, changing the economic operator can lead to an amendment that requires a new competition.[142]

7. Conclusion

First of all, that the provisions in the Public Sector Directive do not apply to the three types of contracts unless so stated (Article 21 for B-services) must

138. Case C-454/06, Pressetext Nachrichtenagentur GmbH v. Austria, APA-OTS Originaltext-Service GmbH and APA Austria Presse Agentur registrierte Genossenschaft mit beschränkter Haftung, [2008] ECR I-4401, paragraph 35. See also Case C-91/08, Wall AG v. La ville de Francfort-sur-le-Main and Frankfurter Entsorgungs- und Service (FES) GmbH, [2010] ECR I-2815, paragraph 38 where the statement in Pressetext where repeated for concession contract.
139. Case C-454/06, Pressetext Nachrichtenagentur GmbH v. Austria, APA-OTS Originaltext-Service GmbH and APA Austria Presse Agentur registrierte Genossenschaft mit beschränkter Haftung, [2008] ECR I-4401, paragraph 36.
140. Case C-454/06, Pressetext Nachrichtenagentur GmbH v. Austria, APA-OTS Originaltext-Service GmbH and APA Austria Presse Agentur registrierte Genossenschaft mit beschränkter Haftung, [2008] ECR I-4401, paragraph 34-37.
141. Case C-91/08, Wall AG v. La ville de Francfort-sur-le-Main and Frankfurter Entsorgungs- und Service (FES) GmbH, [2010] ECR I-2815, paragraph 39.
142. In the Commission's Proposal for a new procurement Directive, it is suggested to introduce rules relating to the performance of the contract, hereunder modification of contracts during their term. See Article 71 of the proposal.

be pointed out. *Strong Segurança* and *the Commission v. Ireland* made this point clear. Thus, for obligations similar to those under the Public Sector Directive to apply to the three types of contracts, the obligations must be direct consequences of the principles of the Treaties.

The Directive's detailed requirements will not apply in the form in which they appear in the Directive, but when the contracting authority holds a competition regarding a contract outside the Directive, time limits must be long enough to allow undertakings to prepare their offers and the selection of tenderers. Moreover, the award of the contract must be based on objective criteria to create transparency and ensure equal treatment of undertakings.

Thus, it is submitted that many obligations similar to those for contracts falling under Directive 2004/18/EC apply for the three types of contracts as a consequence of the principles of the Treaties.

CHAPTER 9

Standstill[1]

1. Introduction

When a contracting authority seeks to enter into a public contract that falls under the Public Sector Directive, the authority is required to wait a certain period after the award decision has been informed to the tenderers until the contract in question can be signed.[2] This waiting period is called a standstill period and aims to give concerned tenderers the opportunity to bring proceedings before the contract has been entered into to ensure that an effective review is conducted.

The standstill obligation is a consequence of the Court of Justice's case law[3] and has been put into clear legislation through the newest amendment of the Public Sector Remedies Directive for contracts, which falls within the Public Sector Directive. This chapter analyses and discusses whether the principles of the Treaties imply that a standstill is also a positive obligation when a contracting authority is entering into one of the three types of contracts. This subject is important because standstill is a measure to ensure that the contract has been awarded correctly and, if not, that complaints can be filed when the possibility of changing the award decision still exists. The question of whether standstill applies outside the Directive has already been disputed before some national courts, but to date the Court of Justice has not ruled on the matter.

1. Some elements of this chapter have been published earlier. See, Hansen, Carina Risvig U. 2011.B. 101 *"Pligt til annoncering af offentlige kontrakter – uden effektiv håndhævelse af reglerne?"*
2. Article 2a of the Public Sector Remedies Directive.
3. Mainly Case C-81/98, Alcatel and others v. Bundesministerium für Wissenschaft und Verkehr, [1999] ECR I-7671 and Case C-212/02, Commission v. Austria, (not reported in the ECR).

Because standstill is an obligation that the contracting authority must observe before signing a contract, it is addressed in part II of the Thesis. This part of the Thesis analyses the obligations derived from the principles of the Treaties that contracting authorities must follow when entering into one of the three types of contracts. However, standstill must also be seen as an enforcement action because its main purpose is to give tenderers sufficient time to analyse the contracting authority's award decision before deciding on whether to bring proceedings before the contract in question has been signed. Standstill, for contracts falling within the Public Sector Directive is also linked to the remedies available for a review body, namely automatic suspension and ineffectiveness (see chapter 11). Nevertheless, because standstill can be a positive obligation for the contracting authority, and not for the review bodies to bear in mind when awarding a contract, I find it natural to place the chapter on standstill in part II of this Thesis.

1.1. Outline

Section 2 examines the subject of standstill, including its meaning and purpose. Section 3 analyses the rules on standstill as stated in the Public Sector Remedies Directive. Section 4 analyses whether standstill is an obligation for the three types of contracts based on the Treaties. In that regard, this section analyses the case law on standstill from the Court of Justice. Section 5 examines the possible length of a standstill period. Section 6 analyses whether a contracting authority is required to state reasons for its award decision when entering into one of the three types of contracts and, if so, the contents of such reasons.

2. What is standstill?

A standstill period is a mandatory period during which the contracting authority is not permitted to sign the contract but must wait until the period expires. The period begins when the tenderers have been informed about the contracting authority's decision on the tenderer awarded the contract (the award decision). However, before the period starts, the contracting authority must inform tenderers on the award decision and state why their tenders were not successful. Therefore, a standstill creates two obligations. Firstly, it gives the contracting authority the duty to inform the tenderers of the award decision and state the reasons for its decision. Secondly, the rules contain a duty for the contracting authority to ensure that a reasonable period has passed between informing the tenderers about the award decision and the conclusion of the contract (the standstill period). In the following, the term *standstill* is used when talking about both requirements (the requirement to inform tenderers and to state reasons and the requirement to wait a certain period), and *standstill period* is used when only discussing the period.

2.1. The purpose of standstill

The rules regarding standstill were added to the Public Sector Remedies Directive through the Amending Remedies Directive in 2007 as a consequence of Court of Justice case law. The purpose of introducing standstill into the Public Sector Remedies Directive was to allow for '... *effective review between the decision to award a contract and the conclusion of the contract in question.*'[4] A standstill period gives tenderers sufficient time to consider whether to bring proceedings before the contract is signed. Giving tenderers sufficient time to analyse and evaluate the contracting authority's reasons for not granting them the contract ensures that a procedure has taken place correctly. A proceeding brought to the review bodies before the signing of the contract allows the contracting authority to correct mistakes, which makes the enforcement system more effective and minimises the overall resources spent by the contracting authority. Therefore, when a contract falls within the Public Sector Directive, a specific minimum amount of time – *the standstill period* – must pass before the contract can be signed. According to the Public Sector Remedies Directive Article 2(1)(a) this standstill period must be a minimum of 10 calendar days when informing the tenderers and candidates by electronic communications, and 15 calendar days when informing the tenderers and candidates by mail.[5]

4. Recital 4 of the Amending Remedies Directive which furthermore state that the lack of a standstill period: '... *sometimes results in contracting authorities and contracting entities who wish to make irreversible the consequences of the disputed award decision proceeding very quickly to the signature of the contract'*.
5. In the Commission's proposal for a Directive of the European Parliament and of the Council amending Council Directives 89/665/EEC and 92/13/EEC, with regard to improving the effectiveness of review procedures concerning the award of public contracts SEC(2006)557, henceforth the proposal for amending the Remedies Directives, it was not an option for the contracting authority to use regular mail. It was stated '... *on which the contract award decision is communicated to the tenderers concerned by fax or electronic means'*. The introducing of two possible standstill periods *'reflects the reality of the 27 Member State, where electronic means, may not be equally widely available in all Member States'*, see in that regard Donnelly, Cathrine *"Remedies in public procurement law in Ireland"* [2009] PPLR, n° 1, pp. 18-41, p. 34.

Before introducing the standstill period, getting the contracting authority to change its award decision was not possible in most Member States, as the contract would already have been signed. However, the General Court has found that the award decision can be changed in situations in which the contract has not yet been signed. In *Antwerpse Bouwwerken v. European Commission*,[6] an undertaking protested a decision made by the Commission regarding a simple calculation error, which resulted in that undertaking not winning the contract. Pointing out the error to the Commission allowed it to redefine its award decision even though it had already announced the contract award to the tenderers.

A few cases before the Danish Complaints Board for Public Procurement discussed whether changing the award decision during the standstill period was possible.[7] However, these cases were handed down before the 'Enforcement Act', which implemented the Amending Remedies Directive, entered into force.[8] Preparatory work for the Enforcement Act now explicitly states that a contracting authority may change the award decision during the standstill period.

Another problem that existed before the adoption of the Amending Remedies Directive was that the national review bodies could not annul a contract. This inability generally meant that tenderers failed to bring proceedings, as the tenderers would not gain anything from doing so. A standstill period ensures that tenderers can complaint at a time when the review body still has the ability to set aside the award decision. The disadvantageous of standstill may be the risk of additional complaints being filed with the review bodies.[9] Fur-

6. Case T-195/08, Antwerpse Bouwwerken v. European Commission, [2009] ECR II-4439.
7. Decision of August 4, 2009, Mölnlycke v. Region Hovedstaden, the Board found that this was not possible because if the contracting authority could change its opinion, this could lead to tenderers seeking to persuade the contracting authority to do so and such a practice would involve a latent risk of unfair influence of the contracting authority. However, in decision of May 26, 2010, M.K Riisager Transport A/S v. Hjørring Kommune, the Board came to the opposite conclusion, even though the legal judge in the case argued that it was not possible due to the same reasons as had been stated in Mölnlycke v. Region Hovedstaden.
8. Act no. 492 of May, 12, 2010, latest amendment Act no 618 of, June 13, 2011, henceforth "the Enforcement Act" (Lov nr. 492 af 12. maj 2010, senest ændret ved lov nr. 618 af 14. juni 2011, håndhævelse af udbudsreglerne m.v.).
9. See, Thorup, Kirsten and Frimodt, Mette in U.2010B.303 *"Standstill Og Opsættende Virkning i Udbudsretten"* footnote 5, wherein it is stated that after the standstill rules entered into force in Denmark the amount of complaints went from 37 in 2006 to 115 in 2009.

thermore, standstill prolongs the procurement process, which a contracting authority must take into consideration when putting a contract out for competition.

Providing a specific period in the legislation improves legal certainty for tenderers in the sense that they know exactly how long they have to file a complaint before the contract is signed. Measures other than a Directive, such as an Interpretative Communication, were considered to determine their sufficiency. However, as can be seen from the Commission's proposal to amend the Remedies Directives, such a Communication was not found appropriate because

'... it could not have guaranteed the application in every Member State of a standstill period which was clearly defined and satisfactory in terms of the various situations covered by the Directives on public procurement'.[10]

The Commission found that with a Communication, differences in interpretations among the Member States regarding the scope of the case law would remain and these different interpretations would not *'... be removed by the Commission's adoption of an interpretative document'*. Therefore, specific rules on standstill were put into the Public Sector Remedies Directive.

Before the Commission proposed to amend the Remedies Directives, it was actively initiating enforcement proceedings against the Member States for lacking standstill rules in their national systems. Thus, at the time of adoption of the Amending Remedies Directive, most Member States had already introduced standstill rules. Therefore, if the Commission had issued a Communication on the matter, it arguably may have been sufficient. Nevertheless, a Directive ensures that a minimum number of days apply equally in all Member States and provides a specific date for the beginning of the standstill period. However, the number of days of the standstill period is the minimum number of days and Member States can choose to introduce longer standstill periods.[11]

In UK an increase of complaints has also been seen in the recent years. See, Trybus, Martin *"An Overview of the United Kingdom Public Procurement Review and Remedies System with an emphasis on England and Wales"* in Treumer, Steen & Lichère, Francois (Eds) *"Enforcement of the EU Public Procurement Rules"* [2011] DJØF p. 201.

10. The explanatory notes to the proposal for amending the Remedies Directive.
11. Italy, for example, has chosen 35 days. See Comba, Mario *"Enforcement of the EU Procurement Rules. The Italian System of Remedies"* in Treumer, Steen & Lichère

3. The standstill obligation under the Public Sector Remedies Directive

According to the Public Sector Remedies Directive, a contracting authority is, as a main rule, obliged to ensure that a standstill period has taken place before the signing of a contract falling within the Public Sector Directive. The standstill period begins on the day after the notice of the award decision has been sent to the concerned tenderers and candidates. According to the Amending Remedies Directive the contracting authority must inform at least *'... any person having or having had an interest in obtaining a particular contract and who has been or risks being harmed by an alleged infringement'.*[12] However, Member States could have chosen to implement time limits for complaints during the earlier phases of the procedure, hence excluding some persons from complaining during the standstill period. For example, in Denmark, the Enforcement Act § 7(2), sets a time limit for complaints regarding prequalification (30 calendar days).[13]

Furthermore, it is a requirement for the contracting authority to inform the tenderers of the award decision and provide 'a summary of the relevant reasons as set out in Article 41(2) of Directive 2004/18/EC, subject to the provisions of Article 41(3) of that Directive' is mandatory.[14] Additionally, the contracting authority must provide a precise statement on the expiration of the standstill period.[15]

Nonetheless, a contracting authority is not required to observe a standstill period in all cases when entering into a public contract. A few derogations are listed in the Public Sector Remedies Directive.[16] The list of derogations is

Francois (Eds) *"Enforcement of the EU Public Procurement Rules"* [2011] DJØF, p. 242. However, most Member States have chosen to implement the minimum period as required in the Public Sector Remedies Directive, such as, for example, Sweden, Denmark, Germany, and UK. See www.puplicprocurementnetwork.org (last visited January 20, 2012) for an overview of how the different Member States have chosen to implement various aspects of the Remedies Directives.

12. The Public Sector Remedies Directive Article 1(3), which according to the Directive Article 2a(1) are the relevant persons to inform. Article 2a(1) states that the Member States shall ensure that: *'... the persons referred to in Article 1(3) have sufficient time for effective review of the contract award decisions taken by contracting authorities'.*
13. For further on time limits see chapter 10.
14. The Public Sector Remedies Directive Article 2a(2).
15. The Public Sector Remedies Directive Article 2a(2).
16. The derogations are found in the Article 2b of the Public Sector Remedies Directive and deals with the following situations: *'(a) if Directive 2004/18/EC does*

exhaustive and is only available for a contracting authority if its Member State has implemented these derogations.[17]

One of these derogations gives the Member States the option not to implement the rules on standstill in situations in which the Public Sector Directive does '*not require prior publication of a contract notice in the Official Journal of the European Union*'.[18] The three types of contracts are all contracts that a contracting authority can enter into without prior publication of a contract notice in the OJ. However, only contracts below the thresholds and service concession contracts fall entirely outside the scope of the Public Sector Remedies Directive.[19] In other words, only if this exception has been implemented in the Member States is it possible to exclude B-services (above the thresholds) from the standstill requirements in the Public Sector Remedies Directive.

In addition to using the derogation for B-services, derogations were primarily intended for situations in which the contracting authority needs to enter into a contract in the case of extreme urgency, according to Public Sector Directive Article 31.[20] However, the derogations are not limited to such situa-

not require prior publication of a contract notice in the Official Journal of the European Union; (b) if the only tenderer concerned within the meaning of Article 2a(2) of this Directive is the one who is awarded the contract and there are no candidates concerned; (c) in the case of a contract based on a framework agreement as provided for in Article 32 of Directive 2004/18/EC and in the case of a specific contract based on a dynamic purchasing system as provided for in Article 33 of that Directive'. If a framework agreement concerns B-service contracts, the contracts will not fall under this provision due to the fact that B-services fall within Article 2b(1) a).

17. Most Member States have implemented all the derogations including Denmark, France, Ireland, the Netherlands, Poland, Romania, and United Kingdom. Germany has only implemented the first derogation partially in such a way that it can only be used when there is a need for extreme urgency in accordance with the Public Sector Directive Article 31, hence not for B-service contracts. See also Burgi, Martin *"A Report about the German Remedies System"* in Treumer, Steen & Lichère, Francois (Eds) *"Enforcement of the EU Public Procurement Rules"* [2011] DJØF, p. 127.
18. Article 2b (1)(a) of the Public Sector Remedies Directive.
19. B-services are covered by the Public Sector Remedies Directive, but can be excluded from many of the provisions therein. See chapter 10, section 3.3 for further on B-services and the Public Sector Remedies Directive.
20. The Amending Remedies Directive Recital 8 states that standstill does not apply where prior publication of a contract notice in the OJ is not necessary: '*... in particular in cases of extreme urgency as provided for in Article 31(1)(c) of Directive*

tions. I believe that if Member States does not implement the derogation for B-services it will be possible to declare a B-service contract ineffective if the requirements in the Public Sector Remedies Directive Article 2d(1)(b) are fulfilled.[21]

Therefore, the derogation in Article 2b(1)(a) of the Public Sector Remedies Directive is highly relevant for B-services. In the Commission's proposal to amend the Remedies Directives,[22] exempting B-services was not an option. Undoubtedly, the Commission wanted the standstill provisions to have covered B-services as well, but the wording gives Member States the power to decide on whether they want to cover B-services of the standstill provisions in their national legislation.[23]

4. Whether EU law requires standstill

As mentioned above, the standstill rules in the Public Sector Remedies Directive are a consequence of the case law from the Court of Justice from primarily two cases, *Alcatel*[24] and the *Commission v. Austria.*[25] Given that the Public Sector Remedies Directive's rules on standstill do not cover all types of contracts, the question is whether some sort of standstill is also required for the three types of contracts as a result of the principles of the Treaties. This question will be analysed in this section by examining at first the Court's case law.

Alcatel concerned a situation in which a contract[26] was awarded to an undertaking and signed on the same day. The other tenderers learned of the con-

2004/18/EC (...). In those cases it is sufficient to provide for effective review procedures after the conclusion of the contract.'

21. This will be elaborated on in chapter 11, section 2.4.
22. The proposal for amending the Remedies Directives.
23. For more on standstill in the Public Sector Remedies Directives, see, for example, Nielsen, Ruth, U.2007B.120, *"Standstill og ugyldighed/uvirksomhed af offentlige kontrakter"*; Golding, Jane and Henty, Paul, *"The new Remedies Directive of the EC: Standstill and ineffectiveness"* [2008] PPLR n° 3, pp. 146-154; Donnelly, Cathrine *"Remedies in public procurement law in Ireland"* [2009] PPLR, n° 1, pp. 18-41; Treumer, Steen & Lichère (Eds) *"Enforcement of the EU Public Procurement Rules"* [2011] DJØF.
24. Case C-81/98, Alcatel and others v. Bundesministerium für Wissenschaft und Verkehr, [1999] ECR I-7671.
25. Case C-212/02, Commission v. Austria, (not reported in the ECR).
26. The contract concerned the supply, installation and demonstration of all the hardware and software components of an electronic system for automatic data transmission to be installed on Austrian motorways.

tracting authority's decision through newspapers and applied for review before a national Austrian court. At the time of the proceedings, the Austrian court only had the power to adopt interim measures and set aside unlawful decisions made by a contracting authority until the award was made. After the award was made, the contracting authority only had the power to determine whether the contract was awarded to the tenderer that submitted the best offer. Thereafter, damages were the only possible remedy. The Austrian court asked the Court of Justice for a preliminary ruling on whether Member States are required to ensure that the contracting authority's award decision is, in any event, open to a procedure that allows an applicant to have that decision annulled if the relevant conditions are met, notwithstanding the possibility of restricting the legal effects of the review procedure to an award of damages once the contract has been concluded. The Court of Justice made it clear that an award decision must *'in all cases [be] open to review in a procedure whereby an applicant may have that decision set aside'*.[27] In that regard, the Court of Justice found that for an undertaking to be awarded damages afterwards was not sufficient.[28]

The Court of Justice made no comment on the duration of such a period or whether 'all cases' also include contracts falling outside the Public Sector Directive. The latter is not surprising because at the time that the Court gave its ruling in *Alcatel*, it had not yet handed down the ruling in *Telaustria*,[29] and that no positive obligations could be derived from the principles of the Treaty regarding the three types of contracts was the most common understanding.[30] Considering the *Alcatel* judgment, establishing a system in which a contracting authority's award decisions could be declared void (or ineffective) instead of introducing a standstill period might have been sufficient. This view is supported by *Arrowsmith*, which stated that,

27. Case C-81/98, Alcatel and others v. Bundesministerium für Wissenschaft und Verkehr, [1999] ECR I-7671, paragraph 43.
28. Case C-81/98, Alcatel and others v. Bundesministerium für Wissenschaft und Verkehr, [1999] ECR I-7671, paragraph 43, where the Court stated also stated: *'... notwithstanding the possibility, once the contract has been concluded, of obtaining an award of damages'*.
29. Case C-324/98, Telaustria Verlags GmbH and Telefonadress GmbH v. Telekom Austria AG, [2000] ECR I-10745.
30. See chapter 1, section 3.1.1.2.

'... the requirements of Alcatel could have been implemented by the alternative approach of allowing for limited set-aside of concluded contracts, and this would have been preferable'.[31]

The reason for *Arrowsmith* preferring this approach is that,

'It seems disproportionately disruptive to require a delay to every contract simply because of the remote possibility of challenge, especially when such disruption is generally opposed by all the participants in the process.' [32]

This might be the case in a Member State such as the UK, where procurement proceedings are rare and time consuming. However, in my opinion, in other Member States for which proceedings take place more often and that have faster systems, declaring the contract void would not be the most effective solution because extra side costs exist for declaring a contract void/ineffective, such as damages to the contracting party and the costs to create a new procurement procedure.

Nevertheless, when separately analysing *Alcatel*, I agree with the view that the case does not lead to an obligation for the contracting authority to have a standstill period before signing the contract. As suggested by *Arrowsmith*, in theory, doing so could be sufficient if a review body is able to declare the contract void/ineffective or terminate the contract. This is also in line with the approach of the Public Sector Remedies Directive with respect to framework contracts, which are awarded after a mini-tender procedure. In these cases, a contracting authority is not required to follow the standstill rules (if Member States have implemented this option). However, if the contract is entered into in breach of the Public Sector Directive (and the value of the contract is above the thresholds in the Public Sector Directive), Member States must ensure that such a framework contract can be declared ineffective.[33] Nevertheless, in *Commission v. Ireland*, the Court of Justice found that

31. Arrowsmith, Sue, *"Implementation of the new EC procurement directives and the Alcatel ruling in England and Wales and Northern Ireland: a review of the new legislation and guidance"* [2006] PPLR n° 3, pp. 86-136.
32. Arrowsmith, Sue, *"Implementation of the new EC procurement directives and the Alcatel ruling in England and Wales and Northern Ireland: a review of the new legislation and guidance"* [2006] PPLR n° 3, pp. 86-136.
33. Article 2d(1)(c) of the Public Sector Remedies Directive. The same applies for dynamic purchasing system. For further on framework agreements and standstill/ineffectiveness see Racca, Gabriella M. *"Derogations from standstill period, ineffectiveness and remedies in the new tendering procedure: efficiency gains vs.*

'... the fact that there is the option of bringing proceedings for the annulment of the contract itself is not such as to compensate for the impossibility of challenging the mere act of awarding the contract concerned, before the contract is concluded'.[34]

This seems to have ended the discussion and have required a standstill period.

Alcatel led to the Commission initiated enforcement actions against some (many) Member States for lack of implementation of the judgment, hereunder Austria,[35] Spain,[36] Ireland,[37] France[38] and Denmark. The Commission dropped its actions against Denmark because the country introduced a standstill period in its legislation.[39] The Commission's quite aggressive approach to initiating enforcement actions against Member States is interesting because the Member States are left to regulate their enforcement systems given the principle of national procedural autonomy. Moreover, for the Commission to initiate proceedings touches on a sensitive issue, which is also probably why the Member States (besides Denmark) did not just change their legislation, even though the cases went all the way to the Court of Justice.

In *Commission v. Austria*,[40] some clarification on the *Alcatel* case was given. The Court of Justice stated in that case that,

'Complete legal protection also requires that it be possible for the unsuccessful tenderer to examine in sufficient time the validity of the award decision. Given the requirement that the Directive ***have practical effect, a reasonable period*** *must elapse between the time*

risk of increasing litigations" in Treumer, Steen & Lichère, Francois (Eds) *"Enforcement of the EU Public Procurement Rules"* [2011] DJØF.

34. Case C-455/08, Commission v. Ireland, [2009] ECR I-225, paragraph 28. The case has been commented by Dunne, Mary *"Requirement to give reasons to unsuccessful tenderers before conclusion of the standstill"* [2010] PPLR, n° 3, NA87-90. She states: *'It was not enough, in the Court's view, that national legislation permitted the Irish courts to annul a contract if found to have been awarded in breach of procurement law.'*
35. Case C-212/02, Commission v. Austria, (not reported in the ECR).
36. Case C-444/06, Commission v. Spain, [2008] ECR I-2045
37. Case C-455/08, Commission v. Ireland, [2009] ECR I-225
38. Case C-327/08, Commission v. France, [2008] ECR I-102. The case is commented by Brown, Adrian, *"Commission of the European Communities v. France (C-327/08): a French provision breaches Remedies Directives 89/665 and 92/13 by jeopardising the effectiveness of the standstill period between notification of the award decision and conclusion of the contract"*, [2009] PPLR, n° 6, NA222-225.
39. The rules on standstill were implemented with "bekendtgørelse nr. 588 af 12. juni 2006". However, the rules are now to be found within the 'Enforcement Act', which entered into force July 2010.
40. Case C-212/02, Commission v. Austria (not reported in the ECR).

when the award decision is communicated to unsuccessful tenderers and the conclusion of the contract in order (...)' [emphasis added].[41]

The Court thereby introduced a reasonable period, in other words a standstill period, between the award decision and the signing of the contract to ensure legal protection for tenderers. The Court of Justice based its ruling in *Commission v. Austria* on the fact that the Public Sector Directive must have practical effect and must ensure that this 'reasonable period' elapse before signing the contract, *'in particular, to allow an application to be made for interim measures prior to the conclusion of the contract'.*[42]

What constitutes '*a reasonable period*' has now been resolved in relation to contracts that fall within the scope of the Public Sector Directive since the Amending Remedies Directive came into force. The Public Sector Remedies Directive now requires that the contracting authority have a standstill period of 10 or 15 calendar days depending on the communication measure used. For the three types of contracts, section 5 below discusses what constitutes sufficient time.

If a contracting authority can breach the rules of the Directive by not giving tenderers the ability to have the contracting authority's decision reviewed, the Directive will not be effective. Once the contract is signed, efficient review is no longer possible. In my opinion, to ensure that the principles of the Treaties (the obligations analysed in chapters 7 and 8) are effective, applying rules on standstill is necessary; thus, contracting authorities are required to ensure a sort of standstill period before signing one of the three types of contracts.

Standstill is not a remedy but is a measure to ensure that individuals can bring proceedings and pursue sufficient remedies. Individuals are entitled to effective judicial protection[43] and, in that regard, the observance of standstill can be an important tool to ensure the effectiveness of a review system. *Pachau* suggests that the principle of effectiveness

41. Case C-212/02, Commission v. Austria (not reported in the ECR), paragraph 23.
42. Case C-212/02, Commission v. Austria (not reported in the ECR), paragraph 23.
43. Article 47 of the Charter of Fundamental Rights of the European Union, states the right of everyone, whose rights and freedoms guaranteed by the law of the Union are violated to an effective remedy before an impartial tribunal. For further on the right to judicial review see chapter 10.

'... could be construed to concern not only ***each remedy separately but also a review system as a whole*** *and require its overall effectiveness, possibly by requiring that one remedy should complement and compensate for the other'* [emphasis added].[44]

Thus, whether the system is effective as a whole is relevant to examine. This argument also supports the view that standstill is necessary. Moreover, *Arrowsmith* questions the logic of excluding B-services from standstill

'unless some other provision is made to ensure that such awards can be effectively challenged', and furthermore argues that, *'Although they are not subject to most of the detailed obligations in the Directives/Regulations, the Remedies Directives on which the Alcatel ruling is based apply to all violations of Community law in procedures covered by the Directives and domestic implementing legislation.'*[45]

However, it must be borne in mind that she is talking about implementation in the UK and not in relation to whether standstill should be regulated at EU level.

Whether standstill is required outside the Directive has been the subject of a few national cases. In an Irish case,[46] the Irish court concluded that even though B-services were excluded from the national legislation on standstill, an obligation for a contracting authority to observe a standstill period when entering into a B-service contract existed in exceptional circumstances. In the specific case, the special circumstances involved factors such as a high contract value and cross-border interest. Several lower courts in France also decided that a reasonable period of time must exist between the award decision and the signing of contracts falling outside the scope of the Procurement Directives, but the Council of State has now ruled out the case.[47] A Belgium

44. Pachnou, Despina, *"Enforcement of the EC. Procurement Rules: The Standard Required of National Review Systems under E.C. Law in the Context of the Principle of Effectiveness"* [2000] PPLR n° 2, pp. 55-74.
45. Arrowsmith, Sue *"A review of the new legislation and Guidance"* [2006] PPLR n° 3, pp. 86-137. The Article is written before the Amending Remedies Directive was published and the standstill requirements dealt with here are the ones derived from the case law.
46. Federal Security Services Ltd v. Chief Constable for the Police Service of Northern Ireland [2009] NICh 3. See for further on the case, McGovern, Patrick *"Standstill Notice in Respect of Part B Services: The Decision in Federal Security Servicese Ltd v. Chief Constable for the Police Service of Northern Ireland and Resource Group Ltd,"* [2009] PPLR n°4, NA181-188.
47. Lichère, Francois *"Enforcement of EU Public Procurement Rules in France"* p. 307 in Treumer, Steen & Lichère, Francois (Eds) *"Enforcement of the EU Public*

court[48] found that no such rules on standstill exist. The fact that the national courts have come to different conclusions on the same matter is interesting and demonstrates the need for clarification on the issue. In my view, if presented with the question, the Court of Justice would likely rule that some sort of standstill must be observed.[49]

Note that although these types of contracts need to observe a standstill period, the standstill provisions in the Public Sector Remedies Directive do not apply. Furthermore, the rules in the Public Sector Remedies Directive require an automatic suspension when a complaint is handed to the review body during the standstill period, but this does not apply to a contract not covered by the standstill provisions (for more on automatic suspension see chapter 10). This condition is applied primarily because automatic suspension is a concrete procedural rule that cannot be derived from any of the principles of the Treaties and is only found in the Public Sector Remedies Directive, which does not cover service concession contracts and contracts below the thresholds. However, if Member States have not implemented the aforementioned derogation for standstill for B-services, then in my view the provision of automatic suspension will also apply to B-services.

5. The length of the standstill period

Assuming that a requirement exists to observe a standstill period for the three types of contracts, the next issue is the specific requirements for such a period. Standstill for the three types of contracts is not an obligation derived from the Public Sector Remedies Directive; instead, it comes from the principles of

Procurement Rules" [2011] DJØF. The French Court case, 29 Bis CE, 19 Janvier 2011, n° 343435.

48. La Cour d'arbitrage, Arrêt n° 179/2005 du 7 décembre 2005.
49. Also the opinion of Treumer, see Treumer, Steen *"The State of Law and Current Issues"* p. 49 in Treumer, Steen & Lichère Francois (Eds) *"Enforcement of the EU Public Procurement Rules"* [2011] DJØF. See also Brown, Adrian *"EU primary law requirements in practice: advertising, procedures and remedies for public contracts out side the procurement directives"* [2010] PPLR n° 5, pp. 169-81, who states: '*... In the interests of ensuring effective remedies for breaches of primary law principles, the Court of Justice may well rule that, at least where there has been some form of bidding procedure, public authorities bear an implied obligation to inform unsuccessful bidders and allow for a standstill period, before entering into the contract or concession, even where that contract or concession falls outside the procurement Directives.*'

the Treaties and its length is not specified but depends on the concrete contract in question. Nevertheless, the period must be long enough to ensure that an effective review can take place. In the aforementioned Irish case,[50] the court seemed to have emphasised elements, such as the value and type of the contract, which must also be considered when determining whether the contract is of cross-border interest (see chapter 6). Regarding the duty to observe standstill, in my opinion, such a duty exists only if the contract in question is of cross-border interest. If a contract is not of cross-border interest, the obligations derived from the principles of the Treaties, namely the principles of equal treatment and transparency, do not apply. Therefore, when these principles do not apply there will be no EU rules that must be ensured to be effective; and hence, standstill will not be a requirement derived from EU law. Nevertheless, the above-mentioned elements should also be taken into account when a contracting authority considers the number of days of a standstill period.

Another element that may be relevant enough to take into account is whether the contracting authority urgently needs the product or service. Under the Public Sector Remedies Directive, a Member State can exclude standstill '*if Directive 2004/18/EC does not require prior publication of a contract notice in the Official Journal of the European Union*',[51] which also includes cases under Public Sector Directive Article 31.[52]

Other factors that may be relevant for consideration include how many tenderers were involved in the procedure and the types of information provided along the way, as well as the criteria used by the contracting authority to award the contract. If only a few tenderers participated in a competition for a contract related to simple products or for a contract awarded on the basis of the price criterion alone, it is my opinion that the length of the standstill period can be relatively short, such as a few days, because in such a situation the tenderers need to examine very little information before deciding on whether to bring proceedings.

The length of the standstill period as stated by the Public Sector Remedies Directive can be used as a guideline; at the very least, the length of the stand-

50. Federal Security Services Ltd v. Chief Constable for the Police Service of Northern Ireland [2009] NICh 3.
51. Article 2a(1)a of the Public Sector Remedies Directive.
52. According to Article 31 c of the Public Sector Directive it is allowed to enter into a contract based on negotiations without prior publication of a contract notice *'(c) insofar as is strictly necessary when, for reasons of extreme urgency brought about by events unforeseeable by the contracting authorities in question (...).'*

still period for contracts outside the Public Sector Remedies Directive cannot be longer than that for contracts falling within the Directive.

The standstill period does not begin until the tenderers have been informed about the award decision.[53] As chapter 10 elaborates on, time limits for complaints do not begin before tenderers have been properly informed. Regarding such time limits, the Court of Justice found in *Uniplex*[54] that if time limits on complaints are introduced, then the tenderers must know exactly when the time limit begins, which will not start until proper information has been provided. In my view, such a requirement to properly inform the tenderers must also apply to standstill.[55] Therefore, contracting authorities must state reasons for their award decisions, which will be elaborated on in section 6.

Finally, the Public Sector Remedies Directive requires the contracting authority to state *'... the exact standstill period applicable pursuant to the provisions of national law transposing this paragraph'*.[56] Thus, a contracting authority must inform tenderers when a given standstill period will expire; in other words, when it plans to sign the contract. Such a requirement becomes even more important in relation to the three types of contracts because, when dealing with standstill outside the Remedies Directive, the amount of days will vary depending on the contract in question. Thus, tenderers must know when the period will expire. Ultimately, a tenderer who participates in a tender procedure bears the risk of knowing the national rules regarding reviews, hereunder standstill in the Member State in which the tenderer participates in a procedure for a public contract.

6. State reasons

6.1. Public Sector Remedies Directive

According to the Public Sector Remedies Directive, that the contracting authority holds a standstill period before signing a contract that comes under the

53. For contracts falling within Public Sector Directive this is precisely stated in the Article 2a (1) of the Public Sector Remedies Directive.
54. Case C-406/08 Uniplex (UK) Limited v. NHS Business Services Authority, [2010] ECR I-817.
55. See also, case C-455/08, Commission v. Ireland, [2009] ECR I-225, paragraph 34, where the Court states: '... *the reasons for the decision to reject their tender must be communicated to the tenderers concerned in sufficient time before the conclusion of the contract, in order to allow the unsuccessful tenderers to bring, in particular, an application for interim measures until such conclusion*'.
56. Article 2a (2) final of the Public Sector Remedies Directive.

Public Sector Directive is not sufficient. When informing the tenderers about the award decision, contracting authorities must also give the tenderers *'... a summary of the relevant reasons as set out in Article 41(2) of Directive 2004/18/EC (...)'.*[57] The reference to Article 41(2) of the Public Sector Directive expanded the obligations under this Directive because this Article only puts obligations on the contracting authority when a tenderer asks for further information. In contrast, the Public Sector Remedies Directive states that information on who was awarded the contract must be accompanied by such reasons following from Article 41(2).

In my opinion, Article 41(2) now also applies to B-services. Thus, contracting authorities must also state reasons when dealing with a B-service contract because the provision, which can exempt standstill, only provides for the option to exempt the standstill **period**. This can be seen in the Directive, where

'Member States may provide that ***the periods*** *referred to in Article 2a(2) of this Directive do not apply in the following cases: (a) if Directive 2004/18/EC does not require prior publication of a contract notice in the Official Journal of the European Union'* [emphasis added].[58]

The Directive only refers to the period and does not state that *'The communication of the award decision to each tenderer and candidate concerned shall be accompanied by the following (...)'*, as Article 2a(2) provides for. This reasoning shows that the Public Sector Remedies Directive has extended Article 41(2) to also apply to contracts regarding B-services.

Thus, the contracting authority must give the rejected tenderer various information such as, for example,

'the ***reasons for the rejection of his tender****, (...), the reasons for its decision of non-equivalence or its decision that the works, supplies or services do not meet the performance or functional requirements,'* and *'the* ***characteristics and relative advantages*** *of the tender selected as well as the name of the successful tenderer or the parties to the framework agreement'* [emphasis added].[59]

57. Article 2a (2) of the Public Sector Remedies Directive.
58. Article 2b of the Public Sector Remedies Directive.
59. Article 41(2) of the Public Sector Directive. For further on this provision see, for example, Steinicke, Michael and Groesmeyer, Lise *"EU's Udbudsdirektiver"*, [2008] 2nd edition, DJØF p. 1038 ff. Arrowsmith, Sue *"The Law of Public and Utilities Procurement"* [2005] 2nd edition, London, Sweet and Maxwell, p. 794.

6.2. Outside the Public Sector Remedies Directive

Given that neither Article 41(2) of the Public Sector Directive nor the Public Sector Remedies Directive apply to contracts below the thresholds and service concession contracts, analysing whether contracting authorities are required to state reasons in such cases is relevant and, if relevant, whether the types of reasons that should be stated for the three types of contracts.

Most national legislations provide for freedom of information requests, which means that contracting authorities within the public sphere are required to submit relevant information to anyone who asks for it. Moreover, that effective judicial review also requires reasons to be stated for a decision on which an EU right is based is also generally accepted under EU law. For example, *Craig and de Burca* stated,

'... the right to effective judicial review also generally requires the giving of reasons for decisions which curtailed or denied a Community right, and must enable the person affected 'to defend that right under the best possible conditions'.[60]

Early in the Court's case law, the Court found that the right to effective judicial review also requires stating decisions. In *Heylens*,[61] a Belgium national was holder of a Belgium diploma and engaged in the activities of a French football club. To practise the occupation of football trainer in France, a person must hold a French or a foreign diploma, which are recognised as equivalent. Heylens' diploma was rejected as equivalent, but no statement of the reason for such a decision was given. The Court first stated that because free access to employment is a

'fundamental right which the Treaty confers individually (...) the existence of a remedy of a judicial nature is essential in order to secure for the individual effective protection for his rights'.[62]

Trepte, Peter *"Public Procurement in the EU"* [2007] Oxford University Press, Second Edition, p. 520.

60. Craig, Paul and Gráinne de Búrca, *"EU Law – Text, Cases and Materials"* [2008], 4th Edition, Oxford University Press, p. 310. See also Tridimas, Takis *"The General Principles of EU Law"* [2006] 2nd edition, Oxford University Press p. 445.
61. Case C-222/86, Union nationale des entraîneurs et cadres techniques professionnels du football (Unectef) v. Georges Heylens and others, [1987] ECR 4097.
62. Case C-222/86, Union nationale des entraîneurs et cadres techniques professionnels du football (Unectef) v. Georges Heylens and others, [1987] ECR 4097, paragraph 14.

Thus, effective judicial review was essential to cover the legality of a decision and *'... presupposes in general that the court (...) may require the competent authority to notify its reasons'*.[63] In the event that the dispute relates to a fundamental right conferred by the Treaty onto an individual, such an individual must *'be able to defend that right under the best possible conditions and have the possibility of deciding, with a full knowledge of the facts, whether there is any point in their applying to the courts'*.[64] Thus, the Court concluded that the authority had a duty to disclose the reasons for the refusal.

Regarding contracts outside the Directive, it is submitted that to ensure protection of an undertaking's rights based on the obligations derived from the principles of the Treaties (analysed in chapters 7 and 8), the principle of effective judicial review requires that the contracting authority states the reasons for its final decisions (such as the award decision and whether to exclude an undertaking during the selection phase). Stating the reasons must take place before the conclusion of the contract for the undertaking to have the genuine possibility of bringing an action.[65]

The obligation to state reasons is an essential procedural requirement, and is important in procurement situations. Stating reasons ensures transparency of the contracting authority's decisions and is, in that regard, a measure to ensure that the right decision has been made (the transparency's control function). In my view, in all cases the contracting authority will be required to state reasons for its decision to reject a tender or a candidate.

The type of information necessary is more difficult to establish in general terms. Regarding the EU Institutions' requirement of stating reasons, such a duty is enshrined in Article 296 TFEU. Inspiration on the content of a reason regarding the three types of contracts might be found in the case law from the General Court regarding complaints over procurement decisions taken by the EU Institutions.

63. Case C-222/86, Union nationale des entraîneurs et cadres techniques professionnels du football (Unectef) v. Georges Heylens and others, [1987] ECR 4097, paragraph 15.
64. Case C-222/86, Union nationale des entraîneurs et cadres techniques professionnels du football (Unectef) v. Georges Heylens and others, [1987] ECR 4097, paragraph 15.
65. In line with the requirement for reasons stated in Case C-212/02, Commission v. Austria, (not reported in the ECR), paragraph 22.

In *Evropaïki Dynamiki,*[66] the General Court recently stated that requirements on the amount of reasons will depend on the circumstances of each case and

'... in particular the content of the measure, the nature of the reasons given and the interest which the addressees of the measure, or other parties to whom it is of direct and individual concern, may have in obtaining explanations'.[67]

In the concrete case, the Court found that the obligation to state reasons is fulfilled if,

'... first of all, to ***informing immediately each tenderer*** *other than the best-ranked, of the reasons for that ranking and if it then informs all such* ***tenderers of the characteristics and relative advantages of the tender of the best-ranked tenderer, together with its name****, within fifteen calendar days of receiving a written request'* [emphasis added].[68]

Thus, that the reasons must be stated immediately can also be derived.[69] Furthermore, the characteristics and relative advantages of a tender must be stated. The type of information that a tenderer must be provided will vary from contract to contract.

As a minimum, the contracting authority must ensure that the reason contains elements such as who was awarded the contract and why the specific tenderer was not awarded the contract, such as because the price was too high or because the tenderer submitted an unconditional tender. Clearly, if a contract concerns simple types of goods and the awarding of the contract is based on the lowest price criterion, then the requirement for the reasons are lower than those for complicated contracts awarded based on criteria for most economically advantageous tender. In all cases, the information required must provide the tenderer with an overview of the substance of the award decision and whether it may have reasons to file a complaint.

66. Case T-298/09, Evropaïki Dynamiki v. Commission, [2011] September 20, 2011, (not yet reported).
67. Case T-298/09, Evropaïki Dynamiki v. Commission, [2011] September 20, 2011, (not yet reported), paragraph 63. See also Case T-57/09, Alfastar Benelux v. Council, [2011] October 20, 2011, (not yet reported), paragraph 25.
68. Case T-298/09, Evropaïki Dynamiki v. Commission, [2011] September 20, 2011, (not yet reported), paragraph 29.
69. Such a requirement can also be seen in the Case T-57/09, Alfastar Benelux v. Council, [2011] October 20, 2011, (not yet reported), paragraph 47. See also Case C-367/95 P, Commission v. Sytraval and Brink's France [1998] ECR I-1719, paragraph 63 and case law cited.

7. Conclusion and suggestions

I submit that when awarding one of the three types of contracts, the principles of the Treaties indicate that the contracting authority is required to ensure that a standstill period has taken place. In that regard, a standstill period is necessary to ensure that the principles of the Treaties can be effectively reviewed.

The length of the standstill period cannot be precisely established but must depend on the contract in question. A tenderer who participates in such a national competition bears the risk of knowing the rules regarding reviews, hereunder standstill in the Member State in which the tenderer participates in a procedure for a public contract. However, the contracting authority is required to state the expiration of the standstill period in its grounds for not awarding the contract to the tenderer. Furthermore, the contracting authority must state reasons for its award decision to the tenderers in order to ensure effective review.

Regarding B-service contracts, the Commission suggests in the proposal for a new Directive that the Directive should fully cover this category of services, thus that B-services are deleted. Deleting B-services also implies that the current services categorised as a B-service will be fully covered by the Remedies Directive and thus by the standstill rules (see chapter 11, section 4).

Regarding service concession contracts, the Commission's proposal suggests that the Remedies Directives cover these types of contracts as well, hereunder the rules on standstill.[70]

70. See Article 46 and 47 of the Proposed Concessions Directive.

PART III

‘Enforcement and Remedies’

CHAPTER 10

Enforcement of the Three Types of Contracts

1. Introduction

This chapter analyses the possibility of bringing a complaint regarding a contracting authority's potential breach of the obligations derived from the principles of the Treaties (the obligations analysed in part II of the Thesis). The chapter focuses on elements such as where can proceedings be brought, who is entitled to bring proceedings, and whether time limits are applicable. Chapter 11 analyses the remedies available for the review bodies.

Unless the Commission brings an enforcement action,[1] disputes will occur before the national courts (or review bodies). Thus, the national review bodies are the ones responsible for determining whether the obligations derived from the principles of the Treaties were complied with.[2]

The Court of Justice has interpreted the law in a very dynamic manner in a number of cases in the area of enforcement in public procurement situations.[3] Indeed, even though the Remedies Directives apply to breaches of the Procurement Directives, and thus breaches are in fact regulated at EU level, the

1. Recalling that the enforcement mechanisms at EU level will not be analysed in this Thesis. See chapter 1, section 4.4.
2. See in that regard case C-324/98, Telaustria Verlags GmbH and Telefonadress GmbH v. Telekom Austria AG, [2000] ECR I-10745, paragraph 63, which states: *'It is for the national court to rule on the question whether that obligation was complied with (...)'*.
3. Treumer, Steen *"Enforcement of the EU Public Procurement Rules: The State of Law and Current Issues"* in Treumer, Steen & Lichère Francois (Eds) *"Enforcement of the EU Public Procurement Rules"* [2011] DJØF, p. 17.

Court of Justice has nevertheless introduced remedies that are not found in the Directive to ensure the effectiveness of the rules.[4]

Effective remedies are important tools to ensure that the obligations derived from the principles of the Treaties are observed. If effective remedies are not available, there is a great risk that the contracting authorities will not ensure the obligations because there are no consequences for not doing so. Therefore, an effective enforcement system also has a preventive effect.

The Award of one of the three types of contracts must take place in a non-discriminative manner and competition for the contract must be created. To ensure this goal, '*... effective and rapid remedies must be available in the case of infringements of Community law in the field of public procurement or national rules implementing that law*'.[5] Enforcement of rules in the Public Sector Directive is an essential part of ensuring that public contracts are open to competition and ultimately awarded to the undertaking that has submitted the best offer. Similarly, the enforcement of the obligations derived from the principles of the Treaties must take place. An effective enforcement system builds confidence among undertakings that public contracts are awarded fairly.

As elaborated on in section 3.3, the Public Sector Remedies Directive covers B-service contracts, but Member States can choose to exclude these contracts from some of the Directive's rules. Because most of the concrete rules in the Public Sector Remedies Directive will be applicable for the enforcement of B-services, these rules will be analysed. Regarding contracts below the thresholds and service concession contracts, this chapter analyses whether the same types of enforcement mechanisms must be available as a consequence of the principles derived from the Treaties.

1.1. Outline

Section 2 examines the relevant principles of the Treaties in relation to enforcement. The principle of national procedural autonomy (section 2.1), the principle of equivalence (section 2.2), the principle of the right to effective judicial protection (section 2.3), and the principle of effectiveness (section

4. Case C-503/04, Commission v. Germany, [2007] ECR I-6153, where the Court found that Germany had a duty to terminate a contract, see chapter 11, section 3.
5. Recital 3 to Directive 89/665/EEC. The Recital refers to the aim of the procurement rules under the Procurement Directive, but as the same aim apply when awarding the three types of contracts (see chapter 2) also in relation to these contracts should effective remedies be available in order to ensure the goal of the procurement rules.

2.4) are examined. Section 3 concerns the Public Sector Remedies Directive. In that regard, sections 3.1 and 3.2 examine the aim and background of the Public Sector Remedies Directive. Section 3.3 elaborates on the contracts covered by the Directive. Finally, some of the Directive's enforcement mechanisms are analysed, including national complaints systems (section 3.4), locus standi (section 3.5) and time limits (section 3.6).

2. The principles of the Treaties

When addressing the enforcement of procurement rules at the national level, the sources of law available include; the Public Sector Remedies Directive, the principles derived from the Treaties and Member States own judicial rules.

The Public Sector Remedies Directive contains judicial rules and remedies. Thus, the rules in this Directive must be applied if it covers the contract. As stated in *Lämmerzahl*,

'When applying domestic law the national court must, as far as is at all possible, interpret it in a way which accords with the objective of Directive 89/665.'[6]

However, in cases where the Public Sector Remedies Directive does not apply, the Member States are left to regulate contract enforcement and remedies in accordance with the principles of the Treaties. Thus, when interpreting whether certain rules and obligations apply at the national level, these principles must be kept in mind.

2.1. The principle of national procedural autonomy

According to the principle of national procedural autonomy, Member States are entitled to set up judicial review in the manner that they find most advantageous. In the absence of EU legislation, the Member States are left to

'... designate the courts having jurisdiction and to determine the procedural conditions governing actions at law intended to ensure the protection of the right which citizens have from direct effect of Community law (...)'.[7]

6. Case C-241/06, Lämmerzahl GmbH v. Freie Hansestadt Bremen, [2007] ECR I-8415, paragraph 62.

Thus, when EU legislation does not exist, Member States are responsible for regulating judicial review of EU law. Therefore, Member States are free to determine the procedural conditions in their own jurisdiction as long as these national rules do not prevent EU law from having full effect (see section 2.2).

2.2. The principle of equivalence and practical possibility

In *Rewe*,[8] the Court found that the national courts should determine the procedural conditions to ensure the protection of the rights derived from EU law and that this position would only be different if the national conditions made exercising these rights practically impossible. The Court stated, '*... it being understood that such conditions cannot be less favourable than those relating to similar actions of a domestic nature'*.[9]

The principle of equivalence means that the same types of remedies must apply to the same situations regardless of whether the rule, which has been breached, is a national rule or an EU rule. The principle also means that a Member State may not make pursuing a breach in the national courts difficult. Thus, the principle of practical possibilities ensures that national rules must not make the exercise of EU rights impossible, and that EU rights receive the same protection as domestic rights. Presumably, this means that if a Member State has national legislation for the three types of contracts, then basing a claim with the national courts regarding a breach of the principles of the Treaties should also be possible.

7. Case C-33/76, Rewe-Zentralfinanz eG and Rewe-Zentral AG v. Landwirtschaftskammer für das Saarland, [1976] ECR 1989, paragraph 5. See also Joined Cases C-6/90 & 9/90, Andrea Francovich and Danila Bonifaci and others v. Italy, [1991] ECR I-5357, paragraph 42, Case C-432/05, Unibet (London) Ltd and Unibet (International) Ltd v. Justitiekanslern, [2007] ECR I-2271, and lately where the dispute concerned a service concession contracts, see Case C-91/08, Wall AG v. La ville de Francfort-sur-le-Main and Frankfurter Entsorgungs- und Service (FES) GmbH, [2010] ECR I-2815, paragraph 63.
8. Case C-33/76, Rewe-Zentralfinanz eG and Rewe-Zentral AG v. Landwirtschaftskammer für das Saarland, [1976] ECR 1989.
9. Case C-33/76, Rewe-Zentralfinanz eG and Rewe-Zentral AG v. Landwirtschaftskammer für das Saarland, [1976] ECR 1989, paragraph 5. See also Case C-91/08, Wall AG v. La ville de Francfort-sur-le-Main and Frankfurter Entsorgungs- und Service (FES) GmbH, [2010] ECR I-2815, paragraph 64. See also Case C-432/05, Unibet (London) Ltd and Unibet (International) Ltd v. Justitiekanslern, [2007] ECR I-2271, paragraph 43.

2.3. The right to effective judicial protection

Another general principle is the principle of the right to effective judicial review. This principle has been enshrined in the European Convention for the Protection of Human Rights[10] and now in the legally binding EU Charter of Fundamental Rights Article 47. This article states that everyone whose rights and freedoms are guaranteed by EU law has the right to effective remedy before an impartial tribunal if such rights and freedoms are violated. The Court of Justice has long acknowledged this principle as a general principle of EU law.[11] Also in procurement cases such as *Loutraki*,[12] where the Court stated:

'In that regard, it is important to note that the principle of effective judicial protection is a general principle of European Union law.'[13]

The principle requires that individuals can bring proceedings for breaches of EU rules, and the principle is essential for safeguarding individuals' rights according to EU law.

2.4. The principle of effectiveness

Perhaps the most important principle when dealing with enforcement at national level is the principle of effectiveness ensuring that the enforcement of EU rules must be effective. That it must be ensures that EU law is effective

10. Articles 6 and 13 of the European Convention on Human Rights. The principle stems from the constitutional traditions of the Member States, see Case C-222/86, Union nationale des entraîneurs et cadres techniques professionnels du football (Unectef) v. Georges Heylens and others, [1987] ECR 4097, paragraph 15. See more on the principle, Tridimas, Takis *"The General Principles of EU Law"* [2006] 2nd Edition, Oxford University Press, p. 443.
11. Case C-222/86, Union nationale des entraîneurs et cadres techniques professionnels du football (Unectef) v. Georges Heylens and others, [1987] ECR 4097, paragraph 14, where the Court also found that the right to effective judicial review also requires the giving of reasons for decisions. The case is also dealt with in chapter 9, section 6.
12. Joined Cases C-145/08 and C-149/08, Club Hotel Loutraki AE, Athinaïki Techniki AE, Evangelos Marinakis v. Ethniko Simvoulio Radiotileorasis, Ipourgos Epikratias (C-145/08) and Aktor Anonimi Tekhniki Etairia (Aktor ATE) v. Ethniko Simvoulio Radiotileorasis (C-149/08), (not yet reported).
13. Joined Cases C-145/08 and C-149/08, Club Hotel Loutraki AE, Athinaïki Techniki AE, Evangelos Marinakis v. Ethniko Simvoulio Radiotileorasis, Ipourgos Epikratias (C-145/08) and Aktor Anonimi Tekhniki Etairia (Aktor ATE) v. Ethniko Simvoulio Radiotileorasis (C-149/08), (not yet reported), paragraph 73. See also Case C-432/05, Unibet (London) Ltd and Unibet (International) Ltd v. Justitiekanslern, [2007] ECR I-2271, paragraph 37.

also follows from Article 4(3) TEU, which states that, '... *The Member States shall take any appropriate measure, general or particular, to ensure fulfilment of the obligations arising out of the Treaties (...)'*. Accordingly, Member States shall take appropriate means to ensure that the obligations derived from the principles of the Treaties are effective.

Early on, the Court of Justice held in *Simmenthal*[14] that the national courts must apply EU law in its entirety, and that:

> *'... any provision of a national legal system (...) which might impair the effectiveness of Community law by withholding from the national court having jurisdiction to apply such law the power to do everything necessary at the moment of its application to set aside national legislative provisions* ***which might prevent Community rules having full force and effect*** *are incompatible with those requirements which are the very essence of Community law'* [emphasis added].[15]

Thus, the principle of effectiveness is essential to bear in mind when analysing enforcement and remedies for the three types of contracts. Regarding the principle of effectiveness, *Pachau* stated that,

> *'... the principle could be construed to concern not only each remedy separately but also a review system as a whole and require its overall effectiveness, possibly by requiring that one remedy should complement and compensate for the other'.*[16]

Therefore, the principle is relevant when applying remedies in a concrete case, but also the review system as a whole must be effective. It is therefore necessary, in my view, to create an enforcement system where remedies and procedural rules supplement each other to ensure the effectiveness of the principles derived from the Treaties.

Thus, despite the principle of procedural autonomy, Member States' procedural rules are, to some extent, limited by other principles of the Treaties, primarily the principle of effectiveness, and Member States are obliged to create an effective review system.

14. Case C-106/77, Amministrazione delle Finanze dello Stato v. Simmenthal SpA, [1978] ECR 629.
15. Case C-106/77, Amministrazione delle Finanze dello Stato v. Simmenthal SpA, [1978] ECR 629, paragraph 22.
16. Pachnou, Despina, *"Enforcement of the EC. Procurement Rules: The Standard Required of National Review Systems under E.C. Law in the Context of the Principle of Effectiveness"* [2000] PPLR n° 2, pp. 55-74.

3. The Public Sector Remedies Directive

3.1. Aim and history

In most fields of EU law, no common procedural rules in relation to review and remedies exist. In fact it is quite unusual that EU rules on remedies exist. However, in later years further enforcement rules have been introduced in various field of EU law.[17] The reason why EU law does not regulate review and remedies in most cases is primarily the result of the principle of national procedural autonomy (section 2.1) as well as the principle of subsidiarity. The latter requires that the EU take actions at the EU level only if considered to be more effective than actions taken at the national level.[18]

Remedies for breaches of EU public procurement rules were found to be necessary in 1989 when the first Remedies Directives were introduced. EU rules on enforcement in procurement cases were introduced because:

'the opening-up of public procurement to Community competition necessitates a substantial increase in the guarantees of transparency and non-discrimination; whereas, for it to have tangible effects, effective and rapid remedies must be available in the case of infringements of Community law in the field of public procurement or national rules implementing that law'.[19]

Regulating enforcement procedures by EU law was found necessary to ensure that effective remedies were available for breaches of procurement rules and that public contracts were open for competition. The existing review mechanism at both national and EU levels were found *'not always adequate to ensure compliance with the relevant Community provisions particularly at a stage when infringements can be corrected'.*[20] Thus, common procedural rules and remedies were found to be necessary to regulate at EU level. The overall aim was to ensure that

17. Other areas where EU legislation exists regarding remedies for the enforcement of EU law are, for example, environmental law and regarding enforcement of Intellectual Property Rights, see Craig, Paul and Búrca, Gráinne de *"EU Law – Text, Cases and Materials"* [2011] 5th Edition, Oxford University Press, p. 218
18. See Article 5(3) TEU, which states: *'Under the principle of subsidiarity, in areas which do not fall within its exclusive competence, the Union shall act only if and in so far as the objectives of the proposed action cannot be sufficiently achieved by the Member States, either at central level or at regional and local level, but can rather, by reason of the scale or effects of the proposed action, be better achieved at Union level'.*
19. Recital 3 of Directive 89/665/EEC.
20. Recital 2 of Directive 89/665/EEC.

'adequate procedures exist in all the Member States to permit the setting aside of decisions taken unlawfully and compensation of persons harmed by an infringement'.[21]

The Public Sector Remedies Directive contains various minimum rules that Member States are obliged to implement. These rules contain measures for structuring a review body, requirements regarding the parties entitled to bring proceedings, *locus standi* and the types of remedies that must be available. The Court of Justice has formulated that the Remedies Directive lies down

'... only the minimum conditions to be satisfied by the review procedures established in domestic law to ensure compliance with the requirements of Community law concerning public contracts'.[22]

The Public Sector Remedies Directive still leaves many choices with the Member States and, as pointed out by *Trepte*,

'The Remedies Directives do not attempt to harmonize the remedies available in all member states, but seek to ensure a minimum level of protection adapted, where necessary, to peculiarities of different national systems.'[23]

The review procedure varies significantly among the Member States depending on how the options in the Public Sector Remedies Directive, hereunder how the voluntary options, have been implemented (see chapter 1, section 4.4).

3.2. The Amending Remedies Directive

In 2007, the Remedies Directives were amended.[24] According to the Commission's proposal to the Amending Remedies Directive, the Directive seeks to *'give greater encouragement to Community enterprises to tender in any*

21. Recital 6 of Directive 89/665/EEC.
22. Case C-492/06, Consorzio Elisoccorso San Raffaele v. Elilombarda Srl and Azienda Ospedaliera Ospedale Niguarda Ca' Granda di Milano, [2007] ECR I-8189, paragraph 21. See also Case C-315/01, Gesellschaft für Abfallentsorgungs-Technik GmbH (GAT) v. Österreichische Autobahnen und Schnellstraßen AG (ÖSAG), [2003] ECR I-6351, paragraph 45. Case C-327/00, Santex SpA v. Unità Socio Sanitaria Locale n. 42 di Pavia, and Sca Mölnlycke SpA, Artsana SpA and Fater SpA, [2003] ECR I-1877, paragraph 47.
23. Trepte, Peter *"Public Procurement in the EU: A Practitioners Guide"* [2007] p. 530.
24. Directive 2007/66/EC.

Member State'.[25] Thus, by ensuring effective review, undertakings rights are better protected, giving them

'... the certainty that they can, if need be, effectively seek effective review if their interests seem to have been adversely affected in procedures for awarding contract'.[26]

Before the Commission proposed to amend the Remedies Directives, the Commission issued a consultation,[27] but the proposal also came as a consequence of the Court's case law.[28] One of the weaknesses of the national complaints systems was that if a contract was awarded directly to an undertaking (without any form of competition) an undertaking interest in the contract could in such a situation, if the contract had already been signed, merely apply for damages.[29] However, because a loss rarely can be proven in such a situation, the award of damages seldom occurs. Thus, the Amending Remedies Directive introduced the possibility for review bodies to declare ineffective certain contracts that were awarded illegally (see chapter 11) and introduced the requirement of standstill to ensure that a contract was not signed immediately (see chapter 9).

3.3. Contracts covered by the Public Sector Remedies Directive

The Public Sector Remedies Directive applies to contracts[30] referred to in the Public Sector Directive Article 1(1) unless *'... such contracts are excluded in accordance with Articles 10 to 18 of that Directive'*. This means that the Pub-

25. The Commission's proposal for a Directive of the European Parliament and of the Council amending Council Directives 89/665/EEC and 92/13/EEC CEE with regard to improving the effectiveness of review procedures concerning the award of public contracts (SEC(2006)195 final), henceforth the proposal for amending the Remedies Directives..
26. The proposal for amending the Remedies Directives..
27. Commission consultation from 2003, questions and answers can be found at: http://ec.europa.eu/internal_market/publicprocurement/infringements/remedies/review_2007_en.htm (last visited January 31, 2012).
28. Mainly Case C-81/98, Alcatel and others v. Bundesministerium für Wissenschaft und Verkehr [1999] ECR I-7671, Case C-26/03, Stadt Halle and RPL Recyclingpark Lochau GmbH v. Arbeitsgemeinschaft Thermische Restabfall- und Energieverwertungsanlage TREA Leuna, [2005] ECR I-1.
29. Recital 3 of the Amending Remedies Directive.
30. What constitutes a contract within the meaning of the Directive is furthermore elaborated on in Article 1 of the Public Sector Remedies Directive, which states: *'Contracts within the meaning of this Directive include public contracts, framework agreements, public works concessions and dynamic purchasing systems'*.

lic Sector Remedies Directive covers all types of contracts that fall within the Public Sector Directive, and that the excluded contracts in Articles 10–18 are not covered.[31]

Since B-services are not a type of contract excluded by Articles 10–18 of the Public Sector Directive,[32] they fall within the scope of the Public Sector Remedies Directive, whereas service concession contracts and contracts below the thresholds do not. This is also the Commission's view, as can be seen in the 2006 Communication that stated,

'This means that in the present context they [the Remedies Directives] apply only to contracts for services listed in Annex II B to Directive 2004/18/EC (...) which exceed the thresholds for application of these Directives. (...). These principles remain unchanged in the recently adopted proposal for a new Directive on review procedures (...).'[33]

Nevertheless, implementing the Directive allows for Member States to exclude B-services from several of the provisions, such as the rules on standstill (see chapter 9) and ineffectiveness (see chapter 11).

In the Commission's proposal for amending the Remedies Directives, the paragraph in Article 1(1) stating, *'unless such contracts are excluded in accordance with Articles 10 to 18 of that Directive'*, was not cited. Therefore, the Council explicitly put the first paragraph into the Directive. Inserting a phrase that expressly states that the Directive does not cover these contracts makes it difficult for the Court of Justice to interpret the rules otherwise, which ultimately ensures legal certainty for the types of contracts falling outside the Public Sector Directive.

Thus, when interpreting the provisions in the Public Sector Remedies Directive, the EU legislator's intent was not to create rules for contracts falling below the thresholds and service concession contracts.

3.4. Review bodies of national complaints systems

The Member States are responsible for determining the competent review bodies to handle complaints. In some Member States, the courts alone decide on whether EU public procurement rules have been breached.[34] In other

31. This can also be seen in Recital 2 of the Amending Remedies Directive that states: *'Directives 89/665/EEC and 92/13/EEC therefore apply only to contracts falling within the scope of Directives 2004/18/EC and 2004/17/EC (...).'*
32. Since B-services have to follow Article 21 of the Public Sector Directive.
33. See the 2006 Communication, section 2.3.2.
34. The Member States even have different types of courts that can handle complaints. Commission's Evaluation Report *'Impact and Effectiveness of EU Public Pro-*

Member States, a separate review body has been given the competence to make decisions in that regard.[35]

A few requirements for the national review systems are found in Article 2 of the Public Sector Remedies Directive. This provision also contains requirements for national review systems when the review body is not a court and, according to the Court of Justice, Article 2(9) is to

'be considered as constituting a specific requirement, including specific guarantees, imposed on the Member States where the authorities responsible for review procedures are not judicial bodies (...)'.[36]

A review body does not need to be a court within the meaning of Article 267 TFEU, but the decisions taken by a review body must be subject for review by another body that constitutes a court within the meaning of Article 267 TFEU.[37] For example, *Unitron*[38] found that the Danish Complaints Board for Public Procurement constituted such a court, and *Hospital Ingenieure* found that the Austrian Vergabekontrollsenat des Landes Wien constituted such a court.[39]

curement Legislation', part 1 SEC(2011) 853 final, p. 69, mentions that in Belgium, France, Ireland, Lithuania, the Netherlands, Portugal, Sweden and the United Kingdom, the review of public procurement decisions is exclusively handled by regular courts. In Portugal and Italy, the administrative courts deal with public procurement disputes. In Ireland, Lithuania, the Netherlands, Sweden and the United Kingdom it is the civil courts. In France and Luxembourg it can be both the administrative and civil courts.

35. Commission's Evaluation Report *'Impact and Effectiveness of EU Public Procurement Legislation'*, part 1 SEC(2011) 853 final, p. 69, states that the following countries have a review body: Austria, Bulgaria, Cyprus, Czech Republic, Denmark, Estonia, Germany, Hungary, Latvia, Malta, Poland, Romania, Slovak Republic, and Slovenia.
36. Case C-570/08, Symvoulio Apochetefseon Lefkosias v. Anatheoritiki Archi Prosforon, [2010] October, 21, 2010 (not yet reported), paragraph 23.
37. Article 2(9) of the Public Sector Remedies Directive.
38. Case C-275/98, Unitron Scandinavia and 3-S, Danske Svineproducenters Serviceselskab v. Ministeriet for Fødevarer, Landbrug og Fiskeri, [1999] ECR I-8291.
39. Case C-92/00, Hospital Ingenieure Krankenhaustechnik Planungs-Gesellschaft mbH (HI) v. Stadt Wien, [2002] ECR I-5553. See also Case C-54/96, Dorsch Consult Ingenieurgesellschaft mbH v. Bundesbaugesellschaft Berlin mbH, [1997] ECR I-4961, where a German, Federal Supervisory Board, was found to constitute a court.

If a review body is not judicial in character, written reasons for their decisions shall always be given, and such decisions must be legally binding.[40]

The Public Sector Remedies Directive allows for the possibility of requiring complainant to notify the contracting authority *'of the alleged infringement and of his intention to seek review'*[41] before launching a complaint to a review body. Some Member States provide for such a mandatory requirement.[42] In many cases, such a requirement results in prolonging the review procedure because a complaint rarely causes a contracting authority to change its decision and, therefore, nothing is gained from such a complaint. Requiring the person desiring to use the review procedure to notify the contracting authority at the time of the launch of the proceedings seems more proportionate and would achieve the same goal.

According to the principle of effective judicial review, pursuing a breach of the obligations derived from the principles of the Treaties in relation to the three types of contracts in the national judicial system should be possible. B-services are covered by the Public Sector Remedies Directive and must ensure the minimum protection given in the Directive. Contracts below the thresholds and service concession contracts are not covered by the Public Sector Directive. Therefore, no requirement exists for specific types of review bodies, hereunder that the same review bodies, that have competence regarding contracts falling within the Public Sector Directive, should also have competence for contracts outside the Public Sector Directive.[43] In fact, even if Member States have not properly implemented the Remedies Directives, a specific body cannot be required for such a purpose. In *Dorsch*,[44]

40. Article 2(9) of the Public Sector Remedies Directive.
41. Article 1(4) of the Public Sector Remedies Directive, which furthermore states: *'provided that this does not affect the standstill period in accordance with Article 2a (2) or any other time limits for applying for review in accordance with Article 2c'*.
42. Commission's Evaluation Report *'Impact and Effectiveness of EU Public Procurement Legislation'*, part 1 SEC(2011) 853 final, p. 69 states that such a requirement exist in: Cypres, Czech Republic, Germany, Greece, Lithuania, Malta, Poland, Slovak Republic and Slovenia. Furthermore, in Finland and Hungary complainants are required to submit a copy of the complaint to the contracting authority.
43. A Member State may also make separate bodies responsible for different aspects of review proceures. See McGowan, David *"Remedies revolution avoided: a note on Combinatie Spijker Infrabouw-De Jonge Konstruktie v. Provincie Drenthe (C-568/08)"* [2011] PPLR n° 3 NA 64-69.
44. Case C-54/96, Dorsch Consult Ingenieurgesellschaft mbH v. Bundesbaugesellschaft Berlin mbH, [1997] ECR I-4961.

Germany had not implemented the Remedies Directive for contracts covered by the Service Directive.[45] The Court of Justice found that the body responsible for breaches of the Works Directive and the Supply Directive does not necessarily, and automatically have competence regarding breaches of the Service Directive.[46] However, the Court was obliged to interpret the rules in conformity with the Service Directive. The German Board later found that it was competent to settle the case.[47]

If a Member State has rules on review of national rules regarding contracts below the thresholds and concession contracts, then because such rules must be interpreted in conformity with EU rules, the review body will be competent to handle breaches of the obligations derived from the principles of the Treaties.[48] However, if national legislation contains no specific judicial requirements, then the complainant must bring the question before the regular courts.

Having established the competent review body, the Public Sector Remedies Directive states that,

'Member States shall take the measures necessary to ensure that, (...) decisions taken by the contracting authorities may be reviewed effectively and, in particular, as rapidly as possible (...).'[49]

This statement is in line with the principle of effectiveness and is considered a mere restatement of the principle.[50] Regarding a rapid procedure, the Directive is silent on requirements for the time it takes complaint systems to deal with a complaint, which is often lengthy. Clearly, although not contrary to the Directive, bringing a proceeding through the regular court system will be lengthier than bringing a proceeding to a specialised review body.

45. Case C-54/96, Dorsch Consult Ingenieurgesellschaft mbH v. Bundesbaugesellschaft Berlin mbH, [1997] ECR I-4961, paragraph 4.
46. Case C-54/96, Dorsch Consult Ingenieurgesellschaft mbH v. Bundesbaugesellschaft Berlin mbH, [1997] ECR I-4961, paragraph 46.
47. See, Priess, Hans-Joachim *"Recent decisions on judicial protection in German public procurement law,"* [1998] PPLR n° 3, CS116-118.
48. In line with Dingel, Dorthe Dahlgaard *"Public Procurement – A Harmonization of the National Judicial Review of the Application of European Community Law"* [1999] Kluwer Law International, p. 161.
49. Article 1(1) of the Public Sector Remedies Directive.
50. Arrowsmith, Sue *"Enforcing the Public Procurement Rules: Legal Remedies in the Court of Justice and the National Courts"* in Arrowsmith, Sue (Ed.) *"Public Procurement in the European Community: Volume IV – Remedies for enforcing the Public Procurement rules"* [1993] Earlsgate Press, p. 50.

3.5. Locus Standi – right to bring proceedings

For B-service contracts, Member States must ensure that

'the review procedures are available, (...) at least to any person having or having had an interest in obtaining a particular contract and who has been or risks being harmed by an alleged infringement'.[51]

That remedies must be available to persons who risk being harmed by an infringement of the public procurement rules give several undertakings the possibility of bringing proceedings. As seen in *Grossmann*,[52] this even includes undertakings that did not participate in the procedure if the undertaking can be considered as '*risk being harmed*'. Thus, if an undertaking has not submitted a bid, showing that the undertaking had an interest in obtaining the contract will arguably be difficult. However, there are many reasons for not submitting a tender; for instance, if the contract notice contained specifications that the undertaking could not live up to and that such specifications were unlawful, if the subject of the contract was later materially changed or, most commonly, if a contract notice was not published at all. Thus, which parties have the right to bring proceedings under the Directive should be interpreted broadly. Since the three types of contracts do not require publishing a contract notice in OJ, undertakings often have difficulty knowing that a potential contract exists; therefore, it is essential that undertakings who did not participate in a competition for the contract are in a situation that gives them the chance to submit a complaint.

Member States can choose to grant persons in addition to the ones expressly stated in the Public Sector Remedies Directive with the right to bring proceedings. This was stated in *Elilombarda*,[53] where the Court found that Member States are not precluded

51. Article 1(2) of the Public Sector Remedies Directive.
52. Case C-230/02, Commission v. Technische Glaswerke Ilmenau GmbH, [2002] ECR I-8977.
53. Case C-492/06, Consorzio Elisoccorso San Raffaele v. Elilombarda Srl and Azienda Ospedaliera Ospedale Niguarda Ca' Granda di Milano, [2007] ECR I-8189.

'... from making those review procedures more widely available under their national laws by enshrining a concept of standing to bring proceedings which is wider than the minimum guaranteed by the directive'.[54]

Thus, Member States can extend the rules on standing, which many Member States have chosen to do. For example, in Denmark, the Competition and Consumer Authority, as well as other authorities and associations (Danish as well as international ones), can bring proceedings before the Complaints Board for Public Procurement. For these associations to have any particular interest in obtaining the contract in question is not necessary.

Regarding the right for consortiums to bring proceedings, the Court of Justice found that if the chance exists that a member has suffered a loss, the consortium will always be required to bring a proceeding,[55] whereas if no loss has occurred then a proceeding can be brought only if provided for by national law. Thus, if a decision has affected an undertaking, the undertaking has the right to bring proceedings.

Private individuals do not have an interest in being awarded the contract, but may wish to file a complaint for other reasons, such as to prevent a certain project from being built. That such individuals would have standing according to the Public Sector Remedies Directive is doubtful. Thus, national law must provide for whether individuals should have such standing. The UK case *Chandler*[56] considered whether a private individual could have standing, which was rejected. Ms Chandler was the mother of children entitled to a place in secondary education in the London Borough of Camden; therefore, she had an immediate interest in the standards for secondary schooling in the borough. However, the Court found

54. Case C-492/06, Consorzio Elisoccorso San Raffaele v. Elilombarda Srl and Azienda Ospedaliera Ospedale Niguarda Ca' Granda di Milano, [2007] ECR I-8189, paragraph 27.
55. Joined Cases C-145/08 and C-149/08, Club Hotel Loutraki AE, Athinaïki Techniki AE, Evangelos Marinakis v. Ethniko Simvoulio Radiotileorasis, Ipourgos Epikratias (C-145/08) and Aktor Anonimi Tekhniki Etairia (Aktor ATE) v. Ethniko Simvoulio Radiotileorasis (C-149/08), [2010] ECR I-4165, paragraph 80.
56. The Court of Appeal in R. (on the application of Chandler) v. Secretary of State for Children, Schools and Families, Court of Appeal (Civil Division), October 9, 2009.

'... that is not the same as showing standing in law for the purposes of bringing judicial review proceedings (...)' and that, *'It would mean that people with no real interest in the question could bring judicial review proceedings'*.[57]

In Denmark, the Complaints Board found has found that individuals do not have the right to review before the Board.[58]

The right to bring proceedings must be available without discriminating against domestic and non-domestic tenderers; thus, burdens should not be placed on foreign undertakings that are not placed on national undertakings.[59]

In my opinion, identifying the parties that should be able to bring complaints regarding concession contracts and contracts below the thresholds must be done in accordance with the provisions of the Public Sector Remedies Directives as well as the Court's case law concerning who has the right to review under the Remedies Directives. I find that the Court of Justice would likely interpret the principle of the right to judicial review in accordance with the Public Sector Remedies Directive's rules on standing.

In my view, there are not – and should not be – any differences between assessing who has the right to bring proceedings for a breach of the Public Sector Directive (hereunder B-services) and who has the right to bring proceedings for breaches of the obligations derived from the principles of the Treaties for contracts below the thresholds and service concession contracts.

3.6. Time limits – limitations periods

It is possible for the Member States to have national legislation regarding time limits for proceedings.

57. The case is commented by Bailey, S.H *"Chandler in the Court of Appeal: the issue of standing: R. (on the application of Chandler) v. Secretary of State for Children, Schools and Families"* [2010] PPLR n° 2, NA68-71. In another case from UK, Richards J in R (Kathro) v. Rhondda Cynon Taff County Borough Council [2001] EWHC Admin 527, the claimants had tried to use the public procurement regime to stop a development nearby to their property. However, the claimants did not show *'to be affected in any way by the choice of tendering procedure'*. Thus, the claimants did not have standing.
58. Neither in decision of July, 14, 2005, Nabofronten v. Østkraft did a group of individuals have standing nor in decision of July, 7, 2006, Heine Petersen v. Økonomisstyrelsen did a consultant for a potential tenderer have a standing.
59. See also Case C-43/95, Data Delecta Aktiebolag and Ronny Forsberg v. MSL Dynamics Ltd, [1996] ECR I-4661, where the Court found that it constituted a breach on grounds of nationality to require security costs for a British plaintiff when it was not required from Swedish plaintiffs.

On the one hand, a time limit allows complaints to be brought before the review bodies as quickly as possible after the contracting authority makes decisions. On the other hand, time limits can result in complaints not being launched before the review bodies. Thus, a time limit must not render it impossible or difficult for tenderers to exercise their rights, and time limits cannot cut them off from bringing proceedings. A balance must exist between the right to bring proceedings and ensuring that the contracting authority can conduct a procedure appropriately. Therefore, tenderers must be given sufficient time to discover a potential breach. The purpose of introducing time limits is primarily to create legal certainty[60] that ensures for the contracting authority that no further complaints are submitted.

Member States are not required to set time limits under the Public Sector Remedies Directive or when falling outside the Directive. Therefore, Member States are free to set time limits for reviews in their national complaints system if they find such limits appropriate.[61] Nevertheless, although it is generally accepted that time limits are compatible with EU law, a few requirements apply. These requirements have been developed in the case law from the Court of Justice. With the Amending Remedies Directive, certain minimum rules on time limits were put into the Public Sector Remedies Directive, but for the Member States to introduce time limits is still voluntary. If Member States do set time limits, they must ensure the minimum requirements in the Directive.

3.6.1. Time limits for B-services

If Member States decide to set time limits in their national legislation for B-services, the Public Sector Remedies Directive calls for minimum time limits in three situations.

The first situation concerns a minimum time limit for review of the decisions made by contracting authorities. If such time limits are introduced, they must be a minimum of 10 or 15 calendar days:[62] 10 calendar days if the con-

60. See mainly Recitals 25 and 27 of Directive 2007/66/EC.
61. The national time limits do not prevent the Commission from bringing enforcement actions. See Case C-17/09, Commission v. Germany, [2010] January, 21 2010 (not yet reported), where the Commission had brought proceedings 10 years after a contract was concluded. The case is commented by Brown, Adrian *"A German city authority beaches the procurement directives by awarding a waste contract without competition over 10 years ago: Commission v. Germany (C-17/09)"* [2010] PPLR n° 3, NA 112-114, who also argue that such a long period could be contrary to the principle of legal certainty as well as good administration.
62. Article 2c of Directive 2007/66/EC.

tracting authority's decision was sent electronically or faxed, or 15 calendar days calculated from the day the notices were sent or 10 days from receipt of the notice. If the time limit concerns a decision not covered by the rules on notice, the time limit must be 10 calendar days from publication of the decision. Member States can choose to implement this option for only some decisions taken by the contracting authority such as, for example, the decision related to which undertakings are prequalified.

The second situation concerns time limits in relation to complaints about the types of contracts that must be declared ineffective.[63] Such a time limit must be a minimum of 30 calendar days, calculated either from the time of publication of a contract award notice in the OJ (if the notice contains details of the decision to directly award a contract) or from the time the contracting authority informed the tenderers and candidates concerned of the conclusion of the contract (provided that this information contains a summary of the relevant reasons as set out in Article 41(2) of Directive 2004/18/EC).[64]

The third situation concerns a time limit for bringing proceedings once a contract has been signed. In that regard, a minimum period of six months applies from the time the contract was entered into, starting from the day the contract was signed. Member States can always choose to set longer time limits.[65]

In my opinion, if Member States want to apply time limits for review in relation to the three types of contracts, the above-mentioned minimum rules in the Directive must be ensured.

3.6.2. Case law from the Court of Justice

Time limits must ensure the effective protection of EU rights. Therefore, time limits can be considered incompatible with EU law if the conditions for such time limits are unclear or if the national courts have too great discretion in determining whether proceedings were brought on time.

In *Universale-Bau,*[66] the Court of Justice held that the Public Sector Remedies Directive does not preclude national legislation, which provides that any application for review of a contracting authority's decision must be commenced within a specific time limit, provided that the time limit in question is reasonable. The Court held that

63. Article 2f (1) a, first sentence, of the Public Sector Remedies Directive.
64. Article 2f (1) a, second sentence, of the Public Sector Remedies Directive.
65. Article 2f (1) b of the Public Sector Remedies Directive.
66. Case C-470/99, Universale-Bau AG, v. Entsorgungsbetriebe Simmering GmbH, [2002] ECR I-11617, paragraph 79.

'setting of reasonable limitation periods for bringing proceedings must be regarded as satisfying, in principle, the requirement of effectiveness under Directive 89/665, since it is an application of the fundamental principle of legal certainty'.[67]

Thus, setting time limits for any of the three types of contracts will not breach the principles of the Treaties.

Even though a time limit as such appears reasonable, for the review bodies to set it aside is possible if it constitutes a breach of the principle of effectiveness. In that regard, it *'render[s] virtually impossible or excessively difficult the exercise of any rights which the party concerned derives from Community* [for tenderers to bring proceedings]*'*.[68] Setting aside a time limit has been done in a few cases.

In *Santex*,[69] the contracting authority stated a clause in the contract notice that undertakings should have certain financial turnover for the last three years to be eligible to bid. Santex did not fulfil this requirement and therefore brought proceedings claiming that this clause constituted an unlawful restriction on competition. However, the national law provided that review should be submitted within 60 days from the day on which the applicant was aware of a potential breach, and this time limit had expired. The Court found that the time limit as such appeared reasonable.[70] However, even though the disputed clause on financial turnover was stated in the contract notice, Santex did not know the contracting authority's interpretation of the clause until the decision to exclude the undertaking. Therefore, the Court found that a plea was permissible according to the Remedies Directive.[71]

In *Lämmerzahl*,[72] an undertaking that participated in a tender procedure brought proceedings claiming that the contract in question was above the thresholds and not, as the contracting authority found, below the thresholds. The Court found that because the contract notice lacked information on the

67. Case C-470/99, Universale-Bau AG, v. Entsorgungsbetriebe Simmering GmbH, [2002] ECR I-11617, paragraph 76.
68. Case C-327/00, Santex SpA v. Unità Socio Sanitaria Locale n. 42 di Pavia, and Sca Mölnlycke SpA, Artsana SpA and Fater SpA, [2003] ECR I-1877, paragraph 55.
69. Case C-327/00, Santex SpA v. Unità Socio Sanitaria Locale n. 42 di Pavia, and Sca Mölnlycke SpA, Artsana SpA and Fater SpA, [2003] ECR I-1877.
70. Case C-327/00, Santex SpA v. Unità Socio Sanitaria Locale n. 42 di Pavia, and Sca Mölnlycke SpA, Artsana SpA and Fater SpA, [2003] ECR I-1877, paragraph 54.
71. Case C-327/00, Santex SpA v. Unità Socio Sanitaria Locale n. 42 di Pavia, and Sca Mölnlycke SpA, Artsana SpA and Fater SpA, [2003] ECR I-1877, paragraph 66.
72. Case C-241/06, Lämmerzahl GmbH v. Freie Hansestadt Bremen, [2007] ECR I-8415.

estimated value of the contract, followed by the contracting authority's evasive conduct in response to the questions of Lämmerzahl, the limitation period *'... must be considered, (...), as rendering excessively difficult the exercise by the tenderer concerned of the rights conferred on him by Community law'*.[73] Therefore, even though the national rule regarding the time limit was permitted, because the contracting authority did not supply the tenderer with sufficient information about the contract, the time limit for review was disregarded. *Dischendorfer* argued in his comment on the case that the time limit should have applied since the tenderer knew that their tender extensively exceeded the thresholds; thus, they were aware that a breach has taken place and should have brought proceedings sooner.[74] I agree with the argument that if a tenderer is obviously aware that a breach took place, then the tenderer should not be able to bring proceedings after the time limit has expired. Economic operators has a certain obligation to make the contracting authority aware of mistakes in a procedure once it is aware that a breach has taken place and that the breach will influence the competition. Thus, as a minimum; it should not be possible to set aside a time limit when bringing proceedings regarding breaches, which the economic operator is already aware of during the procedure.

In *Uniplex*,[75] the undertaking Uniplex participated in a tender procedure and was informed on November 22, 2007 of the award decision. Thereafter, Uniplex requested that the contracting authority grant further information on why its tender was not successful. On December 13, 2007, Uniplex received this information. According to national legislation, proceedings should be

> *'brought* ***promptly*** *and in any event within three months from the date when grounds for the bringing of the proceedings first arose* ***unless the Court considers*** *that there is good reason for extending the period within which proceedings may be brought'* [emphasis added].[76]

73. Case C-241/06, Lämmerzahl GmbH v. Freie Hansestadt Bremen, [2007] ECR I-8415, paragraph 55.
74. Dischendorfer, Martin *"The application of limitation periods under Directive 89/665"* [2008] PPLR n° 2, NA41-47.
75. Case C-406/08, Uniplex (UK) Limited v. NHS Business Services Authority, [2010] (not yet reported).
76. Regulation 47(7)(b) of the Public Contracts Regulations 2006. The provision has been amended as a consequence of the case (with the "Miscellaneous Amendments" Regulations 2011 (SI 2011/2053)), and it is now a requirement that proceedings are commenced within 30 days of the time when the claimant became aware or ought to have

In March 2008, Uniplex initiated proceedings, and the question was whether the time limit began on November 22, 2007 or when the additional information was granted, which was on December 13, 2007. The Court found that the time limit began when the tenderer was properly informed (hence, December 13, 2007) and found that only when a tenderer was

'*... informed of the reasons for its elimination from the public procurement procedure that it may come to an informed view as to whether there has been an infringement of the applicable provisions and as to the appropriateness of bringing proceedings*'.[77] Therefore, the time limit first began '*...from the date on which the* ***claimant knew, or ought to have known****, of the alleged infringement of those provisions*' [emphasis added].[78]

Furthermore, the Court found that a requirement that proceedings are brought 'promptly' was not in accordance with the Public Sector Remedies Directive.[79]

The case *Commission v. Ireland*[80] involved a situation similar to *Uniplex*. The national legislation stated that the review of an award decision

'*shall be made at the* ***earliest opportunity*** *and in any event within three months from the date when grounds for the application first arose unless the Court considers that there is good reason for extending such period*' [emphasis added].[81]

Contrary to the substance in *Uniplex*, the tenderer in *Commission v. Ireland* was not informed about the award decision; instead, the contracting authority merely stated the award of the contract on its own website and in the OJ. As in *Uniplex*, the Court found that such a restriction on bringing proceedings at the earliest opportunity was not permitted.

become aware that the 'grounds for starting the proceedings had arisen'. Henty, Poul *"Public Procurement (Miscellaneous Amendments) Regulations 2011"* [2012] PPLR n° 1, NA50-53 states that *'There is a certain irony to those change, insofar as they stem from (...) Uniplex. That case arose from arguments that the UK rules on time limits were, in many key respects, unfair to claimants. It certainly did not mandate any shortening of limits. It is paradoxical that the upshot of the ruling should be amended limits, which in many respects are even stricter.'*

77. Case C-406/08, Uniplex (UK) Limited v. NHS Business Services Authority, [2010] (not yet reported), paragraph 31.
78. Case C-406/08, Uniplex (UK) Limited v. NHS Business Services Authority, [2010] (not yet reported), paragraph 32.
79. Case C-406/08 Uniplex (UK) Limited v. NHS Business Services Authority, [2010] (not yet reported), paragraph 43.
80. Case C-456/08, Commission v. Ireland, [2010] ECR I-859.
81. Case C-456/08, Commission v. Ireland, [2010] ECR I-859.

The case law from the Court of Justice seems to conclude that time limits are allowed if they begin from the time that the tenderer knows or ought to know that a decision was made.[82] This means that a tenderer must be properly informed before the time limit begins (see also chapter 9 regarding the requirement for a contracting authority to state the reasons for its decisions).

4. Conclusion

Firstly, when looking at the enforcement system for B-services, since the Public Sector Remedies Directive covers these contracts, the same requirements apply as those for contracts falling within the Directive in relation to setting up a review system.

Regarding contracts below the thresholds and service concession contracts, the principle of the right to effective judicial review requires access to the courts for breaches of the principles of the Treaties. This does not mean that the same review bodies as for B-services must be available. In case a Member State does not regulate this right, the right to bring proceedings must be available under the regular national court system.

In my view, the party that has the right to review is considered the same as for complaints regarding contracts, which falls within the Public Sector Remedies Directive primarily because of the principle of the right to effective judicial review. Here, the Court of Justice will most likely interpret this principle in accordance with the Public Sector Remedies Directive. The Court of Justice has been very active regarding the principles derived from the Treaties (the obligations analysed in Part II), and the Court is expected to be active when dealing with reviews of the three types of contracts.

Time limits are not a requirement to implement in the national review systems, neither under the Public Sector Remedies Directive nor under the EU principles. However, when setting time limits for B-services, a few minimum requirements must be met according to the Public Sector Remedies Directive. Furthermore, time limits cannot begin before the tenderer knows, or ought to know, of a decision and cannot render the right to review excessively difficult.

82. This has also been stated in a case from the Danish Complaints Board of Public Procurement, see decision of August 25, 2010, Tegnestuen T plus ApS v. Københavns Kommune.

CHAPTER 11

Remedies

1. Introduction

Having established that a certain undertaking is entitled to bring proceedings and that the review body is competent in settling disputes (as analysed in chapter 10), the next question concerns which remedies the review body has if a contracting authority has breached the obligations derived from the principles of the Treaties. Thus, the aim of this chapter is to analyse the remedies available in national review systems for breaches of obligations.

For B-services, it will first of all be analysed which remedies from the Public Sector Remedies Directive are applicable for breaches of the principles of the Treaties.

Contracts below the thresholds and service concession contracts are left to the principles derived from the Treaties. Thus, potential remedies for breaches of the principles of the Treaties are left to the Member States to regulate (the principle of national procedural autonomy), but these remedies must be in line with the principles of the Treaties. On the one hand, because most of the provisions in the Directive are merely a 'codification' of the principles of the Treaties, arguably the same type of rules apply for contracts below the thresholds and service concession contracts. However, clearly the Court will not interpret these contracts to be covered by the Directive, as seen in *Spijker*,[1] where the Court concluded that because the contract in question was above the thresholds, it fell within the Public Sector Directive, *'... and thus within the scope of Directive 89/665'*.[2] However, this chapter analyses whether remedies similar to those in the Public Sector Remedies Directive apply as a consequence of the principles derived from the Treaties or whether

1. Case C-568/08, Combinatie Spijker Infrabouw-De Jonge Konstruktie and Others v. Provincie Drenthe, [2010] December 9, 2010 (not yet reported).
2. Case C-568/08, Combinatie Spijker Infrabouw-De Jonge Konstruktie and Others v. Provincie Drenthe, [2010] December 9, 2010 (not yet reported), paragraph 41.

the Court of Justice can be expected to find inspiration in secondary legislation (here, the Public Sector Remedies Directive)[3] when deciding on the remedies in a specific case addressing a breach of the principles of the Treaties.

Only very few procurement cases at national level have been initiated for violation of the transparency obligation.[4] Furthermore, whether national courts will rule on the matter is uncertain because the obligations derived from the principles of the Treaties are relatively new and significant time may pass before the question arises in these courts.[5]

Relevant for all three types of contracts is the question of whether remedies not found within the Public Sector Remedies Directive are available based on the principles derived from the Treaties, such as an obligation to terminate a contract that was concluded in breach of the principles of the Treaties. The question was placed before the Court in *Wall.*[6] The Court nevertheless found that, in this case, such remedies could not be derived from EU law. Whether this will always be the case is discussed in this chapter.

1.1. Outline

Section 2 analyses the remedies available in the Public Sector Remedies Directive. The four types of remedies available in the Directive are analysed and discussed for B-services, namely, interim measures (Section 2.1), setting aside decisions (Section 2.2), damages (Section 2.3) and ineffectiveness (Section 2.4). Whether similar remedies can be derived from the principles of the Treaties and, hence, apply to contracts below the thresholds and service concession contracts is also analysed in each section.

3. Treumer, Steen and Werlauff, Erik *"The Leverage Principle: Secondary Law as a Lever for the Development of Primary Community Law"* [2003] ELR n° 1, 28(1) pp. 124-133.
4. Treumer, Steen *"Basis and Conditions for a Damages Claim for breach of the EU Public Procurement Rules"* in Lichère, Francois & Fairgrieve, Duncan (Eds) *"Public Procurement Law: Damages as an effective Remedy"* [2011] Hart, p. 161, who also states in relation to damages that the case law where a claim for damages is brought in this context is presumably very limited.
5. See Treumer, Steen *"The State of Law and Current Issues"* in Treumer, Steen & Lichère Francois (Eds) *"Enforcement of the EU Public Procurement Rules"* [2011] DJØF p. 45 who states: *'national courts (...) presumably will be reluctant to rule that analogue remedies apply outside the scope of the Public Procurement Directives'.*
6. Case C-91/08, Wall AG v. La ville de Francfort-sur-le-Main and Frankfurter Entsorgungs- und Service (FES) GmbH, [2010] ECR I-2815.

Section 3 analyses and discusses whether remedies outside the Public Sector Remedies Directive apply to breaches of the principles of the Treaties when entering into one of the three types of contracts. Section 4 discusses the Commission's proposals for a Directive on Concessions and the proposal for a new Public Sector Directive and their consequences on remedies for concession contracts and B-service contracts. Section 5 provides the conclusion and discusses whether the remedies available are (sufficiently) effective.

2. Remedies available in the Public Sector Remedies Directive

Bringing proceedings both before and after a contract has been signed is possible. The remedies available for the review bodies to use depend on the timing of the proceedings.

The aim of bringing a complaint before the contract has been signed is to stop the procedure and enable the contracting authority to correct errors before the results are final. In that regard, interim measures (as well as setting aside decisions) are relevant. Once the contract has been signed, the contracting authority is no longer able to correct errors. Thus, the remedies available when bringing procedures after the signing of the contract are either damages or seeking to have the contract declared ineffective.

The Public Sector Remedies Directive addresses the following four types of remedies:

1. Interim measures;
2. Setting aside decisions;
3. Damages; and
4. Declaring certain types of contracts ineffective.

The review bodies have been able to use the first three types of remedies through the first Public Sector Remedies Directive, and these remedies apply to B-service contracts. The Amending Remedies Directive introduced the possibility to declare contracts ineffective under specific circumstances.

Sections 2.1 to 2.4 analyse and discuss the remedies in the Public Sector Remedies Directive and whether they apply to B-services. Furthermore, each section discusses whether similar remedies apply for contracts below the thresholds and service concession contracts based on the principles of the Treaties, or whether the Court of Justice can be expected to come to the conclusion that similar remedies apply for these types of contracts based on the principles of the Treaties.

2.1. Interim measures

2.1.1. B-services

When a contracting authority enters into a B-service contract, the review body must be able to grant interim measures in cases in which a complaint has been submitted regarding a breach of the principles of the Treaties (or a breach of Article 23 of the Public Sector Directive). In that regard, the review body must

> '*... take, at the earliest opportunity and by way of interlocutory procedures, interim measures (...) including measures to suspend or to ensure the suspension of the procedure for the award of a public contract or the implementation of any decision taken by the contracting authority*'.[7]

The purpose of interim measures is to allow corrections to the alleged infringement and to prevent further damage to the concerned interests.[8] Interim measures ensure that the contract is not signed (or if the contract was signed, ensure that the contract is not fulfilled) until the review body has settled the case. Thus, interim measures do not finally determine the legal situation,[9] but only ensure that the procedure is put on hold until a final decision that settles the dispute is available.

In procurement situations, interim measures are important because procedures to award public contracts are of short duration, which means that potential infringements need to be dealt with urgently.[10] Thus, interim measures in procurement cases are important because if the contracting authority refuses to delay the signing of the contract, the contract will be concluded and the complainant will, in most cases, only have the possibility to apply for damages.[11]

7. Article 2(1)(a) of the Public Sector Remedies Directive.
8. Article 2(1)(a) of the Public Sector Remedies Directive.
9. Case C-568/08, Combinatie Spijker Infrabouw-De Jonge Konstruktie and Others v. Provincie Drenthe, [2010] December 9, 2010 (Not yet reported), paragraph 61.
10. Recital 5 of the first Public Sector Remedies Directive. Also repeated in Case C-214/00, Commission v. Spain, [2003] ECR I-4667, paragraph 96.
11. Interim measures can also be given to suspend a contract already concluded, which was the case in Case C-194/88 R, Commission v. Italy, [1988] ECR 5647. It is also stated in the preparatory acts to the Danish Enforcement Act that a concluded contract can be suspended. See, 'Forslag til lov om håndhævelse af udbudsreglerne m.v. [2010] Folketingstidende 2009-10, A, L 110', p. 27, [henceforth the proposal for the 'Enforcement Act'].

In my view, the possibility to grant interim measures for B-services are based on the same conditions as for granting interim measures for contracts fully covered by the Public Sector Directive. However, the Public Sector Remedies Directive does not state conditions for granting interim measures.[12] In most Member States, obtaining interim measures is difficult.[13] Moreover, as argued by *Kotsonis*, too strict a test by the national courts can be contrary to the Remedies Directives if it results in regular denial of access to interim measures.[14] Thus, creating a system in the Member State in which interim measures are possible is important to ensure the effectiveness of the enforcement system.

Member States can choose to state conditions for granting interim measures in their national legislation, but the legislation may also be silent on the matter. Thus, it is possible not to have any rules that address the conditions for interim measures. This is to some extent the situation in Denmark, where the 'Enforcement Act' only states that interim measures can be granted if there are 'special reasons',[15] allowing the Complaints Board for Public Procurement to turn to the Court of Justice's case law to determine the crite-

12. Caranta, Roberto *"Many Different Paths, but are They All Leading to Effectiveness?"* in Treumer, Steen & Lichère Francois (Eds) *"Enforcement of the EU Public Procurement Rules"* [2011] DJØF, p. 64, states that the conditions for granting interim relief are more or less the same all over Europe and that the conditions, in substance, are the same as in procedures from the Court of Justice. Trepte, Peter *"Public Procurement in the EU"* [2007] 2nd Edition, Oxford, p. 555 states the procedures are generally available on similar terms in most Member States, but the criteria for the effective implementation vary widely.
13. Treumer, Steen *"The State of Law and Current Issues"* in Treumer, Steen & Lichère Francois (Eds) *"Enforcement of the EU Public Procurement Rules"* [2011] DJØF p. 20 and 30.
14. Kotsonis, Totis *"The basis on which the remedy of damages must be made available"* [2011] PPLR n° 3, NA59-63. *Kotsonis* also refers to a UK case where the judge had expressed doubts as to the compatibility of certain aspect of the court-based test to grant interim measures with the principle of effectiveness. Also in Denmark has it been questioned whether the lack of granting interim measures is contrary to the principle of effectiveness, see, for example, Treumer, Steen *"National håndhævelse af EU's Udbudsregler – er håndhævelsessystemet effektivt på EU-udbudsområdet?* in Treumer, Steen & Fejø, Jens *"EU's udbudsregler – implementering og håndhævelse i Norden"* [2006] DJØF, p. 106, Caranta, Roberto *"Many Different Paths, but are They All Leading to Effectiveness?"* in Treumer, Steen & Lichère Francois (Eds) *"Enforcement of the EU Public Procurement Rules"* [2011] DJØF, p. 64 argues that Italy is presumable the only Member State where courts are quite generous in granting interim measures.
15. The Enforcement Act § 12.

ria that must be met to grant interim measures.[16] This also represents an example of a Member State's review body seeking to find inspiration at the EU level to develop a national regime, in this case for interim measures.[17]

According to Article 279 TFEU, the Court of Justice may prescribe necessary interim measures for cases that come before it. An application before the Court for interim measures must state

> *'the subject-matter of the proceedings, the circumstances giving rise to urgency and the pleas of fact and law establishing a prima facie case for the interim measures applied for'.*[18]

The Court of Justice has occasionally granted interim measures in procurement cases in enforcement proceedings.[19] However, most cases regarding interim measures in procurement situations come from the General Court in relation to tender procedures conducted by the EU institutions, which uses the same conditions. The conditions can be an inspiration for determining the circumstances under which the national courts may grant interim measures.

Three conditions must exist before the Court of Justice grants interim measures. First, the granting of interim measures must be justified (*Fumus boni Juris*). Second, there must be a need for the interim measures and, third, the Court is able to balance the concerned interests.

2.1.1.1. Fumus boni Juris

The first condition calls for justification for granting interim measures. Thus, the complainant must be able to establish a *prima facie* case or, in other words, the complainant must have an arguable case.

16. See, for example, decision of October 16, 2007, Kuwait Petroleum A/S v. Sønderborg Kommune. For further on interim measures in the Danish complaints system, see Thorup, Kirsten & Frimodt, Mette U.2010B 303 *"Standstill og opsættende virkning i udbudsretten";* Treumer, Steen *"Enforcement of the EU Public Procurement Rules: Danish Regulation and Practice"* in Treumer, Steen & Lichère, Francois (Eds) *"Enforcement of the EU Public Procurement Rules"* [2011] DJØF, pp. 162-168.
17. Treumer, Steen & Lichère Francois (Eds) *"Enforcement of the EU Public Procurement Rules"* [2011] DJØF, p. 19.
18. Article 83 (2) of the Court of Justice's Rules of Procedures, (Rules of Procedure of the Court of Justice of 19 June 1991, last amended by 'Amendments to the Rules of Procedure of the Court of Justice', [2011] OJ L 162/17.)
19. See, for example, Case C-194/88 R, Commission v. Italy, [1988] ECR 5647.

Not all breaches that the contracting authority makes can lead to a *prima facie* case. *Arrowsmith* argued that this requirement does not mean that the complainant must show that he is likely to succeed in the main action;[20] however, this argument can be questioned because if a complainant is not likely to succeed, then interim measures are not needed.[21] Moreover, this condition requires that a breach be related to the undertaking seeking to obtain the interim measures. For example, that the undertaking should not have been prequalified or the complaint should lead to an annulment of the contracting authority's decision, meaning that setting the decision aside must be possible.[22]

2.1.1.2. Need for interim measures

The second condition means that a need for interim measures must exist. In that regard, the case should be urgent[23] and interim measures must be necessary to avoid irreparable damages. Regarding this second condition, the General Court has stated that

> *'It must therefore be considered whether it has been shown with a sufficient degree of probability that the applicant* ***is likely to suffer serious and irreparable damage if the interim relief applied for is not granted****'* [emphasis added].[24]

Thus, the need for interim measures is implied in situations in which the applicant is likely to suffer irreparable damages.[25] For example, if the com-

20. Arrowsmith, Sue *"Enforcing the Public Procurement Rules: Legal Remedies in the Court of Justice and the National Courts"* in Arrowsmith, Sue (Ed.) *"Public Procurement in the European Community: Volume IV – Remedies for enforcing the Public Procurement rules"* [1993] Earlsgate Press, p. 27.
21. See also Thorup, Kirsten & Frimodt, Mette U.2010B 303 *"Standstill og opsættende virkning i udbudsretten"* who argue that the Board only will grant interim measures where it is likely that the breach involved would lead to setting aside the contracting authority's decision.
22. See, Thorup, Kirsten & Frimodt, Mette U.2010B 303 *"Standstill og opsættende virkning i udbudsretten"*.
23. The Rules of Procedure, Article 83(2) requires that the applicant states *'the circumstances giving rise to urgency (...)'*.
24. Case T-114/06, Globe SA v. Commission, [2006] ECR II-2627, paragraph 106.
25. The requirement for irreparable appears in procurement cases to have been implied in the sense of irreversible, see, for example, Treumer, Steen *"Enforcement of the EU Public Procurement Rules: The State of Law and Current Issues"* in Treumer, Steen & Lichère, Francois (Eds) *"Enforcement of the EU Public Procurement Rules"* [2011] DJØF, p. 21.

plainant submitted an unconditional tender, he would not have won the contract in any case and, therefore, will not suffer irreparable damage.[26] In procurement contexts, applying for damages is possible in most cases; therefore, the complainant often does not meet the second condition because it will not suffer irreparable damages. In *Capgemini Nederland BV v. the Commission,*[27] the applicant had claimed that the damage it would suffer, would be serious, because if the other undertaking's bid had been rejected then the applicant would have been awarded the contract.[28] The applicant furthermore, argued that the award of the contract, and, *a fortiori*, the execution and performance of this contract, even for the duration of the interim measures proceedings, would make it impossible for the Commission (the contracting authority in the case) to go back on the disputed decision.[29] However, the General Court found that that:

> *'... the rejection of the applicant's bid, were it not justified, could be repaired: the costs of participating in the tender procedure could be quantified and made good, a pecuniary compensation envisaged and the applicant would be free to take part in a fresh call for tenders'.*[30]

The General Court has furthermore, stated that an undertaking that participates in a tender procedure does not have

> *'... an absolute guarantee that it will be awarded the contract, but must always keep in mind the possibility that the contract could be awarded to another tenderer. Under those circumstances, the adverse financial consequences which the company in question would*

26. Which was the situation in the Danish Complaints Board's decision of April 8, 2010 KPI Communications A/S v. IT- og Telestyrelsen and decision of April 3, 2010 KMD v. Frederiksberg Kommune. Or another situation could be if a complainant has not even submitted a tender, see decision of September 9, 2009, Lekolar v. Sydjysk Kommuneindkøb. In the latter situation there will not be a loss and there will be no need for interim measures.
27. See, for example, Case T-447/04 R, Capgemini Nederland BV v. the Commission, [2005] ECR II-257.
28. Case T-447/04 R, Capgemini Nederland BV v. the Commission, [2005] ECR II-257, paragraph 47.
29. Case T-447/04 R, Capgemini Nederland BV v. the Commission, [2005] ECR II-257, paragraph 49.
30. Case T-447/04 R, Capgemini Nederland BV v. the Commission, [2005] ECR II-257, paragraph 57.

suffer as a result of the rejection of its tender have, generally, to be considered to be part of the normal commercial risk which each company active in the market must face'.[31]

On the contrary, if the undertaking does not win the contract, it will be 'excluded' from the market or be in a very weak condition, thus fulfilling the second condition.[32] Thus, an undertaking must be able to show a loss if it is not granted the contract. Additionally, the timing of the complaint can influence the possibility of being granted interim measures.

Often, this second condition is not fulfilled, thus resulting in interim measures not being granted.[33]

2.1.1.3. Balance of interest

If the first two conditions are met, the Court will need to balance interests, which entails considering the complainant's need for interim measures versus the harm that such interim measures can bring to the contracting authority. This balance will depend on the contract in question, hereunder the public need for receiving the service, and the undertaking's need for being granted interim measures.

2.1.2. Contracts below the thresholds and service concession contracts

The Public Sector Remedies Directive does not require Member States' review bodies to grant interim measures in cases related to contracts below the thresholds and service concession contracts. However, in some cases, not granting interim measures can be argued to be contrary to the principles of the Treaties, hereunder the principle of effectiveness and the right to effective review.

31. Case T-511/08, Unity OSG FZE v. Council, [2009] ECR II-10, paragraph 26.
32. See, for example, Case T-511/08, Unity OSG FZE v. Council, [2009] ECR II-10, paragraph 35, where the Court found that: *'interim measures sought could be justified in the circumstances of the present case only if it were apparent that in the absence of such measures the applicant would be in a situation which could endanger its very existence or irretrievably alter its position in the market'*. The case is commented by Varga, Zsófia *"Burden of Proof in Interim Proceedings: Unity OSG FZE v. Council (T-511/08R)"* [2009] PPLR n° 4, NA 128. See also decision from the Danish Complaints Board of March, 23, 2011, AV Form A/S v. 12 by gruppens indkøbscentral.
33. In line with Treumer, Steen *"Enforcement of the EU Public Procurement Rules: Danish Regulation and Practice"* in Treumer, Steen & Lichère, Francois (Eds) *"Enforcement of the EU Public Procurement Rules"* [2011] DJØF, p. 264.

In *Unibet*[34] (a grand chamber decision from the Court of Justice), the Court found that a national court must

'be able to grant the interim relief sought, provided that such relief is ***necessary,*** *(...), in order to ensure the full effectiveness of the judgment to be given on the existence of the rights claimed under Community law'* [emphasis added].[35]

The Court based its finding on the principle of effective judicial protection of an individual's right to require interim measures to be granted *'... where the grant of such relief is necessary to ensure the full effectiveness of the judgment to be given on the existence of such rights'*.[36] Thus, I argue that granting interim measures in review procedures for all three types of contracts must be possible or the principles of the Treaties will not be effective. The requirement for interim measures to be '*necessary*' in *Unibet* is very similar to the second condition of the Court of Justice in relation to interim measures, namely *'the need for interim measures'* (see Section 2.1.1.2). In my view, granting interim measures for contracts below the thresholds and service concession contracts should be interpreted in accordance with the case law from the Court on interim measures.

Furthermore, I see no reason to differentiate between contracts under the Public Sector Directive, hereunder B-services, and service concession contracts and contracts below the thresholds. Thus, if a contracting authority can prevent remedies by signing the contract, such a review system will not be effective and the undertaking should be able to be granted interim measures for serious breaches in which it is at risk of suffering irreparable harm. Thus, interim measures must be available from the national courts when a breach of the principles of the Treaties has taken place in relation to the three types of contracts.

2.1.3. Automatic suspension

In addition to the provision on interim measures, an automatic suspension applies in situations in which a complaint is launched before the review body during the standstill period. In such a situation, the submission of a complaint

34. Case C-432/05, Unibet (London) Ltd and Unibet (International) Ltd v. Justitiekanslern, [2007] ECR I-2271.
35. Case C-432/05, Unibet (London) Ltd and Unibet (International) Ltd v. Justitiekanslern, [2007] ECR I-2271, paragraph 76.
36. Case C-432/05, Unibet (London) Ltd and Unibet (International) Ltd v. Justitiekanslern, [2007] ECR I-2271, paragraph 76.

leads to an automatic suspension of the conclusion of the contract.[37] Thus, the contracting authority cannot enter into the contract before the review body has made a decision on either granting or disregarding further interim measures.[38]

The purpose of the automatic suspension is that seeking review

'shortly before the end of the minimum standstill period should not have the effect of depriving the body responsible for review procedures of the minimum time needed to act, in particular to extend the standstill period for the conclusion of the contract'.[39]

Each Member State must decide on the length of the automatic suspension, as long as it is ensured that it ends after the expiration of the standstill period.[40]

Interestingly, the Public Sector Remedies Directive does not contain an obligation to notify the contracting authority when a complaint has been handed to a review body. If Member States do not provide such a requirement in their national legislation, a contracting authority may be able to sign a contract during a period in which the decision to award a contract is automatically suspended. In such a situation, the review body has no other alternative than to declare the contract ineffective.

The Public Sector Remedies Directive contains no exception for cases in which the contracting authority has signed a contract in good faith and believes that complaints were not submitted. Therefore, establishing a system that ensures that the contracting authority is informed immediately when a review procedure is started is crucial. This notification can be done by specifying an obligation for the review body to inform the contracting authority when a complaint has been launched or by requiring the complainant to simultaneously send a copy of its application of submission to the contracting authority.

37. Article 2(3) of the Public Sector Remedies Directive, which, however, only requires an automatic suspension in cases where the subject matter of the complaint concerns the award decision ct. the wording 'reviews a contract award decision'. In Denmark, the suspension has been extended to apply for all sorts of complaints submitted in the standstill period.
38. Article 2 b of the Public Sector Remedies Directive, which also states that it is possible for the suspension to end when the case is settle in its entirety.
39. Recital 12 of the Amending Remedies Directive.
40. Article 2(3) of the Amending Remedies Directive. In Denmark, for example, the Complaints Board has 30 days from the date of receipt of the complaint to decide upon whether to grant further interim measures.

As analysed in chapter 9, the type of standstill period that applies to the three types of contracts is not the same as the type introduced in the Public Sector Remedies Directive. In my opinion, this also means that when a proceeding is brought before a review body regarding the type of standstill period that applies for the three types of contracts, the complaint need not be automatically suspended. Automatic suspension cannot be said to follow from the principles of the Treaties. However, in my opinion, although a standstill applies for the three types of contracts, such an automatic suspension cannot be derived from the principles of the Treaties.[41]

2.2. Setting aside decisions

The Public Sector Remedies Directive requires that review bodies have the power to *'either set aside or ensure the setting aside of decisions taken unlawfully (...)'.*[42] Before addressing whether a review body can set aside an unlawful decision, exploring what constitutes a decision within the meaning of the Public Sector Remedies Directive, hereunder what types of decisions taken by contracting authorities in relation to the three types of contract constitute a decision within the meaning of the Public Sector Remedies Directive, is relevant.

2.2.1. Decisions

Article 2(1)(b) lists various types of decisions, which must be open for review such as

> *'the removal of discriminatory technical, economic or financial specifications in the invitation to tender, the contract documents or in any other document relating to the contract award procedure'*. The list is not exhaustive.

In several cases, the Court of Justice has dealt with what constitutes a decision, and also in relation to some situations not covered by the Public Sector Directive. The concept of a decision is interpreted broadly.[43] *Stadt Halle*[44] concerned a contract falling within the Directive; however, the contracting

41. Also the opinion of the Danish legislator, see the proposal for the 'Enforcement Act', p. 28.
42. Article 2(1)(b) of the Public Sector Remedies Directive.
43. Trepte, Peter *"Public Procurement in the EU"* [2007] 2nd Edition, Oxford, p. 546.
44. Case C-26/03, Stadt Halle and RPL Recyclingpark Lochau GmbH v. Arbeitsgemeinschaft Thermische Restabfall- und Energieverwertungsanlage TREA Leuna, [2005] ECR I-1.

authority awarded the contract directly, without following procedures in the Directive. The Court first stated that,

'Where a contracting authority decides not to initiate an award procedure on the ground that the contract in question does not, in its opinion, fall within the scope of the relevant Community rules, such a decision constitutes the very first decision amenable to judicial review.'[45]

Thus, the review bodies must be competent in handling disputes related to whether the Procurement Directives apply and matters in which the contracting authority is of the opinion that the Directives did not apply. For example, this will be the case if a contracting authority is of the opinion that a given contract is below the thresholds; such a decision must be open for review. Whether this is also true for potential breaches of the transparency obligation is not as clear. However, examining the case, the Court also stated that

'... every decision of a contracting authority falling under the Community rules in the field of public procurement and liable to infringe them is subject to the judicial review (...).'[46]

This statement indicates that all types of decisions subject to EU law in the field of public procurement fall within the expression of *decision* in the Public Sector Remedies Directive.

In *Hospital Ingenieure*,[47] the Court found that a contracting authority's decision to annul a tender procedure constituted a decision. A decision to annul a tender procedure falls outside the Procurement Directives, but the Court found that such a decision was *'... still subject to fundamental rules of Community law, and in particular to the principles laid down by the EC Treaty on the right of establishment and the freedom to provide services'*.[48] Thereafter, the Court concluded that since the decision to annul the tender procedure was covered by EU law,

45. Case C-26/03, Stadt Halle and RPL Recyclingpark Lochau GmbH v. Arbeitsgemeinschaft Thermische Restabfall- und Energieverwertungsanlage TREA Leuna, [2005] ECR I-1, paragraph 33.
46. Case C-26/03, Stadt Halle and RPL Recyclingpark Lochau GmbH v. Arbeitsgemeinschaft Thermische Restabfall- und Energieverwertungsanlage TREA Leuna, [2005] ECR I-1, paragraph 28.
47. Case C-92/00, Hospital Ingenieure Krankenhaustechnik Planungs-Gesellschaft mbH (HI) v. Stadt Wien, [2002] ECR I-5553.
48. Case C-92/00, Hospital Ingenieure Krankenhaustechnik Planungs-Gesellschaft mbH (HI) v. Stadt Wien, [2002] ECR I-5553, paragraph 42.

'*... it also falls within the rules laid down by Directive 89/665 in order to ensure compliance with the rules of Community law on public contracts*,' and that '*any other interpretation would undermine the effectiveness of Directive 89/665'*.[49]

Moreover, in *Makedoniko Metro*,[50] the disputed decision also concerned annulment of a tender procedure. The Court referred to *Telaustria* and that the general principles of EU law applied to annulment of a procedure. Since these general principles applied to procurement decisions, *'that decision also falls within the rules laid down by Directive 89/665 in order to ensure compliance with the rules of Community law on public contracts'*.[51] Thus, by referring directly to the principles of the Treaties and *Telaustria*, decisions that constitute breaches of the obligations derived from the principles of the Treaties must, in all cases, arguably be open for review.

On one hand, the three types of contracts are subject to the principles of the Treaties when such contracts are entered into; therefore, even though decisions taken in that regard are outside the Public Sector Directive, since EU law contains certain obligations, decisions taken in relation to the three types of contracts must also be open to review. On the other hand, *Hospital Ingenieure* and *Makedoniko Metro* related to contracts falling under the Public Sector Directive and, therefore, a decision to annul a procedure is linked to the rules in the Public Sector Directive, whereas at least service concession contracts and contracts below the thresholds fall fully outside the Public Sector Directive.

In my opinion, when dealing with contracting authorities' decisions taken in relation to the three types of contracts, bringing proceedings must be possible. As seen in chapter 10, based on the principle of effective judicial review, access to the Court must also be open for contracts below the thresholds and service concession contracts. Thus, for the courts to review decisions should clearly also be possible.

The Court of Justice already held that a contracting authority's decision regarding the classification of a contract must be open for review.[52] Addition-

49. Case C-92/00, Hospital Ingenieure Krankenhaustechnik Planungs-Gesellschaft mbH (HI) v. Stadt Wien, [2002] ECR I-5553, paragraphs 48 and 52.
50. Case C-57/01, Makedoniko Metro and Michaniki AE v. Elliniko Dimosio, [2003] ECR I-1091.
51. Case C-57/01, Makedoniko Metro and Michaniki AE v. Elliniko Dimosio, [2003] ECR I-1091, paragraph 70.
52. Case C-411/00, Felix Swoboda GmbH v. Österreichische Nationalbank, [2002] ECR I-10567, paragraph 62, which states: '*... In that regard, it must be observed that the classification of services in Annexes I A and I B to Directive 92/50 is pri-*

ally, a contracting authority's decision to determine whether a contract is of a cross-border interest must, as stated in *SECAP*, be the subject of review.[53] *Trybus* states,

'However, as a crucial limitation, tenderers can only bring proceedings when the contract has relevance for the Internal Market.'[54]

This is apparent in that the obligations derived from the principles of the Treaties apply only if the contract has a certain cross-border interest. However, the decision regarding whether a contract is in fact of cross-border interest, as well as the decision regarding classification of a contract, must be open for review. Thus, the statement is in my view not entirely accurate.

Preliminary considerations and similar concepts do not fall within the meaning of a decision. In *Stadt Halle*,[55] the Court found that

'Not amenable to review are acts which constitute a mere preliminary study of the market or which are purely preparatory and form part of the internal reflections of the contracting authority with a view to a public award procedure.'[56]

To conclude, for the obligations derived from the principles of the Treaties to be effective, decisions taken in relation to the three types of contracts can be subject to review, and decisions that a contracting authority makes when entering into such a contract constitute a decision within the meaning of the Public Sector Remedies Directive.

marily a question of fact for the contracting authority to determine, subject to review by the national courts.'

53. See joined Cases C-147 and C-148/06, SECAP SpA and Santorso Soc. coop. arl v. Comune di Torino, [2008] ECR I-3565, paragraph 30.
54. Trybus, Martin *"An Overview of the United Kingdom Public Procurement Review and Remedies System with an emphasis on England and Wales"* in Treumer, Steen & Lichère, Francois (Eds) *"Enforcement of the EU Public Procurement Rules"* [2011] DJØF, p. 208.
55. Case C-26/03, Stadt Halle and RPL Recyclingpark Lochau GmbH v. Arbeitsgemeinschaft Thermische Restabfall- und Energieverwertungsanlage TREA Leuna, [2005] ECR I-1.
56. Case C-26/03, Stadt Halle and RPL Recyclingpark Lochau GmbH v. Arbeitsgemeinschaft Thermische Restabfall- und Energieverwertungsanlage TREA Leuna, [2005] ECR I-1, paragraph 35.

2.2.1.1. Discretions of the contracting authority

A special category of decisions is the type of decisions that a contracting authority makes when awarding a contract (evaluating the tenders). Such decisions can and will often contain significant discretion as to how the tender should be evaluated, hereunder how many points a tender will receive regarding certain award criterion and similar. When dealing with the three types of contracts, stating beforehand the weighting of the different award criteria when awarding a contract is not necessary.[57] Thus, the contracting authority's discretion might have even more influence on which tenderer will be awarded the contract than for contracts falling within the Public Sector Directive.

The General Court has stated that contracting authorities have wide discretion with regard to factors taken into account when awarding a contract.[58] Given this discretion, the review by the General Court

> *'must be limited to checking that the rules governing the procedure and statement of reasons have been complied with, that the facts found are correct and that there has been no manifest error of assessment or misuse of powers.'*[59]

The General Court also concluded that the burden of proof in such situations is on the claimant (the tenderer).[60]

In Denmark, the Danish Complaints Board has stated that the contracting authority must prove that an award was determined in accordance with the award criteria. For example, in *P.V. Supa OY v. Herlev Kommune*,[61] the contracting authority did not use an evaluation model when evaluating tenders. Instead, a verbal assessment of the tenders was made in relation to the various award criteria. The Board found that the contracting authority must use its discretion to prove that the evaluation was made in accordance with the award criteria, hereunder the weighting. In this case, the contracting authority was able to prove this point.[62]

Although a contracting authority's discretion could be a relevant subject for review, and in principle constitutes a decision within the meaning of the

57. See chapter 8, section 5.2.4.
58. Case T-232/06, Evropaïki Dynamiki v. Commission, [2011] September 9, 2011, (not yet reported), paragraph 180.
59. Case T-232/06, Evropaïki Dynamiki v. Commission, [2011] September 9, 2011, (not yet reported), paragraph 180
60. Case T-232/06, Evropaïki Dynamiki v. Commission, [2011] September 9, 2011, (not yet reported), paragraph 195.
61. Decision of July 12, 2010, P.V. Supa OY v. Herlev Kommune.
62. See, also decision of September 30, 2009, Dansk Erhverv v. Region Nordjylland.

Remedies Directive, the rules for review of such discretion for the three types of contracts cannot be any different than when a contract is covered by the Public Sector Directive. Therefore, unless the review body by national law has been granted other competences, it can only examine whether the contracting authority is in compliance with the formals rules surrounding discretions.

2.2.2. Setting aside

Not all types of unlawful decisions taken by a contracting authority must be set aside. Some decisions may not have an influence on the result of the competition; therefore, arguably they do not necessarily need to be set aside. Thus, assessing the specific circumstances in a given case is relevant.

The Public Sector Remedies Directive is silent on the consequences of setting aside a contracting authority's decision. Whether setting aside a contracting authority's decision affects the contract itself is a topic for discussion. In most Member States, setting aside a decision aims to nullify a decision before awarding the contract and not at annulment of the contract.[63] *Treumer* argues that if the annulment of a decision relates to setting aside the award decision, the contracting authority must make a new award decision or, even in some cases (such as if the contracting authority has used illegal award criteria), a new tender procedure.[64]

In Denmark, on more than one occasion the Complaints board have set aside decisions regarding B-services and contracts below the thresholds.[65] However, despite grave infringements, the Board also maintained a contracting authority's decision.[66]

63. Treumer, Steen *"Enforcement of the EU Public Procurement Rules: The State of Law and Current Issues"* in Treumer, Steen & Lichère Francois (Eds) *"Enforcement of the EU Public Procurement Rules"* [2011] DJØF, p. 32.
64. Treumer, Steen *"Enforcement of the EU Public Procurement Rules: The State of Law and Current Issues"* in Treumer, Steen & Lichère Francois (Eds) *"Enforcement of the EU Public Procurement Rules"* [2011] DJØF, p. 32.
65. See, for example, decision of June, 4, 2009, Eurest A/S v. Copenhagen Business School, decision of February 4, 2011, Intramed A/S v. Region Nordjylland, decision of July 29, 2011, Social-Medicinsk Tolkeservice v. Region Hovedstaden, decision of November 30, 2011, Willis I/S mod Sønderborg Kommune.
66. Decision of September 15, 2009 Almenbo a.m.b.a. v. Den selvejende almene boligorganisation. The Board found that the contracting authority had not been permitted to enter into a contract, without prior advertising (which was required in the national legislation). The Board found that the contracting authority by the breach had violated the procurement rules seriously, but did not annul the decision to enter into

Following from the Directive, decisions that a contracting authority takes regarding B-services must be able to be set aside. Regarding contracts below the thresholds and service concession contracts, because access to the courts must be available (chapter 10) and many decisions made must be open for review (see section 2.2.1), to enable courts to only state that a breach had taken place but not be set aside makes little sense. *Burgi* agues that setting aside decisions

'is a necessity stemming from the fundamental public procurement principles (transparency, competition and non-discrimination) and, of course, the imperative of effectiveness'.[67]

Thus, to also ensure that the obligations derived from the principles of the Treaties are effective, it is submitted that unlawful decisions taken in relation to these contracts can be set aside.

2.3. Damages

This section addresses damages for a contracting authority's breach of the EU procurement rules.[68] Remedies must be available to ensure the effectiveness of the EU procurement rules, and one such remedy is damages to *'persons harmed by an infringement'.*[69] Nothing is mentioned in the Public Sector Remedies Directive as to how damages should be awarded. The Directive

the contract. The Board emphasised that the complainant, despite being aware of the breach, had submitted a complaint late and that the length of the contract was only one year.

67. Burgi, Martin *"A Report about the German Remedies System"* in Treumer, Steen & Lichère Francois (Eds) *"Enforcement of the EU Public Procurement Rules"* [2011] DJØF, p. 131.
68. Only damages for breaches of the procurement rules are examined and not for breaches of contractual obligations in case a contract is declared ineffective or terminated for other reasons contrary to the conditions in the contract. In such a case it might be possible for the contracting authority's contract party to be awarded damages based on other grounds if national law provides for it. See, for example, Treumer, Steen *"Enforcement of the EU Public Procurement Rules: The State of Law and Current Issues"* in Treumer, Steen & Lichère Francois (Eds) *"Enforcement of the EU Public Procurement Rules"* [2011] DJØF p. 39. See also Arnould, Joul *"Damages for performing an Illegal contract – the other side of the Mirror: Comments on Three Recent Judgments of the French Council of State"* [2008] PPLR n° 17, NA 274.
69. Article 2(1)(c) of the Public Sector Remedies Directive.

merely states that damages must be available.[70] However, Member States are able to

'provide that where damages are claimed on the grounds that a decision was taken unlawfully, the contested decision must first be set aside by a body having the necessary powers'.[71]

Thus, Member States are responsible for creating a system that allows damages for contracts covered by the Public Sector Remedies Directive, and can make damages depending on whether a contracting authority's decision has been set aside.

Whether damages are in fact granted varies among the Member States;[72] therefore, for an undertaking to identify whether damages are an option to pursue in a concrete case can be difficult. In some Member States, the conditions for damages for breaches of the procurement rules in relation to a contract falling within the Public Sector Directive is the same as for breaches of the national rules or the principles of the Treaties.[73]

The right to damages under the Remedies Directive has been argued not to give a further protection under the general principles of EU law (Member States liability cases, Section 2.3.2)[74] and that the conditions for damages un-

70. Article 2(1)(c) of the Public Sector Remedies Directive.
71. Article 2(5) of the Public Sector Remedies Directive.
72. For information on various systems on damages in different Member States see the Special issue of PPLR edited by Treumer, Steen *"Damages for violations of the EC Procurement Rules"*, PPLR [2006] n° 4, pp. 159-240, Treumer, Steen & Lichère Francois (Eds) *"Enforcement of the EU Public Procurement Rules"* [2011] DJØF, Lichère, Francois & Fairgrieve, Duncan (Eds) *"Public Procurement Law: Damages as an effective Remedy"* [2011] Hart, Treumer, Steen *"Damages for Breach of the EC Public Procurement Rules from a Danish Perspective"* [2004] European Business Organization Law Review, For a Swedish perspective see Leffler, Henrik *"Damages for liability for breach of EC Procurement Law: Governing Principles and Practical Solutions"* [2003] PPLR n° 4, pp. 151-174.
73. This, is for example, the situation in Denmark, where the Complaints Board in theory grant damages for breaches of the Treaties principles when awarding one of the three types of contracts, but it is rather difficult to obtain them. Regarding goods and services see the present author in Hansen, Carina Risvig *"Pligt til annoncering af offentlige kontrakter – uden effektiv håndhævelse af reglerne?"*, in U.2011B.101. However, regarding works contracts below the thresholds, damages have been awarded more often.
74. Arrowsmith, Sue *"Enforcing the Public Procurement Rules: Legal Remedies in the Court of Justice and the National Courts"* in Arrowsmith, Sue (Ed.) *"Public Pro-*

der the Remedies Directive should be interpreted in this light.[75] However, the Member State may also incur liability under less strict conditions on the basis of national law.

Because contracts below the thresholds and service concession contracts are not covered by the Directive, national law, or damages on grounds of the case law on Member States liability is the only grounds on which damages can be awarded for breaches taken in relation to these contracts. According to the Court of Justice, the principle of liability for damage caused to individuals as a result of breaches of EU law for which the Member State is responsible is *'inherent in the system of the Treaty'*.[76] Thus, for principles of the Treaties to be effective, it is my opinion that awarding damages on the principle of state liability must be possible. In *Köbler*,[77] the Court of Justice stated that,

'the full effectiveness of those rules [The EU rules edt.] would be called in question and the protection of those rights would be weakened if individuals were precluded from being able, under certain conditions, to obtain reparation when their rights are affected by an infringement of Community law attributable to a decision of a court of a Member State adjudicating at last instance'.[78]

Thus, in order to ensure undertakings rights are ensured, it must be possible to claim damages based on the conditions for Member States' liability, as developed in case law.[79]

In addition to the case law on Member States liability (discussed in Section 2.3.2), the Court of Justice recently addressed the conditions for damages in a few cases. Because this case law is applicable to B-service contracts, some observations on these rulings are made in Section 2.3.1.

curement in the European Community: Volume IV – Remedies for enforcing the Public Procurement rules" [1993] Earlsgate Press, p. 52.

75. Leffler, Henrik *"Damages for liability for breach of EC Procurement Law: Governing Principles and Practical Solutions"* [2003] PPLR n° 4 pp. 151-174, p. 154. Treumer, Steen *"The State of Law and Current Issues"* in Treumer, Steen & Lichère Francois (Eds) *"Enforcement of the EU Public Procurement Rules"* [2011] DJØF, p. 46.
76. Case C-224/01, Gerhard Köbler v. Austria, [2003] ECR I-10239, paragraph 30.
77. Case C-224/01, Gerhard Köbler v. Austria, [2003] ECR I-10239.
78. Case C-224/01, Gerhard Köbler v. Austria, [2003] ECR I-10239, paragraph 33.
79. In line with Treumer, Steen *"Basis and Conditions for a Damages Claim for breach of the EU Public Procurement Rules"* in Lichère, Francois & Fairgrieve, Duncan (Eds) *"Public Procurement Law: Damages as an effective Remedy"* [2011] Hart, p. 161, with reference to other authors in footnote 77.

2.3.1. Case law under the Remedies Directive

In *Strabag*,[80] the Court found that Member States were not permitted to make damages conditional upon the infringement being culpable. The Court first stated that the conditions for damages '*... in principle comes under the procedural autonomy of the Member States, limited by the principles of equivalence and effectiveness*'.[81] However, although damages were for the Member States to determine, the Court found that examining whether Article 2(c) of the Remedies Directive precludes a national provision for which damages are only available when the contracting authority was at fault was necessary.[82]

The Court's examination first referred to the fact that Member States were permitted to introduce time limits in their national legislation and limit the review bodies' powers to damages after award of a contract.[83] The Court concluded that damages could only be a procedural alternative for which the possibility of being awarded damages is

> '*... no more dependent than the other legal remedies provided for in Article 2(1) of Directive 89/665 on a finding that the contracting authority is at fault*'.[84] Otherwise, '*the tenderer who has been harmed by an unlawful decision of a contracting authority is nevertheless deprived of the right to damages in respect of the damage caused by that decision, where the contracting authority is able to rebut the presumption that it is at fault*'.[85]

80. Case C-314/09, Stadt Graz v. Strabag AG and Others, [2010] September 30, 2010 (not yet reported). In the case, the undertaking Strabag, which had submitted the second best tender, brought proceedings claiming that the undertaking which had been awarded the contract had submitted an unconditional tender. The national court held that the award of the contract had been unlawful as the tender had not been conditional. The national court of first instance held that the action for damages was well founded, and that decision was upheld on appeal. The last instance court asked the Court of Justice for a preliminary ruling as to whether the national conditions for damages were contrary to the conditions in the Remedies Directive.
81. Case C-314/09, Stadt Graz v. Strabag AG and Others, [2010] 30 September 2010 (not yet reported), paragraph 34.
82. Case C-314/09, Stadt Graz v. Strabag AG and Others, [2010] 30 September 2010 (not yet reported), paragraph 34.
83. Article 2(6) of the Remedies Directive (now Article 2(7)).
84. Case C-314/09, Stadt Graz v. Strabag AG and Others, [2010] 30 September 2010 (not yet reported), paragraph 39.
85. Case C-314/09, Stadt Graz v. Strabag AG and Others, [2010] 30 September 2010 (not yet reported), paragraph 41.

The Court found that such a situation is contrary to the aim of the Remedies Directive.[86] Thus, the Court concluded that granting damages cannot rely on the contracting authority being in fault.[87] *Treumer* finds that the approach in *Strabag* seems indirectly *'to rule out that a Member State make damages for breaches of EU public procurement law conditional of a "sufficiently serious breach" or "substantial" breaches'*.[88] Moreover, *Caranta* argues in line with this that the ruling in *Strabag* can be interpreted to state that illegality is a sufficient condition for liability, and thus the case law on damages for breach of procurement rules is more demanding than the general rule on liability for breaches of EU law.[89]

In *Spijker*,[90] the Court was asked whether criteria for the award of damages applied according to EU law. The Court found that Article 2(c) gives

> *'concrete expression to the principle of State liability for loss and damage caused to individuals as a result of breaches of EU law for which the State can be held responsible'*.[91]

Furthermore, the Court stated that the case law had not yet set out more detailed criteria on the basis of which damage must be determined.[92] Thus, according to the principle of national procedural autonomy, Member States must regulate damages under the conditions that the principles of equivalence

86. Case C-314/09, Stadt Graz v. Strabag AG and Others, [2010] 30 September 2010 (not yet reported), paragraph 43.
87. The case is commented by Kotsonis, Totis *"The basis on which the remedy of damages must be made available"* [2011] PPLR n° 3, NA59-63, who argues that the Court's ruling would apply to all remedies in the Remedies Directive, thus neither interim measures or the setting aside of decisions can require the establishment of fault.
88. Treumer, Steen *"Enforcement of the EU Public Procurement Rules: The State of Law and Current Issues"* in Treumer, Steen & Lichère, Francois (Eds) *"Enforcement of the EU Public Procurement Rules"* [2011] DJØF, p. 39.
89. Caranta, Roberto *"Many Different Paths, but are They All Leading to Effectiveness?"* in Treumer, Steen & Lichère Francois (Eds) *"Enforcement of the EU Public Procurement Rules"* [2011] DJØF, p. 71.
90. Case C-568/08, Combinatie Spijker Infrabouw-De Jonge Konstruktie and Others v. Provincie Drenthe, [2010] December 9, 2010 (Not yet reported).
91. Case C-568/08, Combinatie Spijker Infrabouw-De Jonge Konstruktie and Others v. Provincie Drenthe, [2010] December 9, 2010 (Not yet reported), paragraph 87.
92. Case C-568/08, Combinatie Spijker Infrabouw-De Jonge Konstruktie and Others v. Provincie Drenthe, [2010] December 9, 2010 (Not yet reported), paragraph 88.

and effectiveness are complied with.[93] The Court referred to *Strabag*, paragraph 33, in which it merely emphasised that the Remedies Directive laid down minimum conditions, and that national law must ensure that the review procedures were effective. Thus, Member States must establish grounds for damages, provided that these conditions are in accordance with the principle of effectiveness and equivalence.[94] The ruling in *Spijker* does not elaborate further on the conditions set in *Strabag*. This is peculiar because, as *Treumer* states, *'this case law appears to cause more confusion than clarity'*.[95] *Caranta* states that one reason for the different outcome in the two cases could be that the Court in *Spijker* asked a '*totally open question.*'[96] Whether the Court will follow the *Spijker* ruling in the future when it is asked to rule upon damages remains to be seen. Thus, at the moment, the state of the law regarding the conditions for damages is unclear.[97]

Regarding contracts below the thresholds and service concession contracts, in my view the rulings in *Strabag* and *Spijker* cannot be transferred to these types of contract. These cases are only relevant for B-services and the Court of Justice cannot be expected to find inspiration in the Remedies Directive to place such peculiar and contradictory conditions on the two types of contracts, as the case law is built on the general need for an effective remedies system under the Directive. For the Court to interpret this case law to be applicable to these contracts would be far-reaching and contrary to the principle of national procedural autonomy.

93. Case C-568/08, Combinatie Spijker Infrabouw-De Jonge Konstruktie and Others v. Provincie Drenthe, [2010] December 9, 2010 (Not yet reported), paragraph 90.
94. Case C-568/08, Combinatie Spijker Infrabouw-De Jonge Konstruktie and Others v. Provincie Drenthe, [2010] December 9, 2010 (Not yet reported)
95. Treumer, Steen *"Basis and Conditions for a Damages Claim for breach of the EU Public Procurement Rules"* in Lichère, Francois & Fairgrieve, Duncan (Eds) *"Public Procurement Law: Damages as an effective Remedy"* [2011] Hart, p. 160.
96. Caranta, Roberto *"Many Different Paths, but are They All Leading to Effectiveness?"* in Treumer, Steen & Lichère Francois (Eds) *"Enforcement of the EU Public Procurement Rules"* [2011] DJØF, p. 73.
97. See also Treumer, Steen *"Basis and Conditions for a Damages Claim for breach of the EU Public Procurement Rules"* in Lichère, Francois & Fairgrieve, Duncan (Eds) *"Public Procurement Law: Damages as an effective Remedy"* [2011] Hart, p. 160.

2.3.2. Member States' liability

A contracting authority can be liable for breaches of the principles derived from the Treaties when awarding one of the three types of contracts based on the conditions governing Member States liability.

The conditions for damages have developed since the Court gave its ruling in *Francowich.*[98] In this case, the Court found that a Member State is required to grant damages for a breach of EU law for which it is responsible. The conditions governing Member State liability have been further explained in a number of cases, perhaps most comprehensively in *Brasserie du Pêcheur*,[99] and such conditions can be summarised as follows:

- The rule of law infringed must be intended to confer rights on individuals;
- The breach must be sufficiently serious; and
- There must be a direct causal link between the breach of the obligation resting on the State and the loss sustained by the injured party.[100]

The three conditions are cumulative. The following sections make some observations on the three conditions in relation to the obligations derived from the principles of the Treaties.

2.3.2.1. Confer rights on individuals

The rule of law infringed must be intended to confer rights on individuals. When dealing with breaches in relation to the three types of contracts, the rules that can be breached are the principles derived from the Treaties. In that regard, a breach can take place when a contracting authority enters into a contract without following the transparency obligation (as analysed in chapter 7). However, a breach can also relate to other breaches of the principles of equal treatment and transparency, such as a breach of the positive obligations discussed in chapter 8.

98. Joined Cases C-6/90 & 9/90, Andrea Francovich and Danila Bonifaci and others v. Italy, [1991] ECR I-5357.
99. Joined cases C-46/93 and C-48/93, Brasserie du Pêcheur SA v. Bundesrepublik Deutschland and The Queen v. Secretary of State for Transport, ex parte: Factortame Ltd and others, [1996] ECR I-1029.
100. Joined Cases C-6/90 & 9/90, Andrea Francovich and Danila Bonifaci and others v. Italy, [1991] ECR I-5357, paragraph 40. See also the opinion of Advocate General Jacobs delivered on 11 July 2002, in Case C-112/00, Eugen Schmidberger, Internationale Transporte und Planzüge v. Austria, [2003] ECR I-5659 paragraph 20-21.

The obligations derived from the principles of the Treaties aim to ensure undistorted competition by guaranteeing open and equal access to public contracts. The undertaking's right relates primarily to ensuring that the principles of equal treatment and transparency are upheld (see chapters 7 and 8). Thus, the principles confer rights to undertakings when a contracting authority awards one of the three types of contracts.

2.3.2.2. Sufficiently serious breach

The second condition is that the breach must be sufficiently serious. The Court has stated that a sufficiently serious breach takes place when the Member State manifestly and gravely disregards the limits to its discretion.[101]

The set of procurement rules is dynamic; thus, a breach of the principles of the Treaties cannot *per se* be categorised as a sufficiently serious breach. For a contract falling within the Directive and entered into without a contract notice, the Court of Justice found the failure to publish a contract notice in the OJ is the most serious breach of the procurement rules.[102] This may indicate that for a contracting authority to enter into one of the three types of contracts without creating competition for the contract would also constitute a sufficiently serious breach.

For example, *Treumer* suggests that a sufficiently serious breach could be the case for a contract that has been concluded with a tenderer who should have been excluded because of, for example, illegal state aid or technical dialogue prior to the submission of bids,[103] thus indicating that a breach of the principle of equal treatment can be considered as sufficiently serious under some circumstances. Such breaches are serious because they have an impact on competition for the contract and, ultimately, who will be awarded the contract.

101. Joined cases C-46/93 and C-48/93, Brasserie du Pêcheur SA v. Bundesrepublik Deutschland and The Queen v. Secretary of State for Transport, ex parte: Factortame Ltd and others, [1996] ECR I-1029, paragraph 55. Other considerations to be taken into account, according to paragraphs 56-57 are clarity and precisions of the rules, the measure of discretions left to the authorities, whether the breach was intentional, whether any error of law excusable etc.
102. Case C-26/03, Stadt Halle and RPL Recyclingpark Lochau GmbH v. Arbeitsgemeinschaft Thermische Restabfall- und Energieverwertungsanlage TREA Leuna, [2005] ECR I-1, paragraph 37.
103. Treumer, Steen, *"Towards an obligation to Terminate Contracts Concluded in Breach of the EC Public Procurement Rules: End of Status of Concluded Public Contracts as Sacred Cows".* [2007] PPLR n° 6, pp. 371-386, p. 378.

I agree that in some situations a breach of the principles of the Treaties can be sufficiently serious, but in most situations a breach should not be regarded as such. Whether the breach was clear will always depend on the concrete circumstances taken into consideration. The Court of Justice has developed the obligations applicable to the three types of contracts and the legal certainty of these obligations is very weak because the Court's expected rulings on specific matters are unpredictable. Furthermore, as seen in Part I of the Thesis, establishing the correct nature of a contract and determining whether the contract has a cross-border interest, thus establishing whether the principles of the Treaties apply, can be difficult. Thus, regarding damages for the three types of contracts, considering all types of breaches of the principles sufficiently serious would be very strict.

On the other hand, entering into a contract directly without any form of competition for the contract will often be a sufficiently serious breach of the EU public procurement rules. In my opinion, a clear breach of the free movement provisions would also be a clear breach of the Treaty, such as, for example, a situation in which a contracting authority stated a make without following the statement with 'or equivalence'. Furthermore, illegal award criteria may be considered sufficiently serious, but may also depend on the influence that such criteria can have on who was awarded the contract. Not waiting to sign the contract until the expiry of a standstill period may also be considered sufficiently serious if such an action deprived a tenderer from bringing proceedings. However, in such a situation material rules presumably should also have been breached.[104] In any case, it is submitted that a breach can only be considered serious if it influences who was awarded the contract.

2.3.2.3. Direct causal link

The third condition of requiring a direct causal link between the breach of the obligation resting on the Member State and the loss sustained by the injured party can occur at more than one level.

First, that the contracting authority's infringement resulted in the tenderer not being awarded the contract and therefore suffering a loss of profit is possible.

104. As will be seen in section 2.4 regarding ineffectiveness, this is also what the EU legislator has chosen as a ground for ineffective where standstill, which has deprived the tenderer from applying for review combined with an infringement the Public Sector Directive, which has affected the chances of the tenderer applying for a review to obtain the contract can lead to ineffectiveness.

Second, that any loss occurred related only to the cost to participate in the tender procedure because the tenderer would not have won the contract is also possible. For a contract entered into directly without any form of competition, very often a potential tenderer cannot prove the loss because it has neither suffered a loss from competing for the contract nor can it prove that it would have won the contract had it been put out for competition.

2.3.3. Conclusion regarding damages

Obtaining damages for a contracting authority's breach of the principles derived from the Treaties is difficult because breaches of such principles related to entering into one of the three types of contracts are most likely not to constitute a sufficiently serious breach. However, in my view certain breaches, such as entering into a contract directly without any type of competition, are sufficiently serious breaches of the principles of the Treaties. Yet, when addressing the direct award of a contract, proving a loss will not be possible in most cases. Thus, it is my opinion that the effectiveness of the EU rules is not ensured if damages are the only possible remedy.

2.4. Ineffectiveness

Certain types of contracts falling within the Public Sector Directive must, according to this Directive, be declared as ineffective if a breach of the EU procurement rules has occurred.[105]

The concept of ineffectiveness is a new EU concept and the assumption is that the Court of Justice will interpret it this way.[106] That a contract is being considered ineffective must lead to '*... that the rights and obligations of the parties under the contract should cease to be enforced and performed*'.[107] National law is to decide on the consequences of a contract considered ineffective,[108] and national law may provide for the retroactive cancellation of all contractual obligations (*ex tunc*) or may limit the scope of the cancellation to those obligations that still have to be performed (*ex nunc*). In the latter case,

105. Article 2d of the Public Sector Remedies Directive.
106. Regarding ineffectiveness as a new concept see, for example, Clifton, Michael-James *"Ineffectiveness – The New Deterrent: Will the New Remedies Directive Ensure Greater Compliance with the Substantive Procurement Rules in the Classical Sectors?"* [2009] PPLR n°4, pp. 165-184, p. 168, who states: *'It is perhaps unsurprising that the Commission turned to a new term (...) after so many other formulations, which necessarily have long and specified histories in the jurisdiction of the Member States had been used in the waste case (Commission vs. Germany).'*
107. Recital 21 of the Amending Remedies Directive.
108. Article 2 d (2) of the Public Sector Remedies Directive.

Member States shall provide for the application of alternative sanctions within the meaning of Article 2e(2).[109] However, Member States are not required to implement alternative sanctions, and if they do not provide such alternatives then the contract must be declared ineffective *ex tunc*. Because there are various consequences to a contract being declared ineffective, such consequences will vary among the Member States.

For example, in Denmark the Complaints Board for Public Procurement is responsible for establishing whether a contract is ineffective *ex nunc* or *ex tunc*. The key rule is that contracts are declared ineffective *ex nunc* except for cases in which it is possible to return the goods to the contractor in the same condition as they were delivered.[110] In other Member States, the courts have not been given the option to decide on the most appropriate action. For example, Germany has provided for the *ex tunc* possibility,[111] whereas the UK has only provided for ineffectiveness *ex nunc*.[112] Because ineffectiveness is a new remedy in most Member States,[113] the Court of Justice has yet to rule on the matter.[114]

109. Article 2 d (3) of the Public Sector Remedies Directive. These alternative sanctions must be either fines or shortening of the duration of the contract.
110. See the proposal for the 'Enforcement Act', p. 34. So far only two contracts have been declared for ineffective. See decision of January 3, 2012, Danske Arkitektvirksomheder v. Thisted Gymnasiumog HF-kurser, where the Board declared the contract for ineffective *ex nunc*, and provided for a fine of 80.000 DKK (approximately 11.000 Euro). Also decision of January 13, 2012, Danske arkitektvirksomheder v. Skanderborg Gymnasium had a contract been entered into directly and the contract was declared ineffective *ex nunc* and an alternative sanction was sat at 45.000 DKK (approximately 6000 Euro).
111. Burgi, Martin *"A Report about the German Remedies System"* in Treumer, Steen & Lichère Francois (Eds) *"Enforcement of the EU Public Procurement Rules"* [2011] DJØF, p. 138.
112. Trybus, Martin *"An Overview of the United Kingdom Public Procurement Review and Remedies System with an emphasis on England and Wales"* in Treumer, Steen & Lichère, Francois (Eds) *"Enforcement of the EU Public Procurement Rules"* [2011] DJØF, p. 222.
113. Except for France, where a similar possibility existed also before the Amending Remedies Directive. See Lichère, Francois & Gabayet, Nicolas *"Enforcement of the EU Public Procurement Rules in France"* in Treumer, Steen & Lichère, Francois (Eds) *"Enforcement of the EU Public Procurement Rules"* [2011] DJØF, p. 314.
114. Except for a preliminary reference in Case C-348/10, Norma-A and Dekom, [2011] November 11, 2011 (not yet reported) regarding whether ineffectiveness applied before the expiry of the transposition date of the Amending Remedies Directive, which the Court found it did not.

However, a breach of the EU procurement rules alone does not lead to ineffectiveness (*per se*) but must be established by an independent review body. Therefore, the Member States must ensure that *'a contract is considered ineffective by a review body (...) or that its ineffectiveness is the result of a decision of such a review body'*.[115] The review bodies must then declare a contract ineffective and a contracting authority cannot itself make such a decision.[116]

2.4.1. Types of contracts that can be declared ineffective

According to the Public Sector Remedies Directive, three types of breaches of the EU procurement rules must lead to the contract being considered ineffective by a review body.

The first type of infringement concerns the situation in which the contracting authority has awarded a contract without prior publication of a contract notice in the OJ as required by the Public Sector Directive. None of the three types of contracts require prior publication of a contract notice before being awarded. However, such contracts cannot be entered into directly, thus ensuring the obligations derived from the principles of Treaties. This does not mean that one of the three types of contracts must be declared ineffective if entered into without any form of competition because the Public Sector Remedies Directives only calls for contracts to be declared ineffective that requires prior publication of a notice in the OJ. Thus, the three types of contracts are never covered by this situation, but if the contracting authority has mistaken a service contract for a service concession contract and therefore failed to publish a contract notice in the OJ but followed the obligations applicable to service concession contracts when entered into that contract, such a service contract will be covered by the provisions in Article 2d and constitute an illegal direct award of a contract.

The second type of infringement that can cause a contract to be declared ineffective is a situation when a contracting authority is in breach of the rules regarding standstill or automatic suspension that at the same time has deprived the tenderer from applying for review, in combination with an infringement of the Public Sector Directive that affected the tenderer's chance

115. Article 2d(1) of the Public Sector Remedies Directive.

116. Burgi, Martin *"A Report about the German Remedies System"* in Treumer, Steen & Lichère Francois (Eds) *"Enforcement of the EU Public Procurement Rules"* [2011] DJØF p. 137 states regarding ineffectiveness in Germany that *'Hence, the award of a contract is not ineffective per se but always implies an application and the respective decision of an independent review body.'*

to obtain the contract. If the contracting authority has only breached the rules on standstill or automatic suspension, the review bodies have the discretion to deem ineffectiveness proportionate.[117]

The three types of contracts are not required to have a standstill period as that provided for in the Public Sector Remedies Directive. Contracting authorities must, however, ensure a similar standstill period in order to ensure the effectiveness of the obligations derived from the principles of the Treaties (see chapter 9 for the discussion of standstill). Therefore, in my opinion, the three types of contracts cannot be considered ineffective in relation to this provision. However, if Member States have not included an exception in their national legislation for B-services regarding the standstill rules, a contract regarding a B-service can be declared ineffective if the contracting authority signed the contract during the standstill period and material rules were breached.

The third type of infringement that can lead to declaring a contract ineffective relates to framework agreements and dynamic purchasing systems, and is only an option if the contracting authority failed to follow the standstill rules in the Remedies Directive. However, such a contract can only be declared ineffective when the contract value is above the thresholds stated in the Public Sector Directive.[118] Applying a limitation on contract value also indicates that ineffectiveness was never intended to apply for contracts below the thresholds. In my view, framework agreements concerning B-services are not covered by this situation because B-services are not required to follow the rules in the Public Sector Directive.

The Directive states two exceptions to declaring a contract for ineffective. The first exception is when the review body finds 'overriding reasons relating to a general interest' to justify a contract not being declared ineffective.[119] The second is when a certain procedure for prior publications was used. These two exceptions are discussed below.

2.4.2. Exception 1: Overriding reasons relating to a general interest

In some cases, the review body can choose not to declare a contract ineffective if it finds that '... *overriding reasons relating to a general interest require*

117. Article 2e(1) of the Public Sector Remedies Directive.
118. Article 2b last indention of the Public Sector Remedies Directive
119. Article 2d(3) of the Public Sector Remedies Directive.

that the effects of the contract should be maintained'.[120] What constitutes *overriding reasons relating to a general interest* is not regulated in the Public Sector Remedies Directive, which merely states that economic interest related to the contract's effectiveness may be regarded as overriding reasons only if

'in exceptional circumstances ineffectiveness would lead to disproportionate consequences. However, economic interests directly linked to the contract concerned shall not constitute overriding reasons relating to a general interest'.[121]

Therefore, it can be argued that the exception of overriding reasons has very limited scope.

2.4.3. Exception 2: Prior publication of a notice – ex ante transparency

The Public Sector Remedies Directive contains another possible exception to ineffectiveness, which can be used under certain situations.[122] It cannot be used to avoid other sanctions than ineffectiveness.[123]

In order to use this exception, the contracting authority must be of the opinion that the award of a contract is permissible without following the rules in the Public Sector Directive and, hence, does not publish a contract notice in the OJ. Furthermore, the contracting authority must publish an *ex ante* transparency notice in the OJ

'expressing its intention to conclude the contract and the contract has not been concluded before the expiry of a period of at least 10 calendar days with effect from the day following the date of the publication of this notice'.[124]

120. Article 2(d)(3) of the Public Sector Remedies Directive, which furthermore states *'In this case, Member States shall provide for alternative penalties within the meaning of Article 2e (2), which shall be applied instead'*.
121. Article 2(d)(3) of the Public Sector Remedies Directive, which furthermore finds that such economic interests directly linked to the contract include: *'... inter alia, the costs resulting from the delay in the execution of the contract, the costs resulting from the launching of a new procurement procedure, the costs resulting from the change of the economic operator performing the contract and the costs of legal obligations resulting from the ineffectiveness'*.
122. The conditions can be found in Article 2d)4) of the Public Sector Remedies Directive.
123. Which has also been stated by the Danish Complaints Board in decision of December 5, 2011, Konica Minolta Business Solutions Denmark AS v. Erhvervsskolen Nordsjælland.
124. Article 2 d(4) of the Public Sector Remedies Directive.

If such a notice is published and no economic operators have challenged the validity of the direct awarding during a minimum 10-day waiting period (a sort of standstill period),[125] the contract can be concluded and its ineffectiveness can no longer be invoked at a later stage. In that regard, it is a requirement that

'the contracting authority considers that the award of a contract without prior publication of a contract notice in the Official Journal of the European Union is permissible'.[126]

From the wording of the Public Sector Remedies Directive, the contracting authority must objectively 'consider' the award of the contract to be permissible, indicating that review bodies cannot consider whether awarding the contract was in fact permissible. Thus, whether the contracting authority considered correctly by taking into account whether the contracting authority was acting in good faith. *Treumer* suggested that a review body should be able to declare a contract ineffective in certain situations. The Danish legislator seems to have suggested this choice by stating in the preparatory works regarding the Danish implementation of the Remedies Directive that [my translation]

'if the Complaints Board at a later time considers that the contracting authority has made a manifest error of assessment regarding whether the contract was covered by the Procurement Directives, the Board can declare the contract for ineffective'.[127]

According to Recital 26 of the amending Remedies Directive, that a review body can declare a contract ineffective in certain situations was introduced to ensure legal certainty. Thus, arguably, legal certainty will not exist if disregarding the contracting authority's decision is a possibility. Based on that conclusion, the Danish Complaints Board determined in *Konica Minolta Business Solutions Denmark AS v. Erhvervsskolen Nordsjælland* that the Board is not competent to declare a contract ineffective if the contracting au-

125. Recital 26 of the Amending Remedies Directive furthermore states: *'The voluntary publication which triggers this standstill period does not imply any extension of obligations deriving from Directive 2004/18/EC or Directive 2004/17/EC.'* Thus, requirements such as to state reasons in accordance with the Public Sector Directive Article 41 does not apply. Similar, if a complaint is brought before the review bodies in this 'voluntary standstill period', it will not have automatic suspension.
126. Article 2d(4) of the Public Sector Remedies Directive.
127. See the proposal for the 'Enforcement Act', p. 21.

thority followed the conditions to ensure *ex ante* transparency. Thus, it was not possible to set the contracting authority's discretion aside.[128]

However, according to Recital 20 of the Amending Remedies Directive, the Directive *'should not exclude the application of stricter sanctions in accordance with national law.'* Thus, because Member States are not required to implement the 'ex ante transparency exception', national law could arguably provide for a stricter use of the exception. Thus, the Complaints Board may have come to another conclusion had the exception been stated directly in the Danish legislation instead of the preparatory works.

If a contracting authority wishes to use this derogation and has doubts about whether the contract is a service concession contract or a B-service contract, or whether the value of the contract falls below the thresholds, the contracting authority should prior to concluding the contract have followed the obligations derived from the principles of the Treaties when awarding the contract. Otherwise, other remedies might occur.

3. Remedies not listed in the Public Sector Remedies Directive

The question of whether remedies exist for breaches of the EU procurement rules not listed in the Public Sector Remedies Directive, hereunder the question of whether a contracting authority has a duty to terminate a contract, is even more important for the three types of contracts than for contracts falling within the Public Sector Directive because these contracts are not covered by either the provisions in the Directive regarding standstill or ineffective as well as it is difficult to obtain damages for breaches of the principles derived from the Treaties.

Before the Court of Justice's ruling in *Commission v. Germany*,[129] most authors were of the opinion that a duty to terminate contracts did not exist.[130]

128. See decision of December 5, 2011, Konica Minolta Business Solutions Denmark AS v. Erhvervsskolen Nordsjælland. See also decision of November 3, 2011, Finn Frogne A/S v. Rigspolitiet.
129. Case C-503/04, Commission v. Germany, [2007] ECR I-6153.
130. See, for example, Treumer, Steen *"National håndhævelse af EU's Udbudsregler – er håndhævelsessystemet effektivt på EU-udbudsområdet?"* in Treumer, Steen & Fejø, Jens *"EU's udbudsregler – implementering og håndhævelse i Norden"* [2006] DJØF, p. 107, footnote 33 for references to academics arguing such a duty did not exist. However, Treumer argues that it should be possible to terminate a contract based on the principle of effectiveness.

However, the Court came to the opposite conclusion in the case and found that Germany was obliged to terminate two contracts. Thereby, the Court of Justice introduced a new form of remedy not found in the Remedies Directives. The case was the first and only of its kind that found that, in some situations, Member States have a duty to terminate contracts awarded illegal by a contracting authority (the case is examined in section 3.1).

In *Wall*,[131] the Court stated that a duty to terminate the contract did not exist regarding a service concession contract, but because the Court used the wording 'in every case', the discussion of whether remedies exist outside the Directive did not conclude with the case (the case is examined in Section 3.2). Whereas *Commission v. Germany* dealt with the question in relation to an enforcement proceeding, *Wall* was a preliminary ruling. Some of the arguments placed before the Court in *Commission v. Germany* (and that the Court dismissed) may have a greater impact in national courts.

Thus, Section 3.3 discusses whether breaches of the obligations derived from the principles of the Treaties can lead to a duty to terminate one of the three types of contracts, taking into consideration the arguments in the above two cases and their potential relevance at the national level.

3.1. Commission v. Germany

In July 2007, the Court of Justice found in *Commission v. Germany*[132] that Germany failed to fulfil its obligations according to Article 258 TFEU. The Court found that Germany had not adopted the necessary means to live up to the Court's ruling in two earlier cases. In these cases,[133] the Court of Justice stated that the municipality of Bockhorn, by concluding a contract for the collection of its wastewater for a term of at least 30 years with a private undertaking without following the procedures in the prior procurement Directive, failed to fulfil its obligations under EU law. Additionally, the city of Braunschweig concluded a contract under which a private undertaking was made responsible for residual waste disposal using thermal processing for a period of 30 years by applying the 'negotiated procedure without prior publication of a contract notice' when there were no grounds for doing so.

After the judgments in these cases, the contracts were not terminated even though the German government informed the two municipalities that the provisions regarding awarding of contracts should be upheld. The municipalities

131. Case C-91/08, Wall AG v. La ville de Francfort-sur-le-Main and Frankfurter Entsorgungs- und Service (FES) GmbH, [2010] ECR I-2815.
132. Case C-503/04, Commission v. Germany, [2007] ECR I-6153.
133. Joined cases C-20/01 and C-28/01, Commission v. Germany [2003] ECR I-3609.

were in that regard encouraged to inform the government on the measures taken to ensure that similar breaches would not exist in the future. However, the German government did not order the municipalities to terminate the contracts in question. The Commission initiated proceedings against Germany for not terminating the contracts, as it had not *'fulfilled the judgment of the case'* according to Article 258 TFEU. Therefore, the *Commission v. Germany* was primarily a case dealing with the question of whether Germany fulfilled its duties under the Treaties by not taking the necessary means to ensure that the disputed contracts were concluded in compliance with the Court of Justice's previous cases.

Therefore, when analysing the scope of the case, it is essential to highlight that the case resolved the relationship between Germany and the EU and not the relationship between a German contracting authority and a harmed tenderer. It is unclear from the case whether the duty to terminate a contract can only be an issue under enforcement proceedings. The case may have had a wider scope, which I will argue in section 3.3.[134] Moreover, some of the intervening Member States in the case and Germany argued that the principles of legal certainty and protecting legitimate expectations, the principle *pacta sunt servanda*, preclude that the contract in question should be terminated.[135] Nevertheless, the Court found that these arguments could not justify the non-implementation of a judgment that established a failure to fulfil obligations under an enforcement proceeding.[136] Section 3.3 discusses these arguments and whether they can apply at national level.

3.2. Wall AG

In *Wall AG,*[137] a German court (Landgericht Frankfurt am Main) asked the Court of Justice about the remedies available for breaches of the principles of the Treaties when entering into a service concessions contract. The city of Frankfurt published a call for tenders in a newspaper regarding a service concession contract concerning the operation, maintenance and service and cleaning of 11 toilet systems for a period of 16 years. Two of those systems were to be built and payment for the concession consisted of user fees for the

134. For a similar point, see Treumer, Steen, *"Towards an obligation to Terminate Contracts Concluded in Breach of the EC Public Procurement Rules: End of Status of Concluded Public Contracts as Sacred Cows"*. [2007] PPLR n° 6, pp. 371-386.
135. Case C-503/04, Commission v. Germany, [2007] ECR I-6153, paragraph 31.
136. Case C-503/04, Commission v. Germany, [2007] ECR I-6153, paragraph 32.
137. Case C-91/08, Wall AG v. La ville de Francfort-sur-le-Main and Frankfurter Entsorgungs- und Service (FES) GmbH, [2010] ECR I-2815.

toilets and the right to use the systems for commercials. The contract was awarded to the company Frankfurter Entsorgungs- und Service GmbH (FES) using Wall AG as a subcontractor. The contract stated that a change of subcontractor only was possible with permission from the City. Later, FES asked Wall and another company, DSM, to bid for the delivery of the two toilet systems. DSM was awarded the contract and the City was asked if changing the subcontractor was permissible. The City responded that it was of the opinion that FES alone was responsible for the contract.

Thereafter, Wall AG launched proceedings at the national court ordering FES not to fulfil the contract with DSM and that the City was not permitted to accept the change of the subcontractor. The national court referred five questions to the Court of Justice. One of these questions related to whether a breach of the principles of the Treaties, namely the principle of transparency when entering into – and changing a contract – could lead to a duty to terminate a contract.

The opinion from Advocate General *Bot* argued that no EU rules regulate remedies for such a breach.[138] According to *Bot*, the reasoning in *Commission v. Germany* could not be transferred to service concessions contracts because, first of all, no EU legislation exists regarding the awarding of a service concession contract and, secondly, ensuring that the contract in question is a regular contract or a concession contract is difficult. Therefore, the national courts should decide on remedies for such breaches of the principles derived from the Treaties.[139]

The Court of Justice came to the same conclusion but without any references to *Commission v. Germany* or to the Public Sector Remedies Directive. The Court found that the transparency obligation

'do not require the national authorities to terminate a contract or the national courts to grant a restraining order ***in every case*** *of an alleged breach of that obligation in connection with the award of service concessions'* [emphasis added].[140]

138. Opinion of General Advocate, Yves Bot, delivered on October 27, 2009 in Case C-91/08, Wall AG v. La ville de Francfort-sur-le-Main and Frankfurter Entsorgungs- und Service (FES) GmbH, [2010] ECR I-2815, paragraph 124.
139. Opinion of General Advocate, Yves Bot, delivered on October 27, 2009 in Case C-91/08, Wall AG v. La ville de Francfort-sur-le-Main and Frankfurter Entsorgungs- und Service (FES) GmbH, [2010] ECR I-2815, paragraphs 139-142.
140. Case C-91/08, Wall AG v. La ville de Francfort-sur-le-Main and Frankfurter Entsorgungs- und Service (FES) GmbH, [2010] ECR I-2815.

The Courts reference to *'in every* case*'* indicates that such an obligation could exist in some circumstances.

The Court's reasoning in the case is peculiar. First, the Court stated that

'in the absence of European Union rules, it is for the domestic legal system of each Member State to regulate the legal procedures for safeguarding rights which individuals derive from European Union law'[141] (the principle of national procedural autonomy).

However, the Member States are not entirely left to regulate the field of remedies, which the Court also acknowledged by stating that some requirements apply to the national systems. The Court stated that

'Such procedures must be no less favourable than similar domestic procedures (principle of equivalence) and must not render practically impossible or excessively difficult the exercise of rights conferred by the law of the European Union (principle of effectiveness).'[142]

Thus, the Court merely referred to the principles of the Treaties without adding any new substance to them. The Public Sector Directive does not cover service concession contracts, but contracting authorities concluding them are bound by the principle of the Treaties and must follow the obligations analysed in Part II of this Thesis. Thus, these obligations are a part of EU law. Moreover, Member States must ensure that effective enforcement and remedies take place in such situations.

Although the Court found that no remedies existed according to EU law, the case resulted in a preliminary ruling asking for remedies at the national level and that the Court could have found otherwise had the question been placed in an enforcement proceeding. *Treumer* argues that the Court most likely considers itself competent to terminate a contract and that it will likely apply the rationale in *Commission v. Germany* within a few years.[143]

Because the Court in *Wall* left the determination of the procedures and remedies for the three types of contracts to the Member States, the Member States must create an effective enforcement system. *Brown* states that, *'It is submitted that this devolved approach is entirely sensible and respects gen-*

141. Case C-91/08, Wall AG v. La ville de Francfort-sur-le-Main and Frankfurter Entsorgungs- und Service (FES) GmbH, [2010] ECR I-2815
142. Case C-91/08, Wall AG v. La ville de Francfort-sur-le-Main and Frankfurter Entsorgungs- und Service (FES) GmbH, [2010] ECR I-2815, paragraph 34.
143. Treumer, Steen *"Enforcement of the EU Public Procurement Rules: The State of Law and Current Issues"* in Treumer, Steen & Lichère, Francois (Eds) *"Enforcement of the EU Public Procurement Rules"* [2011] DJØF, p. 35.

eral EU law principles, including that of subsidiarity'.[144] However, in my opinion, if Member States do not provide for effective remedies in their system, the requirement for termination of contracts as in *Commission v. Germany* could be invoked to make the obligations effective. Another point is that *Wall* deals with a harmed tenderer and not the interest of the EU, as was the case in *Commission v. Germany*. Therefore, the national court using the national remedies must resolve such a case. Therefore, that the Court of Justice in time will 'create new remedies' for these types of breaches of the EU rules is possible.

3.3. Termination of one of the three types of contracts?

Without a doubt, as a main rule, a breach cannot lead to a duty to terminate a contract.[145] In *Commission v. Germany*, the dispute concerned direct awarding of a contract, which has been stated in the most serious breach of the procurement rules.[146] Thus, other remedies were necessary because in such a case damages could not be awarded. As argued by *Treumer*, *'It would indeed be a paradox if what is considered the most serious violation of the public procurement rules (...) would be the most difficult to challenge and have corrected.'*[147]

However, the Court of Justice did not say anything in *Commission v. Germany* regarding the possibility that breaches other than the direct awarding of a contract could lead to a duty for a contracting authority to terminate a contract. Hence, stating whether other types of breaches can lead to a duty to terminate a contract is difficult, if even at all possible. *Treumer* states,

> '*... that it will take a careful examination of the concrete circumstances in each individual case to establish whether there is an obligation to terminate a contract concluded in*

144. Brown, Adrian *"Changing a sub-contractor under a public services concession: Wall AG v. Stadt Frankfurt am Main (C-91/08)"* [2010] PPLR n° 5, p. 160-166.
145. In line with Treumer, Steen *"National håndhævelse af EU's Udbudsregler – er håndhævelsessystemet effektivt på EU-udbudsområdet?* in Treumer, Steen & Fejø, Jens *"EU's udbudsregler – implementering og håndhævelse i Norden"* [2006] DJØF p. 107.
146. Case C-26/03, Stadt Halle and RPL Recyclingpark Lochau GmbH v. Arbeitsgemeinschaft Thermische Restabfall- und Energieverwertungsanlage TREA Leuna, [2005] ECR I-1, paragraph 37.
147. Treumer, Steen *"The discretionary powers of contracting entities – towards a flexible approach in the recent case law of the European Court of Justice?"* [2006] PPLR n° 3, pp. 71-85.

breach of the EC public procurement ***rules and that it will not be the main rule that a breach leads to such an obligation***' [emphasis added].[148]

As a main rule it is for the Member States to decide on the effects of the annulment of a decision. This can be seen in Article 2(7) of the Public Sector Remedies Directive, which states that:

'The effects of the exercise of the powers referred to in paragraph 1 on a contract concluded subsequent to its award shall be determined by national law. Furthermore, (...) a Member State may provide that, after the conclusion of a contract following its award, the powers of the body responsible for the review procedures shall be limited to awarding damages to any person harmed by an infringement.'[149]

In *Commission v. Germany*, according to Germany (and supported by the intervening Member States), this provision allows for the Member States to provide in their national legislation that after the conclusion of a contract, bringing an action can give rise to only an award of damages and thus the rescission of that contract is excluded.

However, the Court disregarded this argument in *Commission v. Germany* and stated that,

'... the second subparagraph of Article 2(6) of Directive 89/665, [now Article 2(7)] *(...) relates, as is apparent from its wording, to the compensation which a person harmed by an infringement committed by a contracting authority may obtain from it. That provision, because of its specific nature, cannot be regarded also as regulating the relations between a Member State and the Community in the context of Articles 226 EC and 228 EC'.*[150]

Therefore, the Public Sector Remedies Directive does not influence the consequences of a case that is dealt with under an enforcement procedure. However, a dispute before a national court will deal with the relationship between a contracting authority and a harmed tenderer; therefore, Article 2(7) might have greater value before a national court. The Public Sector Remedies Directive does not cover contracts below the thresholds and service concession contracts, meaning that Article 2(7) likely does not have any influence on disputes regarding breaches of the principles when one of these contracts is awarded. However, in that regard the principle of national procedural auton-

148. Treumer, Steen, *"Towards an obligation to Terminate Contracts Concluded in Breach of the EC Public Procurement Rules: End of Status of Concluded Public Contracts as Sacred Cows"*. [2007] PPLR n° 6 pp. 371-386, p. 384.
149. Article 2(7) of the Public Sector Remedies Directive.
150. Case C-503/04, Commission v. Germany, [2007] ECR I-6153, paragraph 35.

omy applies. Thus, in my opinion, if Member States explicitly put in their national legislation that one of the three types of contracts cannot be terminated, great arguments are required to come to the opposite conclusion, which will be argued below that in some cases this might be possible.

Therefore, since the overall enforcement regime in the Member States must be effective, in my view that a contract could be terminated based on the principle of effectiveness if other remedies are not available cannot be excluded, which will be discussed below. *Treumer* points out some of the following issues for consideration: the breach of the EU public procurement rules must be sufficiently serious, whether the contract has an impact on the Internal Market if it is not terminated, the degree of completion of the contract, the public interest and the interest of the contract party of the contracting authority.[151] I will further discuss these issues below. Other arguments for not terminating a contract, such as those claimed by Germany in *Commission v. Germany*, will also be considered.

3.3.1. Sufficiently serious breach

Section 2.2.3 already analysed this condition with respect to the three types of contracts in relation to damages. The analysis concluded that not many types of breaches of the Treaties constitute a sufficiently serious breach, but a breach such as entering into a contract directly without any type of competition is a sufficiently serious breach of the principles of the Treaties.

3.3.2. Impact on the Internal Market

Another factor to consider when analysing whether a breach can lead to a duty to terminate a contract is whether not terminating the contract will have an impact on the Internal Market.[152] This requirement is not to be mistaken with whether a contract is of a cross-border interest (as analysed in chapter 6). A contract can be of cross-border interest without having a significant impact on the Internal Market.

I submit that, as a main rule, the three types of contracts do not have a significant impact on the Internal Market that is arguably present before a duty to terminate a contract exists according to EU law. However, exceptions to

151. Treumer, Steen, *"Towards an obligation to Terminate Contracts Concluded in Breach of the EC Public Procurement Rules: End of Status of Concluded Public Contracts as Sacred Cows."* [2007] PPLR n° 6, pp. 371-386.
152. Treumer, Steen, *"Towards an obligation to Terminate Contracts Concluded in Breach of the EC Public Procurement Rules: End of Status of Concluded Public Contracts as Sacred Cows."* [2007] PPLR n° 6, pp. 371-386.

this main rule may exist, such as a very long and high value service concession contract or a contract regarding a B-service that very limited undertakings have an interest in obtaining. Therefore, in a concrete case, the argument regarding the impact on the Internal Market could have some value.

3.3.3. Degree of completion of the contract – and the public interest

The degree of completion of the contract and the public interest are complex factors and depend very much on the contract in question, if they are relevant for discussion at all. If the service has already been fulfilled or the goods have been delivered, then discussing whether such a contract should be terminated makes little sense.[153] The arguments also seem to be secondary to whether the breach is sufficiently serious and whether the contract has an impact on the Internal Market. The notion of considering the public interest when deciding on whether to terminate a contract can also be seen in the Public Sector Remedies Directive, which contains the possibility of considering whether a contract should be declared ineffective if *'overriding reasons relating to a general interest require that the effects of the contract should be maintained'.*[154] In my opinion, the same sort of overriding reasons must also be taking into consideration when dealing with 'termination of a contract'.

However, these arguments must be interpreted as very limited exceptions when analysing whether a contract should be terminated. If a sufficiently serious breach of the Treaties is present (such as direct award of a contract), and the contract has an impact on the Internal Market, these arguments must be very strong to avoid creating a duty to terminate the contract in question.

3.3.4. Pacta sunt servanda and legitimate expectations

The Court of Justice also dismissed the arguments of *pacta sunt servanta* and legitimate expectations because EU law stands above such principles. However, in my opinion, the Court did not dismiss *pacta sunt servan* as a general statement that the national courts could not apply this argument. Therefore, that these arguments could have led to another result in a case between the contracting authority and a harmed tenderer is possible. In contrast, since these arguments determine whether an EU right is considered effective, they are presumably very weak and insufficient before a national court as well. If a contracting authority has entered into a service concession contract and the

153. Which is also why the Public Sector Remedies Directive has the possibility to issue a fine instead.
154. See section 2.4.2.

concessionaire in such a case has already invested in very expensive equipment, then the interest of the concessionaire could result in not terminating the contract.

3.4. Conclusion

As a main rule, I submit that a duty to terminate one of the three types of contracts does not exist. A court-developed duty to terminate a contract that has not been regulated by the EU legislator would lead to stricter rules compared with the types of contracts covered by the Public Sector Remedies Directive. Thus, as a main rule, it cannot be required that one of the three types of contracts to be terminated.

Nevertheless, if Member States do not provide for (other) effective remedies in their national enforcement system, the Court of Justice will likely conclude in a concrete case (where the above elements speak for a termination) that the contract must be terminated to ensure that the system is effective. Thus, it remains to be seen what the Court will rule in a concrete case.

4. The Commission's new proposals

The Commission's proposal for a new Directive on Concessions suggests that the Remedies Directives should apply to concession contracts above the thresholds. The aim of covering concessions by the Remedies Directives is

> *'to guarantee effective channels for challenging the award decision in court and provide minimal judicial standards which have to be observed by contracting authorities or entities'*.[155]

The proposal places concessions in line with contracts fully covered by the Public Sector Directive, thus also the rules of standstill as well as the possibility to declare a contract for ineffective will apply if the proposal is adopted.

Also, the proposal for a new Public Sector Directive will have consequences for B-services and the remedies available. Since the Public Sector Remedies Directive merely applies to contracts referred to in the Public Sector Directive Article 1(1) unless *'... such contracts are excluded in accordance with Articles 10 to 18 of that Directive'*. This means that these contracts falls within the Public Sector Remedies Directive. This will also mean that

155. See the explanatory memorandum to the Proposed Concessions Directive, p. 7. See also Articles 44 and 45.

the rules on standstill and ineffectiveness will apply. For example, the rules on standstill currently states that contracts where a contract notice is not mandatory can be excluded from the standstill (see chapter 9), because the proposal suggest making it mandatory to publish a sort of contract notice this will also lead to a requirement for standstill since B-services will no longer fall into this category. The same goes for the ineffectiveness provisions where currently B-services cannot lead to ineffectiveness, as it is not required to publish a contract notice in the OJ. Again by making it mandatory to do so, this will in my view lead to the possibility of declaring such contracts for ineffective.

The proposal does not mention these potential consequences for remedies.

In my view, I find it welcoming to introduce remedies for both service concession contracts as well as for B-services. As seen above, the remedies available is to some extent unclear and especially standstill would lead to a guarantee that it is possible to bring proceedings at a time where the award decision can still be changes.

5. Summary of findings

B-services contracts are covered by the remedies available in the Public Sector Remedies Directive, but can be excluded from being declared ineffective. In such cases, the same conditions for granting interim measures, setting aside decisions and damages, are available for breaches of the principles derived from the Treaties.

The Directive does not cover service concession contracts and contracts below the threshold. However, in my opinion interim measures must be available for situations in which they need to ensure the effectiveness of the principles. The Court is expected to find inspiration in its own case law to state the conditions that make such measures available when national legislation has not provided such.

Many decisions made by the contracting authority must be open for review; in my view, this also includes decisions made when awarding one of the three types of contracts to ensure the effectiveness of the obligations derived from the principles of the Treaties, as analysed in chapters 7 and 8. This statement also holds for elements such as determining the value of the contract and the nature of the contract (for example, whether a B-service or a service concession contract). Such categorisation decisions must be open for review since they constitute decisions within the meaning of the Public Sector Remedies Directive. Moreover, the subject of whether a contract has a cross-border interest must be open for review.

Damages must exist for these types of contracts based on Member States' liability case law. However, such damages can be difficult to obtain because a breach of the principles of the Treaties are rarely sufficiently serious.

With respect to the overall system of enforcement, first of all, a standstill period must be ensured to guarantee the effectiveness of the obligations derived from the principles of the Treaties. If standstill is not ensured, other possible remedies must be available, such as damages or the possibility of contract termination. Thus, the effectiveness of the enforcement system as one is the important factor.'[156] Therefore, the review system as a whole must be effective. It is my opinion that this is not the case with the current state of law because whether the discussed potential remedies are applicable and whether a standstill must be applied are unclear. If Member States do not regulate their national review procedures, the Court of Justice will likely conclude in a concrete case that an obligation to terminate a contract exits.

To conclude, it is my opinion that the current remedies are not sufficiently effective based on EU law. However, Member States may have implemented other remedies to ensure an effective system for the three types of contracts.

156. In line with Pachnou, Despina, *"Enforcement of the EC. Procurement Rules: The Standard Required of National Review Systems under E.C. Law in the Context of the Principle of Effectiveness"* [2000] PPLR n° 2, pp. 55-74.

CHAPTER 12

Summary of findings

1. Introduction

The aim of this Thesis was to analyse, clarify and discuss which positive obligations derived from EU law, in a public procurement law context, a contracting authority must apply when entering into one of the three types of contracts and how these obligations can be enforced.

In order to answer these questions, the Thesis was split in three parts. In this summary of findings, the main conclusions from each part of the Thesis will be examined. Furthermore, I will discuss whether there is a need for legislation for the three types of contracts. In that regard the Commission's recent proposal for changing the Public Sector Directive as well as the proposal for a new Directive on Concessions, are discussed.

2. Part I 'Introduction, definitions and foundations'

Chapter 2 of this Thesis examined the aim of the EU procurement and the principles of the Treaties. It was concluded that also the aim of the principles of the Treaties is to ensure undistorted competition by guaranteeing open, equal access to public contracts. In order to pursue this aim, contracting authorities must apply the principles of the Treaties when awarding one of the three types of contracts. It was argued that the principle of non-discrimination does not have an independent function in procurement context, and that the interpretation of the principles is the same under the Directive as under the Treaties.

Chapter 3 contains an analysis of the definition of a service concession contract found within the Public Sector Directive. It was seen that defining a service concession contract can be a difficult task as neither the definition itself nor the case law from the Court of Justice is clear on the matter. The chapter concludes, that the main difference between a regular service contract and a service concession contracts is that the consideration in a service concession contract consists of the right to exploit the service. Hence, the economic operator must bear the risk of profiting from the contract by being exposed to elements such as competition from the market, financing and whether he is guaranteed payment. It was concluded that the risk arising from operating the service must be substantial, but that the risk, according to the Court of Justice, can be limited in cases due to legislation in a specific sector (most likely only in the utilities sector). In these cases, the *transferred* risk must still be significant, which means that the risk that is present despite the legislation in the area must be transferred. By looking at the above these elements, it is necessary from case to case to make a calculation of the risk and this calculation can be difficult to make.

Chapter 4 examined when a contract falls below the thresholds. It was concluded that there were two reasons for excluding contracts below the EU thresholds from the procedural rules in the Public Sector Directive. Firstly, it is assumed that contracts below the threshold are not of cross-border interest. Secondly, the thresholds are set to ensure that the EU complies with the GPA.

Chapter 5 concerned the subject of B-service contracts and why these contracts were excluded from the Procurement Directives. It was concluded that B-service contracts were excluded from the procedural rules in the Public Sector Directive on the assumption that these types of contracts were not of cross-border interest. The contracting authority bears the burden of proof that the contract in question has been classified correctly.

Chapter 6 concerned an analysis of the EU concept of cross-border interest. The principles of the Treaties only apply if the contract in question is of 'certain cross-border interest'. The analysis of when a contract is of cross-border interest has been placed in part I of the Thesis because 'cross-border interest' is considered an essential requirement for the principles of the Treaties to apply and not as an obligation that can be derived from the principles of the Treaties. When a contract can be said to be of 'certain cross-border interest' depends on the specific contract in question, and will only cover the situation where a non-domestic undertaking wishes to directly tender for the contract, hence only direct cross-border interest is necessary. The contracting authority must in all cases make a concrete assessment, by including elements such as the value of the contract, language elements, the complexity of the works or services to be performed, the location for the performance of the contract, national legal requirements, the type of contract and the duration of the contract. Whether a contract is of certain cross-border interest is for the contracting authority to determine, based on a hypothetical analysis of the market and contract in question. The contracting authority's decision must be open for review, and in such a situation it is most likely that it will be for the contracting authority to bear the burden of proof of whether its assessment was correct when a procedure takes place in national courts.

3. Part II 'Positive obligations derived from the principles of the Treaties'

This Part of this Thesis relates to the obligations derived from the principles of the Treaties that contracting authorities must apply when awarding one of the three types of contracts.

Chapter 7 analysed the transparency obligation. Thus, according to the principle of transparency the contracting authority must ensure that a contract has been put out for some sort of competition before entering into the contract. This is necessary in order to ensure competition for the contract and to ensure equal treatment of undertakings, which is the overall aim of the EU public procurement rules. By ensuring competition, the contracting authority will create better access to public contract as well as ensuring getting better value for money. In some cases this it will be necessary to advertise a contract beforehand, if it is not possible for the contracting authority to create sufficient amount of competition for the contract by other means.

Chapter 8 discussed and examined whether other types of positive obligations could be derived from the principles of the Treaties. In that regard it was concluded that some requirements do apply, as these are a consequence of the principles of the Treaties and not the Public Sector Directive.

Chapter 9 concerned an analysis of the rules of standstill. Despite the fact that B-services contracts fall within the Public Sector Remedies Directive whereas contracts below the thresholds and service concession contracts do not, all tree types of contracts are excluded from the Directives rules on standstill. Nevertheless, a similar requirement for standstill can be found to exist based on the principles of the Treaties, mainly the principle of effectiveness. Article 41(2) of the Public Sector Directive applies to B-service contracts and leads to the conclusion that the contracting authority must provide reasons for its award decisions in accordance with that provision. Stating reasons for contracts below the thresholds and service concession contracts are also a necessity due to the principle of effective judicial review.

4. Part III 'Enforcement and Remedies'

Part III of the Thesis aimed at analysing the enforcement system and remedies available for breaches of the obligations derived from the principles of the Treaties when awarding one of the three types of contracts.

Chapter 10 examined the enforcement mechanism available in the Member States. In that regards, as the Public Sector Remedies Directive applies for B-services, the Directive sets requirements as to the review system, locus standi, as well as certain remedies for breaches of the obligations derived from the principles of the Treaties. Regarding contracts below the thresholds and service concession contracts, the principle of right to effective judicial review require access to the national courts for breaches of the EU rules. This does not mean that the same review bodies as for B-services should be available, but if a Member State does not regulate which review body has jurisdiction, the right to bringing proceedings must be available under the regular national court system. Time limits are not a requirement to have in national review systems, but when setting time limits for B-services a few minimum requirements must be met according to the Public Sector Remedies Directive. Such time limits must be appropriate and start to run from the tenderer know or ought to have known of a decision and not render the right to review excessively difficult.

Chapter 11 dealt with remedies available for breaches of the obligations derived from the principles of the Treaties. Even though only B-services are covered by the Public Sector Remedies Directive, some remedies must be available in the national courts for service concession contracts and contracts below the threshold.

Many decisions taken by the contracting authority must be open for review, including decisions taken when awarding one of the three types of contracts. This also goes for decisions such as determining the value of the contract, whether a contract has a cross-border interest as well as the nature of the contract, for example, whether a contract is a B-service or a service concession contract.

Damages must exist for these types of contracts based on the case law for Member States liability, but can be difficult to obtain as a breach of the principles of the Treaties very rarely can constitute a sufficiently serious breach.

All the three types of contracts are not covered by the ineffectiveness provision in Article 2 (d) (unless Member States have not implemented the exception for standstill for B-services). Finally, it was concluded that remedies derived from EU law outside the Public Sector Directive, does not, as a main rule exist. Only in exceptional situations where a sufficiently serious breach has taken place and where the contract has an impact on the Internal Market can there exist an obligation to terminate a contract. Thus, it was found that the current remedies are not sufficiently effective.

5. Need for new legislation?

The Thesis has focused on answering what the current legal rules is, *de lege lata*, without asking whether new legislation is needed. In this final section, I will make some observations as to whether legislation is needed for the three types of contracts. Legislation could be introduced at either national level or EU level.

5.1. National legislation

As mentioned in the introduction to this Thesis most Member States have national legislation regarding B-services and contracts below the thresholds. In that regard many Member States have chosen to apply the same rules for the three types of contracts as for those falling within the Public Sector Directive, in order to be on the safe side. Such 'over implementation'[1] might be transparent and ensures the equal treatment of economic operators, but it also places unnecessary burdens for contracting authorities to conduct, sometimes rather complicated, procedures for these contracts. It is my assumption that a flexible regime, leaving choices to the concrete contracting authority, is the best solution. However, I reckon that the principle of legal certainty has led many Member States to implement detailed national regulation for contracts outside the Directives, and that in some Member States this has been the preferred way to create legal certainty for contracting authorities – and even something the contracting authorities in that Member States have come to appreciate since they then know exactly which rules to follow.

When looking upon whether something should be regulated at EU level; it is relevant to bear in mind that Member States have judicial autonomy and there can be many reasons for not regulating a field at EU level (or regulating at all). According to the principle of subsidiarity, which is embodied in Article 5(3) and (4) TEU, the Union only acts (regulates) in areas which do not

1. In the Commission's Green Paper of EU public procurement policy Towards a more efficient European Procurement Market, COM (2011) 15, footnote 26, this concept is called 'gold-plating' and refers to the situation where Member States have national regulation which contain further requirements than can be derived from EU law.

fall under its exclusive competence, '*insofar as the objectives of the proposed action cannot be sufficiently achieved by the Member States (...) but can rather (...) be better achieved at Union level*'. Therefore, the EU should only regulate when the same objective cannot be achieved at national level.

Ensuring that the obligations derived from the Treaties, are applied by contracting authorities in cases where the contract is of cross-border interest, are in my view best ensured at national level. However, one must take into account that it is necessary to know when the Public Sector Directive covers a contract, and as was seen in chapter 3, the definition of service concession contracts is not clear, and a clearer definition should in my view be set at EU level since the concept of a service concession contract is a EU concept.

Regarding the positive obligations derived from the principles of the Treaties for contracting authorities when awarding one of the three types of contracts, these leads to an obligation to create competition for the contract. It was concluded that advertising in that regard is not necessary in all cases. If discussing whether it will be appropriate to introduce an obligation to advertise a contract beforehand – either at EU level or national level depends on from which side of the table the rules are looked upon.

From an undertaking perspective the aim of such a mechanism would presumably be to get better access to public contracts, but at the same time some undertakings will also be exposed to competition from non-domestic undertakings tendering for a contract in the first undertaking's Member State. From a contracting authority perspective advertising will in many cases lead to more competition for the contract, which ultimately would mean better value for money. However, an important element is that conducting a procedure can be rather costly and the need to evaluate more tenders (and the cost for this) will risk not being proportionate. Even though, it will be more costly, it will nevertheless create legal certainty as to which rules and obligation to behave in accordance with.

If taken the Member State perspective introducing obligations at EU level might not be inline with the intention and specific circumstances of each Member State, hereunder the principle of national procedural autonomy.

5.2. EU legislation

Introducing EU legislation in this field would ensure that the rules in all Member States are identical. This could be a useful tool for undertakings that take part in cross-border competitions, because they will be aware of the rules in the Member States. The Commission has recently published a new proposal for a new Directive on Concessions as well as a proposal for a new Public Sector Directive. These will be examined below.

5.2.1. The Proposed Concessions Directive

By proposing a Directive on Concessions it is the Commission's intention that creating specific obligations in the field of concessions will increase legal certainty on one hand by providing contracting authorities with clear rules incorporating the Treaty principles governing the award of concessions and on the other hand by giving economic operators with some basic guarantees with regard to the award procedure.[2] Thus, it does not seem from at least the explanatory notes, that it is the intention to create legislation which goes further than what already can be said to apply as a consequence of the principles of the Treaties. Taking a closer look at the proposal itself this does, however, not seem to be the case and it is my opinion that the proposal places obligations, which cannot be said to derive from the Treaty.

The Proposed Concessions Directive contains a new definition on what constitute a service concession contract, which has been elaborated on in chapter 3. It is my opinion that this new definition is highly welcome, as defining what constitute a concession has been seen to be a difficult task.

The Commission proposes to cover service concession contracts by a sort of similar regime as the Proposed Procurement Directives but with the intention of creating a more flexible – simpler regime – a sort of "light regime".

A brief look at the framework of the Directive, shows that the Proposed Concessions Directive is rather extensive; containing a total number of 53 Articles, indicating at a first view that this is not a 'light regime'. A closer look at the Proposed Concessions Directive also shows that many of the provisions found in the proposal are similar to those found within the Proposed Procurement Directive. This being elements such as many of the definitions, including that on contracting authorities and entities, many of the similar exclusion provisions, the provisions related to technical specifications, life cycle and life cycle-costing, the rules on performance of concessions etc.[3] The fact that the proposal covers a high number of the same provisions as the Proposed Procurement Directive makes it difficult to see that what is actually being proposed in relation to concessions is intended to be a 'light regime'.

It is well known that the obligations derived from the principles of the Treaties only apply if the contract in question is of certain cross-border inter-

2. The Proposed Concessions Directive, See explanatory note, p. 5.
3. See, for example, Article 4 and 4, section II regarding exclusions, Article 32, Article 40, Title III: Rules of performance of concessions (Articles 41-43) of the Proposed Concessions Directive.

est.[4] By setting a threshold for service concession contracts this threshold is set to ensure that concessions with a clear cross-border interest are covered.[5] Thus, with the thresholds in the Proposed Concessions Directive this, according to the Commission, indicates that above the threshold the contract is *clearly* of cross-border interest it at the same times indicates that below the threshold the contract *can be* of cross-border interest, hence it will still be necessary for contracting authorities to make a concrete evaluation of the contract in question to determine whether the contract is covered by the principles of the Treaties. However, as the thresholds for service concession contracts starts at EUR 2.500.000[6], and taking into account that concessions contracts often have a long duration not many concessions will fall out of this regime. Thus, it would have been more appropriate to indicate that below the thresholds it is the assumption that the contract is not of cross-border interest. In fact, despite the fact that this threshold only requires contracting authorities to publish a contract notice, it can be discussed whether the threshold sat is too low as it seems to cover many service concession contracts, which are not of cross-border interest.

Article 26 of the proposal is particularly relevant to notice. This provision introduces a requirement to publish a 'concession notice'. The notice must contain a minimum amount of information such as estimated value, time frame for delivery, and conditions for participating in the competition hereunder selection and award criteria. Thus, it will no longer be possible to invite candidates to participate before a concession notice has been published. The reason for this can perhaps be found in Recital 10, which states that:

'In view of the detrimental effects on competition, awarding concessions without prior publication should only be permitted in very exceptional circumstances. This exception

4. For service concession contracts, some sort of cross-border interest was mentioned in Case C-231/03, Consorzio Aziende Metano v. Comune di Cingia de' Botti, [2005] ECR I-7287. See also for below-threshold contracts, Case C-412/04, Commission v. Italy, [2008] ECR I-619. For B-service contracts, cross-border interest was stated in the Case C-507/03, Commission v. Ireland, [2007] ECR I-9777.
5. See Recital 18, which states: *"The thresholds should reflect the clear cross-border interest of concessions to economic operators located in other Member States."* Recital 6 furthermore states that the threshold reflects *"the manifest cross-border interest of concession contract"*.
6. See Article 5 (2): *"Services concessions the value of which is equal to or greater than EUR 2 500 000 but lower than EUR 5 000 000 other than social services and other specific services shall be subject to the obligation to publish a concession award notice in accordance with Articles 27 and 28."*

should be limited to cases where it is clear from the outset that a publication would not trigger more competition, notably because there is objectively only one economic operator who can perform the concession.'[7]

Thus, the requirement for advertising is based on the assumption that this will create more competition for the contract. The Proposal does in that regard not introduce any *requirements to use a specific procedure. According to the explanatory note:*

'This solution allows contracting authorities and contracting entities to follow more flexible procedures when awarding concessions notably reflecting national legal traditions and permitting the award process to be organised in the most efficient way. However, the proposal establishes a number of clear procedural safeguards to be applied to the award of concessions notably during negotiations. These safeguards aim at ensuring that the process is fair and transparent.'[8]

However, despite the fact that procedures do not exists, all the procedures in the Procurement Directives can as a starting point be used. Furthermore, as a minimum Article 34 sets out some general principles applicable when awarding a concession and Article 35 a set of procedural guarantees. These principles being e.g. that a tender must comply with the selection criteria set and that award criteria must be stated beforehand. It is permitted to negotiate as long as the principle of equal treatment is complied with and if wishing to limit the number of participants this shall be done in a transparent manner based on pre-defined non-discriminatory criteria. Contrary to the negotiated procedure under the Proposed Procurement Directive it is also permitted to negotiate with one (or more) tenderers after the submission of tenders. It is not a requirement to use the same award criteria as under the Public Sector Directive Article 53, but the criteria must be objective and linked to the subject matter of the contract and the criteria must be stated in the contract notice either weighted or in descending order of importance.[9] Thus, it is not necessary to award the concession to the economic operator submitting the lowest price or the most economical advantageous tender, but the award criteria must be objective. In my opinion all the above are elements that shows that in

7. Recital 10 furthermore states: *"Only situations of objective exclusivity can justify the award of a concession without publication to an economic operator, where the situation of exclusivity has not been created by the contracting authority or contracting entity itself in view of the future award procedure, and where there are no adequate substitutes, the availability of which should be assessed thoroughly."*
8. P. 7 of the Proposed Concessions Directive.
9. Article 39(2) and (3) of the Proposed Concessions Directive.

fact the Proposed Concessions Directive is in fact in many ways more flexible than the Proposed Procurement Directive.

Nevertheless, it is clear that many provisions could be deleted as they do not add anything further to the 'light regime' as they are voluntary to use. Furthermore, the proposal suggests a time limit of 52 days, which is higher than the one found in the new Proposed Procurement Directive. This is rather peculiar as many service concession contracts are not very complex and it should be possible to award them fast and effective and hence, in my view the time limit should be shortened.

Another distinctive feature is that the proposal also suggests that the Remedies Directives should apply to concession contracts above the thresholds.[10] The proposal places concessions in line with contracts fully covered by the Public Sector Directive, thus also the rules of standstill as well as the possibility to declare a contract for ineffective will apply if the proposal is adopted.

Overall, the proposal will create legal certainty for some types of service concession contracts above the thresholds. Furthermore, it creates clarity when a contract is to be considered as a service concession contract and finally it can be assumed that there will be created more competition for these types of contracts. As many of the provisions in the proposed Directive are identical to the once proposed in Directive for the Public Sector it might have been a better option to include concession by this Directive instead of proposing a new separate Directive.

Furthermore, the proposal does first of all not resolve the question of obligations derived from the principles of the Treaties below the threshold suggested in the Directive. Thus, if the Directive is adopted it will still leave many questions unanswered such as the subject of whether cross-border interest will be relevant to take into consideration below the thresholds sat in the Directive, and in that regard obliged to follow the principles of the Treaties.

5.2.2. The Proposed Procurement Directive

The Proposed Procurement Directive suggests deleting the two-tier regime for services. This would mean that B-service contracts would be fully covered by the Directive.

However, a special regime for Social services such as health and education services is introduced in the Directive as well.[11] According to the pro-

10. See Articles 44 and 45 of the Proposed Concessions Directive.
11. Other services are also suggested to be covered by this regime such as cultural services, compulsory social security services, benefit services, religious services, see

posal, such services: '*continue by their very nature to have a limited cross-border dimension, namely what are known as services to the person, such as certain social, health and educational services.*'[12] The 'Cross-border Report' had showed that many B-services already had high cross-border bidding and it therefore seems reasonable to cover these contracts fully by the Directive. According to the proposal:

> *'The results of the Evaluation on the Impact and Effectiveness of EU Public Procurement Legislation [footnote left out] demonstrated that the exclusion of certain services from the full application of the Directive should be reviewed. As a result, the full application of this directive is extended to a number of services (such as hotel and legal services, which both showed a particularly high percentage of cross-border trade).'*[13]

Thus, the proposal suggest that contracting authorities awarding such contracts shall publish a contract notice, make the result of the procedure known, and leave it up to the Member States to implement appropriate procedures for the award of these contracts. The procedure should comply with the principles of transparency and equal treatment.[14]

As elaborated on in chapter 11, the consequence of the Commission's proposal would in my view be that this new 'social' regime will be fully covered by the Remedies Directive, hereunder the rules on standstill and ineffectiveness.

In my view, the annexes should be reconsidered and some B-services should therefore be categorised as A-services. However, there is still a need for two categories, since many of the current B-services still represent a kind of service that is assumed not to have cross-border interest, especially in areas such as social services and healthcare. Nevertheless, not all Member States experience the same development of competition in the same sectors. Therefore, it might be more proportionate to allow Member States themselves to regulate the rules regarding these services.

It is doubtful that the proposal will be adopted in is current content. It could very well be expected that there will be high debate about B-services as the proposal in that regard limits Member States prerogative to regulate these contracts as well as it is possible that many Member States have special tradi-

further in Annex XVI. The services listed in this annex are currently the ones found in Annex II B, category 24-26 and some services from the category 27, 'other services', which has a social character.

12. Recital 11 of the Proposed Procurement Directive..
13. Recital 10 of the Proposed Procurement Directive..
14. See Articles 74–76 of the Proposed Procurement Directive.

tions for certain types of contracts and that these vary in the Member States. Thus, it will be very interesting to see what the result will be.

The fact that the Commission has chosen to propose to cover service concession contracts and B-services fully by a given secondary regime shows the importance of these contracts and that it is essential that certain rules apply to ensure undistorted competition by guaranteeing open, equal access to public contracts, and that it is the Commission's view that this will best take place at EU level. It remains to be seen whether the Council and the Parliament agree.

Legislation

The Treaty of Lisbon amending the EU Treaty and the EC Treaty. Reference is made to the Consolidated versions of the Treaty on European Union and the Treaty on the Functioning of the European Union, [2008] C 115.

The Charter of Fundamental Rights of the European Union (2000/C 364/01).

Regulations

1049/2001 of the European Parliament and of the Council of 30 May 2001 regarding public access to European Parliament, Council and Commission documents, [2001] OJ L 145/43.

1605/2002 of 25 June 2002 on the Financial Regulation applicable to the general budget of the European Communities, [2002] OJ L 248/1.

1998/2006 of 15 December 2006 on the application of Articles 87 and 88 of the Treaty to de minimis aid, [2006] OJ L 379/5.

1370/2007 of 23 October 2007 on public passenger transport services by rail and by road, [2007] OJ L315/1.

1008/2008, on common rules for the operation of air services in the Community, [2003] OJ L 293/3.

1251/2011 of 30 November 2011 amending Directives 2004/17/EC, 2004/18/EC and 2009/81/EC of the European Parliament and of the Council in respect of their application thresholds for the procedures for the awards of contract, [2011] OJ L 319/43.

Directives

71/305/EEC of 26 July 1971 concerning the co-ordination of procedures for the award of public works contracts, [1971] OJ L 185/5.

77/62/EEC of 21 December 1976 coordinating procedures for the award of public supply contracts, [1977] OJ L13/1.

89/440/EEC of 18 July 1989 amending Directive 71/305/EEC concerning coordination of procedures for the award of public works contracts, [1989] OJ L 210/1.

89/665/EEC of 21 December 1989 on the coordination of the laws, regulations and administrative provisions relating to the application of review procedures to the award of public supply and public works contracts, [1989] OJ 395/33.

92/13/EEC of 25 February 1992 coordinating the laws, regulations and administrative provisions relating to the application of Community rules on the procurement procedures of entities operating in the water, energy, transport and telecommunications sectors, [1992] OJ L 76/14.

92/50/EEC of 18 June 1992 relating to the coordination of procedures for the award of public service contracts, [1992] OJ L 209/1.

93/36/EEC of 14 June 1993 coordinating procedures for the award of public supply contracts, [1993] OJ L 199/1.
93/37/EEC of 14 June 1993 concerning the coordination of procedures for the award of public works contracts, [1993] OJ L 199/54.
2004/17/EC of the European Parliament and of the Council of 31 March 2004 coordinating the procurement procedures of entities operating in the water, energy, transport and postal services sectors, [2004] OJ L 134/1.
2004/18/EC of the European Parliament and of the Council of 31 March 2004 on the coordination of procedures for the award of public works contracts, public supply contracts and public service contracts, [2004] OJ L 134/114.
2007/66/EC of the European Parliament and the Council of 11 December 2007 amending Council Directives 89/665/EEC with regard to improving the effectiveness of review procedures concerning the award of public contracts, [2007] OJ L 335/31.
2009/81/EC of the European Parliament and of the Council of 13 July 2009 on the coordination of procedures for the award of certain works contracts, supply contracts and service contracts by contracting authorities or entities in the fields of defence and security, and amending Directives 2004/17/EC and 2004/18/EC, [2009] OJ L 216/76.

Proposals

Proposal for a first directive of the Council on the co-ordination of procedures for the conclusion of public works contract, Supplement to Bulletin of the European Economic Community No 9/19, 1964, p.12.
proposal for a Directive relating to the Coordination of Procedures on the award of public service contract COM(90)72, OJ C23/1.
Proposal to the Service Directive, [1991] COM(91)322 final, OJ C250/4.
Proposal for a Directive of the European Parliament and of the Council amending Council Directives 89/665/EEC and 92/13/EEC CEE with regard to improving the effectiveness of review procedures concerning the award of public contracts, SEC(2006)557
Proposal for a Directive of the European Parliament and the Council on procurement by entities operating in the water, energy, transport and postal services sectors, COM(2011) 895 final.
Proposal for a Directive of the European Parliament and the Council on public procurement, COM(2011) 896 final
Proposal for a Directive of the European Parliament and the Council on the award of concession contracts COM(2011) 897 final

Communications and other Commission documents

White Paper, *'Completing the Internal Market'* [1985] COM(85)310.
Communication from the Commission to the European Parliament regarding the Council's common position on the proposal for a Directive coordinating the procedures on the award of public service contracts, [1992] SEC (92) 406.
Green Paper *'Public Procurement in the European Union: Exploring the way'*, [1996] COM (1996) 583.
Commission Interpretative Communication on Concessions under Community Law (2000/C121/02)
Commission's Green Paper on Public Procurement Partnerships, [2004] COM(2004)327.
Communication from the Commission to the European Parliament, the Council, The European Economic and Social Committee and the Committee of the Regions on public-

private partnerships and community law on public procurement and concessions, [2005] COM(2005)569

Commission Interpretative Communication on the Community law applicable to contract awards not or not fully subject to the provisions of the Public Procurement Directives, [2006] OJ C179/2.

European Code of Best Practices facilitating access by SME´s to Public Procurement Contracts SEC(2008)2193.

Communication from the Commission to the European Parliament, the Council, the Economic and Social Committee of the Regions *'Single Market Act Twelve levers to boost growth and strengthen confidence'*, (SEC(2011) 467 final).

Commission Green Paper on the modernisation of EU public procurement policy Towards a more efficient European Procurement Market, COM (2011)15. (the Green Paper on Modernisation)

Commission Evaluation Report Impact and Effectiveness of EU Public Procurement Legislation, part 1 SEC(2011) 853 final.

Commission Evaluation Report Impact and Effectiveness of EU Public Procurement Legislation, part 2 SEC(2011) 853 final.

Commission Staff Working Document – Commissions Impact Assessment on an Initiative on Concessions, SEC(2011) 1588 final.

List of Judgments and Decisions

The Court of Justice

Case C-5/69, Franz Völk v. S.P.R.L. Ets J. Vervaecke, [1969] ECR 295 *150*

Case C-33/76, Rewe-Zentralfinanz eG and Rewe-Zentral AG v. Land-wirtschaftskammer für das Saarland, [1976] ECR 1989 *254*

Case C-106/77, Amministrazione delle Finanze dello Stato v. Simmenthal SpA, [1978] ECR 629 *256*

Case C-120/78, Rewe-Zentral AG v. Bundesmonopolverwaltung für Branntwein, [1979] ECR 649 *40, 200*

Case C-810/79, Peter Überschär v. Bundesversicherungsanstalt für Angestellte, [1980] ECR 2747 *57*

Case C-76/81, SA Transporoute et travaux v. Minister of Public Works, [1982] ECR 417 *211*

Case C-96/81 Commission v. Netherlands, [1982] ECR 1791 *117*

Case C-249/81, Commission v. Ireland, [1982] ECR 4005 *46*

Case C-283/81, Srl CILFIT and Lanificio di Gavardo SpA v. Ministry of Health, [1982] ECR 3415 *32, 33*

Case C-286/81, Criminal proceedings against Oosthoek's Uitgevers maatschappij BV, [1982] ECR 4575 *155*

Joined cases C-177/82 and C-178/82, Van de Haar [1984] ECR 1797 *150*

Case C-269/83, Commission v. France, [1985] ECR 837 *150*

Case C-103/84, Commission v. Italy, [1986] ECR 1759 *150*

Case C-222/86, Union nationale des entraîneurs et cadres techniques professionnels du football (Unectef) v. Georges Heylens and others, [1987] ECR 4097 *244, 245, 255*

Case C-31/87, Gebroeders Beentjes BV v. the Netherlands, [1988] ECR 4635 *34, 45, 54, 214, 216*

Case C-45/87, Commission v. Ireland, [1988] ECR 4929 *155, 184, 197*

Case C-3/88, Commission v. Italy, [1989] ECR 4035 *154*

Case C-194/88 R, Commission v. Italian Republic, [1988] ECR 5647 *276, 278*

Case C-243/89, Commission v. Denmark, [1993] ECR I-3353 *52, 154, 155, 194, 211*

Case C-340/89, Irène Vlassopoulou v. Ministerium für Justiz, Bundes- und Europaangelegenheiten Baden-Württemberg, [1991] ECR I-2357 *200*

Joined Cases C-6/90 & 9/90, Andrea Francovich and Danila Bonifaci and others v. Italian Republic, [1991] ECR I-5357 *254, 296*

Case C-41/90, Klaus Höfner and Fritz Elser v. Macrotron GmbH, [1991] ECR I-1979 *154, 155*

Case C-76/90, Manfred Säger v. Dennemeyer & Co. Ltd., [1991] ECR I-4221 *200*

General Court

Case T-57/09, Alfastar Benelux v. Council, [2011] October 20, 2011, (not yet reported) *246*

Case T-298/09, Evropaïki Dynamiki v. Commission, [2011] September 20, 2011, (not yet reported) *246*

Opinions of Advocates Generals

Opinion of Advocate General Pergola delivered on February, 9, 1998 in the Case C-360/96, Gemeente Arnhem and Gemeente Rheden v. BFI Holding BV, [1998] ECR I-6821 *45, 79, 80, 88, 89, 162*

Opinion of Advocate General Fennelly delivered on May 18, 2000 in the Case C-324/98, Telaustria Verlags GmbH and Telefonadress GmbH v. Telekom Austria AG, [2000] ECR I-10745 *21, 65, 72, 74, 75, 79, 81, 92, 161, 162, 164, 186, 167*

Opinion of Advocate General Jacobs delivered on July 11 2002, in Case C-112/00, Eugen Schmidberger, Internationale Transporte und Planzüge v. Republik Österreich [2003] ECR I-5659 *151, 296*

Opinion of Advocate General Stix-Hackl delivered on April 12, 2005, in Case C-231/03, Consorzio Aziende Metano v. Comune di Cingia de' Botti, [2005] ECR I-7287 *39, 121, 122, 126, 13, , 140, 167, 168, 169, 173, 195, 324*

Opinion of Advocate General Jacobs delivered on June 2, 2005 in Case C-525/03 Commission v. Italy, [2005] ECR I-9405 *38*

Opinion of Advocate General Stix-Hackl delivered on September 14, 2006, in Case C-532/03, Commission v. Ireland, [2007] ECR I-11353 *37, 39*

Opinion of Advocate General Sharpston delivered on January 18, 2007, in Case C-195/04, Commission v. Finland, [2007] ECR I-3351 *166, 171, 180*

Opinion of Advocate General, Ruiz Jarabo Colomer delivered on November 27, 2007 in Joined Cases C-147/06 and C-148/06 SECAP SpA v. Comune di Torino and Santorso, [2008] ECR I-3565 *109*

Opinion Advocate General Kokott delivered on March 13, 2008 in Case C-454/06, Pressetext Nachrichtenagentur GmbH v. Republik Österreich (Bund), APA-OTS Originaltext-Service GmbH and APA Austria Presse Agentur registrierte Genossenschaft mit beschränkter Haftung, [2008] ECR I-4401 *19, 55, 56, 64, 136, 172, 221, 222, 224*

Opinion of Advocate General Bot delivered on October 27, 2009 in Case Case C-91/08, Wall AG v. La ville de Francfort-sur-le-Main and Frankfurter Entsorgungs- und Service (FES) GmbH, [2010] ECR I-2815 *35, 45, 46, 47, 56, 140, 144, 176, 222, 223, 224, 254, 274, 306, 307, 308, 309, 310*

Opinion of Advocate General Mengozzi delivered on June 29, 2010, in Case C-226/09, Commission v. Ireland, [2010] November 18, 2010 (not yet reported). *61, 62, 64, 111, 141, 146, 174, 175, 184, 187, 189, 220, 221*

Opinion of Advocate General Mazák delivered on September 9, 2010 in Case C-274/09, Privater Rettungsdienst und Krankentransport Stadler v. Zweckverband für Rettungsdienst und Feuerwehralarmierung Passau, [2011] March 10, 2011 (not yet reported) *71, 78, 79, 83, 84, 90, 93, 96, 142, 144, 145, 176*

Opinion of Advocate General, Yves Bot, delivered on October 27, 2009 in Case C-91/08, Wall AG v. La ville de Francfort-sur-le-Main and Frankfurter Entsorgungs- und Service (FES) GmbH, [2010] ECR I-2815 *35, 45, 46, 47, 56, 60, 140, 144, 176, 222, 223, 224, 254, 274, 306, 307, 308, 309, 310*

Opinion of Advocate General Kokott in Case C-368/10, Commission v. The Netherlands, (not ruled yet), delivered on December 15, 2011 *196, 198*

National cases

Cases from Scotland, Wales, England, Northern Ireland and Ireland can be found at www.bailii.org. Cases from the Danish Complaints Board for Public Procurement can be found at www.klfu.dk.

Denmark

Danish Complaints Board for Public Procurement

List of literature

A

Arnould, Joel *"Procedures for awarding low-value contracts in France: the Region Nord-Pas-de-Calais case"* [2006] PPLR n° 2, NA66-69

Arnould, Joul *"Damages for performing an Illegal contract-the other side of the Mirror: Comments on Three Recent Judgments of the French Council of State"* [2008] PPLR n° 17, NA 274.

Arrowsmith, Sue *"The Law of Public and Utilities Procurement"* [1996] 1st Edition, London, Sweet and Maxwell

Arrowsmith, Sue *"The Law of Public and Utilities Procurement"* [2005] 2nd Edition, Sweet and Maxwell

Arrowsmith, Sue and Kunzlik, Peter (Eds.) *"Social and Environmental Policies in EC Procurement Law"* [2009] Cambridge University Press

Arrowsmith, Sue (Edt.) *"EU Public Procurement Law: An Introduction"* [2010] Asia Link Project, can be found at http://www.nottingham.ac.uk/pprg/publications/short-textbooks.aspx (last visited January 4, 2012).

Arrowsmith, Sue *"Enforcing the Public Procurement Rules: Legal Remedies in the Court of Justice and the National Courts"* in Arrowsmith, Sue (Edt.) *"Public Procurement in the European Community: Volume IV – Remedies for enforcing the Public Procurement rules"* [1993] Earlsgate Press.

Arrowsmith, Sue *"Public Private Partnerships and the European Procurement rules: EU Policies in Conflict?"* [2000] CMLR n° 37, pp. 709-737

Arrowsmith, Sue *"The entity coverage of the EC procurement directives and UK regulations: a review"* [2004] PPLR n° 2, 59-86

Arrowsmith, Sue, *"Implementation of the new EC procurement directives and the Alcatel ruling in England and Wales and Northern Ireland: a review of the new legislation and guidance"* [2006] PPLR n° 3, pp. 86-136.

Arrowsmith, Sue *"A review of the new legislation and Guidance"* [2006] PPLR n° 3, pp. 86-137.

B

Bailey, S.H *"Chandler in the Court of Appeal: the issue of standing: R. (on the application of Chandler) v. Secretary of State for Children, Schools and Families"* [2010] PPLR n° 2, NA68-71

Barnard, Cathrine *"Derogations, Justifications and the Four Freedoms: Is State Interest Really Protected?"* in Barnard, Cathrine & Odudu, Okeoghene (Eds) *"The Outer Limits of European Union Law"* [2009] Hart.

Barnard, Cathrine *"The Substantive Law of the EU"*[2010], 3rd Edition, Oxford University Press

Berg, Henrik *"Udbud med forhandling – og hvordan forhandler man?"* in Hagel-Sørensen, Karsten (edt.) *"Aktuel Udbudsret"* [2011] DJØF.

Bianchi, Tiziana & Guidi, Valentina *"The Comparative Survey on the National Public Procurement Systems across the PPN"*, which can be found at: www.publicprocurementnetwork.org/ (last visited January 4, 2012).

Bovis, Christopher *"EU public procurement law"* [2007] Elgar European Law.

Bovis, Christopher *"The effects of the principle of transparency and accountability"* in Hofmann, Herwig and Türk, Alexander (Eds.) *"Legal challenges in in EU administrative law: towards an integrated administration"* [2009] Edward Elgar Publishing limited.

Braun, Peter *"A Matter of Principle(s) – The Treatment of Contracts Falling Outside the Scope of the European Procurement Directives"* [2000] PPLR n° 1, pp. 39-49.

Braun, Peter, *"Requirement to state reasons for procurement decisions: a note on the recent cases of the General Court"*, [2011] PPLR n° 2, NA19-23.

Broberg Morten *"Preliminary References by Public Administrative Bodies: When Are Public Administrative Bodies Competent to Make Preliminary References to the European Court of Justice?"* [2009] ELR n° 15, pp. 207–221

Brown, Adrian *"Seeing Through Transparency: the Requirement to Advertise Public Contracts and Concessions Under the EC Treaty"* [2007] PPLR n° 1, pp. 1-21.

Brown, Adrian *"The Overlap between EC procurement principles and the safeguard procedures laid down in Directive 93/42/EC concerning medical devices: a note on C-6/05 Medipac-Kazandazidis AE v. Venizelio-Pananio"* [2007] PPLR n° 6, NA 159-162

Brown, Adrian *"Application of the directives to contracts with not-for-profit organisations and transparency under the EC Treaty: a note on Case C119/ 06 Commission v. Italy"* [2008] PPLR n° 3, NA96-99.

Brown, Adrian, *"When do changes to an existing public contract amount to the award of a new contract for the purposes of the EU procurement rules? Guidance at last in Case C-454/06"* [2008] PPLR n° 6, NA253-267.

Brown, Adrian *"Incorrect categorisation of a tramway contract as a works concession by an Italian municipality: Commission v. Italy (C-437/07)"* [2009] PPLR n° 2, NA55-58.

Brown, Adrian, *"Commission of the European Communities v. France (C-327/08): a French provision breaches Remedies Directives 89/665 and 92/13 by jeopardising the effectiveness of the standstill period between notification of the award decision and conclusion of the contract"*, [2009] PPLR n° 6, NA222-225.

Brown Adrian *"A German city authority beaches the procurement directives by awarding a waste contract without competition over 10 years ago: Commission v. Germany (C-17/09)"* [2010] PPLR n° 3, NA 112-114

Brown, Adrian *"Helmut Muller GmbH v. Bundesanstalt fur Immobilienaufgaben (C-451/08): clarification on the application of the EU procurement rules to land sales and development agreement"* [2010] PPLR n° 4, NA125-130.

Brown, Adrian *"EU primary law requirements in practice: advertising, procedures and remedies for public contracts outside the procurement directives"* [2010] PPLR n° 5, pp. 169-181.

Brown, Adrian *"Changing a sub-contractor under a public services concession: Wall AG v. Stadt Frankfurt am Main (C-91/08)"* [2010] PPLR n° 5, pp. 160-166.

Brown, Adrian *"The grant of concessions to operate casinos in Austria without competitive tendering"* [2011] PPLR n° 2, NA13-16.

Burgi, Martin *"A Report about the German Remedies System"* in Treumer, Steen & Lichére Francois (Eds.) *"Enforcement of the EU Public Procurement Rules"* [2011] DJØF.

Burnett, Michael *"A new EU Directive on Concessions – the right Approach for PPP?"* [2008] EPPPL n° 3, pp. 107-115.

C

Cahill, Dermot *"The Ebb and Flow, the Doldrums and the Raging Tide: Single Market Law's EBB and Flow over Services of General Economic Interest, the Legal Doldrums over Services of General Interest, and the Raging Tide of Article 106(2) (ex Art 86(2)) over State Aid & Public Procurement"* [2010] EBLR, pp. 629-662.

Caranta Roberto, Trybus Martin (Eds.) *"The law of green and social procurement in Europe"* [2010] DJØF

Caranta, Roberto *"Many Different Paths, but are They All Leading to Effectiveness?"* in Treumer, Steen & Lichére Francois (Eds.) *"Enforcement of the EU Public Procurement Rules"* [2011] DJØF.

Clifton, Michael-James *"Ineffectiveness – The New Deterrent: Will the New Remedies Directive Ensure Greater Compliance with the Substantive Procurement Rules in the Classical Sectors?"* [2009] PPLR n°4, pp. 165-184.

Casalini, Dario *"Beyond EU Law: the new "public house"* in Ølykke, Grith, Hansen, Carina Risvig and Tvarnø, Christina D. *"EU Public Procurement – Modernisation, Growth and Innovation"*, DJØF, July 2012.

Comba, Mario *"Enforcement of the EU Procurement Rules. The Italian System of Remedies"* in Treumer, Steen & Lichére Francois (Eds.) *"Enforcement of the EU Public Procurement Rules"* [2011] DJØF.

Comba, Mario & Treumer, Steen (Eds.) *"The In-house Providing in European Law"* [2010] DJØF

Craig, Paul and Búrca, Gráinne de *"EU Law – Text, Cases and Materials"* [2011] 5th Edition, Oxford University Press.

Craig, Poul & Trybus, Martin *"England and Wales"* in Noguellou, Rozen & Ulrich, Stelkens (eds.) *"Droit comparé des Contrats – Publics Comparative Law on Public Contracts"* [2010] Brussels Bruylant.

D

Dethlefsen, Peter & Pedersen, Claus Kaare *"Tilbudsloven: Bygge & Anlæg"* [2002] Thomson

Dingel, Dorthe Dahlgaard *"Public Procurement – A Harmonization of the National Judicial Review of the Application of European Community Law"* [1999] Kluwer Law International.

Dischendorfer, Martin *"The application of limitation periods under Directive 89/665"* [2008] PPLR n° 2, NA41-47.

Donnelly, Cathrine *"Remedies in public procurement law in Ireland"* [2009] PPLR n° 1, pp. 18-41.

Drijber, Jan Berend & Stergiou, Hélène *"Public Procurement Law and Internal Market Law"* [2009] CMLR n° 46, pp. 805-846.

Dunne, Mary *"Requirement to give reasons to unsuccessful tenderers before conclusion of the standstill"* [2010] PPLR n° 3, NA87-90.

F

Fabricius, Jesper *"Offentlige indkøb i praksis"* [2010] 1st Edition, Thomson.

Fugou, Cao in Tvarnø, Christina (Eds.) *"PPP – An international analysis in a legal and economic perspective"* [2010] Asia Link.

G

Gaffney, John *"The Obligation to advertise contracts under the EC Treaty: recent actions by the Commission"* [2003] PPLR n° 3, NA60-61.

Graells, Albert Sánchez *"Public Procurement and the EU Competition Rules"* [2011] Hart.

Golding, Jane and Henty, Paul, *"The new Remedies Directive of the EC: Standstill and ineffectiveness"* [2008] PPLR n° 3, pp. 146-154.

H

Hansen, Carina Risvig *"Chapter 8, Treaty requirements for contracts 'outside' the procurement Directives"* in Trybus, Martin, Caranta, Roberto & Edelstam, Gunille (Eds.) *"EU Law and Public Contracts"* [2012] Bruylant, Brussels forthcoming,

Hansen, Carina Risvig *"Pligt til annoncering af offentlige kontrakter – uden effektiv håndhævelse af reglerne?"*, in U.2011B.101.

Hansen, Carina Risvig *"Defining a service concession contract, Will the proposed new definition of service concession contracts increase legal certainty in the field of concessions?"* in Ølykke, Grith, Hansen, Carina Risvig and Tvarnø, Christina D. *"EU Public Procurement – Modernisation, Growth and Innovation"*, DJØF July 2012.

Hartley, TC *"The Foundations of European Union Law"* [2010] 7. Edition, Oxford University Press

Hebly, Jan M. *"European Public Procurement – Legislative History of the 'classic' Directive 2004/18/EC"* [2006] Kluwer Law.

Hartlev, Kristian & Liljenbøl, Morten Wahl *"Ændringer af udbudte kontrakter"* in Hagel-Sørensen, Karsten (Edt.) *"Aktuel Udbudsret"* [2011] DJØF.

Hatzis, Nicholas *"The legality of SME development policies under EC procurement law"* in Arrowsmith, Sue and Kunzlik, Peter (Eds.) *"Social and Environmental Policies in EC Procurement Law"* [2009] Cambridge University press, p. 350.

Henty, Poul *"A note on Sidey v. Clackmannanshire Council and Pyramid Joinery and Construction Limited"* [2010] PPLR n° 6, NA237-241.

Henty, Poul *"Public Procurement (Miscellaneous Amendments) Regulations 2011"* [2012] PPLR n° 1, NA50-53.

Henty, Paul *"Chandler in the Court of Appeal: public procurement issues – R. (on the application of Chandler) v. Secretary of State for Children, Schools and Families"* [2010] PPLR n° 2, NA64-67

Hesselink, Martjin *"A European Legal Method? On European Private Law and Scientific Method"* [2009] ELJ, Vol. 15, n° 1, pp. 20–45.

Hesselink, Martijn W *"A Toolbox for European Judges"* in in Neergaard, Ulla, Nielsen, Ruth and Roseberry, Lynn (Eds.) *"European Legal Method – Paradoxes and Revitailisation"* [2010] DJØF.

Hordijk, Erik Pijnacker & Meulenbelt, Maarten *"A Bridge Too Far: Why the Commission's Attempts to Construct an Obligation to Tender Outside the Scope of the Public Procurement Directives Should be Dismissed"* [2005] PPLR n° 3, pp. 120-130.

K

Kaukoris, C.N. *"Do the Member States posses judicial procedural autonomy?"* [1997] CMLR n° 34, pp. 1389-1412.

Kekelekis, Mihalis and Rusu, Ioana Eleonora *"The award of public contacts and the notion of "internal operator" under Regulation 1370/2007 on public passenger transport services by rail and by road"* [2010] PPLR n° 6, 198-216.

Kotsonis, Totis *"The role of risk in defining a services concession contract: Wasser- und Ab-wasserzweckverband Gotha und Landkreisgemeinden (WAZV Gotha) v. Eurawasser Aufbereitungs- und Entsorgungsgesellschaft mbH (C-206/08) (WAZV)"*, [2010] PPLR n° 1, NA4-12.

Kotsonis, Totis *"The basis on which the remedy of damages must be made available"* [2011] PPLR n° 3, NA59-63.

Krugner, Matthias *"The principles of equal treatment and transparency and the Commissions Interpretative Communication on Concessions"* [2003] PPLR n° 5, pp. 181-207.

Krüger, Kai *"Critical comments on the new procurement directives, preceding the Nordic adaption"* in Treumer, Steen and Fejø, Jens (Eds.) *"EU's Udbudsregler – implementering og håndhævelse i norden"* [2006] DJØF

L

Leffler, Henrik *"Damages for liability for breach of EC Procurement Law: Governing Principles and Practical Solutions"* [2003] PPLR n° 4, pp. 151-174.

Lichére, Francois & Gabayet, Nicolas *"Enforcement of the EU Public Procurement Rules in France"* in Treumer, Steen & Lichére, Francois (Eds.) *"Enforcement of the EU Public Procurement Rules"* [2011] DJØF

M

Madell, Tom & Indén, Tobias *"Offentlig-Privat Samverkan"* [2010] Iustus Förlag.

McCrudden, Christopher *"EC public procurement law and equality linkages: founations for interpretations"* in Arrowsmith, Sue and Kunzlik, Peter (Eds.) *"Social and Environmental Policies in EC Procurement Law"* [2009] Cambridge University press.

McGowan, David, *"Consortia member rights and classification of mixed contracts: a note on Club Hotel Loutraki (C-145/08 and C-149/08)"* [2010] PPLR n° 5, N174-179.

McGowan, David *"Concessions: rescue, risk and remuneration – a note on Privater Rettungsdienst und Krankentransport Stadler v. Zweckverband fur Rettungsdienst und Feuerwehralarmierung Passau (C-274/09)"* [2011] PPLR n°4, NA128-131.

McGowan, David *"Remedies revolution avoided: a note on Combinatie Spijker Infrabouw-De Jonge Konstruktie v. Provincie Drenthe (C-568/08)"* [2011] PPLR n°3, NA 64-69.

McGovern, Patrick *"Standstill Notice in Respect of Part B Services: The Decision in Federal Security Servicese Ltd v. Chief Constable for the Police Service of Northern Ireland and Resource Group Ltd"*. [2009] PPLR n°4, NA181-188.

Monti, Giorgio & Davies, Gareth & Chalmers, Damian *"European Union Law"*, [2010] Cambridge University Press.

N

Neergaard, Ulla *"The Concept of Concessions in EU Public Procurement Law Versus EU Competition Law and National Law"* in Treumer, Steen and Nielsen, Ruth (Eds.) *"The New EU Public Procurement Directives"* [2005] DJØF.

Neergaard, Ulla & Nielsen, Ruth *"Where Did the Spirit and Its Friends Go? On the European Legal Method(s) and the Interpretation Style of the Court of Justice of the European Union"* in Neergaard, Ulla, Nielsen, Ruth and Roseberry, Lynn (Eds.) *"European Legal Method – Paradoxes and Revitailisation"* [2010] DJØF.

Neergaard, Ulla *"Pligt Til Udbud Af Koncessionskontrakter Om Tjenesteydelser I Henhold Til EU-Retten?"* in U. 2006B. 299.

Neergaard, Ulla *"Public service concessions and related concepts – the increased pressure from Community law on Member States' use of concessions"* [2007] PPLR n° 6, pp. 387-409. Neergaard, Ulla, Nielsen, Ruth and Roseberry, Lynn (Eds.) *"European Legal Method – Paradoxes and Revitalisation"* [2010] DJØF.

Neergaard, Ulla, Nielsen, Ruth, Roseberry, Lynn (Eds.) *"The Role of Courts in Developing a European Social Model – Theoretical and Methodological Perspectives"* [2010] DJØF.

Nielsen, Ruth *"Udbud af offentlige kontrakter"* [1998] 1st Edition, DJØF.

Nielsen, Ruth *"Udbud af offentlige kontrakter"* [2010] 4th Edition, DJØF.

Nielsen, Ruth and Neergaard, Ulla *"EU Ret"* [2010] 6th Edition, DJØF.

Nielsen, Ruth and Tvarnø, Christina *"Retskilder & Retsteorier"* [2011] 3rd Edition, DJØF.

Nielsen, Ruth *"Standstill og ugyldighed/uvirksomhed af offentlige kontrakter"* in U.2007B.120.

Neumayr, Florian, *"Value for money v. equal treatment: the relationship between the seemingly overriding national rationale for regulating public procurement and the fundamental E.C. principle of equal treatment"* [2002] PPLR n° 4, pp. 215-234.

P

Pachnou, Despina, *"Enforcement of the EC. Procurement Rules: The Standard Required of National Review Systems under E.C. Law in the Context of the Principle of Effectiveness"* [2000] PPLR n° 2, pp. 55-74.

Petersen Zsofia *"Below-threshold contract awards under EU primary law: Federal Republic of Germany v. Commission (T-258/06)"* [2010] PPLR n° 6, NA 215-220

Priess, Hans-Joachim *"Recent decisions on judicial protection in German public procurement law,"* [1998] PPLR n° 3, CS116-118.

Poulsen, Sune *"Om henvisning til varemærker ved udbud af offentlige kontrakter"* in U.2008B.41.

R

Racca, Gabriella M. *"Derogations from standstill period, ineffectiveness and remedies in the new tendering procedure: efficiency gains vs. risk of increasing litigations"* in Treumer, Steen & Lichére, Francois (Eds.) *"Enforcement of the EU Public Procurement Rules"* [2011] DJØF.

S

Stergiou, Hélène, *"The Increasing Influence of Primary EU Law on EU Public Procurement Law: Must a Concession to Provide Services of General Economic Interest be*

Tendered?" in Van de Gronden, Johan *"EU and WTO law on services: Limits to the realization of general interest policies within the services market"* [2008] Kluwer.

Smith, Susie *"No obligation to apply specific provisions in the Public Sector Directive to contracts for Annex II B services: Strong Seguranca SA v. Municipio de Sintra (C-95/10)"* [2011] PPLR n° 4, NA 125-127.

Steinicke, Michael *"Varernes frie bevægeligthed og offentlige indkøb"* [2001] DJØF.

Steinicke, Michael and Groesmeyer, Lise *"EU's Udbudsdirektiver"* [2008] 2nd Edition, DJØF.

Stergiou, Hélène *"Public Procurement Law and Health Care: From Theory to Practice"* Research Chapters in law 2/2010. Can be found at www.coleurop.be .

Szydlo, Marek *"Contracts beyond the scope of the EC procurement Directives – who is bound by the requirement for transparency"* [2009] ELR n° 34, vol. 5, p. 720-737.

T

Thorup, Kirsten and Frimodt, Mette *"Standstill Og Opsættende Virkning i Udbudsretten."* in U.2010B.303.

Timmermans, William and Gelders, Mike *"Standstill Obligations in European and Belgian Public Procurement Law"* [2005] PPLR n° 6, pp. 265-290

Trepte, Peter *"Transparency requirements"* in Treumer, Steen and Nielsen, Ruth (Eds) *"The New EU Public Procurement Directives"* [2005] DJØF.

Trepte, Peter *"Public Procurement in the EC"* [1993] 1st Edition, CCH Editions Limited.

Trepte, Peter *"Public Procurement in the EU"* [2007] 2nd Edition, Oxford.

Treumer, Steen *"National håndhævelse af EU's Udbudsregler – er håndhævelsessystemet effektivt på EU-udbudsområdet?* in Treumer, Steen & Fejø, Jens *"EU's udbudsregler – implementering og håndhævelse i Norden"* [2006] DJØF.

Treumer, Steen *"Ligebehandlingsprincippet"* [2000] DJØF.

Treumer, Steen & Lichére Francois (Eds.) *"Enforcement of the EU Public Procurement Rules"* [2011] DJØF.

Treumer, Steen *"Enforcement of the EU Public Procurement Rules: The State of Law and Current Issues"* in Treumer, Steen & Lichére, Francois (Eds.) *"Enforcement of the EU Public Procurement Rules"* [2011] DJØF.

Treumer, Steen *"Enforcement of the EU Public Procurement Rules: Danish Regulation and Practice"* in Treumer, Steen & Lichére, Francois (Eds.) *"Enforcement of the EU Public Procurement Rules"* [2011] DJØF.

Treumer, Steen *"Basis and Conditions for a Damages Claim for breach of the EU Public Procurement Rules"* in Lichére, Francois & Fairgrieve, Duncan (Eds.) *"Public Procurement Law: Damages as an effective Remedy"* [2011] Hart .

Treumer, Steen *"The Selection of Qualified Firms to be Invited to Tender under the E.C Procurement Directives"* [1998] PPLR n° 6, pp. 147-154.

Treumer, Steen *"Damages for Breach of the EC Public Procurement Rules from a Danish Perspective"* [2004] European Business Organization Law Review, Vol 5, n° 3, pp. 563-577.

Treumer, Steen *"The discretionary powers of contracting entities – towards a flexible approach in the recent case law of the European Court of Justice?"* [2006] PPLR n° 3, p. 71-85.

Treumer, Steen and Werlauff, Erik *"The Leverage Principle: Secondary Law as a Lever for the Development of Primary Community Law"* [2003] ELR n° 1, 28(1) pp. 124-133.

Treumer, Steen, *"Towards an obligation to Terminate Contracts Concluded in Breach of the EC Public Procurement Rules: End of Status of Concluded Public Contracts as Sacred Cows."* [2007] PPLR n° 6, pp. 371-386.

Treumer, Steen (Edt.) *"Special issue of Public Procurement Law review"* [2009] PPLR n° 3, pp. 103-164.

Treumer, Steen (Edt.)*"Damages for violations of the EC Procurement Rules"*, [2006] PPLR n° 4, pp. 159-240.

Tridimas, Takis *"The role of the Advocate General in the Development of Community law: Some Reflections"* [1997] CMLR n° 34, pp.1349-1387.

Tridimas, Takis *"The General Principles of EU Law"* [2006] 2nd Edition, Oxford University Press.

Trybus, Martin *"Public Contracts in European Union Internal Market Law: Foundations and Requirements"* in Nogouelleou, Rozen and Stelkens, Ulrich (Eds.) *"Comparative Law on Public Contracts"* [2010] Brussels Bruylant

Trybus, Martin *"An Overview of the United Kingdom Public Procurement Review and Remedies System with an emphasis on England and Wales"* in Treumer, Steen & Lichére, Francois (Eds.) *"Enforcement of the EU Public Procurement Rules"* [2011] DJØF

Tryfonidou, Alina *"The Outer Limits of Article 28 EC: Purely Internal Situations and the Development of the Court's Approach through the Years"* in Barnard, Cathrine & Odudu, Okeoghene (Eds) *"The Outer Limits of European Union Law"* [2009] Hart.

Tvarnø, Christina (Edt.) *"PPP – An international analysis in a legal and economic perspective"* [2010] Asia Link Project can be found at: http://www.cbs.dk/Forskning/Institutter-centre/Projekter/EU-Asia-Inter-University-Network-for-Teaching-and-Research-in-Public-Procurement-Regulation/Menu/Publications/Menu/Textbooks (last visited January 4, 2012)

Tvarnø, Christina *"PPPs in an international legal, economic and political perspective"* in Tvarnø, Christina (Edt.) *"PPP – An international analysis in a legal and economic perspective"* [2010] Asia Link.

W

Wang, Ping *"Public-Private Partnerships under the EU Public Procurement Rules"* in Tvarnø, Christina (Edt.) *"PPP – An international analysis in a legal and economic perspective"* [2010] Asia Link.

V

Varga, Zsófia *"Burden of Proof in Interim Proceedings: Unity OSG FZE v. Council (T-511/08R)* [2009] PPLR n° 4, NA 128.

Wahl, Morten Liljenbøl *"Ændringer i bestående kontraktforhold – udbudsretlige udfordringer i Offentlig-Private Partnerskaber (OPP)"* in TBB2010.15.

Wiggen, Janicke *"Public procurement rules and cooperation between public sector entities: the limits of the in-house doctrine under EU procurement law"* [2011] PPLR n° 5, pp. 157-172

Williams Rhodri *"The European Commission's interpretative Communication under Community Law"* [2000] PPLR n° 5, NA105-110.

Williams, Rhodri *"Contracts Awarded Outside the Scope of the Public Procurement Directives"* [2007] PPLR n° 1, NA1-10.

Ø

Ølykke, Grith Skovgaard *"Regulation 1370/2007 on Public Passenger Transport Services"* [2008] PPLR n° 3, NA84.

Ølykke, Grith Skovgaard *"How does the Court of Justice of the European Union pursue competition concerns in a public procurement context?"* [2011] PPLR n° 6, pp. 179-192.

Ølykke, Grith *"Abnormally low Tenders – with an emphasis on public tenderers"* [2010] DJØF.

Abstract of the Thesis

The Thesis concerns the rules and obligations laid upon contracting authorities when awarding a contract that does not fall fully within the Public Sector Directive and how these obligations can be enforced in national courts.

The Public Sector Directive applies to certain public contracts and requires contracting authorities to follow a detailed set of rules when awarding public contracts. However, for a range of reasons, not all types of public contracts fall within the Public Sector Directive. Three such types of contracts which are either not covered, or not fully covered, by the Public Sector Directive are: service concession contracts, contracts below the EU thresholds and B-service contracts.

When contracting authorities are awarding public contracts they are obliged to follow the EU Treaties, and the principles derived therefrom. The case law from the Court of Justice has shown that the principles of the Treaties imply certain positive obligations for contracting authorities, which must be observed before a contract can be awarded and signed. However, it is unclear what the precise content of these obligations consists of. Thus, the aim of the Thesis is to analyse, clarify and discuss which positive obligations derived from EU law that a contracting authority must apply when entering into one of the three types of contracts and how these obligations can be enforced.

The Thesis is divided into three parts.

Part I 'Introduction, Definitions and Foundations'

Part I of the Thesis consists of 6 chapters.

Chapter 1 contains the introduction to the Thesis. In this chapter the aim of the Thesis is explained as well as the methodological approach taken (traditional legal method). Furthermore, various delimitations made in the Thesis are elaborated on.

Chapter 2 contains a discussion on the aim and principles of the EU procurement rules. This is carried out in order to establish the grounds for interpretation of the principles of the Treaties. The chapter concludes that the overall aim of the procurement rules, found within the principles of the Treaties, is to ensure undistorted competition by guaranteeing open, equal access to public contracts. In order to pursue this aim, contracting authorities must apply the principles of the Treaties when awarding one of the three types of contracts. It was argued that the principle of non-discrimination does not have an independent function in procurement context, and that the interpretation of the principles is the same under the Directive as under the Treaties.

Chapters 3-5 contain the definitions of the three types of contracts and discuss why these contracts have been excluded from the Procurement Directives. These chapters were found necessary for the subject of the Thesis in order to establish whether a contract falls within, or outside the Public Sector Directive. The task of defining a service concession contract is complicated as neither the definition in the Public Sector Directive nor the case law from the Court of Justice is clear on the matter. It was concluded that the main difference between a regular service contract and a service concession contracts is that the consideration in a service concession contract consists of the right to exploit the service. Hence, the economic operator must bear the risk of profiting from the contract by being exposed to elements such as competition from the market, financing and whether he is guaranteed payment. It was concluded that the risk arising from operating the service must be substantial, but that the risk, according to the Court of Justice, can be limited in cases due to legislation in a specific sector (most likely only in the utilities sector). In these cases, the *transferred* risk must still be significant, which means that the risk that is present despite the legislation in the area must be transferred.

Regarding contracts below the thresholds (chapter 4) it was concluded that there were two reasons for excluding contracts below the EU thresholds from the procedural rules in the Public Sector Directive. Firstly, it is assumed that contracts below the threshold are not of cross-border interest. Secondly, the thresholds are set to ensure that the EU complies with the GPA.

Regarding B-service contracts it concluded that B-service contracts were excluded from the procedural rules in the Public Sector Directive on the assumption that these types of contracts were not of cross-border interest. Finally, it was concluded that the contracting authority bears the burden of proof that the contract in question has been classified correctly.

Chapter 6 contains an analysis of the subject of 'cross-border interest'. The principles of the Treaties only apply if the contract in question is of 'certain cross-border interest'. Whether a contract can be said to be of 'certain cross-border interest' depends on the specific contract in question, and will only cover the situation where a non-domestic undertaking wishes to directly tender for the contract, hence only direct cross-border interest is necessary. The contracting authority must in all cases make a concrete assessment, by including elements such as the value of the contract, language elements, the complexity of the works or services to be performed, the location for the performance of the contract, national legal requirements, the type of contract and the duration of the contract. Whether a contract is of certain cross-border interest is for the contracting authority to determine, based on a hypothetical analysis of the market and contract in question. The contracting authority's decision must be open for review, and in such a situation it is most likely that it will be for the contracting authority to bear the burden of proof of whether its assessment was correct when a procedure takes place in national courts.

Part II 'Positive obligations derived from the principles of the Treaties'

Part II of the Thesis includes an analysis of the positive obligations derived from the principles of the Treaties that a contracting authority is required to follow when entering into one of the three types of contract. Part II consists of 3 chapters.

Chapter 7 addresses the transparency obligation and questions the necessity of advertising the contract beforehand. The chapter explores the Court of Justice's case law and concludes that a contracting authority must ensure that a contract has been put out for some sort of competition before entering into the contract. This is necessary in order to ensure competition for the contract and to ensure that equal treatment of undertakings takes place, which is the overall aim of the EU public procurement rules.

In some cases it will be necessary to advertise a contract beforehand if it is not possible for the contracting authority to create sufficient amount of competition for the contract by other means.

Chapter 8 analyses the existence of other types of obligations derived from the principles of the Treaties, other than the transparency obligation that a contracting authority must ensure when awarding one of the three types of contracts. The chapter explores whether requirements similar as those in the Public Sector Directive exists. It was found that in some cases similar requirements do exist.

Chapter 9 analyses whether a contracting authority is required to state reasons for its decisions when awarding one of the three types of contracts and whether contracting authorities are obliged to respect a standstill period before a contract can be signed. The chapter reaches the conclusion that in order to ensure that the principles of the Treaties are effective some sort of standstill period must be ensured. Furthermore, Article 41(2) of the Public Sector Directive applies to B-service contracts and leads to the conclusion that the contracting authority must provide reasons for its award decisions in accordance with that provision. Stating reasons for contracts below the thresholds and service concession contracts are also a necessity due to the principle of effective judicial review.

Part III 'Enforcement and Remedies'

Part III of this Thesis analyses how the obligations derived from the principles of the Treaties can be enforced. This part of the Thesis is divided into two chapters.

Chapter 10 relates to the enforcement mechanism that must be available before the national courts. The chapter addresses elements such as who is entitled to bring proceedings and where proceedings can be brought. Accordingly, the chapter examines the rules in the Public Sector Remedies Directive and discusses whether these rules apply to the three types of contracts and if similar rules apply based on the EU principles. The chapter finds that B-service contracts fall within the Public Sector Remedies Directive, and therefore the same requirements for a national review system, as for contracts falling within the Directive apply for such contract. Regarding contracts below the thresholds and service concession contracts, the principle of right to effective judicial review and other principles of the Treaties lead to the conclusion that access to the courts for breaches of the principles of the Treaties must be available. It was furthermore concluded that time limits are not a requirement to have in national review systems, but when setting time limits for B-services a few minimum requirements must be met according to the Public Sector Remedies Directive. Such time limits must be appropriate and start to run from the tenderer know or ought to have known of a decision and not render the right to review excessively difficult.

Chapter 11 analyses, which remedies must be available at the national courts. The chapter discusses whether remedies in the Public Sector Remedies Directive apply as well as analysing whether remedies that are not to be found in the Directive exist. It was seen that most of the Directive's remedies are available for B-services and that in some cases similar remedies can be found to apply for service concession contracts and contracts below the thresholds as a consequence of the principles of the Treaties.

Finally, *chapter 12* includes a summary of the findings in this Thesis.

Index